W9-AGM-375

Conservative Constraints
North Carolina and the New Deal

Twentieth-Century America Series
Dewey W. Grantham, General Editor

Conservative Constraints

North Carolina and the New Deal

Douglas Carl Abrams

UNIVERSITY PRESS OF MISSISSIPPI
Jackson & London

Manufactured in the United States of America

95 94 93 92 4 3 2 1

The paper in this book meets the guidelines for permanence and durability of the Committee on Production Guidelines for Book Longevity of the Council on Library Resources.

Library of Congress Cataloging-in-Publication Data

Abrams, Douglas Carl, 1950-
Conservative constraints : North Carolina and the New Deal / Douglas Carl Abrams.
p. cm. — (Twentieth-century America series)
Includes bibliographical references and index.
ISBN 0-87805-559-2
1. North Carolina—Politics and government—1865-1950. 2. New Deal, 1933-1939—North Carolina. 3. Conservatism—North Carolina—History—20th century. I. Title. II. Series.
F259.A27 1992
975.6′042—dc20 91-48025
CIP

British Library Cataloging-in-Publication data available

To Linda, wife and colleague

Contents

Preface

Scholars have examined the workings of the New Deal in most states and large cities, but North Carolina, a leading southern state in population, agriculture, and business, has not received book-length treatment. This book is an effort to meet that need, considering primarily political and administrative history, although with attention to economic, social, and black history.

Not every aspect of North Carolina's experience in the Depression and New Deal could be developed fully, and topics such as relief, blacks, women, and the impact of New Deal programs on cities and counties warrant separate studies. My work concludes with 1940, except for finishing stories of agencies that had begun before that year. The Tennessee Valley Authority had no impact on North Carolina until after 1940 and therefore is not included.

Organizing a book on the New Deal is a challenge because so much happened at once. The focus is on the activities of both New Deal agencies and state government. New Deal strategies of relief, recovery, and reform were addressed at the state level. Throughout the 1930s, three men symbolized the diverse reactions in North Carolina to the New Deal: Senator Josiah W. Bailey, staunch opponent; ambassador and newspaperman Josephus Daniels, avid New Dealer; and governor, lawyer, and lobbyist O. Max Gardner, pragmatic conservative torn between cooperation and resistance.

I am happy to acknowledge my debts to many people and organizations. Bob Jones University granted me a generous leave and financial assistance. The history department of the University of Maryland awarded me a Hearst Fellowship to assist in one summer's research. Participation in George B. Tindall's National Endowment for the Humanities summer seminar and William E. Leuchtenburg's Project '87 seminar aided research on this project. Library staffs in New York, Washington, D.C., North Carolina, and South Carolina were gracious and helpful, especially the staff members at the National Archives, who kindly assisted me in my research for over a year. Special thanks also go to the North Carolina Mutual Life Insurance Company for permission to use the Spaulding Papers. For helpful comments on the manuscript at various stages I thank Anthony J. Badger, George H. Callcott, and Horace Samuel Merrill. Charles W. Eagles criticized Chapter 6, for which I am grateful. I greatly appreciate the thorough evaluation of the manuscript by Richard L. Watson, Jr. His queries helped me refine aspects of the study.

Special thanks goes to Keith W. Olson of the University of Maryland, for his professional expertise and friendship. My thanks go to Dewey W. Grantham, general editor of the Twentieth-Century America Series, for his careful help with the manuscript. I am grateful to all who helped make this a better book. Errors that remain are my responsibility alone.

One special joy of this project was the opportunity to spend lots of time in my native state, and my brother Billy Abrams and his wife, Becky, graciously shared their home with me when I did research in North Carolina. I thank my children, Jessica and Benjamin, for their patience.

My greatest debt is to my wife, Linda, a fellow historian. Dedication of the book to her is small payment for her encouragement, criticism, proofreading, and selfless spirit. "She opens her mouth in wisdom, and the teaching of kindness is on her tongue" (Prov. 31:26).

Guide to Manuscript Collections

Special Collections Department, Duke University Library, Durham, N.C.
- Papers of Josiah W. Bailey
- Papers of Graham A. Barden
- Papers of Santford Martin

East Carolina Manuscript Collection, East Carolina University, Greenville, N.C.
- Papers of Richard T. Fountain
- Papers of Franklin Wills Hancock, Jr.
- Papers of John A. Lang, Jr.
- Papers of Allen J. Maxwell

Franklin D. Roosevelt Library, Hyde Park, N.Y.
- Papers of Lorena Hickok
- Papers of Franklin D. Roosevelt

Library of Congress, Washington, D.C.
- Papers of Josephus Daniels
- Papers of the National Association for the Advancement of Colored People

National Archives, Washington, D.C.
- Papers of the Agricultural Adjustment Administration, Record Group 145
- Papers of the Civilian Conservation Corps, Record Group 35
- Papers of the Farm Security Administration, Record Group 96
- Papers of the National Recovery Administration, Record Group 9
- Papers of the National Youth Administration, Record Group 119
- Papers of the Rural Electrification Administration, Record Group 221
- Papers of the Social Security Administration, Record Group 47
- Papers of the Works Progress Administration, Record Group 69

North Carolina Mutual Life Insurance Company, Durham, N.C.
- Papers of Charles Clinton Spaulding

North Carolina Department of Archives and History, Raleigh, N.C.
Papers of the Governors—O. Max Gardner, cited as Governors' Papers (G); J. C. B. Ehringhaus, cited as Governors' Papers (E); and Clyde R. Hoey, cited as Governors' Papers (H)
Papers of J. C. B. Ehringhaus—Private Collection, cited as Ehringhaus Papers (P)
Papers of Thad S. Ferree

North Carolina State Records Center, Raleigh, N.C.
Papers of the North Carolina Emergency Relief Administration

Southern Historical Collection, University of North Carolina, Chapel Hill, N.C.
Papers of James O. Carr
Papers of Jonathan Daniels
Papers of the Federal Writers' Project
Papers of O. Max Gardner
Papers of John H. Kerr
Papers of Howard W. Odum
Papers of Lindsay C. Warren

Southern Oral History Program Collection, University of North Carolina, Chapel Hill, N.C.
Interviews of Jonathan Daniels, Edwin Gill, Sam Ervin, Guy B. Johnson, and Capus Waynick

Introduction

Since the 1940s historians have debated how much change the New Deal brought. From a Washington perspective, the reforms of the 1930s appeared momentous. At a local level, however, those programs to reverse the Depression seemed limited because they encountered resistance.[1] In North Carolina a strong Democratic organization, a pervasive probusiness ideology, and a states'-rights tradition severely constrained the New Deal. President Franklin D. Roosevelt, Washington bureaucrats, and New Dealers in the state never completely overcame the obstructions, despite the president's popularity. In per capita allocation of New Deal expenditures for 1933–39 the state ranked last in the nation. Governor O. Max Gardner, forged an agenda of retrenchment and a balanced budget from 1929 to 1933 that persisted after he left office. His successors, John C. B. Ehringhaus and Clyde R. Hoey, in the words of newspaper editor Josephus Daniels, also worshiped the "Great God Boodgit." Instead of relief, jobs, or regulation of business, they tenaciously fought for tight fiscal policies, implementation and preservation of the sales tax, and a climate favorable to business. A "little New Deal" was never a serious possibility in the state. Conservatives, with no interest in the welfare state, were too strong. They co-opted the popular appeal of Roosevelt with rhetoric supporting the New Deal, and the president strengthened New Deal critics by working with them. Liberals in the state, proposing weak candidates and an ideology virtually limited to opposition to the sales tax and the Democratic "machine," offered little alternative. As a poor, rural state, North Carolina had neither the money to fund an extensive welfare state nor the urban base to create strong support for the New Deal.

Liberals such as Jonathan Daniels and state representative Ralph W. McDonald challenged the status quo and sought permanent change through the New Deal to help the poor, tenant farmers, and urban workers. Conservatives, however, generally resisted Roosevelt's reformist

1. For a discussion of New Deal historiography, see the Bibliographical Essay.

goals, preferring to protect the interests of business and large landowners. Historian James T. Patterson's definition of *conservative* is apt for North Carolina. Acknowledging that no two conservatives were alike, he concluded that the "unifying factor . . . was opposition to most of the domestic program of the New Deal." Conservatives, he argued, feared federal power and bureaucracy, deficit spending, labor unions, and welfare programs. He labeled many who served in Congress in the 1930s as conservative, despite a high percentage of votes for New Deal measures.[2]

But votes tell only part of the story. Politicians supported Roosevelt overwhelmingly in part because of pressure from constitutuents, and, skillful at evasion, they often kept their own feelings quiet, a strategy typical of North Carolina's congressional delegation. In some cases they voted for a program yet opposed its operation or changed their views over time. Frequently, loyalty to party, a program, or a leader, like Roosevelt or Gardner, was more important than ideas. The vote on the National Recovery Administration (NRA), for example, illustrates the need for caution in matching votes and ideological labels. In the Senate, Josiah W. Bailey voted for it, yet many prominent progressives voted no, believing it was too favorable to big business. The New Deal was not always synonymous with liberalism. Wilbur J. Cash explained the contradictions by describing the South in the 1930s as "unanalytical now as it had always been"; it did not realize that the New Deal ran "counter to its established ideas and values." Political scientists Earl Black and Merle Black, examining modern southern politics, concluded that embracing the New Deal did not make southerners liberal. On the contrary, they argued, "Southern whites became progovernment from sheer necessity; their options were limited and their short-term self-interest clear." Southerners received economic help but experienced few immediate threats from Washington. Though southerners turned to the national government out of economic desperation, Black and Black pointed out that they remained fundamentally conservative.[3] These authors' conclusions clarify the relationship between North Carolinians and the New Deal and show that the labels *liberal* and *conservative* had meaning in

2. Patterson defines a conservative in the House as one who opposed the New Deal 25 percent or more on key votes and in the Senate at least 12 percent on key votes. By that standard, North Carolina's Senator Bailey and Congressman Clark were conservative. See James T. Patterson, *Congressional Conservatism and the New Deal* (Lexington: University of Kentucky Press, 1967), pp. vii, 339, 342, 347–49.

3. W. J. Cash, *The Mind of the South* (New York: Vintage Books, 1941), p. 377; Earl Black and Merle Black, *Politics and Society in the South* (Cambridge, Mass.: Harvard University Press, 1987), pp. 214–15.

the 1930s and clarify general attitudes about the New Deal, expressed not only in votes but also in other actions.

Politicians, businessmen, and farmers all sought largesse from Washington but resisted threats to the socioeconomic status quo. Textile executives, seeking help for an ailing industry, initially embraced the NRA, but when the results were unions, strikes, higher wages, regulations, and an ineffective NRA, they soured on reform. Tobacco companies needed no federal assistance and resisted an NRA code until a few months before the Supreme Court invalidated the agency. Similarly, tobacco growers, both landowners and tenants, overwhelmingly endorsed the Agricultural Adjustment Administration (AAA) because it created improvement in prices, but as the decade progressed they revealed a resilient conservatism. Farmers hoped to limit the New Deal to price increases for crops, and through the American Farm Bureau Federation they resisted relief for urban areas and fought funding for the Resettlement Administration (RA) and the Farm Security Administration (FSA). Confident that they no longer needed crop controls, they rejected them for 1939 only to return to them the next year, when prices fell. The farmers' liberalism, like the New Dealism of the textile executives, merely cloaked economic self-interest; there was little enthusiasm for genuine reform. The AAA may have brought short-term recovery with higher prices, but in the long run the success of the tobacco program perpetuated a one-crop economy.

Local forces restricted the welfare state. Farmers and businessmen fought New Deal relief as a threat to cheap labor. Ehringhaus and Hoey refused to meet requirements for matching funds for federal relief. Tar Heel politicians and businessmen had a different premise than federal relief administrator Harry L. Hopkins: for them, the question was not one of doing more but why do so much. State Democrats were more concerned with patronage battles than with relief. Statistics for per capita relief reflected the lack of enthusiasm. North Carolina ranked forty-third in Federal Emergency Relief Administration (FERA) receipts and last in Works Progress Administration (WPA) expenditures. Though the New Deal enlarged the state's responsibility for welfare, the state welfare department survived controls by the New Deal relief bureaucracy. Furthermore, despite the millions spent for relief, chronic rural poverty remained. Blacks in the state encountered more adversity than social or economic progress. The 1930s for them served as a painful down payment for postwar gains.

By 1938 the New Deal had ceased as a vital reform movement in the state. Conservatives remained entrenched in the Hoey administration, and liberal opposition fizzled. Court packing, recession, and Roosevelt's attempted purge of southern conservatives in 1938 compelled Senator Bailey and former governor Gardner to close ranks with other New Deal opponents on the national level.

The North Carolina experience in the 1930s underscores a dimension of the New Deal story often overlooked when scholars focus primarily on the president, Congress, or the bureaucracy. Examining the application of relief and reform programs on a state level provides a more realistic picture of the New Deal's performance. Liberal reform impulses encountered countervailing conservative forces that were especially strong in North Carolina. Historians have been too eager to blame Roosevelt for the shortcomings, but a more accurate judgment might be to credit his enemies for thwarting the New Deal. Gardner, Ehringhaus, Hoey, and men like them in other states proved that entrenched conservatism could successfully constrain reform. The point is not that the New Deal failed but that North Carolina conservatives frustrated its goals. By 1938 the federal government had poured $440 million in grants and loans into the state, dramatically improved tobacco prices, and through the public works projects made a substantial record of physical achievement. More remarkable, however, was how little North Carolina's society, economy, and politics had changed by the end of the decade.[4]

North Carolina epitomized southern problems in the 1930s. Frank Freidel observed that southern leaders developed an "embarrassing ambivalence" toward FDR and the New Deal. Even southern conservatives recognized the need for an economically revitalized New South and appreciated the president's popularity, but they also sensed a threat to the status quo. The welfare state undermined the paternalism of landowners over the poor, and wage regulation along with prolabor legislation challenged the authority of mill owners and tobacco company executives. These assaults on the socioeconomic elites generated opposition in North Carolina that stymied the New Deal. Because of this

4. James T. Patterson, *The New Deal and the States: Federalism in Transition* (Princeton: Princeton University Press, 1969), 191–92, 202–7; Anthony J. Badger, *North Carolina and the New Deal* (Raleigh: North Carolina Division of Archives and History, 1981), p. 96. In his introduction Badger states that "ambiguity characterized the impact of the New Deal on North Carolina," but in his conclusion he admits that "perhaps the most striking aspect of the New Deal experience in North Carolina was the pervasiveness of a conservative, business-oriented ideology that survived the changes wrought by the New Deal." For a discussion of the focus on constraints on the New Deal see Harvard Sitkoff, "Introduction," in Sitkoff, ed., *Fifty Years Later: The New Deal Evaluated* (Philadelphia: Temple University Press, 1985), p. 8.

conservative opposition, the New Deal accomplished least in a region where Roosevelt enjoyed greatest popular support among the masses.[5]

Though opponents checked reform in the 1930s, the New Deal, as Dewey W. Grantham noted, "nourished forces that eventually began to reconstruct the region's political affairs." In fact, the conservative response to the New Deal foreshadowed the postwar fracture of the Democratic party and the emergence of the two-party South. For established Democratic leaders, some issues loomed more important than party, as the 1928 Hoover-Smith battle revealed. Threats to business, the bureaucratic leviathan of the welfare state, and the prospect of new elements like blacks and labor in politics, overrode loyalty to the Democratic party. Furthermore, the urban-North bias of the New Deal made the national Democratic party increasingly liberal while southern influence waned. Tar Heel Democrats like Josiah Bailey fought that trend, and perhaps during the 1930s they met the challenge, but as Grantham pointed out, the "threat remained, and it promised to grow larger in the future."[6]

North Carolina's hostility to reform in the 1930s refutes the state's progressive image. According to Richard N. Current, the state's progressive reputation was firmly in place by the 1920s, born of Governor Charles B. Aycock's educational advances earlier in the century, the state's industrial leadership in the South, and Governor Cameron A. Morrison's road-building program during the "business progressivism" of the 1920s. Prominent sociologist Howard W. Odum and President Frank Porter Graham at the University of North Carolina reinforced the image. By the late 1940s, several writers bolstered that positive portrait. North Carolina was "beyond doubt one of the most important, alive, and progressive states in the union," declared John Gunther in 1947. That same year Jonathan Daniels described his native state as the "most advanced Southern state," showing signs of "enlightened maturity."

5. George Brown Tindall, *The Emergence of the New South, 1913–1945* (Baton Rouge: Louisiana State University Press and the Littlefield Fund for Southern History of the University of Texas, 1967), pp. 389–90, 608, 618–23; Cash, *Mind of the South*, pp. 373–77, 415, 417; Frank Freidel, *FDR and the South* (Baton Rouge: Louisiana State University Press, 1965), pp. 35–36, 46; Dewey W. Grantham, Jr., *The Democratic South* (Athens: University of Georgia Press, 1963), pp. 69–70, 96; Grantham, *The Regional Imagination: The South and Recent American History* (Nashville: Vanderbilt University Press, 1979), p. 202.

6. Grantham, *Democratic South*, pp. 73–74, 96; Grantham, *Regional Imagination*, pp. 13, 20, 203. For a careful analysis of the emerging two-party South in the postwar era see Alexander P. Lamis, *The Two-Party South* (New York: Oxford University Press, 1984).

With the label "progressive plutocracy" political scientist V. O. Key, Jr., in 1949 created an image that persisted for more than a generation. Though he recognized the pervasive influence of an "economic oligarchy," he sensed a progressive "spirit" and praised the state's economic development, race relations, emphasis on education, and orderly government. In the late 1940s, with W. Kerr Scott in the Governor's Mansion, Frank Porter Graham appointed to the United States Senate, and a crusading, liberal *Raleigh News and Observer*, the popular label seemed justified.[7]

In recent years, however, scholars have challenged Key's assessment of postwar North Carolina. Since the 1940s the state has been a "political plutocracy that lives with a progressive myth," charged Jack Bass and Walter DeVries in 1976. Though Tar Heel leaders accept the myth as fact, the level of economic development, social problems, race relations, the influence of business, and a conservative congressional delegation point to a different North Carolina. In the 1940s, when Key wrote, the state ranked forty-fifth in per capita income and last among the states in average manufacturing wage. Since the 1940s North Carolina has remained near the bottom in wealth and state services. In 1971 the state ranked forty-ninth in average weekly earnings from manufacturing. Also in the 1970s controversies like the Wilmington 10, the Joan Little case, J. P. Stevens's battles with unions, the Department of Health, Education and Welfare's suit over desegregation of the University of North Carolina, and the political potency of Senator Jesse Helms all have diminished the state's progressive image.[8]

The record of the 1930s suggests that *progressive* is not a fair label for that decade either because state leaders used progressive rhetoric to mask a staunch conservatism. Deliberately and at times unwittingly, Max Gardner, the state's most prominent Democrat, confused his terminology. According to his biographer, he declared North Carolina to be a "conservative, progressive state." "I am at heart a progressive yet I have

7. Richard N. Current, "Tarheels and Badgers: A Comparative History of Their Reputations," *Journal of Southern History* 42 (February 1976): 3–30; John Gunther, *Inside U.S.A.* (New York: Harper and Brothers, 1947), pp. 718–21; V. O. Key, Jr., *Southern Politics in State and Nation* (New York: Vintage Books, 1949), pp. 205, 211, 214; Jonathan Daniels, *Tar Heels: A Portrait of North Carolina* (New York: Dodd, Mead, 1947), p. 325.

8. Jack Bass and Walter DeVries, *The Transformation of Southern Politics: Social Change and Political Consequence since 1945* (New York: Basic Books, 1976), pp. 219, 247; William H. Chafe, *Civilities and Civil Rights: Greensboro, North Carolina, and the Black Struggle for Freedom* (New York: Oxford University Press, 1980), p. 4; Merle Black, "North Carolina: The 'Best' State?" in *Politics and Policy in North Carolina*, ed. Thad L. Beyle and Merle Black (New York: MSS Information Corporation, 1975), p. 15; *New York Times*, February 22, 1978.

been forced into the position of taking my place in the minds of a great many of my dearest friends as a reactionary," he confided on another occasion, as reported by a contemporary, R. Mayne Albright. In 1932, justifying his tight fiscal policy, Gardner blamed the expansionist programs of the 1920s, when the state was "aflame with the passion of progress." Actually, there was not much progress in the 1920s. In 1927 North Carolina ranked forty-fifth in the per capita cost of government, a pattern that persisted in the succeeding decades. In 1940 in per capita income the state placed forty-third, only a slight improvement from forty-fifth in 1929, despite the New Deal.

Yet rhetoric glossed over the social and economic realities. When Gardner proclaimed in a 1932 *Saturday Evening Post* article that North Carolina was "cleaning house," or in an address to the Kentucky legislature that "new conditions demand new remedies," he touched on an old Progressive theme of efficiency and also revealed a flexibility that seemed broad-minded. His personality and charm gave him the image of an enlightened politician. In 1938, when a National Economic Council report labeled the South the nation's number one economic problem, Governor Hoey responded, "I must insist that North Carolina does not fit into that classification." He cited the state's leadership in agriculture and industry and its ranking fourth in the payment of federal taxes. Ignoring the problems and perpetuating the Progressive myth, he added, "I regard my state as a stalwart, supporting member of the family rather than a problem child."[9]

The state's economic and political leaders used North Carolina's Progressive myth to help thwart change in the New Deal era. Promoting a forward-looking image for the state was part state patriotism, part southern oratory, but also deceptive. Gardner advised Hoey in his 1936 gubernatorial bid, against a strong New Dealer, to appear more liberal. For Hoey's 1937 inaugural address Gardner gave similar advice. Conservatives found that co-opting the New Deal with speeches, not action,

9. David Leroy Corbitt, ed., *Public Papers and Letters of Oliver Max Gardner, Governor of North Carolina, 1929–1933* (Raleigh: Council of State, State of North Carolina, 1937), pp. 406, 679–80; radio address by Gardner, May 7, 1932, Gardner Papers; Samuel Huntington Hobbs, Jr., *North Carolina: Economic and Social* (Chapel Hill: University of North Carolina Press, 1930), pp. 220–21; R. Mayne Albright, "O. Max Gardner and the Shelby Dynasty," Part 1, *State* 50 (April 1983): 8; Joseph L. Morrison, *Governor O. Max Gardner: A Power in North Carolina and New Deal Washington* (Chapel Hill: University of North Carolina Press, 1971), p. 62; David Leroy Corbitt, ed., *Addresses, Letters and Papers of John Christoph Blucher Ehringhaus, Governor of North Carolina, 1933–1937* (Raleigh: Council of State, State of North Carolina, 1950), p. 138; Lindley S. Butler and Alan D. Watson, eds., *The North Carolina Experience: An Interpretive and Documentary History* (Chapel Hill: University of North Carolina Press, 1984), p. 403.

proved effective. As historian William H. Chafe observed, for true liberals "the enemy was elusive and flexible." Furthermore, Chafe added, the progressive image "acted as camouflage, obscuring . . . underlying social and economic realities." Worn by conservative leaders, the progressive mask protected North Carolina from change by either insiders or outsiders. The state was fine, its leaders were good politicians, civil, open-minded, and cautious, demanding consensus before acting on major public issues. New Deal social, political, and economic conflict, the conservative argument went, was not for North Carolina. Besides, in the South, and especially in North Carolina, progressivism meant good government, free of corruption, and favorable to business. For the state's plutocracy, of course, that was the ideal situation.[10]

During the 1930s the state's genuine progressives were on the sidelines. Howard Odum served as assistant director of Herbert Hoover's Committee on Social Trends, which made him sympathetic to Hoover and his ideal of voluntarism. Though Odum voted for FDR in 1932 and worked briefly with relief, he was uneasy about the centralizing trend of the New Deal, which violated his concept of regionalism. Tagged by some as a Republican, the old Progressive remained a "reluctant" New Dealer. Frank Porter Graham, at the insistence of state politicians, remained president of the University of North Carolina, defended free speech, organized labor, and sharecroppers, but had little impact on the New Deal in the state. Josephus Daniels, publisher and editor of the *Raleigh News and Observer,* the most prominent Tar Heel liberal, served as ambassador to Mexico in the 1930s. His absence and the silence of other liberals encouraged pragmatic politicians like Max Gardner and conservative ideologues like Josiah Bailey to fight hard and in the end successfully against the New Deal.[11]

10. Bass and DeVries, *Transformation of Southern Politics*, p. 226; Chafe, *Civilities and Civil Rights*, pp. 6–8, 338–39. Chafe has a superb analysis of the state's progressive "mystique," which he treats in connection with the civil rights movement in Greensboro, North Carolina.

11. Chafe, *Civilities and Civil Rights*, p. 3; Michael O'Brien, *The Idea of the American South, 1920–1941* (Baltimore: Johns Hopkins University Press, 1979), pp. 48–49, 59–60, 80–81.

Conservative Constraints
North Carolina and the New Deal

CHAPTER 1

Setting the Stage

In the South, according to novelist James Dickey, one could hardly call the events following October 1929 a crash because "things just sagged a little more."[1] The response of the Gardner administration to the first three years of the Depression was equally undramatic. The governor's actions signified a cautious tone that persisted in state government for over a decade. Because of his ties to business, economy in government overrode concerns for relief, despite burgeoning unemployment and declining crop prices. The primary focus was on balancing the budget through retrenchment and giving property tax relief. The debate revolved around how little, not how much, state government could do to fight the economic decline. His opposition's failure in the debate and at the polls foreshadowed the weakness of New Dealers in the state. In four years Gardner consolidated his political power, and his handpicked successor following after the election of 1932 entrenched the conservative regime in Raleigh.

Like the rest of the United States, North Carolina suffered immensely during the early years of the Depression. In 1929 the state ranked forty-fifth in per capita income and no better than ninth in the South, well below the average for the region. Because per capita income was so low already, North Carolina experienced the smallest decline in real per capita income from 1929 to 1933 of any state. The economic crisis was a result of dramatically low crop prices. In 1930, for example, Nash County in the tobacco-growing east had 3,500 foreclosures on its 5,280 farms. Throughout the 1920s tobacco always sold above 20 cents a pound, but by 1931 it dipped to 8.4 cents a pound. Cotton likewise plummeted from 16.6 cents a pound in 1929 to 5.97 cents in 1931. From 1928 to 1932 the value of all crops produced in the state dropped more than half, and by 1932 cash farm income declined to a mere third of what it had been for 1928. From 1929 to 1931 the state's industry suffered as the "value added by manufacture" figure for North Carolina fell 50 percent. By September 1931 approximately one hundred thousand workers were unem-

1. James Dickey, narrator, "One-Third of a Nation," WJWJ-TV/South Carolina ETV, Beaufort, South Carolina, 1981.

ployed, and by late 1932, 25 percent of the population had received some form of relief. Bank failures mounted, too, with eighteen in 1929, and in 1930 depositors lost $56 million when ninety-three banks collapsed. The diary entries of Fay Webb Gardner, the state's first lady, captured the despair in Raleigh during late 1931: "All depressed about rumors of Commercial Bank here closing tomorrow. To bed at 12 but not much sleep. Times are tragic! . . . Another rainy gloomy day. Max and I head-achy after a sleepless night. The bank closed as predicted—thousands lost their all. Runs being made on two other banks. City in a turmoil."[2]

The Depression brought extreme adversity to thousands of North Carolina tenant farmers. Low prices, overproduction, and lack of credit to buy seed and fertilizer forced landlords to release tenants and sharecroppers, and by 1932 an estimated fifteen to twenty thousand tenants had been displaced. Tenancy dominated agriculture in the eastern part of the state, and by 1925 in over thirty counties more than half of the farmers were tenants. Small cotton and tobacco farms formed the basis of the state's agriculture. From 1910 to 1925 North Carolina led the nation in the increase in farm tenancy. These small tobacco and cotton farms adapted readily to tenancy because neither crop required large amounts of land or capital and both produced cash at harvest. In 1925, though North Carolina had the second largest farm population in the nation and ranked second in the number of farms, it placed last in number of cultivated acres per farm. In 1930 about three-fourths of the population resided outside towns, and the prevalence of tenancy and sharecropping illustrated the chronic poverty of the rural South made worse by the Depression.[3]

North Carolina's relatively balanced economy tempered the economic crisis brought on by reverses in agriculture. In 1929 the state led the nation in textile production. It ranked first in the region in industrial

2. U.S. Department of Commerce, Bureau of the Census, *Fifteenth Census of the United States: 1930, Abstract of the Fifteenth Census of the United States* (Washington, D.C.: U.S. Government Printing Office, 1933), p. 464; Hugh Talmadge Lefler and Albert Ray Newsome, *North Carolina: The History of a Southern State*, 3d ed. (Chapel Hill: University of North Carolina Press, 1973), p. 606; Thomas Sellers Morgan, Jr., "A Step toward Altruism: Relief and Welfare in North Carolina, 1930–1938" (Ph.D. dissertation, University of North Carolina, 1969), p. 21; Calvin B. Hoover and Benjamin U. Ratchford, *Economic Resources and Policies of the South* (New York: Macmillan, 1951), p. 50; Grace Rutledge Hamrick, *"Miss Fay": A Biography of Fay Webb Gardner* (Boiling Springs, N.C.: Gardner-Webb College, 1978), p. 29; Badger, *North Carolina and the New Deal*, pp. 1–2, 7.

3. *Abstract of the Fifteenth Census*, pp. 15, 19; Hobbs, *North Carolina*, pp. 90–93, 335; Lefler and Newsome, *North Carolina*, p. 577; Badger, *North Carolina and the New Deal*, p. 3.

development, including the number of establishments, value of output, capital, and number of wage earners. More than one-fourth of the country's cotton textile mills were in North Carolina. Overproduction and destructive price competition caused problems for the textile industry, but the state's tobacco industry fared well after 1929. The piedmont section monopolized the tobacco industry, producing well over one-half of the country's cigarettes. The consumption level remained constant while the price tobacco companies paid for tobacco declined, and profits increased from $115 million in 1927 to $145 million in 1930. That level was maintained through 1932.[4]

The inauguration of Governor O. Max Gardner in 1929 gave those piedmont business interests an ally for the political battles ahead. Writing in 1949, V. O. Key argued that an "economic oligarchy had held sway" in North Carolina for half a century. The influence of the manufacturing and banking elite in Winston-Salem, Charlotte, Greensboro, and Durham pervaded the state's economic and political life. Corporate interests provided campaign funds for cooperative politicians, who would favor conservative, probusiness policies in the legislature in Raleigh. Max Gardner's career validates Key's assessment of North Carolina politics. Gardner symbolized the harmony between the state's political and economic interests, typifying the solicitude for business development that George B. Tindall identified as the key to progressivism by the 1920s. Combining old southern bourbonism and progressivism, Gardner did not fear change as long as it aided business, but he feared reform at the expense of what Tindall called the bourbon "organic traditional community with its personal relationships, its class distinctions, its habits of deference." Gardner's conservative core would determine his response not only to the Depression but later to the New Deal.[5]

In the state Senate before World War I, Gardner had a reputation as "a forward-looking businessman—but not extremely progressive," according to his biographer. His record was "conservative enough." For textile interests he fought a child labor bill; he cultivated rich friends such as James A. Gray of Reynolds Tobacco Company and Robert M. Hanes of Wachovia Bank. Jonathan Daniels, liberal editor of the *Raleigh News*

4. Lefler and Newsome, *North Carolina*, pp. 580–82; Hoover and Ratchford, *Economic Resources*, p. 116; Hobbs, *North Carolina*, p. 80; "Cotton Textile Industry" folder [n.d.], NRA Papers; Anthony J. Badger, "The New Deal and North Carolina: The Tobacco Program, 1933–1940" (Ph.D. dissertation, University of Hull, 1974), pp. 4, 10.

5. George B. Tindall, *The Persistent Tradition in New South Politics* (Baton Rouge: Louisiana State University Press, 1975), pp. xii, 22, 58–59, 72; Key, *Southern Politics*, pp. 211, 214.

and Observer and frequent critic of Gardner, remembered him as "probably the most fascinating political figure in this century in North Carolina." Though a "straight" businessman, close to the conservative elements, Gardner had, according to Daniels, a "politician's understanding" that business had to build its position in the community. In 1925 with two others Gardner organized the Cleveland Cloth Mills, which produced rayon dress goods. A year later he had his own sales office in New York, and by 1928 with stock ventures and bank interests he had accumulated a modest six-figure fortune. As landlord of a model mill village, Gardner believed that "we cannot build a prosperous citizenship on low wages" and increased wages for his workers. As an enlightened mill owner, Gardner sought to discourage unions by paying better wages and to overcome the low-wage philosophy of competing mill operators in the lower South that caused destructive competition in the textile industry. When labor strife in Gastonia in 1929 tarnished the state's reputation, Gardner did his best to achieve justice by punishing those responsible for the mob violence.[6]

The 1928 election campaign in North Carolina proved pivotal in the state's political history. Since 1900 conservative Senator Furnifold M. Simmons had dominated the state's Democratic party. Though from the east, Simmons enjoyed close ties with piedmont financial interests and with a loyal network of followers that gave him control of the party for a generation. That changed in 1928 in the bitter race between Herbert C. Hoover and Alfred E. Smith. Simmons refused to support Smith, a "wet" Catholic, and resigned as national Democratic committeeman from North Carolina. Gardner declared, "I won't desert the captain of my ship!" and worked hard for the Smith ticket, though Hoover carried North Carolina and Gardner's congressional district. Afterward Simmons's power declined and Smith supporters Gardner, Josiah W. Bailey, J. C. B. Ehringhaus, Clyde R. Hoey, and Samuel J. Ervin, Jr., rose to prominence in state politics.[7]

In 1928 Gardner ran unopposed in the Democratic gubernatorial primary. Since losing the gubernatorial nomination in 1920 to a Simmons-backed candidate, he had deferred to the tradition of rotating the governorship between the east and west. In 1924 it was the east's turn,

6. Interview of Jonathan Daniels by Daniel J. Singal and George B. Tindall, March 22, 30, 1972, Southern Oral History Program Collection; Morrison, *Gardner*, pp. 22–23, 26, 42, 44, 62–63.

7. Key, *Southern Politics*, p. 213; Morrison, *Gardner*, pp. 49–51; interview of Edwin Gill by Archie K. Davis, September 10, 12, October 2, 1974, Southern Oral History Program Collection; Albright, "Shelby Dynasty," Part 1, p. 9.

and he endorsed the choice of the Simmons organization. For that "accommodation" he received the nomination in 1928 by virtual acclamation, quite a feat in a one-party state. Gardner had carefully built his own organization, in some instances befriending those who opposed him in 1920 and courting Simmons's conservative financial support. Jonathan Daniels recalled how politically "smart" Gardner was, how he did not "cherish animosities" but hoped to make everyone his friend. Daniels remembered Gardner's charm: "He was terribly ingratiating, and he loved to do anybody a favor." Edwin M. Gill, longtime state treasurer and once Gardner's personal secretary, described him as one of the most magnanimous men he had ever known in public office, particularly generous to his former foes. R. Mayne Albright, in 1948 an "antimachine" candidate for governor, knew Gardner as a "large, confident, and forceful man." The trademark of his career, according to his biographer, was the "Gardner handshake, Gardner personality . . . the Gardner oratory."[8]

When he entered the Governor's Mansion in 1929, Gardner was a probusiness conservative but pragmatic enough to adapt to changing circumstances, whether Progressivism, Depression, or New Deal. His opposition to Simmons before the 1920s and his youthfulness gave him a progressive image, whether deserved or not. In 1908 Gardner backed the candidate for governor who defeated Simmons's choice. That same year Josephus Daniels, an agrarian liberal and supporter of William Jennings Bryan, asked him to organize hundreds of Young Men's Democratic Clubs. In 1915 he became the youngest ever to serve as president pro tem of the state Senate. Two years later, at thirty-three, he became lieutenant governor with no Democratic opposition in the primary. When he battled the Simmons organization unsuccessfully in 1920 for the governorship, he supported women's suffrage and represented the postwar generation in the state that for the first time transcended old Reconstruction issues.[9]

Gardner expressed the hope that "when the historian comes to write of my administration . . . he will be able to say of me . . . I at least kept my head and resisted the pressure of quacks and demagogues." As governor he certainly "kept his head" and exhibited a staunch, even stubborn, conservative position. His first year in office, before the

8. Morrison, *Gardner*, pp. 26, 45, 49; interview of Edwin Gill by Archie K. Davis, September 10, 12, October 2, 1974; Albright, "Shelby Dynasty," Part 1, pp. 8–9; interview of Jonathan Daniels by Charles Eagles, March 9–11, 1977, Southern Oral History Program Collection; interview of Thad Eure by Carl Abrams, June 21, 1983.

9. Albright "Shelby Dynasty," Part 1, p. 8; Morrison, *Gardner*, pp. 19, 22, 25, 30.

Depression set in, Gardner responded to business progressivism the same way he reacted to the economic crisis, calling for retrenchment and property tax relief. Progressivism in the 1920s in North Carolina meant efficiency in government and expanding public services such as roads and schools, but not welfare legislation, protection of labor, or regulation of business. Good government meant fostering business development, synonymous with progress. Consequently, a huge debt accumulated during the 1920s, rising from $13 million in 1920 to over $178 million in January 1929. In the decade North Carolina probably had the greatest expansion of any state save Florida. In 1931 the state's per capita debt ranked second highest in the country. George Tindall had called North Carolina the "exemplar of business progressivism."[10]

In March 1929, even before the October stock market crash, Governor Gardner called for retrenchment. "Today, at the direction of the public mind, we are about to enter a period of descending public expenditures and tax levies," he warned. By June 1929 he had reduced the state budget by almost $1.5 million. The Wall Street collapse increased fervor for cutbacks, and several months into the Depression he commissioned a special Brookings Institution study to determine how to reorganize state government. Drawing upon that report, Gardner recommended to the 1931 General Assembly some drastic measures for centralizing state government, thereby increasing its efficiency and decreasing its costs. He proposed a 10 percent cut in state salaries, consolidation of the state university system, a general reorganization of state government, and consolidation of some counties. The legislature responded by revamping the highway department and several other agencies such as the university and the health and agriculture departments. In 1932 the governor boasted that in the first two years of his administration the legislature had reduced appropriations by $3.5 million and the most recent General Assembly by $6 to $7 million per year. "Retrenchment and reform," he argued in 1932, "is still . . . the most important single question faced by city administration, by state . . . administration, and faced by the national government." The challenge for government, according to Gardner, was "to put its house in order to survive the economic storm."[11]

10. Tindall, *Persistent Tradition*, pp. 58–59; Tindall, *Emergence of the New South*, pp. 368–69; Gardner speech, May 7, 1932, Gardner Papers; Lefler and Newsome, *North Carolina*, p. 605; Lent D. Upson to Harry Hopkins, November 12, 1934, Governors' Papers (E); Hoover and Ratchford, *Economic Resources*, p. 196; Morrison, *Gardner*, p. 102; Badger, *North Carolina and the New Deal*, pp. 7–8.

11. Address by Gardner, May 7, 1932, Gardner Papers; Corbitt, ed., *Public Papers and Letters of Gardner*, pp. xxii, 97–98, 370–72; Lefler and Newsome, *North Carolina*, p. 607; Elmer L. Puryear, *Democratic Party Dissension in North Carolina, 1928–1936* (Chapel Hill: University of North Carolina Press, 1962), pp. 62, 90.

Just as he sensed the public sentiment for cutting government services even before the Depression, Gardner also realized before October 1929 that North Carolinians demanded property tax relief. His inaugural address sounded that theme, and in March 1929, he demanded that the General Assembly reduce property taxes. Total state and local tax levies increased by 195 percent between 1920 and 1929. The time of burgeoning public services and taxation had ended. In a 1928 report, the state Tax Commission called attention to the alarming increase in local tax delinquency and concluded that the state must reduce the property tax. After the 1929 crash, property taxes became even more unbearable, and demands for tax relief grew louder. By December 1932, in part because of nonpayment of taxes, thirty-four of North Carolina's one hundred counties and seventy-seven towns had defaulted.[12]

Although property taxes as a percentage of all taxes declined from 85 percent in 1920 to 60 percent in 1929, landowners demanded more relief. State government provided some relief by assuming responsibility for services previously supported locally, administering them more economically and financing them with bond programs. This trend lessened the need for local taxes. In an early 1929 message to the legislature, Gardner proposed that the state assume the responsibility of maintaining some secondary roads and increasing aid to the public schools so as to reduce the county tax burden. The economic crisis of the next few months made that policy even more desirable. In 1930, however, as delinquent taxes mounted to $7.5 million on more than 150,000 pieces of property, the governor refused to call a special session of the legislature to deal with demands for further tax relief.[13]

The 1931 General Assembly wrestled for nearly five months with the question of tax relief. Though by 1931 only 52 percent of state taxes came from property, down 8 percent from 1929, much remained to be done. To ease the local property tax burden, the legislature dramatically assumed control of all state roads and provided support for a six-month school term. This action meant relief at the county level, but the state had to find a way to fund these new responsibilities. The controversy centered on the proposed MacLean bill to finance the school program from revenue other than an additional state property tax. The governor did not support the measure because there was little consensus on funding

12. Corbitt, ed., *Public Papers and Letters of Gardner,* pp. 97–98; Hoover and Ratchford, *Economic Resources*, p. 196; B. U. Ratchford, "The Financial Crisis in North Carolina," *South Atlantic Quarterly* 32 (January 1933): 44, 46; *Raleigh News and Observer,* February 8, 1933.

13. Corbitt, ed., *Public Papers and Letters of Gardner,* pp. xx, 165; Hobbs, *North Carolina*, p. 229; Lefler and Newsome, North Carolina, pp. 606-7.

alternatives; various interests fought the institution of sales or luxury taxes. A year later, Gardner called the sales tax "a perversion of the equitable basis of taxation." A compromise revenue bill placed a fifteen cent ad valorem tax on property and increased corporate income and franchise taxes. A gasoline tax supported the new state highway system. The General Assembly's assumption of control of schools and roads reduced the property tax load overall by more than $12 million, the biggest dollar reduction in property taxes in the history of the state.[14]

Consistent with his policies of retrenchment and tax relief, Gardner established a low-key relief effort for the one hundred thousand unemployed and the twenty thousand displaced tenants. The legislature never contributed to relief for the unemployed. Gardner's Live-at-Home program encouraging farmers to grow enough food for family and livestock, while producing cotton and tobacco for cash surplus, attracted popular attention, but he never expected it to resolve all relief needs. As the Depression deepened, counties, churches, and private charities could not handle the increasing relief needs. In December 1930 Gardner formed the Governor's Council on Unemployment and Relief (GUR), and though its funds were limited, it coordinated local relief efforts for two winters. The state and counties, through the Public Welfare Department, cared for a small number of dependents. The 1931 General Assembly provided the first state subsidy ever for county welfare work, paying the county welfare superintendent to serve as a truant officer. Despite these efforts, distress continued, and the executive secretary of GUR complained that the needs were increasing. Counties, cities, and community chests could not satisfy the relief needs. The state clearly needed outside help.[15]

But state officials could not decide on the nature of federal aid they would seek. The governor's relief administrator and conservative Senator Bailey rejected the federal La Follette-Costigan bill, which called for federal grants to states for unemployment relief. Bailey told the

14. Address by Gardner, May 7, 1932, Gardner Papers; Ratchford, "Financial Crisis," pp. 49, 54; Lefler and Newsome, *North Carolina*, pp. 607–8; Puryear, *Democratic Party Dissension*, pp. 72–78, 90; Corbitt, ed., *Public Papers and Letters of Gardner*, pp. xxxiii, 383, 679–80.

15. Morgan, "Step toward Altruism," p. 21; Gardner to C. A. Williams, November 24, 1931, R. W. Henninger to Josiah W. Bailey, March 2, 1932, Governors' Papers (G); J. S. Kirk, Walter A. Cutler, and Thomas W. Morse, eds., *Emergency Relief in North Carolina: A Record of the Development and the Activities of the North Carolina Emergency Relief Administration, 1932–1935* (Raleigh: Edwards and Broughton, 1936), pp. 22–23; North Carolina State Board of Charities and Public Welfare, *Biennial Report, 1930–1932*, p. 8; R. W. Henninger to Bailey, January 16, 1932, Bailey Papers; Badger, *North Carolina and the New Deal*, p. 9.

governor he opposed the dole and would vote for it only to prevent a revolution and "to keep the people alive until election day." Besides, he pointed out that such a relief measure would primarily aid large cities and would give President Herbert Hoover huge amounts of funds to dispense in an election year. Josephus Daniels, castigating the monopolies and power companies for the present conditions, argued for the relief measure because the state's tenant farmers were in pitiful shape. Nonetheless, President Hoover's opposition killed the La Follette-Costigan bill.[16]

In July 1932 Congress established the Reconstruction Finance Corporation (RFC). Senator Bailey supported it only as an emergency measure and only after Congress added an amendment providing for farm loans. The RFC loaned money for relief in the state. To administer the funds, Gardner created the Governor's Office of Relief (GOR) in September 1932, and this state agency worked with county welfare departments and private agencies to meet relief needs. The RFC program also provided for work relief, and in November 1932 more than one hundred projects were operating in various counties. Cities and counties received RFC grants for their own relief organizations. Between October 1, 1932, and May 31, 1933, North Carolina received almost $6 million in RFC loans. The state and local governments produced over $2 million in matching funds. By October 1932, GOR had 56,697 people on either work or direct relief. The RFC loaned $4.6 million to approximately forty thousand North Carolina farmers.[17]

The record of the Gardner administration on relief, taxes, and retrenchment was similar to that in many states in the early Depression years. Because extensive borrowing was out of the question and revenues from property taxes declining, North Carolina, like other states, seriously considered a sales tax. Although he refused to "soak the rich," as liberals in the state wanted, by increasing business taxes, especially on utilities and tobacco companies, Gardner did compromise, accepting a slight raise in corporate taxes to avoid the unpopular sales tax before the 1932 election. Mounting retrenchment and meager relief efforts underscored the sanctity of the balanced budget. Gardner seemed most concerned about North Carolina's credit rating among New York bank-

16. Bailey to Gardner, February 5, 1932, Josephus Daniels to Bailey, February 13, 1932, Bailey to S. A. Ashe, February 18, 1932, R. W. Henninger to Bailey, February 23, 1932, Bailey Papers.

17. Bailey to E. S. Parker, January 12, 1932, Bailey Papers; *Raleigh News and Observer*, March 21, May 22, 1932; Kirk, Cutler, and Morse, eds., *Emergency Relief in North Carolina*, pp. 23–24; Morgan, "Step toward Altruism," pp. 58, 60–61, 68, 70.

ers and meeting the state's bond obligations. The governor resisted calls for extreme cuts, and North Carolina remained solvent. Retrenchment and property tax relief, initially a response to the expansion of public services in the 1920s, gained strength under Gardner as strategies against the Depression. Gardner's obsessive fiscal conservatism established the policies of state government for a decade, and the results did not bode well for the New Deal in the state.[18]

The 1932 election campaign centered on a factional struggle between Gardner's organization and eastern insurgents for control of state government. In the gubernatorial campaign, insurgents Richard T. Fountain and Allen J. Maxwell attacked both the administration's choice, John C. B. Ehringhaus, as the "machine" candidate and the record of the Gardner administration. The senatorial contest between incumbent Cameron Morrison and challenger Robert R. Reynolds resembled theater more than politics. Reynolds mocked Morrison's wealth and clowned his way through the primary. In the two major state races Ehringhaus survived and Reynolds produced a major upset. In the presidential race, North Carolina's Democratic leaders settled early on Franklin Roosevelt as their choice.

Gardner faced the 1932 campaign as the clear leader of the North Carolina Democratic party, and Simmons was now a former senator living in New Bern, out of politics. In the 1928 campaign Simmons had isolated himself from the majority of the party leaders, and many old guard stalwarts joined Cameron Morrison in endorsing Smith. At the 1928 state convention Simmons had to join forces with his old enemy Josephus Daniels to win a majority of delegates for Cordell Hull over Al Smith. With the senator on the defensive at the convention, Josiah Bailey, leader of the Smith forces, declared that "the Simmons machine is sunk, and without a trace." In August 1928, when Simmons announced that he would not vote for either presidential nominee, former governor Cameron Morrison replaced him as the state's national committeeman. "There is more to the Democratic party in North Carolina than prohibition and Senator Simmons, God bless him," proclaimed Morrison.[19]

During his four years as governor, Gardner strengthened his control of the party. Despite Simmons's opposition, the 1929 legislature restricted absentee voting and passed the secret ballot, thereby inhibiting election

18. Badger, *North Carolina and the New Deal*, pp. 8–9; Patterson, *New Deal and the States*, pp. 26–27.

19. John Robert Moore, *Senator Josiah William Bailey: A Political Biography* (Durham: Duke University Press, 1968), pp. 46–51, 54.

abuses by the old Simmons organization. In May 1929 J. Crawford Biggs, a Gardner ally, became the first chairman of the state board of elections to oppose Simmons in a long time. In 1930 North Carolina gained two new United States senators. Lee Slater Overman died, and Gardner appointed Cameron Morrison to his seat. His naming Morrison, who had already announced as a candidate for 1932, showed Gardner's willingness to absorb political opposition for Morrison had been his rival in 1920, a longtime old guard Democrat, and, until 1928, a Simmons ally. A little later, the new senator returned the favor by depositing money in and rescuing Shelby's First National Bank, where Gardner, a bank director, had his Cleveland Cloth Mills funds.[20]

But far more dramatic was Josiah Bailey's defeat of Simmons in November 1930. After vacillating between Wilsonian Progressivism and association with the Simmons organization before the early 1920s, Bailey lost the governor's race in 1924 against the "machine." In 1928 as the leader of the Smith forces, he championed party regularity. In 1930, when Bailey took on Simmons, he carried eighty-four out of a hundred counties and won by seventy thousand votes. Bailey had both Gardner's and Morrison's support. Simmons's association with Hoover, whom he indirectly aided in 1928, and the Depression were enormous political liabilities, made worse by Bailey's tireless two-year campaign.[21]

On the eve of the 1932 campaign, Gardner was clearly the most influential politician in the state. Though Senator Bailey fought for things important to him, he usually deferred to Gardner on matters relating to state government. An especially welcome visitor at the Governor's Mansion, Bailey shared Gardner's conservative political views and probusiness perspective as well as cordial friendship. Unlike Simmons, whose power rested on a network of local supporters in counties, Gardner built his strength on elected and appointed state officials. The centralization of state government and his friends in the highway and revenue departments enabled him to create an organization that supplanted Simmons's. Gardner appointed eleven of his legislative lieutenants to state positions they helped create. Sam Ervin, Ehringhaus's Burke County campaign manager in 1932, remembered that Gardner's organization "worked like a dynamo," running state government and controlling appointments and candidacies. Ervin, a political ally, de-

20. Richard L. Watson, Jr., "A Southern Democratic Primary: Simmons vs. Bailey in 1930," *North Carolina Historical Review* 42 (Winter 1965): 23–24; Morrison, *Gardner*, pp. 72–73.

21. Watson, "Southern Democratic Primary," pp. 22–23, 39, 43–45; Morrison, *Gardner*, p. 70; Moore, *Bailey*, pp. v, 25, 46.

scribed Gardner as "very intelligent," a man of "tremendous ability," and an "able, colorful speaker." In contrast, Ervin recalled Simmons as highly respected but not personally popular, an "adroit political organizer." According to Ervin, Simmons depended on his political network because he lacked charisma and delivered "dull, dry, prosaic" speeches on the stump. Nonetheless, Gardner, like Simmons before him, maintained an upper hand in North Carolina politics through personal prominence, political allies, and ability to raise campaign funds from corporate interests. Neither exercised dominance to the degree of the Byrd machine in Virginia, but both fostered a clear community of interests compatible to their conservative supporters. During the 1930s a small establishment of political and business leaders, headed by Max Gardner, not a tight political machine, dominated Tar Heel politics.[22]

Several prominent Democrats decided not to challenge Gardner's choice of a successor. The most prominent noncandidate in 1932 was seventy-year-old Josephus Daniels, champion of prohibition, former navy secretary, and easily the state's most important liberal. Daniels had built a reputation as a loyal Democrat and a fierce opponent of corporate interests, especially the tobacco and textile companies. A fellow editor called his newspaper the "most fearless . . . in the South on economic and industrial issues."[23] Daniels favored unions and criticized Gardner's handling of the 1929 Gastonia textile strike. He also wanted the tax burden shifted from the small property holders to the utilities and tobacco companies. Daniels had pushed consistently for greater regulation of the power companies. He sought relief for farmers and backed efforts to reduce crop surpluses. He fought the Gardner administration's reductions in public school appropriations. In a campaign for governor, Daniels could expect support from tenant farmers in the east, small property owners, schoolteachers, and professionals.[24]

Despite his commitment to these issues, Daniels decided in early February 1932 not to enter the race for governor, claiming that his major reason was a pledge he had made forty years earlier never to run for office. The *News and Observer*, he explained, had always been an

22. Puryear, *Democratic Party Dissension*, p. 152; Key, *Southern Politics*, pp. 211, 213–14; Morrison, *Gardner*, p. 167; Moore, *Bailey*, pp. 89, 123–24; Daniels, *Tar Heels*, pp. 324–25; Albright, "Shelby Dynasty," Part 1, p. 9; interview of Samuel J. Ervin, Jr., by Richard Dabney, January 8, August 2, 1974, Southern Oral History Program Collection; Hamrick, "*Miss Fay*," p. 25.

23. Hugh Talmadge Lefler, ed., *North Carolina History Told by Contemporaries* (Chapel Hill: University of North Carolina Press, 1965), p. 435.

24. E. David Cronon, "Josephus Daniels as a Reluctant Candidate," *North Carolina Historical Review* 33 (October 1956): 457, 459–60.

independent newspaper, dedicated to the Democratic party but never to any faction or organization. To campaign for elective office, he believed, would damage his integrity as a journalist. He urged his supporters to back a candidate who favored a taxing policy of getting the money "where the money is."[25]

There were other reasons for Daniels's decision. The most compelling was a serious automobile accident in January 1932, which confined him to bed for a month. In addition, the newspaper staff opposed his entering the race. His son Jonathan Daniels recalled that his "very energetic" father was "eager to do it" but faced "violent" opposition from the family, particularly Mrs. Daniels. A realist, Daniels knew that his popularity in the east would be insufficient to overcome the party organization's strength in the populous piedmont. He understood better than anyone that the outcome would be uncertain at best, and at his age he lacked the will for a tough political battle. Furthermore, a bank failure wiped out his life's savings and jeopardized the *News and Observer*, and only a $25,000 loan from Bernard Baruch eased Daniels through the Depression. Unfortunately for the insurgents, they lost their best candidate. The voters, too, missed a gubernatorial contest based on a serious ideological discussion of the issues.[26]

In March 1932, General Albert L. Cox, a world war hero, surprised his backers by declining to enter the race. Several days later Willis Smith, Speaker of the House during the 1931 legislature, and Thomas A. McNeil, a leader in the drive for tax reduction, decided not to run for governor. During this time, Angus D. MacLean of Beaufort County, a leader in the 1931 General Assembly for state support of the six-month school term without a tax on land, declared that he would not be a candidate for health reasons.[27]

Richard T. Fountain of Edgecombe County was left as the major insurgent challenger, and in July 1931 he announced his candidacy. Fountain, an easterner, a lawyer, former judge, member of the legislature, Speaker of the House from 1927 to 1929, and since 1929 the lieutenant governor, drew support from the agricultural east, the base for the insurgents. Though less firmly than Josephus Daniels, he favored

25. Reprint from *Raleigh News and Observer*, February 15, 1932, Box 674, Josephus Daniels Papers.

26. Joseph L. Morrison, *Josephus Daniels: The Small-d Democrat* (Chapel Hill: University of North Carolina Press, 1966), p. 161; Cronon, "Josephus Daniels," pp. 461–64; unidentified newspaper clipping by J. C. Baskervill, July 13, 1931, Box 129.19, Fountain Papers; interview of Jonathan Daniels by Singal and Tindall, March 22, 30, 1972.

27. *Raleigh News and Observer*, February 29, March 6, 10, 17, 1932.

the interests of certain unions, teachers, and the small farmers who were particularly angry over the low prices paid by the tobacco companies for their crop. He joined eastern politicians in advocating a tax policy that placed a greater burden on the corporations and relieved the small farm owners, and in general he fought for agricultural over business interests. The tobacco-growing east continued as a source of liberal resistance to the conservative machine politics because of the large number of white tenant farmers and a preponderance of small farms.[28]

Rivalry between agrarian interests and the political machine, ongoing since the 1890s, involved more than an ideological battle and revealed the limits of North Carolina's agrarian liberalism. The 1932 contest signaled a revolt against the Gardner organization and a struggle for personal power. Fountain, for example, opposed Gardner's government reorganization plan because it would create a more powerful and centralized state government in Raleigh with more Gardner-appointed officials. Centralization offended Fountain's Jeffersonian beliefs, but it also angered him because it would strengthen the political establishment. In 1932, the insurgent candidate for governor was more interested in attacking the machine than in promoting liberal issues.[29]

Gardner's vigorous support for John C. B. Ehringhaus in the 1932 Democratic primary reinforced the "machine" image, the establishment of the so-called "Shelby Dynasty," named for Gardner's hometown. Following the custom of the east-west rotation for electing governors, 1932 was the east's turn. Ehringhaus hailed from the east, Elizabeth City, but electoral strength for both the Simmons and Gardner organizations was centered in the populous piedmont and western counties. Gardner wanted conservative, probusiness policies important to that section continued through his ally Ehringhaus. Secretary of State Thad Eure, a Gardner protégé who began his tenure in that office in the 1930s, argued that although the Gardner organization was not as strong as Simmons's, Ehringhaus never would have been elected without Gardner's support. He was hardly known west of Raleigh, Eure remembered. In backing Ehringhaus, Gardner was exhibiting his tactic of merging with his political opposition; in the 1920 gubernatorial campaign Ehringhaus had backed Gardner's opponent.[30]

Gardner and Ehringhaus prepared thoroughly for the 1932 challenge.

28. Puryear, *Democratic Party Dissension*, pp. 94–95, 100, 120; Key, *Southern Politics*, pp. 215, 217.

29. Puryear, *Democratic Party Dissension*, pp. v–vi, 231, 234.

30. Interview of Thad Eure by Abrams, June 21, 1983; Key, *Southern Politics*, pp. 217, 220.

Though not prominent statewide, Ehringhaus, a lawyer, had been active in party politics as a state legislator from 1905 to 1907 and solicitor from 1911 to 1923. He had coauthored a bill that gave eastern North Carolina its teacher training college in Greenville. In 1928 he worked hard for the Smith-Gardner ticket; he traveled twelve thousand miles at his own expense, visited ninety-five counties, and delivered nearly sixty speeches. Though not a member of the 1931 General Assembly, Ehringhaus lobbied for Gardner's proposals among eastern politicians. Tyre Taylor, Gardner's counsel and Young Democrats organizer, planned for the 1932 Ehringhaus candidacy. To strengthen ties to the west, Ehringhaus named Major Lennox P. McLendon, a former mayor of Chapel Hill and a prominent official in the American Legion, as his statewide manager. Property tax relief advocate Angus D. MacLean, Congressman Lindsay Warren in the east, and Congressman Alfred Lee Bulwinkle from the west endorsed him. Senator Bailey worked on his behalf, though not publicly. The *Greensboro Daily News*, whose part-owner also served as the Gardner-appointed chairman of the State Highway Commission, editorially supported him, as did the *Raleigh Times* and the *Charlotte Observer*.[31]

In the announcement of his candidacy on August 15, 1931, Ehringhaus called for a "program of progress" but also for a balanced budget and "a strict but sane economy." He reminded voters that "social" progress could not precede "material" progress.[32] His emphasis on economy in government and preservation of the state's credit meshed with Gardner's Depression policies. He endorsed Gardner's centralization of state bureaucracies and declared that taxation was the single most important issue. Five days after his announcement, Ehringhaus described the sales tax as "too high a price to pay" for property tax relief because it would hurt the "impoverished laborer, the back-broken tenant farmer and the hard-pressed merchant." Although he had not been involved in the 1931 legislative tax fight, Ehringhaus was vulnerable on the tax issue because many of his supporters worked with tobacco companies against a luxury tax, and that cooperation cost him support among eastern tobacco farmers. His association with Gardner was also a problem in the

31. H. M. London, ed., *North Carolina Manual, 1933* (Raleigh: North Carolina Historical Commission, 1933), p. 127; Warren to W. H. S. Burgwyn, February 24, 1932, L. P. McLendon to Herbert C. Bonner, March 30, 1932, Warren to Ehringhaus, April 3, 1932, Box 8, Warren Papers; pamphlet, *Ehringhaus the Democrat*, [1932], Box 129.14, Fountain Papers; *Raleigh News and Observer*, March 4, April 19, 1932; Bailey to L. P. McLendon, March 14, 1932, Bailey Papers; Puryear, *Democratic Party Dissension*, p. 99; Albright, "Shelby Dynasty," Part 1, p. 10.

32. Press release, August 20, 1931, Box 3, Carr Papers.

east because the governor equivocated on the tax question and opposed the MacLean bill, an effort to remove property taxes as the basis for school support, a popular cause in the east.[33]

Yet in 1932 Ehringhaus enjoyed several advantages. Though backed by the political establishment, he did not have a long record of public service to defend, an advantage in a Depression year when incumbency was a liability. He could pose as an outsider, a potato farmer, not a state official like both of his primary opponents. Ehringhaus, a skillful campaigner, avoided controversial issues and made few enemies.[34]

The last candidate to announce for governor, Commissioner of Revenue Allen J. Maxwell, proved troublesome to the Gardner organization. Since the 1915 statewide primary law, no gubernatorial primary attracted more than two major candidates, except in 1920. Maxwell announced in September 1931, only one month after Gardner endorsed Ehringhaus. As a member of the administration since 1929, Maxwell had hoped for the governor's blessing, especially because he had the support of one of Gardner's key aides, Fred Morrison. Though he approved of Gardner's policies in general, Maxwell posed a serious threat to the organization from the right because he called for even greater retrenchment in government. He appealed for the election of a General Assembly and an administration committed to a thorough revamping of the tax system and to trimming government at every political level. His austerity platform calling for greater economy and the readjustment of spending by all levels of government appeared too stern and unpleasant, and affected groups such as schoolteachers opposed it. Maxwell, more conservative than Ehringhaus, obscured the clash between the insurgents and the administration forces.[35]

Though the candidates announced nearly a year before the June 4 primary, interest in the campaign lagged through the spring of 1932. The kidnapping of Charles Lindbergh's baby son on March 1 dominated the headlines, and economic troubles diverted attention from politics. Candidates failed to debate fundamental economic issues, thereby contributing to the lack of interest. Instead, Richard Fountain made the Gardner administration the focal point of the campaign. Their feuds in

33. *Raleigh News and Observer,* April 10, 1932; Puryear, *Democratic Party Dissension,* pp. 93, 96; press release, August 20, 1931, Carr Papers.

34. Puryear, *Democratic Party Dissension,* pp. 101, 120.

35. Key, *Southern Politics,* p. 212; Puryear, *Democratic Party Dissension,* pp. 94–95, 101; Morrison, *Gardner,* p. 105; newspaper clippings, *Greensboro Daily News,* September 30, 1931, *Fayetteville Observer,* October 31, November 21, 1931, *Rocky Mount Telegram,* December 23, 1931, Box 95.5, Maxwell Papers.

the 1929 and 1931 legislatures continued into 1932. Fountain attacked the governor for postponing for two years a revaluation of property for tax purposes. Fountain supported the MacLean bill and wanted the state's six-month school term to be financed by another source than an ad valorem property tax. He attacked Gardner's short ballot proposal, an attempt to make several council of state offices appointive rather than elective, because it would put state bureaus, boards, and commissions beyond the reach of the people. He reminded the voters that Gardner was leaving a $6 to $8 million deficit for the next governor and General Assembly. Fountain eagerly associated Ehringhaus with Gardner, charging that the governor had dictated the choice of his successor and coerced state employees, particularly highway department personnel, into backing Ehringhaus. Fountain declared that his opponent had the support of the tobacco companies, utilities, and machine stalwarts.[36]

Ehringhaus was on the defensive for most of the campaign. Stating emphatically that his administration would be his own, he challenged his critics to check his campaign contributions as proof that he was free from the influence of special interests. Fountain, he reminded voters, as a recent Speaker of the House and present lieutenant governor, had to share responsibility for the state's economic woes. As Fountain's antiadministration rhetoric intensified, Ehringhaus countered by accusing him of attacking the Democratic party. Ehringhaus's charge of disloyalty received editorial support from the conservative *Charlotte Observer* and the *Greensboro Daily News*. These editors defended Gardner's integrity, praised Ehringhaus, derided Fountain's ability and ambition, and concluded that his attacks would only aid the Republican party in November. Fountain's ally, the *Raleigh News and Observer*, helped him little because its policy was never to endorse a candidate during a Democratic primary.[37]

In contrast to the machine issue, the candidates generally agreed on tax questions. Revenue Commissioner Maxwell presented the most detailed economic plan, which called for property revaluation, security for bank deposits, and readjustment of government expenditures as tax revenues declined. All three candidates agreed that the fifteen cent ad valorem property tax should be ended, and all three opposed a state

36. Editorial, *Raleigh News and Observer*, February 29, April 10, May 10, June 5, 1932; address, May 9, 1932, Box 139.14, Fountain Papers; Puryear, *Democratic Party Dissension*, pp. 98, 103, 105, 115.

37. Puryear, *Democratic Party Dissension*, pp. 101–2; *Raleigh News and Observer*, April 10, May 14, 1932; Lefler, ed., *North Carolina History*, pp. 434–35; editorial, *Charlotte Observer*, June 3, 1932; editorial, *Greensboro Daily News*, June 2, 1932.

sales tax as an alternate source of revenue. If economic conditions warranted a sales tax, Fountain favored placing it on luxuries, Ehringhaus would leave the issue for the legislature, and Maxwell remained opposed to any sales tax. The state's deficit and the public mood against burdensome property taxes made a sales tax likely, but no candidate for governor in 1932 dared admit it.[38]

On June 4, 1932, Ehringhaus's strength in the west gave him a lead over Fountain of over 47,000 votes, but Fountain and Maxwell's combined total of over 217,000 versus Ehringhaus's 162,000 demonstrated the strength of opposition to Gardner's choice. On June 15 Fountain called for a runoff, yet he faced several disadvantages in a head-on battle with Ehringhaus. Several of Maxwell's supporters joined the administration forces. Fountain suffered from a critical shortage of funds. On June 16 the state Democratic convention in Raleigh, dominated by Gardner and Ehringhaus men, drafted a platform commending the present administration, thereby weakening Fountain's attacks. The last week in June the nomination of Franklin Roosevelt in Chicago diverted attention from the runoff. Nonetheless, Fountain intensified his charges against the machine by claiming that highway department employees carried voters to the polls on June 4 and alleging that in one county there was absentee ballot fraud. He revealed his liberalism by advocating an immediate cash payment of the soldiers' bonus and reminding voters of his preference for the luxury tax over a sales tax. He defended himself against charges that his attacks on Ehringhaus were "Republican" speeches, arguing that the Democratic party was large enough for everyone. On July 2, though the turnout was surprisingly large, and despite the consolation that Ehringhaus had the smallest victory margin on record for a major office in a runoff, Fountain's challenge fell about thirteen thousand votes short. The eastern insurgents battled the Gardner-Ehringhaus organization and press to a virtual standoff, but the administration survived a severe test, two major primary opponents, and a close runoff.[39]

The bitter gubernatorial primary in 1932 did not match the drama of the senatorial race. Former governor Cameron Morrison, appointed in

38. Press release, August 20, 1931, Box 3, Carr Papers; newspaper clipping, *Burlington Daily Times-News*, April 5, 1932, Governors' Papers (E); *Raleigh News and Observer*, June 5, 1932; address, [1932], Box 129.14, Fountain Papers; Puryear, *Democratic Party Dissension*, pp. 98, 101.

39. Puryear, *Democratic Party Dissension*, pp. 105, 108–10, 112, 119; *Raleigh News and Observer*, June 16, 19, July 3, 4, 1932; political handbill, June 25, 1932, and pamphlet, Box 129.14, and press release, June 28, 1932, Box 129.6, Fountain Papers; H. M. London, ed., *North Carolina Manual, 1939* (Durham: Christian Printing Co., 1939), p. 97.

1930 to finish the term of the late senator Lee S. Overman, faced a challenge from political maverick Robert Reynolds, state labor commissioner Frank Grist, and Judge Tam C. Bowie. Early in the campaign, Morrison considered none of the three a serious threat. He had been a fairly popular governor in the early 1920s, known for his expansive road-building and education programs. At sixty-three in 1932, he had a career in state politics reaching back to the white supremacy drives of the 1890s, and after his marriage to a wealthy widow his generous campaign contributions to fellow Democrats further strengthened his ties to the party establishment. Morrison joked that his wife used her money to fight the devil through the Presbyterian church, and if any were left he used it to fight the devil through the Democratic party. Governor Gardner, Senator Bailey, and Congressman Warren supported his candidacy. Yet during his three decades of party activity, Morrison had made enemies. His ties to the old Simmons organization hurt him after Bailey ousted Simmons in 1930. In his brief tenure as a senator, Morrison supported Frank McNinch as Hoover's nominee to the Federal Power Commission, and that appointment reopened the wounds of 1928, when McNinch, a Democrat with ties to Duke Power Company, had backed Hoover over Smith. Morrison's action, intended to reunite the party, created a furor among former Smith partisans. To make matters worse, Morrison defended Duke Power and its foundation by calling it a great beneficent institution. Furthermore, those who favored property tax relief in the 1931 General Assembly protested that Senator Morrison lobbied against it. Traditionally a United States senator did not interfere with the legislature, and his poor judgment cost him support.[40]

Bob Reynolds of Asheville, called by his biographer "a showman, an orator, and a flim-flam man of the highest order," seemed incapable of defeating Cameron Morrison.[41] Married four times, a "wet," with little money, no statewide organization, and a "slacker" during the world war, Reynolds had lost previous races for Congress, lieutenant governor, and the U.S. Senate. In 1910 he successfully ran for district solicitor. He prepared for 1932 by taking a trip around the world the year before and sending voters back home postcards from exotic places. In the midst of the Depression Reynolds attacked the wealthy, and millionaire Mor-

40. *Raleigh News Observer,* March 15, April 22, 23, June 5, 1932; Warren to J. L. Horne, Jr., May 19, 1932, Box 8, Warren Papers; Bailey to William B. Jones, March 5, 21, 1932, Bailey Papers; Gardner to Cameron Morrison, February 5, 1932, Gardner Papers; Morrison, *Gardner,* p. 106.

41. Julian McIver Pleasants, "The Senatorial Career of Robert Rice Reynolds" (Ph.D. dissertation, University of North Carolina, 1971), p. 725.

rison was the perfect target. In a campaign that resembled vaudeville more than politics, Reynolds severely criticized Morrison for being a friend of big business, specifically Duke Power and the tobacco companies. Before large crowds he mocked Morrison's ostentatious wealth, his limousine, his fancy clothes, and his luxurious apartment in Washington's Mayflower Hotel; he enjoyed waving a Mayflower Hotel menu before the audience while exclaiming that Senator Morrison ate caviar, Russian fish eggs, instead of "good ole North Carolina hen eggs." He exaggerated his own poverty by borrowing money, stamps, gas, and automobiles and by staying with friends instead of in hotels. The public never knew he traveled frequently in a private plane throughout the campaign. In a serious vein, Reynolds called for repeal of prohibition and for government control and taxation of liquor. He advocated a balanced federal budget, taxes on corporations, guaranteed bank deposits, and payment of the soldiers' bonus.[42] Reynolds, like Fountain, did not challenge conservatives with bold liberal alternatives.

On June 4 the forty-seven-year-old Reynolds stunned the political establishment by winning a thirteen-thousand-vote margin over Morrison; but without a majority, a runoff primary was necessary. Shaken from his overconfidence, Morrison quickly set up a campaign organization, and administration forces rallied to his side. The *Charlotte Observer* cautioned against panic and continued its ardent editorial support for its native son. Before the first primary, neither Morrison nor his friends had worked very hard. Reynolds polled strongly in the east and mountains, while Morrison held firm in the piedmont. Gardner knew that the Reynolds forces encouraged Fountain to call for a runoff and thereby increase the turnout in the east. Ousted candidate Tam C. Bowie, a "dry," surprised the state by endorsing Reynolds, but the other first primary casualty, Frank Grist, backed Morrison. The attention party members gave the Democratic National Covention in Chicago the last week of the runoff made it more difficult for Morrison to catch up. Furthermore, that convention's platform calling for repeal of the Eighteenth Amendment enhanced Reynolds's "wet" position and embarrassed Morrison. On July 2, the primary date, it did not really matter, for Reynolds beat Morrison by almost a two-to-one margin, the largest ever for a Democratic primary. Journalist Gerald W. Johnson viewed

42. Pleasants, "Robert Reynolds," pp. 30, 37, 49, 51, 66, 68, 70, 76, 86, 90; Puryear, *Democratic Party Dissension*, pp. 137–40; Arthur L. Shelton, "Buncombe Bob," *American Mercury* 27 (October 1932): 140–41, 143; *Raleigh News and Observer*, March 25, 1932; Alan A. Michie and Frank Ryhlick, *Dixie Demagogues* (New York: Vanguard Press, 1939), pp. 233, 235.

Reynolds's election as a North Carolina version of "Blease-ism," while Senator Bailey, fearing something worse than Populism, recognized that Reynolds perhaps had "caught the imagination of the distressed and the enthusiasm of the younger element in the party." Reynolds's dramatic campaign, his personality, his exploitation of discontent with wealth, Depression, and prohibition, his demagoguery, his timely position on repeal of prohibition, and Morrison's errors all joined to win a victory for "Our Bob." Also in the runoff, the "machine" seemed more concerned about rescuing Ehringhaus than Morrison.[43]

North Carolina Democrats fought over their nominees for governor and senator but not over their choice for the presidential nomination. By 1931 party leaders in the state settled on Roosevelt, considered a part-time southerner because of his stays in Warm Springs, Georgia, and believed the most likely one to deliver the party from former nominee Al Smith and Democratic National Chairman John J. Raskob. Former Secretary of War Newton D. Baker and Virginia Governor Harry Flood Byrd stirred some interest, but Roosevelt's support held firm through early 1932. Josephus Daniels, Roosevelt's former boss in the Wilson administration Navy Department, remained in constant communication with the New York governor and had supported him since 1930. Gardner also joined the forces of a fellow governor, as did Senators Bailey and Morrison, along with the state's congressmen. Confident of the North Carolina delegation's endorsement of Roosevelt, party leaders decided against any preconvention organization in the state for fear that formal activity on behalf of their candidate might provoke opposition. They feared prohibitionist efforts for Byrd of Virginia. On June 16 at the state convention, Roosevelt's and James A. Farley's courtship of the party regulars paid off when the delegation instructed for the New York governor. The state convention elected Gardner chairman of the delegation and also endorsed the record of his administration. "My position in the party is today unchallenged," Gardner confided to New York stockbroker John W. Hanes before he headed for Chicago.[44]

43. *Raleigh News and Observer*, June 8, 14, July 3, 4, 1932; editorial, *Charlotte Observer*, June 7, 1932; Gardner to John W. Hanes, June 21, 1932, Gardner Papers; Puryear, *Democratic Party Dissension*, pp. 148, 151–52; Moore, *Bailey*, p. 89; Pleasants, "Robert Reynolds," p. 141; London, ed., *North Carolina Manual, 1939*, p. 105; Gerald W. Johnson to Bailey, July 4, 1932, Bailey to Johnson, July 6, 1932, Bailey Papers.

44. Gardner to John W. Hanes, June 21, 1932, Gardner Papers; Bailey to FDR, February 8, 1932, Bailey Papers; Josephus Daniels to FDR, May 4, 1932, Box 95, Josephus Daniels Papers; *Raleigh News and Observer*, June 28, 1932; Aubrey Lee Brooks, *A Southern Lawyer: Fifty Years at the Bar* (Chapel Hill: University of North Carolina Press, 1950), pp. 138, 141; Tindall, *Emergence of the New South*, pp. 386–88; interview of Jonathan Daniels by Eagles, March 9–11, 1977.

Though President Hoover had carried the state in 1928, Democrats did not worry because of his present unpopularity. Ehringhaus and Reynolds had no serious Republican opposition. Some Democrats, however, worried about the prohibition issue because their national platform called for repeal while the Republican one did not. Ehringhaus, "dry," and Reynolds, "wet," agreed that the question must be settled by a referendum. The state Democratic party remained united for the campaign. Ehringhaus attacked Hoover for taxation that was impoverishing and for excessive federal spending. Gardner, claiming his identification with the conservative wing of the party for the past twenty years, in a note assured Roosevelt that business interests supported the ticket. Josephus Daniels wrote a campaign article for the *Saturday Evening Post* entitled "Franklin Roosevelt as I Know Him" and in September made a western campaign swing for FDR. Senator Bailey's former political manager handled Roosevelt's effort in the state, which climaxed on October 25 with a visit by Roosevelt to North Carolina, where he spoke to ten thousand people at the Raleigh fairgrounds. FDR's majority on November 8, the largest ever recorded in the state by any candidate, exceeded that of either Ehringhaus or Reynolds. North Carolina voters thoroughly repudiated Hoover's stewardship of the nation's economy.[45]

On the eve of the New Deal, after weathering over three years of depression, North Carolinians had established the state's pattern for the 1930s. The Gardner administration, especially the 1931 legislature, and the 1932 campaign further entrenched conservative control. In four years Gardner built a political organization that replaced Simmons's, and the election of Ehringhaus perpetuated that conservative hold on state government. The Gardner years also revealed the paucity of agrarian liberalism, whether in the legislature or the 1932 campaign. The liberals, opponents of the machine, showed great strength at the polls in a losing gubernatorial race but also revealed ideological weakness by seldom venturing beyond the tax question. Little in the Fountain or Reynolds campaigns anticipated the New Deal; both seemed more intent on defeating the organization than having state government fight the Depression. Instead, the agenda remained conservative, and the issue of the decade was how little state government could do.

Along with persistent conservatism, North Carolinians in 1932 ex-

45. Gardner to FDR, July 22, 1932, Gardner Papers; Bailey to FDR, November 16, 1932, Bailey Papers; *Raleigh News and Observer*, October 2, 15, 26, November 9, 1932; Gardner to FDR, August 4, 1932, Presidential Personal File 393, Roosevelt Papers; Morrison, *Josephus Daniels*, pp. 164–66.

hibited an ambivalence that would continue throughout the decade. They placed hope in Roosevelt to bring economic recovery, and the forces for change from Washington would often clash with the economic and political oligarchy's preference for the status quo. Max Gardner understood this ambivalence. In a letter to Roosevelt in July 1932, he demonstrated a flexibility, an understanding of change, as well as a need to remain on good terms with the likely next president, important to Gardner because he would soon be a lawyer-lobbyist in New Deal Washington. "What this nation needs is a strong man with a sense of social justice," he confided to Roosevelt. "If I were Roosevelt," he continued, "I would become more liberal." "I think your idea of a new deal should be emphasized," he added. North Carolina conservatives like Gardner remained open-minded about prospects for reform in Washington, and as long as it helped the state and did not threaten their power, they would cooperate.[46] The New Deal's plan for business provided the first test.

46. Gardner to FDR, July 22, 1932, Gardner Papers.

CHAPTER 2

Business and the National Recovery Administration

During Roosevelt's first Hundred Days as president, Congressman Robert L. Doughton of North Carolina supported legislation in the House aimed at economic recovery. In June 1933 Congress passed the National Industrial Recovery Act that created the National Recovery Administration to regulate industrial wages, hours, and production and the Public Works Administration (PWA) to spur business and provide work relief. Cotton textile leaders in the state, beset by overproduction and destructive competition, sought help through the NRA. Their relationship to this agency over the next two years mirrored the ambiguous attitude of Tar Heel business and political leaders toward the New Deal: initial enthusiasm born of economic self-interest with no commitment to reform turned to stout opposition when the program proved ineffective. North Carolina businessmen needed assistance, they perceived the NRA as helpful, and they supported it. Cotton textile industrialists helped draft the first NRA code, and generally state businessmen dominated their respective code authorities. In the months ahead, however, as the NRA resulted in higher wages, strikes, and union activity, opposition galvanized. Tobacco companies in the state, in a virtual mockery of the NRA, stalled in their negotiations and avoided a code until a few months before the agency ended. The power of business, along with the NRA's modest goals, thwarted recovery in the state.

Business executives in the state welcomed the New Deal's assistance, for the period 1930 to 1933 had brought dramatic decline, and North Carolina, the most industrialized southern state, sensed those economic reverses perhaps more keenly than others in the region. North Carolina, and the South as a whole, did not suffer as greatly as the rest of the nation because it lacked significant amounts of heavy industry. After 1930, despite losses, the Tar Heel State retained its regional industrial supremacy. The 1930 total value of manufacturing in the state equaled approximately $1.3 billion, and by 1933 the figure fell to $878 million. Sales dropped significantly from 1929 to 1935, yet another sign that the state's industry was not recovering. Wholesale trade sales fell almost $140 million, and retail trade sales plummeted $182 million over the six-year period.[1]

As industry suffered, the state's workers retained little hope for improving their wages. Seven percent of North Carolina's population worked in textile, furniture, and tobacco manufacturing establishments, and by far the largest number of that group were the 158,504 textile workers, over 40 percent of whom were women. From 1929 to 1933 wages in the cotton textile industry declined by 25 percent, while the number of wage earners remained fairly constant. With its huge employment, value added by manufacturing, and factories scattered throughout the piedmont, textiles dominated industry in the state. This industry's troubles did not portend well for the state's economic recovery. By 1933 North Carolina's per capita income was 56 percent of the national average. The state ranked thirty-ninth nationally and in the middle of the southern states. Seven southern states had lower per capita incomes.[2]

The cotton textile industry led the way in cooperating with the NRA, an enthusiasm sought by New Deal promoters and symbolized by the Blue Eagle, emblem of the NRA. Initially, state textile manufacturers demonstrated enthusiasm for an agency that promised to stabilize their industry through coordination with that industry's trade association. Roosevelt's recovery program offered predictability and planning of costs, marketing, employment, and wages. The NRA sought to accomplish what the textile producers had been striving for since 1926, when they formed their trade association, the Cotton Textile Institute (CTI), to limit production, end price cutting, and reduce competition. The 1920s had been a disastrous decade for textiles, and the manufacturers responded well to the voluntary trade association movement. By 1930, 80 percent of the industry had voluntarily restricted production.[3]

As further encouragement to industry, the NRA provided for a tempo-

1. Hoover and Ratchford, *Economic Resources*, pp. 116–17; Lefler and Newsome, *North Carolina*, p. 630; U.S. Department of Commerce, Bureau of the Census, *Sixteenth Census of the United States: 1940, Census of Business*, Vol. 1: *Retail Trade, 1939* (Washington, D.C.: U.S. Government Printing Office, 1941), p. 58; Vol. 2: *Wholesale Trade* (Washington, D.C.: U.S. Government Printing Office, 1942), p. 261.

2. Hoover and Ratchford, *Economic Resources*, p. 50; North Carolina Department of Labor, *Biennial Report, 1934–1936*, pp. 45–46; "Statistical Materials: No. 1, The Cotton Textile Industry," December 1935, NRA Papers; Lefler and Newsome, *North Carolina*, p. 581.

3. George B. Tindall, "The 'Colonial Economy' and the Growth Psychology: The South in the 1930s," *South Atlantic Quarterly* 64 (Autumn 1965): 466; Tindall, *Emergence of the New South*, p. 433; Badger, "New Deal and North Carolina," pp. 52–54.

rary relaxation of antitrust legislation, briefly abandoning the ideal of competition. The government clearly wanted to use the trade associations to steady and regiment the sluggish economy. The partnership of government and the trade association, which the NRA achieved, represented a definite shift from the voluntarism of the Cotton Textile Institute to coercion. The trade association could use government power to accomplish the purposes of a majority of its members so it was little wonder that the editor of the *Charlotte Observer*, mouthpiece for the textile interests, supported the CTI and its efforts to control the cotton textile industry. In an early May 1933 editorial, he boasted that the CTI had Roosevelt's backing and that the government was not a "controlling" factor but a "cooperative agency." He argued that the CTI needed the power of the government to force into line the "rebellious ten percent" in the textile industry that would not go along with the CTI system.[4]

North Carolina business and political leaders responded to Roosevelt's recovery program with a mixture of enthusiasm, caution, and opposition. The state congressional delegation voted overwhelmingly for it. Robert L. Doughton, chairman of the Ways and Means Committee and floor leader for the bill in the House, called it "one of the most important pieces of legislation that has perhaps ever been considered by the Congress within the history of our country." Doughton, typical of conservative southern Democrats whose support was vital to the New Deal, followed Roosevelt's leadership and worked behind the scenes for his programs. The seventy-year-old farmer from the mountains defended the NRA on the House floor by pointing to the emergency and stressing confidence in the administration. The NRA provided a "middle course" between monopoly and ruinous competition. "Flexible remedies are always necessary in emergencies," he continued. He acknowledged that the measure gave "unprecedented power and authority" to the president but added that the nation faced "unprecedented conditions." "Chatter and hair-splitting about the Constitution will find little sympathy among the American people," he warned. Fellow Tar Heel and dean of the House Edward W. Pou chaired the Rules Committee and expedited passage of the NRA. Calling it the "capstone" of the recovery program, Pou said it was necessary "to bring this nation out of the bottomless pit of hell in which we found ourselves." "It is very true that under this bill," he continued, "the president . . . is made a dictator

4. Louis Galambos, *Competition and Cooperation: The Emergence of a National Trade Association* (Baltimore: Johns Hopkins University Press, 1966), pp. 196, 201–2; editorial *Charlotte Observer*, May 9, 1933.

over industry for the time being, but it is a benign dictatorship." Curiously, in the Senate the more conservative Josiah Bailey voted for it, while the more New Dealish Robert Reynolds voted no, as some liberals did, because they believed it favored big business.[5]

Former governor Max Gardner typified those ambivalent to the New Deal. In 1933, after four years as governor and with his personal finances critically low because of reverses in textiles and the stock market, Gardner moved to Washington and became a lawyer-lobbyist for such clients as the Cotton Textile Institute and the National Aeronautical Organization. He resigned as North Carolina's Democratic national committeeman to remove any possibility of conflict of interest. Gardner commanded substantial fees, which supplemented his income as owner of the Cleveland Cloth Mills in Shelby. Having served as governors together, Gardner and Roosevelt remained on excellent terms. Gardner had such easy access to Roosevelt that he could take a cab to the White House and walk right in to speak with the president. As a frequent adviser to Roosevelt, Gardner was the state's most influential figure for the NRA and an important liaison between the New Deal and big business.[6]

Gardner, along with other conservative Democrats, initially backed the NRA as a temporary measure to meet the immediate emergency. On a more practical level, Gardner represented those upper South mill owners who dominated the textile industry and who sought protection from competing newer firms of the lower South through production controls, whether enacted by the CTI or the NRA. A political realist and a loyal Democrat, Gardner appreciated Roosevelt's popularity and the public mood. In public and with avid New Dealers, Gardner appealed for strong action on the part of the administration and urged his business friends to support the changes or risk something worse. If the president "does not come through with something big and radical," Gardner confided to Josephus Daniels, "we are lost." In an address to the Raleigh Chamber of Commerce, Gardner described the New Deal as a shift from a "civilization built around a survival of the fittest . . . and rugged individualism" to a "drive in cooperation." Gardner compared the date of

5. *Congressional Record,* 73d Cong., 1st sess. (1933), pp. 3611, 4188, 4201–3, 4207, 4373, 5694, 5700, 5861; Tindall, *Emergence of the New South,* pp. 608–9; William E. Leuchtenburg, *Franklin D. Roosevelt and the New Deal, 1932–1940* (New York: Harper & Row, 1963); p. 58.

6. Badger, "New Deal and North Carolina," pp. 119–20; Gardner to J. Wallace Winborne, October 12, 1933, Gardner Papers; interview of Edwin Gill by Archie K. Davis, September 10, 12, October 2, 1974.

the passage of the eight-hour day to July 4, 1776, and observed that "one of the marvels of this age is the manner in which the standpatters, the Bourbons, and the recalcitrants have been forced to take their places in the ranks and keep step with that great social and economic drill master, Franklin D. Roosevelt."[7]

His hearty support for the NRA placed Gardner in the vanguard of moderate southern mill men. To his business and political associate in Cleveland County Odus M. Mull, Gardner defended his support for higher wages for mill workers by exclaiming that "I am in no sense a socialist!" Gardner noted with pride and vindication that, after several months under the NRA, textile employment and wages had improved dramatically.[8]

Despite his enthusiasm for the NRA, which he believed in the best interest of the textile industry, Gardner remained a conservative businessman with strong ties to corporate interests in North Carolina, and he understood the risks of a too radical recovery program. To his more conservative business allies, Gardner simultaneously complained about the Roosevelt administration and tried to reassure them. To S. Clay Williams of the Reynolds Tobacco Company, Gardner expressed concern during the first Hundred Days that the president might have set a bad example by attempting more than he could handle. Gardner embraced the NRA but fretted over the rest of the New Deal. By the spring of 1934 he warned Roosevelt repeatedly that pushing Congress to pass more and more new legislation risked forcing too much upon the country and might be a "colossal blunder." Writing to his friend Benjamin B. Gossett, a prominent Charlotte textile executive, Gardner remarked that more conservative policies were needed from Washington. In 1935, Gardner complained to Gossett that nearly one-third of the nation on relief was "living off the taxpayers," and he feared a collapse of the relief system that would mean even more radical measures.[9] Throughout the first two years of the New Deal, Gardner's political loyalty never overrode his cautious and tentative private ambiguity toward the New Deal.

Although southern industrialists like Gardner praised aspects of the New Deal recovery program that worked in their best interests, more

7. Newspaper clipping, *Winston-Salem Journal,* January 27, 1934, Gardner to P. D. McLean, July 17, 1933, to Josephus Daniels, February 20, 1933, Gardner Papers; Galambos, *Competition and Cooperation*, p. 160; Patterson, *New Deal and the States*, p. 31.

8. Gardner to FDR, May 5, 1933, to O. M. Mull, July 26, 1933, newspaper clipping, *Raleigh News and Observer,* Januay 27, 1934, Gardner Papers.

9. Gardner to S. Clay Williams, April 7, 1933, to Edwin Gill, March 23, 1934, to Ben B. Gossett, March 27, April 13, 1934, April 3, 1935, Gardner Papers.

perceptive ones foresaw problems. The NRA stood in stark contrast to the New South economic growth philosophy. Those few textile mill owners who wished to expand production with no limits were horrified by the NRA proposal to restrict hours of operation in the factories. Some owners knew that such restriction would allow the New England textile mills to regain some of the competitive edge that they had lost in the last few decades to the more expansive southern industry. The NRA labor philosophy also posed a serious threat to the low-wage tradition that was a key part of New South economic growth. Government support for collective bargaining and unionization for mill workers clashed with southern insistence on cheap labor as an advantage in their competition with northern industry. Thus the passage of the recovery act by Congress presented a dilemma for southern and Tar Heel industrialists. The NRA appeared simultaneously attractive and threatening.[10]

After Congress enacted the legislation, attention in North Carolina centered during the early summer of 1933 on the establishment of the code for the cotton textile industry. The twenty members of the code committee were major national figures in the industry. George A. Sloan, president of the Cotton Textile Institute, chaired the committee. Other key members of the group were Thomas M. Marchant, president of the American Cotton Manufacturing Association, which had headquarters in Charlotte, North Carolina; and Ernest Hood, head of the Boston-based National Association of Cotton Manufacturing. Prominent mill owners made up the rest of the code committee. Only about half were southerners, and that was surprising because the cotton textile industry was a predominantly southern industry. In 1933 the region produced 70 percent of the nation's cotton goods.

About one-fifth of the committee came from North Carolina, an indication of the state's leadership in the industry; more than one-fourth of the nation's cotton goods establishments were in North Carolina. State textile leaders Charles A. Cannon, Stuart W. Cramer, Jr., and Benjamin B. Gossett served on the NRA code authority. Former governor Max Gardner worked feverishly with the president's committee that formulated the recovery act during the Hundred Days, and he urged the president's men to name his fellow textile manufacturer and close friend Ben Gossett of Charlotte to the code committee. Gardner felt comfortable with men like Gossett writing the regulations for the textile industry. Charles A. Cannon, son of the founder of Cannon Mills and president of the textile giant since 1921, served on Gardner's State

10. Tindall, "'Colonial Economy'" pp. 466–67.

Highway Commission and assisted state government in obtaining credit during the Depression. Shy, though a tough competitor, Cannon proved an innovator with his aggressive advertising. In 1932 he led the North Carolina Cotton Manufacturers Association. Stuart Cramer, mill owner, engineer, and Duke Power executive, helped organize the CTI and other professional textile associations. A leader in state Republican politics, Cramer served on Hoover's Organization on Unemployment Relief. Cannon and Cramer, both public-spirited and eager for NRA assistance, suited Roosevelt's plans for industrial recovery.[11]

Industry representatives dominated the code-making process. The original code called for a minimum wage of ten dollars a week for the South and eleven dollars for the North for a forty-hour workweek. The industry won a key point when the code placed a two-shift limit on mill production and established controls on new factories entering the industry and expansion of ones already in existence. Through these provisions, industry leaders hoped to control those troublesome manufacturers who had refused to cooperate with the CTI's voluntary controls since the 1920s. Government gained a key concession from industry in the original code—recognition of the right of unions to organize.[12]

Despite the gains, George Sloan of the CTI reported in early June 1933 that two-thirds of the industry favored a change in the code, undoubtedly because of the concessions on labor and the minimum wage. Labor also complained and, after the code hearings in June, won some important points. Largely because of pressure from labor, the code authority increased the minimum wage to twelve dollars a week in the South and thirteen dollars in New England. At the code hearings the audience cheered when textile executives announced plans to abolish child labor, and the code prohibited the employment of any child under sixteen. To placate the industry, the NRA delegated the major responsibility for administration of the code to the CTI. The trade association would collect statistics on wages, hours, operation of machinery, production, stocks, and orders, and then furnish the NRA with reports. On balance, the code represented a triumph of business over labor.[13]

11. "Cabinet Committee Report on Cotton Textile Industry," August 21, 1935, "Cotton Textile Industry" folder [n.d.], George R. Dickson, "History of Code of Fair Competition for the Cotton Textile Industry," NRA Papers; Gardner to Ben B. Gossett, May 15, 1933, Gardner Papers; Marjorie W. Young, ed., *Textile Leaders of the South* (Anderson, S.C.: James R. Young, Publisher, 1963), pp. 41, 735, 739, 744; William S. Powell, ed., *Dictionary of North Carolina Biography*, Vol. 1: *A–C* (Chapel Hill: University of North Carolina Press, 1979), pp. 319, 455.

12. Galambos, *Competition and Cooperation*, pp. 213–14.

13. Code of Fair Competition for the Cotton Textile Industry, July 17, 1933, memo, June 9, 1933, NRA Papers; Galambos, *Competition and Cooperation*, pp. 219–20, 223–24; Leuchtenburg, *Franklin D. Roosevelt and the New Deal*, p. 65.

The southern branch of the textile industry registered a major victory when the government accepted the North-South wage differential, so important to the South in maintaining a competitive edge over the New England mills. The Southern States Industrial Council argued the southern mill owners' case effectively before the NRA code authority. The council's defense of the wage differential ranged from arguments based on practical economics, regional differences, and tradition, to those built on paternalism, racism, and sexism. It pointed out that the southern industry was less mechanized and as a result relied more on manpower. Since the South employed more laborers and labor was more costly than machines, southern industry had to pay lower wages than the northern industry with its modern machines and highly skilled workers. Mechanization, this circular argument continued, was not as necessary for the South because white workers could earn a "comfortable living without exerting too much effort," and there was an "abundant supply of Negro labor of subnormal capabilities" that precluded blacks becoming skilled machine operators. In North Carolina mills, over 40 percent of the workers were women but few were in skilled positions, and owners worried that northern mills could employ skilled female workers more cheaply than the South could employ skilled male workers.[14]

Factories in the South were generally not located near large markets, and freight rates increased production and distribution costs. These extra expenses made the owners less able to pay wages comparable to those of New England, the committee believed. Southern manufacturers also claimed that climate caused lower production in the South because the heat and humidity reduced the speed, accuracy, and productivity of workers. One mill owner frankly stated that southern textiles, as a low-wage industry, merited the wage differential. Some owners convinced themselves that mill employees, many just off the farm, were accustomed to low wages, and others argued that the NRA must consider the benefits of the mill village in pondering wage levels.[15]

Not all southerners agreed with the businessmen that the South deserved a wage differential. Jonathan Daniels, liberal, ardent New Dealer, who in 1933 took over as editor of the *Raleigh News and Observer* when his father left to become Roosevelt's ambassador to Mexico, vigorously condemned the principle behind a wage difference

14. "Summary of Outstanding Factors Justifying a Wage Differential between the South and Other Sections of the Country," from the Wage Differential Committee of the Southern States Industrial Council, NRA Papers; North Carolina Department of Labor, *Biennial Report, 1934–1936*, p. 45.

15. "Summary Justifying a Wage Differential," W. D. Anderson, "Notes for Statement in Washington," June 16, 1933, NRA Papers.

for the two regions. He bristled at the NRA's accommodation of the southern arguments about cost-of-living differences, need to attract industry, and the presence of unskilled blacks. Daniels argued that a wage differential thwarted equal recovery in the South and that it "damns them all to a sectional poverty in a rich nation." Daniels wanted the NRA to use the force of government to improve the lot of the workingman, not to sanction low wages.[16]

In the face of opposition from men such as Daniels to the NRA textile code, industry leaders viewed the result as a major victory for their industry and trade association, the CTI. Under the code, the government would cooperate with industry to strive to bring stability to a suffering business. In one sense the trade association triumphed, not the government or industry, because the CTI had effectively represented the manufacturers, helped shape public policy, and the Roosevelt administration followed its leadership. The code pleased the government as well as cotton manufacturers. Roosevelt pressured the industry for quick action on the NRA's first code, and the textile industry's expeditious creation of a code earned the goodwill of NRA director Hugh Johnson and President Roosevelt. Government-industry consensus on minimum wages, production controls, and the length of the workweek overcame the challenges from labor unions and southern manufacturers.[17]

At the end of 1933, after several months of following the NRA code, cotton textile mills reported a net profit of over $13.4 million, or a 4 percent increase of profits to net worth. Workers, too, enjoyed some progress. Employment in cotton textiles jumped from 314,000 in March 1933 to 465,000 by April 1934. In the summer of 1934 workers averaged $11.54 for approximately 36.5 hours though the average for the South was about $9.70. Before the code a typical mill employee in the South was paid $8.50 for a fifty-hour workweek. The $11.54 average weekly wage in July 1934 for the entire cotton textile industry was a decline in dollars from the $15.65 average for 1929, but when the NRA economists adjusted the July 1934 wage to the cost of living, it totaled about $15, no real decline. The NRA officials concluded in September 1934 that cotton textiles enjoyed a better "upward adjustment" than most industries after adoption of NRA codes. Although the government recognized some improvement, its economists were pessimistic about the prospects for

16. Charles W. Eagles, "Prudent Rebel: Jonathan Daniels and Race Relations" (Ph.D. dissertation, University of North Carolina, 1978), pp. 51–53.

17. Galambos, *Competition and Cooperation*, pp. 199–201, 206–9, 226.

increasing real wages in the immediate future. The NRA had not solved the roots of the wage problem such as low consumption, low production, and a reduced workweek, but actual money wages seemed to be as high as practicable under present conditions.[18]

In 1934 the industry's enthusiasm for the NRA cotton textile code cooled considerably. As long as the code promised to serve their interests, manufacturers cooperated. But after several months, although the crisis eased, it was clear that the NRA could not solve chronic overproduction. Powerful government bureaucracy now threatened the industry with red tape and restrictions. Mill owners complained about higher wages, higher cotton prices, and processing taxes. Rural areas feared higher wages would draw workers to cities. Businessmen in the state mistrusted a New Deal that endorsed collective bargaining, and labor unrest in the summer of 1934 brought industry's honeymoon with the NRA to an end amid mounting hostility and frustration.[19]

The administration's agricultural program of crop reduction and processing taxes assessed to industry to finance benefit payments to farmers caused the price of cotton to rise. In 1933, for example, North Carolina alone produced seventy-six thousand fewer bales of cotton than it did in 1929. Despite the wage differential, wages in the South under the code increased by as much as 50 to 100 percent, higher than the increase in the North. Industry officials viewed the trend as dangerous to the South, and they warned that if not corrected it could lead to increased unemployment because of closings or mechanization. In late spring 1934 disgruntled manufacturers in North Carolina threatened to shut down one week in May, June, and July and not to follow the NRA proposal for reducing the number of hours of operation without reducing workers' pay. George Sloan, CTI chairman, disagreed with those mill owners and pushed for a thirty-six-hour week with no change in pay scales, despite the overproduction and reduced demand that plagued the industry. Sales of cotton cloth for the last two weeks of April 1934 amounted to less than half of production. NRA Director Hugh Johnson approved of the

18. George Dickson, "History of Code of Fair Competition for the Cotton Textile Industry," V. S. von Szeliski, "Wage Differential in the Cotton Textile Industry," August 14, 1934, Szeliski, "What Wage Rise, If Any, Is Possible in the Cotton Textile Industry?" September 4, 1934, Clement Winston, "Preliminary Abstract of Work on Labor Compliance Activities of the Cotton Textile Industry Code Authority," December 1, 1935, NRA Papers.

19. Ellis W. Hawley, "The New Deal and Business," in *The New Deal*, Vol. 1, *The National Level*, ed. John Braeman, Robert H. Bremner, and David Brody (Columbus: Ohio State University Press, 1975), p. 65; Patterson, *New Deal and the States*, p. 116; Tindall, *Emergence of the New South*, pp. 437–38.

proposal to reduce production so the mills could share the declining business.[20]

The long-term failure to resolve the wage problem brought on the largest strike in American history up to that time. In September 1934, textile union leaders demanded union recognition, an end to the stretch-out, and a thirty-hour week with no pay cut. Spurred by NIRA 7(a), workers challenged the management bias of the code authority and uncovered a weakness in the New Deal's associative philosophy, the government's close relationship with industry as evidenced by the NRA and the CTI.[21]

Frustrations like those felt by workers at Tanner's Stonecutter Mills in Spindale began to mount. The company fired union members and increased production. Workers walked out when the appeals board dismissed complaints, and they walked out again after losing what they veiwed as an unfair union vote. In the end Hugh Johnson sided with management. This incident and a similar one at Max Gardner's Cleveland Cloth Mills caused unionists in North Carolina to lose faith in the NRA. The New Deal had not followed the advice of Haynes Willoughby, a Durham cotton mill worker: "The quicker the government learns the boss class cannot be trusted and builds a wall of protection around it the better it will be for all."[22]

Labor's prospects for success were never good. Despite NIRA 7(a), which provided collective bargaining rights, only an estimated 35 percent of North Carolina textile workers joined the union. The southern worker's attitude, linked to the agrarian tradition, was simultaneously highly individualistic and deferential to authority. Unskilled workers were scattered among many small mills across North Carolina, and isolation hampered unionization. Small mills encouraged a close relationship between officials and workers, and the paternalism of the mill village weakened the leverage of the textile worker. One survey of five hundred families in four North Carolina mill towns revealed that about 70 percent lived in company-owned housing. Hostility of manufacturers

20. H. H. Pixley, "Wage Differential," May 11, 1934, George Sloan to Hugh Johnson, May 19, 1934, "Statistical Material: No. 1, The Cotton Textile Industry," December 1935, NRA Papers; newspaper clipping, *Raleigh News and Observer*, May 13, 1934, Gardner Papers; Tindall, *Emergence of the New South*, p. 437; *Tindall*, "'Colonial Economy'" p. 468.

21. Galambos, *Competition and Cooperation*, p. 266; Tindall, *Emergence of the New South*, pp. 509–11.

22. Jacquelyn Dowd Hall, James Leloudis, Robert Korstad, Mary Murphy, LuAnn Jones, and Christopher B. Daly, *Like a Family: The Making of a Southern Cotton Mill World* (Chapel Hill: University of North Carolina Press, 1987), pp. 324, 327–28.

and state government toward unions also thwarted any advances by organized labor. Cheap wages lured industry, but unionization meant high wages and no growth.[23]

Mill owners took a tough stand. Many employers refused to deal with the United Textile Workers Union (UTW) and blacklisted workers who joined. Spofford Mills at Wilmington ignored an employee committee and dismissed the union committeemen. In Hickory, Highland Cordage Mills fired workers who joined the UTW. Management in Lumberton discharged workers for distributing a labor newspaper and for talking with a labor organizer. Despite Section 7(a), collective bargaining remained illusory to textile workers.[24]

Although most mill owners and the general business community in the South doggedly opposed unionism, certain large textile leaders of the upper South became friendlier to the idea, even if only out of self-interest. They wanted to end the competition from mills in the Deep South that used even cheaper labor. In North Carolina, owners such as Kemp P. Lewis pushed this point of view. Even the *Charlotte Observer*, mouthpiece for the manufacturers, on the eve of the September 1934 strike stoutly defended workers' right to organize and strike as "belonging to the essential sovereignty of the citizen." The newspaper carefully added that workers also had a right to remain unorganized and to work during a strike if they so chose. The *Greensboro Daily News* criticized the mill owners for refusing to confer with union representatives in NRA code disputes over wages and hours. The editor argued that resisting reasonable government-sponsored mediation showed a lack of leadership on their part, and their stance placed them in an unfavorable light with the public. After one year, of the New Deal and the NRA labor had gained some support among newspaper editors.[25]

Cotton textile workers needed more than sympathy and enlightened New South attitudes to solve their problems. Novelist Martha Gellhorn, as a field representative for Harry Hopkins, described Gaston County, scene of ugly labor strife five years earlier, as a "terribly frightening picture" and a "place to go to acquire melancholia." One Charlotte textile worker complained of economic woes after the NRA code in-

23. J. F. Taylor to Hugh Johnson, June 2, 1934, NRA Papers; Jennings J. Rhyne, *Some Southern Cotton Mill Workers and Their Villages* (Chapel Hill: University of North Carolina Press, 1930), pp. 204–5, 210; Lefler and Newsome, *North Carolina*, p. 583; Tindall, *Emergence of the New South*, p. 523.

24. Irving Bernstein, *Turbulent Years: A History of the American Workers, 1933–1941* (Boston: Houghton Mifflin, 1970), p. 303.

25. Editorial, *Charlotte Observer*, September 3, 1934; Cash, *Mind of the South*, p. 400; editorial, *Greensboro Daily News*, September 1, 1934.

creased wages from $11.50 to $12.00 a week because grocery bills were higher as a result of increased prices under the NRA and rent went from free to $1.50 a week. For the first year of the NRA, objections to code wages and hours made up about half of the complaints to the Cotton Textile National Industrial Relations Board. In July 1933, one month before the recovery act was passed, the average hourly wage reached a low of twenty-three cents. By October 1934 the average for cotton textiles had jumped to thirty-eight cents, still well below the fifty-five cents an hour average for all industry in the United States. From July 1933 to August 1934, average weekly wages for male textile workers in the South increased only five cents, while for southern women wages jumped almost two dollars. Both sexes lagged several dollars behind New England workers. Paychecks shrank because of reduced work-weeks. Thomas F. McMahon, international president of the United Textile Workers of America, protested Hugh Johnson's order to reduce production by 25 percent, effective June 4, 1934. That reduction meant a substantial wage loss. When mill owners reduced production, wages, and employees, they reverted to the stretch-out, assigning more work to fewer people, and resentment against the stretch-out constituted about one-fourth of all complaints to the NRA code authority. Textile labor wanted union recognition and government support in the battle with management.[26]

Workers constantly complained about the stretch-out. One exasperated union man in North Carolina declared: "The government ain't ever helped us textile workers. As soon as they pass something the mill figures some way to get around it." A Durham mill worker, equally frustrated by the effect of the NRA, protested that the "New Deal's made all mill jobs heavy." Mill owners, he argued, "stretch the stretchout," speeding up the machines to get the same production with less labor and time. "The mills is makin' the same amount of goods in three and four days as they used to make in a full week. Anybody'll tell you that," he added.[27]

Industry's control over the NRA code authority and labor's weakness were evident in the way the NRA handled workers' complaints. Domi-

26. Winston, "Labor Compliance," Thomas F. McMahon to Hugh Johnson, May 29, 1934, NRA Papers; Galambos, *Competition and Cooperation*, pp. 257, 261; Bernard Bellush, *The Failure of the NRA* (New York: Norton, 1975), p. 177; Bernstein, *Turbulent Years*, pp. 299–300; Hall et al., *Like a Family*, pp. 302–3.

27. Federal Writers' Project, *These Are Our Lives* (Chapel Hill: University of North Carolina Press, 1939), pp. 139, 209; John L. Robinson, *Living Hard: Southern Americans in the Great Depression* (Washington, D.C.: University Press of America, 1981), p. 152; Bernstein, *Turbulent Years*, p. 299.

nated by the Cotton Textile Institute, the code authority investigated all labor violations arising under NIRA 7(a) after receiving labor complaints from the Cotton Textile National Industrial Relations Board, the complaint committee. No labor representative sat on the code authority or complaint committee. The five investigators the authority hired all had industry backgrounds; industry paid their salaries. They operated out of New York City and did not initiate investigations but only responded to complaints. The code authority usually ignored violations related to the stretch-out, discrimination, production, or excessive hours. Rarely did it force wage restitution on industry. Out of a sample of about eight hundred labor complaints received through September 15, 1934, the code authority adjusted only sixty-one. It rejected the rest or exonerated management. In the spring of 1934 the NRA compliance division began investigating complaints, but labor saw little improvement because an inefficient government agency had just replaced the CTI-dominated code authority. Certainly the handling of labor violations defied the spirit of the NRA.[28]

By the end of the summer of 1934, textile workers had reached their limit. The textile code had been a humiliation for the union, and the code authority had ignored UTW President Thomas F. McMahon and included no textile worker. Faced with a 25 percent industry reduction in early June, workers agreed not to strike when granted a seat on the complaint committee. In the coming weeks, reductions and stretch-outs diminished code wage increases and the complaint procedure neutralized the promise of Section 7(a). For textile workers the NRA had become a fraud.[29]

After a summer of bitter wildcat strikes that failed, the United Textile Workers, joined by the rival Textile Workers Union, called for a strike to begin on Monday, September 3, 1934. The unions sought recognition and minor points, while industry and the code authority insisted on the status quo. Timing favored the industry; inventories were excessive. Though UTW membership had grown from 15,000 in 1933 to 270,000 in 1934, the union was weak in the South and had little money to conduct an effective strike. The Roosevelt administration, moreover, opposed the strike. Nonetheless, labor planned to strike; on Sunday, September 2, about 2,000 textile workers from the Carolinas met in Charlotte to receive strike instructions. One reporter noted the "evangelistic fervor"

28. Winston, "Labor Compliance," NRA Papers; Galambos, *Competition and Cooperation*, pp. 232, 246.
29. Bernstein, *Turbulent Years*, pp. 301, 304, 306.

of the union members, and when a chorus of amens greeted UTW Vice-President Francis J. Gorman's radio address, he compared it to an "old-time southern camp meeting." Workers were serious about shutting down the seven hundred mills in the two states in their "battle for human justice."[30]

The strike lasted three weeks. On the first day of the strike almost one hundred textile mills in North Carolina closed as workers joined the nationwide walkout. Gaston, Cleveland, Mecklenburg, and Durham counties reported all mills closed. At Town Park in Gastonia, scene of violence five years before, 5,000 strikers held a spectacular Labor Day parade, a first for that part of the country. By the second day, half of the 160,000 textile workers in North Carolina and South Carolina had walked off the job. Violence spread as "flying squadrons," numbering anywhere from 200 to 1,000 strong, set out in automobile caravans, urged workers to join the strike, and occasionally battled police. The size and effectiveness of the flying squadrons in closing mills were new in the American labor movement. Governor Ehringhaus announced that he would use troops to stop any violence and protect property. By the third day the governor ordered 300 troops to Marion and Concord to prevent bloodshed between flying squadrons and workers who wished to break the picket lines. The strike leader in North Carolina denounced the lawlessness of the squadrons, and other labor leaders called Ehringhaus's action unnecessary. According to the *New York Times*, the Carolinas resembled a "war zone" as state militia reopened mills with a display of "shot guns, revolvers, bayonets, and machine guns." By September 14, the governor had called out 2,100 men and mills slowly began reopening under guard protection.[31]

The North Carolina press generally supported Governor Ehringhaus's intervention on behalf of the mill owners. The *Charlotte Observer* argued that maintenance of peace was essential and local authorities might prove insufficient. Besides, the editor pointed out that the public, mill owners, and nonstriking workers had rights as well as labor. Newspapers carried rumors about the violence associated with the flying squadrons. There were stories of their destroying machines, tearing

30. *Charlotte Observer,* September 3, 1934; *New York Times*, September 3, 1934; Galambos, *Competition and Cooperation*, pp. 257, 261–62; Badger, "New Deal and North Carolina," p. 56.

31. Harriet O'Berry to J. Allan Johnstone, September 4, 1934, NCERA Papers; *Charlotte Observer,* September 4, 5, 6, 8, 15, 1934; *New York Times*, September 4, 5, 8, 1934; Lefler and Newsome, *North Carolina*, p. 641; Galambos, *Competition and Cooperation*, p. 262.

down factory gates, shutting off power, throwing rocks, blocking trains, and stabbing people.[32]

Josephus Daniels and the *News and Observer* sympathized with the strikers. Writing to President Roosevelt in the midst of the strike, Daniels noted that North Carolina had more cotton mills than any other state and that semifeudalism prevailed in some areas because mill owners insisted on running their factories with no interference. He related that owners had repudiated collective bargaining and had increased the work load through the stretch-out. He described the lack of progress under the NRA and called George Sloan the "voice of reaction." Daniels warned Roosevelt that the mill owners would not concede to the strikers and with a note of sympathy added that "it makes me heartsick to see soldiers beat them down, even though they make demands greater than the industry can stand in days of weak demand." Daniels insisted that the strikers receive federal relief benefits, and during the peak period of the labor unrest the state's relief agency added almost seven thousand cases.[33]

For Josephus Daniels, the NRA and the New Deal were not liberal enough. Roosevelt named him ambassador to Mexico after overlooking him for a cabinet position Daniels sought. From Mexico, Daniels had little impact on New Deal domestic legislation, but through his newspaper and party ties, he influenced public opinion in North Carolina. Daniels, perhaps more progressive in 1933 than he had been during his days with William Jennings Bryan and Woodrow Wilson, castigated fellow Progressives for "backsliding." He feared that Roosevelt leaned to the right and was "too blamed conservative." At first he enthusiastically accepted the NRA and its labor provisions calling for the protection of collective bargaining and a ban on child labor. He approved of higher wages, shorter hours, and increased employment.[34]

In 1934 Daniels soured on the National Recovery Administration. With an unbridled liberalism free from the pragmatism of elective office, Daniels resisted Roosevelt's accommodationist posture to conservatives. Daniels had almost made a career of opposing utilities and tobacco companies, and he resented the suspension of antitrust laws. He believed that the codes favored big producers and that Hugh Johnson

32. Editorial, *Greensboro Daily News*, September 6, 1934; A. L. Fletcher to Ehringhaus, September 8, 1934, Governors' Papers (E).

33. Josephus Daniels to FDR, September 17, 1934, Box 95, Josephus Daniels Papers; "Relief Cases Due to the Strike," October 18, 1934, NCERA Papers.

34. E. David Cronon, "A Southern Progressive Looks at the New Deal," *Journal of Southern History* 24 (May 1958): 152–54, 158, 175–76.

prosecuted small violators rather than large ones. Daniels favored Johnson's dismissal but viewed his replacement, S. Clay Williams of R. J. Reynolds Tobacco Company, as the opposite of what the New Deal should be. Daniels warned Roosevelt that Williams had never worked for "your" causes in North Carolina. A lobbyist for his company's interests, Williams had refused collective bargaining, paid low wages, and even resisted a code for his own industry. In September 1934, Daniels staunchly defended the textile strikers, but their efforts failed before the power of the business-dominated NRA textile board.[35]

On September 23, after more workers returned to their jobs and more mills reopened, the weakened strikers responded to a plea from President Roosevelt and ended the walkout. A mediation board resolved the labor unrest in a clear victory for the industry and the code. Labor did not achieve industrywide collective bargaining, shorter hours, or higher wages but only the creation of a new labor relations board for handling complaints. For the next several months that board adjusted 2,478 out of 2,751 complaints, but that was small consolation to textile labor, which clearly had lost a battle with industry. The NRA had not stood up to the pressures of business, and for textile workers in North Carolina, NIRA 7(a) remained an unfulfilled hope. The New Deal's promises stirred labor and captured public attention through the strike, but permanent gains still lay in the future.[36]

The strike that one reporter called the "greatest industrial conflict in the history of the South" ended with dashed hopes for Tar Heel labor. Maintaining troops had cost the state $5,000 a day, and one picketer died in a clash at Belmont between strikers and the state militia. Strikers, who pinned their hopes on dramatic intervention from Roosevelt only to be disappointed, admitted that the twin enemies of "force and hunger" killed the strike. Otis Hardison, a Wilmington cotton mill worker, had joined the UTW and struck in 1934. He lost his eighteen-dollar-a-week mill job and was evicted from company housing. Sustained for a while by his oldest son's monthly Civilian Conservation Corps (CCC) check, Hardison sold his furniture and moved to Durham where he landed another mill job. Nobody asked questions, and many Wilmington strikers came to Durham and Durham strikers to Wilmington. Other workers were not so lucky. On September 24, employers told twenty-five hundred strikers in Concord they were not needed, and in

35. Josephus Daniels to FDR, October 1, 1934, Box 95, Josephus Daniels Papers; Cronon, "Southern Progressive," pp. 154, 156–58.

36. *Charlotte Observer,* September 23, 1934; Galambos, *Competition and Cooperation,* p. 264; Winston, "Labor Compliance," NRA Papers.

Roanoke Rapids mill owners advised four thousand strikers to apply individually for their old jobs. The strike left a bitter legacy. In November 1934, Martha Gellhorn described Gaston County workers who "live in terror of being penalized for joining unions; and the employers live in a state of mingled rage and fear against this imported monstrosity: organized labor." Rosa Holland, a Marion mill worker, recalled years later that after the 1934 strike she dared not mention the union for fear of being fired again. Mildred Shoemaker, a textile worker in Burlington, thought the strike leaders were "hoodlums," and economic necessity forced her back to work when the National Guard protected the plant. George Dobbin, a Durham mill worker, complained about the New Deal and NRA but retained faith in Roosevelt the man: "biggest-hearted man we ever had in the White House . . . picked us up out of the mud and stood us up." Roosevelt enjoyed the adoration of North Carolina workers, according to selective interviews, despite policies that sometimes failed them. George Dobbin and thousands like him in the state separated Roosevelt from the adverse effects of the NRA.[37]

By May 1935, when the Supreme Court invalidated the NRA, the cotton textile code authority had failed both business and labor. The NRA had not restored profits for most of the mills. The year 1933 had been good for the industry, but in 1934 over half the cotton textile firms registered deficits. Only during 1936–37, after the NRA ended, did 1929 levels of profitability return. The NRA protected and strengthened the New England mills and thereby provided more competition for the South. The recovery act did improve workers' conditions, providing better pay, more employment, and a shorter workweek. Though the New Deal fell short of its major goals for North Carolina's cotton textile industry, the NRA made modest progress and built a foundation for future improvement.[38]

The state's third largest industry, wooden furniture manufacturing, cooperated with the NRA in a pattern similar to textiles. Both industries had been suffering from depressed conditions since the mid-1920s. In the highly competitive furniture industry profits declined and production increased, compounding the economic crisis that followed the stock

37. *New York Times*, September 5, 20, 21, 23, 25, 1934; Ann Banks, ed., *First Person America* (New York: Knopf, 1980), pp. 128–30; Federal Writers' Project, *These Are Our Lives*, pp. 210–11; Bernstein, *Turbulent Years*, pp. 314–15. For a critical assessment of New Deal labor policy see James A. Hodges, *New Deal Labor Policy and the Southern Cotton Textile Industry, 1933–1941* (Knoxville: University of Tennessee Press, 1986), pp. 128–29; Hall et al., *Like a Family*, p. xv.

38. Galambos, *Competition and Cooperation*, p. 285; Tindall, *Emergence of the New South*, p. 470.

market crash of 1929. In North Carolina the drop was never as severe as it was in other furniture-manufacturing states. In 1925 North Carolina led the country in the production of wooden furniture and placed fifth in all furniture manufacture, and in 1929 its factories built 8.7 percent of the national total. Statistics for 1931 revealed that the state produced 10.1 percent of the nation's furniture, placing North Carolina second only to New York. Virginia, ranking sixth, was the only other southern state in the top eleven.[39]

Although North Carolina's furniture industry declined after the onset of the Depression, the rate of decline never matched that of the industry as a whole, and by 1933 the state's relative position had improved. From 1929 to 1933 the number of furniture-manufacturing establishments in the state dropped by one-third and the value of their products fell more than 50 percent, but for the eleven major furniture-manufacturing states the value of products declined almost 70 percent. The number of employees in the industry in the state decreased by almost one-fourth for the same period, while for the top eleven states, the number of workers plummeted by approximately 50 percent.[40]

For an industry in need and with an administration eager to assist, the NRA and the furniture manufacturers formulated and implemented a code with little fanfare or difficulty. Of the twenty-two code authority members, six came from North Carolina. Two key industry people from the state on the committee were Finley H. Coffey and James T. Ryan, president and secretary respectively of the Southern Furniture Manufacturing Association, headquartered in High Point because a majority of southern furniture factories operated within a 250-mile radius of the town. The furniture code authority placed one of its two regional administrative agencies in High Point in recognition of the state's key role in the industry. The code covered almost 2,000 manufacturers nationwide with approximately 117,000 employees. Like the cotton textile code, the one for furniture called for a minimum wage differential for North and South. The result was thirty cents an hour for the South and thirty-four cents for the North. Amazingly, so few southern furniture manufacturers complained about the minimum that some NRA officials wondered whether the wage rates should have been higher. Southern industry people did not react to it generally as a burden even though in June 1933,

39. Alexander Sachs, "Material Bearing on Furniture Industry," October 3, 1933, Robert Irwin and F. A. Coffey to NRA, October 6, 1935, NRA Papers; Lefler and Newsome, *North Carolina*, p. 582.

40. Sachs, "Material Bearing on the Furniture Industry," Robert K. Lyle, "The Furniture Manufacturing Industry," August 1935, NRA Papers.

68 percent of southern workers in furniture factories earned less than the code minimum wage.[41]

Other code specifications included a forty-hour workweek with an eight-hour day. The code abolished child labor and required that time and a half be paid for labor before and after the seven-to-five-o'clock shift. The latter provision effectively limited production. Throughout the two-year operation of the code, wages advanced well beyond the minimum for the industry as a whole, as well as for the South. The average hourly wage in 1929 for all furniture manufacturing was 46.7 cents. In 1933 the figure dropped to 36.6 cents, but the following year it reached 44.4 cents an hour, almost up to the 1929 level. In the South for July 1933, before the institution of the code, the hourly average wage had dropped to 26.1 cents and by December 1933, after a few months of the code's operation, had climbed to 38.7 cents. In May 1935, when the Supreme Court abruptly ended the NRA, the Southern Furniture Manufacturing Association favored the continuance of the basic code, the wage levels, and the operation schedules, claiming that the public welfare required it. The guidance of the NRA and general economic recovery helped rescue the industry. By 1937 the southern furniture-manufacturing industry had shown considerable growth with more workers and a higher value of its products. One industry leader, James E. Broyhill, sustained growth and yearly profits in his plants during the 1930s, but he was a Republican and fought the New Deal, especially the NRA. He worked well with his congressman, Robert Doughton, who shared his conservative views.[42]

The only serious rift between the North Carolina furniture industry and the New Deal centered on federal relief in financing government-run furniture factories. Two such projects, in Reidsville, West Virginia, and Nashville, Tennessee, caught the attention of the state's furniture manufacturers, and they resented the government competition with private enterprise. They protested vigorously, and Senator Bailey joined with attacks on the "communistic set-up." No such projects were attempted in North Carolina. Relief officials reassured nervous busi-

41. Robert Irwin and F. A. Coffey to NRA, October 6, 1933, Hugh Johnson to FDR, November 18, 1933, J. D. Kershner to C. R. Niklason, September 26, 1934, Walter S. Giele, "History of the Furniture Manufacturing Industry Code," October 29, 1935, NRA Papers.

42. Hugh Johnson to FDR, November 18, 1933, H. H. Pixley, "Wage Differential," May 11, 1934, Giele, "History of the Furniture Code," Lyle, "The Furniture Manufacturing Industry," NRA Papers; *Raleigh News and Observer,* May 30, 1935; Hoover and Ratchford, *Economic Resources,* p. 159; William Stevens, *Anvil of Adversity: Biography of a Furniture Pioneer* (New York: Popular Library, 1968), pp. 107, 117.

nessmen that those experimental operations paying higher than average wages were not economical and therefore were not likely to endure.[43]

The NRA's experience with tobacco companies contrasted dramatically with that of cotton textiles and furniture. The NRA depended on voluntary cooperation and had no success in the code negotiations with the obstinate cigarette manufacturers. Tobacco companies in North Carolina, prosperous despite the Depression, did not need the NRA. Unlike textiles, tobacco companies did not suffer from overproduction and extreme competition. Promises of immunity from antitrust action had no appeal for the oligopolistic industry. Both parties signed the temporary President's Reemployment Agreement in August 1933, which remained in force while they negotiated a code. Hearings for the code did not begin until August 21, 1934. During the negotiation process Roosevelt startled liberals by naming S. Clay Williams of R. J. Reynolds Tobacco Company, the manufacturers' chief negotiator, as chairman of the new National Industrial Recovery Board, which ran the NRA when Hugh Johnson stepped down. Roosevelt apparently had given up hope for an effective code, but on February 10, 1935, with little enthusiasm, he signed one. After almost two years in the making, the code survived until May 1935, when the Supreme Court declared the NRA unconstitutional.

The cigarette manufacturers' code brought mixed results. Industry officials agreed to a minimum wage of thirty cents an hour, lower than the cotton textile minimum. Companies abolished child labor and recognized collective bargaining rights, although unions touched the industry only slightly. Industry executives agreed that prices should increase only if costs did, a policy they did not follow from 1933 to 1935. To their credit, the companies complied with wage guidelines during the brief operation of the code. In May 1935, unemployment among tobacco workers remained at a high 24 percent. The President's Reemployment Agreement and the code ironically brought adversity to the predominantly black workers. As wages increased, whites and machines replaced unskilled black workers. On balance, tobacco companies made a mockery of the NRA by resisting a code and paying wages so low that their employees went on relief. North Carolina's tobacco companies were run by strong conservative businessmen who successfully circumvented New Deal interference.[44]

43. Bailey to W. L. Simpson, July 21, 1934, J. T. Ryan to Bailey, February 18, 1935, speech by Bailey [1933–35?], Bailey Papers.

44. "Cigarette, Snuff, Chewing, and Smoking Manufacturing Industry Code," [January 25, 1935], C. W. Dunning, "History of the Cigarette, Snuff, Chewing, and Smoking Tobacco Manufacturing Industry Code," October 1, 1935, Charles S. Johnson, "The Tobacco Worker: A Study of Tobacco Factory Workers and Their Family," 1935, p. 78, NRA Papers; Badger, *North Carolina and the New Deal*, pp. 33–36.

Senator Josiah Bailey symbolized the old bourbon, conservative southern Democrat who spoke for North Carolina industrialists and bankers. His early skepticism of the New Deal and the NRA had hardened as it had for most Tar Heel businessmen. Roosevelt's election strengthened Bailey's political power in the state because he controlled federal patronage, despite his differences with Roosevelt. Though he never equaled Gardner as a power in state politics, he coexisted with the machine as an independent political force. Gardner and Bailey maintained cordial ties. Friend and foe regarded Bailey as intellectually capable, politically shrewd, and thoroughly conservative.[45]

Tobacco company executives in the state found in Senator Bailey a kindred spirit. He voted for the recovery act, but from 1933 to 1935 he at times grudgingly supported and also attacked the NRA. He was torn between philosophical opposition to the agency and party loyalty to a Democratic administration. He predicted the NRA's failure and complained that it aided larger businesses at the expense of smaller ones and that it damaged business in the South. In May 1934, Bailey delivered the first Democratic attack on Hugh Johnson and the NRA in the Senate. He had expressed a willingness to experiment in dealing with the economic crisis, but he did not see the need for basic changes in the nature of the federal government. Bailey explained to his constituents that he would not be a rubber stamp because representative government and states' rights were at stake. He did not intend to sacrifice liberty for the president's popularity. In mid-1934 Bailey was included in the *Washington Post*'s list of anti-New Deal conservative Democratic senators, but he remained a potent political force in a state whose citizens revered Franklin Roosevelt. After his reelection in 1936, Bailey would lead an overt, organized assault on the New Deal.[46]

Bailey did not escape criticism in the state. Jonathan Daniels, the new editor of the *Raleigh News and Observer*, scolded Bailey for lacking party loyalty because he supported the administration only about half the time. Daniels compared Bailey's excuses about "convictions" to Simmons's explanation for his opposition to Smith in 1928. Bailey's occasional opposition during the first Hundred Days troubled Josephus Daniels, who confided to the president that Bailey was "off the reservation," and he could do nothing to help the situation. Even the *Charlotte*

45. Moore, *Bailey*, p. v; Patterson, *Congressional Conservatism*, pp. 27, 29; Cash, *Mind of the South*, p. 434.

46. Press release, May 7, 1933, Bailey to Hugh Johnson, August 23, 1933, to C. A. Cannon, August 25, 1933, to John A. Goode, January 30, 1934, to Drew Pearson and Robert S. Allen, June 15, 1934, Bailey Papers; *Raleigh News and Observer*, May 25, 1934; Moore, *Bailey*, p. 105; Patterson, *Congressional Conservatism*, p. 27.

Observer expressed disdain at Bailey's behavior. His early votes against certain New Deal measures offended the editor's sense of balance between conviction and party loyalty. Throughout the period 1933–35, Bailey defended his actions and couched his public comments in a way that obscured his position.[47]

Before the Supreme Court invalidated the NRA on May 27, 1935, the program had become ineffective and had lost popular support. Congressional leaders, concerned over the NRA's fostering of monopolies, prompted an investigation, and the report that resulted concluded that the NRA under Johnson had favored large businesses. Consumers complained about higher prices. Businessmen feared that their partnership with government had ended as government regulation gradually replaced self-regulation. In September 1934, under pressure from business, labor, consumers, and the president, Hugh Johnson resigned. Southern manufacturers received more good news in early 1935 when George Sloan resigned as president of the Cotton Textile Institute. Southern textile owners believed that in his key role in the NRA textile code authority, Sloan had not paid enough attention to their needs, and consequently the New England mills had gained on them.[48]

The NRA's demise elicited a mixed response in North Carolina. Though Senator Bailey voted in committee one week before the court decision to extend the agency for eleven months, he later agreed that the Supreme Court was right. Now everyone could "breathe on his own," he argued, adding that the economy in the state was doing so well that "if we can just get it out of the heads of the people that there is a depression, we will be all right."[49] "Simply to preserve the good that has been accomplished," Congressman Doughton introduced a joint resolution to continue until April 1, 1936, an NRA that conformed to the Court decision in *Schechter Poultry Corporation v. United States.* Doughton pointed to the NRA's successes: greater employment, higher wages, improved working conditions, a shorter workweek, the end of child labor, and rights for labor. "Challenge that if you will," he dared Republican critics. The House passed the resolution easily, and no North Carolina member voted against it.[50]

47. Editorial, *Raleigh News and Observer,* May 8, 1933; Josephus Daniels to FDR, April 19, 1933, August 25, 1934, Box 95, Josephus Daniels Papers; editorial, *Charlotte Observer,* May 4, 1933; Patterson, *Congressional Conservatism,* p. 28.

48. Galambos, *Competition and Cooperation,* pp. 267, 270.

49. Bailey to FDR, May 20, 1935, to G. S. Ferguson, Jr., September 28, 1935, Bailey Papers.

50. *Congressional Record,* 74th Cong., 1st sess. (1935), pp. 8736, 8882–83, 9318–19.

Both Governor Ehringhaus and Max Gardner were alarmed over the NRA's end and suggested that voluntary agreements replace the codes. Textile leaders pledged voluntary compliance. Cotton textiles in the South could not afford a price war with northern mills, especially with inventories still high. Unions threatened to strike if the industry returned to pre-NRA conditions. The American Cotton Manufacturing Association, meeting in Charlotte, voted to maintain the NRA code. By 1936, however, enthusiasm for cooperation had waned, and individualistic practices returned. The Cotton Textile Institute ceased its efforts for voluntary compliance. A survey by the Southern States Industrial Council revealed about 45 percent of southern businessmen opposed the NRA, and thus several industries in the region other than textiles, including tobacco companies, found little to lament with NRA's passing.[51]

In its two years of existence the NRA never solved industry's economic problems, but it did bring a measure of recovery. Nationally, the gross national product improved, unemployment dropped, and weekly earnings and corporate profits climbed. In the South, the textile and tobacco industries rose above 1929 levels. North Carolina maintained its supremacy in the South, increasing its total value of manufacturers from $878 million in 1933 to $1.1 billion by 1935. During these two years the retail trade of the state increased 14.4 percent, income tax collections moved up 16.2 percent, bank deposits jumped 70.2 percent, and automobile registration 32.7 percent. Critics of the NRA, conservative businessmen and politicians, pointed out that general economic improvement and the impact of other New Deal agencies contributed more than the NRA to the upturn. The agency's failure to reorganize the economy, as well as its coziness with big business, disappointed many North Carolinians, and its encouragement of labor angered industry.[52]

Industry in the state had an uneven record from 1935 until World War II. With the lapse of the NRA, North Carolina businessmen expected economic improvement, and in the spring of 1937 in mill towns like Gastonia optimism prevailed as prices, profits, and employment picked up. Overproduction eventually plagued textiles again, however, and the

51. Joel Gordon, "Audit and Analysis of the Statement Issued by the Southern States Industrial Council on What Should Be the Future of the NRA," March 15, 1935, NRA Papers; Ehringhaus to FDR, June 1, 1935, Governors' Papers (E); *Raleigh News and Observer,* May 30, June 2, 8, 1935; Badger, "North Carolina and the New Deal," p. 64.

52. "Report of Semi-Annual Coordinating Meeting of Representatives of Federal Departments and Agencies in North Carolina," December 18, 1935, NCERA Papers; Lefler and Newsome, *North Carolina*, p. 630; Tindall, *Emergence of the New South*, pp. 446, 470; Ellis W. Hawley, *The New Deal and the Problem of Monopoly* (Princeton: Princeton University Press, 1966), pp. 131–32; Bellush, *Failure of the NRA*, pp. 176–77.

industry declined in the 1937 recession. Textile executives angrily denounced presidential policies as the cause. North Carolina businessmen, hating the New Deal they no longer believed useful, fought a third term for Roosevelt, and many backed Wendell L. Willkie.[53]

Staunch conservatism among North Carolina businessmen thwarted New Deal ambitions for acceptance of unions in the state. They accepted wage and hour regulation and the abolition of child labor but stiffly resisted organized labor. With the president's backing, Congress passed the National Labor Relations Act, popularly known as the Wagner Act, in 1935 to secure the collective bargaining rights lost through the Court's invalidation of the NRA. This reform legislation of the second Hundred Days went further than the NRA. The act provided that by a majority vote in a referendum workers could select their collective bargaining agents, outlawed "unfair labor practices," and created the National Labor Relations Board to enforce the provisions. The Senate approved the Wagner Act by a vote of sixty-three to twelve. Bailey was one of only four Democrats to vote against it. He argued that it would increase tension between labor and business and lead to strikes. Reynolds, in the Virgin Islands on Senate business, did not vote. The House passed it without a recorded vote. Of the North Carolina delegation, only Harold D. Cooley defended the bill for the record. "The spirit of the Blue Eagle lives on and will continue to live until the American laborer is freed from the bondage of economic slavery," he declared. Law, not "industrial warfare," should secure collective bargaining rights for workers.[54]

The Wagner Act did little to promote organized labor in the state. Textile owners rejected industrywide bargaining so labor battles had to be fought plant by plant. For example, in February 1938, the Textile Workers' Organizing Committee (TWOC) won elections at three Erwin Mills plants in North Carolina, but the company, led by former NRA code authority member Kemp P. Lewis, balked at a contract that increased wages. Not until 1941, after a walkout, another union election victory, and two interventions by the National Labor Relations Board, did the company and union settle on a contract with a minimal wage increase. The unsuccessful strike in June 1938 at the Cone White Oak Mills near Greensboro revealed labor's weakness. After two frustrating weeks, realizing their impotence, the workers, faced with a choice

53. Galambos, *Competition and Cooperation*, p. 281; Tindall, *Emergence of the New South*, p. 438; Badger, *North Carolina and the New Deal*, pp. 36–38.

54. *Congressional Record*, 74th Cong., 1st sess. (1935), pp. 7681, 9704, 9731; Moore, *Bailey*, p. 115; Pleasants, "Robert Reynolds," p. 217; Tindall, *Emergence of the New South*, pp. 512–13; Leuchtenburg, *Franklin D. Roosevelt and the New Deal*, p. 151.

between John L. Lewis and the mill owner Benjamin Cone, cried "Give us Cones." As a Baptist mill preacher despaired, "The multi-million-airy is hard to beat." A female textile worker added: "The government can say it'll make the Cones let everybody that wants to join the union but the Cones is still totin' the keys to the mill." The failure of the TWOC, part of the Congress of Industrial Organizations (CIO), to unionize textile workers in the state in 1937 was described by historian James A. Hodges as "a dramatic example of the limits of New Deal labor policy." Delays in organizing and the recession in the fall of 1937 helped large mills like Cannon and Burlington to remain free of unions.[55]

Company executives and probusiness politicians in the state responded angrily to labor trouble in general and particularly to the sit-down strikes in Detroit, led by the CIO. Employers ignored the Wagner Act, fired workers, and evicted them from company housing. Representative Lindsay Warren denounced the sit-down strikes as "lawless and un-American." Cooley, usually a defender of labor and collective bargaining, said that labor had to use reason, not "brute force." "This romance of violence is ladened with evil," he warned. Senator Bailey criticized the sit-down strikes, but Senator Robert R. Reynolds voted for a resolution condemning both labor for those actions and business for resistance to the Wagner Act.[56]

The Wagner Act rendered little aid to tobacco workers. Reynolds Tobacco Company avoided unions, but in 1937 Liggett and Myers and the American Tobacco Company recognized the Tobacco Workers International (TWI) of the American Federation of Labor. Jim Wells, TWI organizer for the successful strike in 1939 against Liggett and Myers in Durham, admitted that some workers liked unions, some were "plain scared," and some considered the company a "fairy godmother." Ultimately, the Wagner Act and the CIO had little impact on North Carolina. As Pete Daniel has observed, the South remained a "stronghold of antiunion sentiment." In 1939 North Carolina ranked forty-seventh in unionization, and only 4.2 percent of the state's nonagricultural work force belonged to unions; by 1968 the figure rose to less than 7.5 percent. But the New Deal did help labor. State troops were no longer used

55. Tindall, *Emergence of the New South*, pp. 513, 517–19, 521; Hodges, *New Deal Labor Policy*, pp. 5, 172–75; Tom E. Terrill and Jerrold Hirsch, eds. *Such as Us: Southern Voices of the Thirties* (New York: Norton, 1978), pp. 163–64; Badger, *North Carolina and the New Deal*, p. 38.

56. *Congressional Record*, 74th Cong., 1st sess. (1935), pp. 3290–91, 2915–16; Moore, *Bailey*, pp. 139–40; Pleasants, "Robert Reynolds," p. 302; Badger, *North Carolina and the New Deal*, pp. 37–38; Bailey to Horace Williams, January 19, 1937, to Charles H. Neal, January 25, 1937, Bailey Papers; Bernstein, *Turbulent Years*, p. 621.

against strikers. The threat of unions, with collective bargaining rights, improved wages and working conditions. The federal government's intervention neutralized the paternalism of the mill owners. Textile manufacturers eliminated child labor and implemented the forty-cent-an-hour federal minimum wage in 1942, three years ahead of schedule. In 1943 the TWI won a union election at Reynolds Tobacco Company.[57]

Roosevelt charged Interior Secretary Harold L. Ickes with responsibility for another program aimed at economic recovery. Created under the National Industrial Recovery Act in June 1933, the Public Works Administration sought to stimulate business activity with large expenditures for public works, indirectly providing work relief. The PWA provided 30 percent of the money for nonfederal projects as a grant and loaned the remaining 70 percent to a county, city, or state. Many North Carolina municipalities could neither afford to incur huge debts to the PWA nor manage clearance for the loans because of numerous defaults, and local cooperation with the PWA lagged. Secretary Ickes, fiscally conservative, made no loans unless the city, county, or state had proper financial security. In awarding loans the PWA considered debt limits, tax levels, budgets, state and local construction laws, and legal questions concerning project contracts and labor. Because of numerous defaults in the state, the Local Government Commission scrutinized all PWA loans to municipalities.[58]

Red tape, Ickes's cautious manner, competition from the Civil Works Administration (CWA), a work relief agency, resistance to high relief wages, and the bankruptcy of so many municipalities gave the PWA a slow start in the state, and it contributed less to economic recovery than other New Deal efforts. Former highway department chairman Frank Page and University of North Carolina engineering dean Herman G. Baity headed the Advisory Committee on Public Works for the state. By December 1933 the PWA had received only 120 applications for 230 projects, but work had begun on projects funded totally by the federal government. Not until 1934, after the close of the CWA, did PWA projects such as slum clearance, public housing, highway construction,

57. Banks, ed., *First Person America*, p. 158; Tindall, *Emergence of the New South*, pp. 512, 521; Pete Daniel, *Standing at the Crossroads: Southern Life since 1900* (New York: Hill and Wang, 1986), p. 127; Lefler and Newsome, *North Carolina*, pp. 642–43; Nannie M. Tilley, *The R. J. Reynolds Tobacco Company* (Chapel Hill: University of North Carolina Press, 1985), pp. 382–83; Badger, *North Carolina and the New Deal*, pp. 38–39.

58. Public Works Administration, Division of Information, *America Builds: The Record of the PWA* (Washington, D.C.: U.S. Government Printing Office, 1939), p. 220; *Raleigh News and Observer*, December 31, 1933; Morgan, "Step toward Altruism," p. 116; George Brown Tindall, *America: A Narrative History*, 2d ed. (New York: Norton, 1988), 2:1122.

conservation work, and building hospitals and schools begin in earnest. The PWA spent millions on construction at Fort Bragg in Fayetteville, improving the Cape Fear River and expanding the Blue Ridge Parkway. In 1934 the PWA allotment for North Carolina, including federal and nonfederal projects, totaled $22,086,313. Duke Power Company opposed PWA public power projects, particularly a Greenwood, South Carolina, power plant, making the novel argument that the public utility would reduce the company's profits and curtail its philanthropy. Ickes and North Carolina New Dealers were not impressed.[59]

After a sluggish start, the PWA received stimulation from the 1935 Emergency Relief Appropriations Act. In early 1936 director Baity announced that the PWA had spent $20 million in the state and that 95 percent of the projects planned in 1933 were completed. A second program begun in 1935 was 30 percent completed. In 1937, Roosevelt, in a retrenchment mood, virtually stopped PWA pump-priming, but one year later, to combat the recession, he substantially increased funds for the agency. By 1940 the PWA had built schools, hospitals, city halls, courthouses, libraries, and water and sewer systems, established flood control projects, and made harbor improvements throughout the country, all at an estimated cost of $6.1 billion. In seven years, the PWA had projects in all but three of the nation's 3,071 counties. In North Carolina, the PWA sponsored 903 projects at an estimated cost of $86.1 million. As few as 1,152 people worked on PWA projects during its "inactive" period in March 1938, but the number of workers had increased to 6,938 by June 1939. One year later the number working under the PWA in the state declined to 238, and in June 1941 the PWA ceased operations. PWA regulations required matching funds from state and local governments for nonfederal projects, and by 1938 North Carolina and its local governments had contributed $13.3 million to PWA projects.[60]

Sluggish participation by local governments kept North Carolina from getting its full share, and Baity described himself as "perfectly sick over

59. Ickes to Ehringhaus, July 27, 1933, Governors' Papers (E); Ickes to Bailey, March 6, 1934, Bailey Papers; *Raleigh News and Observer,* December 31, 1933; PWA, *America Builds*, p. 221; Cronon, "Southern Progressive," pp. 160–61; Lefler and Newsome, *North Carolina*, p. 615.

60. Unfortunately, the full story of the PWA in North Carolina will never be known because Harold Ickes had the agency's records destroyed. Catlin, "Relief and Economic Statistics: N.C.," April 1938, WPA Papers; Federal Works Agency, *The First Annual Report: Federal Works Agency, 1940* (Washington, D.C.: U.S. Government Printing Office, 1940), pp. 133, 154, 308–10, 318–19; PWA, *America Builds*, pp. 221–22; *Raleigh News and Observer,* February 11, June 16, 1936, North Carolina Collection Clipping File through 1975, University of North Carolina Library, Chapel Hill.

the whole business." Continued pressure from power companies also thwarted PWA activity in the state. Utility companies delayed the legislature's compliance with PWA programs in the late 1930s, and Duke Power went to court to stop a municipal power plant in High Point. By 1940 that city still had no public power facility.[61]

By 1940, as a result of New Deal largesse and the probusiness policies of the state's governors, North Carolina's economy exhibited relative strength. In March 1940, the percentage seeking work or on work relief dipped to 8.8, best in the nation and impressively lower than the 15.2 percent national average. For the decade North Carolina had the highest percentage increase in per capita net income in the nation, although in 1940 still only 55 percent of the national average. While nine southern states declined industrially, North Carolina remained in first place in the region. The state's first advertising campaign, by the Department of Conservation and Development, produced remarkable results in the last four years of the decade. Tourist business jumped from $36 million to $102 million annually; four hundred new industries moved to the state and spent $125 million on industrial expansion. State government, bent on retrenchment during the 1930s, ended the decade with an $8 million surplus.[62]

61. *Raleigh News and Observer,* September 25, 1935, North Carolina Collection Clipping File through 1975, University of North Carolina Library, Chapel Hill; Badger, *North Carolina and the New Deal,* pp. 51–52.

62. David Leroy Corbitt, ed., *Addresses, Letters and Papers of Clyde Roark Hoey, Governor of North Carolina, 1937–1941* (Raleigh: Council of State, State of North Carolina, 1944), pp. xiv–xvii, 558–59; *Raleigh News and Observer,* December 29, 1940; North Carolina Department of Labor, *Biennial Report, 1938–1940,* p. 59; Donald S. Howard, *The WPA and Federal Relief Policy* (New York: Russell Sage Foundation, 1943), p. 672; Hoover and Ratchford, *Economic Resources,* pp. 50, 119, 132; Hayes, "South Carolina and the New Deal," p. 524.

CHAPTER 3

Farmers and the Agricultural Adjustment Administration, 1933–1935

The Agricultural Adjustment Administration, created by Congress in May 1933, had more impact on North Carolina than any other New Deal measure. The state's farmers, like its textile executives, embraced a New Deal recovery program designed to improve prices that had been hurt by overproduction. Independent, individualistic farmers voted overwhelmingly for production controls, led by tobacco growers, who simply wanted higher prices. Their support continued as the AAA achieved that goal. Unlike the NRA, the AAA tobacco program worked. For the nation overall the AAA did not restore parity or farm income, but tobacco was an exception, important for a state that produced 40 percent of the U.S. crop. Cotton in the state followed the national pattern of weak recovery. This first AAA program operated through the 1935 crop season until the Supreme Court ended it in January 1936.[1]

Despite its success, the AAA experience revealed the conservative nature of both the New Deal and the state's farmers. Tobacco growers endorsed the AAA's limited goal of price recovery because it met their immediate economic needs. New Deal agricultural officials catered to landowners through local, decentralized administration, and most New Deal funds provided rental and benefit payments and loans to "middle-class" farmers, not assistance for sharecroppers and tenants. The state's farmers, secure with higher prices and a virtual monopoly on growing

1. For a thorough account of the AAA tobacco program in North Carolina see Anthony J. Badger, *Prosperity Road: The New Deal, Tobacco, and North Carolina* (Chapel Hill: University of North Carolina Press, 1980), pp. 198, 217–18, 223, 229; see also Badger, *North Carolina and the New Deal*, pp. 25, 29; Theodore Saloutos, *American Farmer and the New Deal* (Ames: Iowa State University Press, 1982), pp. 256–57; Richard S. Kirkendall, "The New Deal and Agriculture," in *The New Deal*, Vol. 1, *The National Level*, ed. Braeman, Bremner, and Brody, pp. 83, 105; Robert F. Hunter, "The AAA between Neighbors: Virginia, North Carolina, and the New Deal Farm Program," *Journal of Southern History* 44 (November 1978): 567.

tobacco, resisted the expansion of the New Deal to aid labor, the urban poor, or tenants. They were motivated by self-interest, not agricultural reform, and cooperation in production controls did not destroy their conservatism.

Economic need overshadowed fears of federal intervention in agriculture. For a state that was three-fourths rural, a drop in cash farm income from $321 million in 1928 to approximately $98 million in 1932 meant a significant economic crisis. North Carolina agriculture faced other difficulties, for as Theodore Saloutos pointed out, farmers had a "whole series of interrelated problems." North Carolina was a state of small farms, each averaging about 64.5 acres. By 1930 the state had the second largest farm population in the United States but ranked forty-eighth in cultivated acres per farm. Between 1920 and 1930 the number of farms rose 3.7 percent, while the acres per farm decreased 9.8 percent. From 1910 to 1925 the state also led the nation in the increase of farm tenancy, as tenants in the tobacco and cotton counties of the east continued to subdivide farmland. Consequently, the number of farms increased while their size decreased. Small, uneconomical, and inefficient farms were widespread. North Carolina's two major crops, tobacco and cotton, did not require large amounts of land or capital, but they required a high ratio of labor to land and capital.[2]

In addition to the low per capita production, the state encountered other agricultural problems shared by other states in the South and nation. The scarcity of land and its rising costs, dependency on single crops and inability to diversify, low income worsened by unstable prices and marketing procedures, and difficulty in obtaining credit while becoming more dependent on it because of the increasing costs of farm machinery threatened the future of agriculture. Chronic overproduction kept the prices of farm commodities down, and a shrinking world market, especially for cotton, compounded the problem. The crash of 1929 made worse an agricultural depression in progress since the early 1920s.[3]

Between 1929 and 1932 North Carolina farmers and political leaders wrestled unsuccessfully with the problem of low prices. Per pound

2. *UNC Newsletter,* September 25, 1935, PC 246.9, Ehringhaus Papers (P); *Abstract of the Fifteenth Census,* pp. 503, 512; Hobbs, *North Carolina,* pp. 92–93, 335; Hoover and Ratchford, *Economic Resources,* pp. 284, 291; Saloutos, *American Farmer and the New Deal,* p. 14.

3. Monroe Lee Billington, *The Political South in the Twentieth Century* (New York: Charles Scribner's Sons, 1975), pp. 64–65; Sidney Baldwin, *Poverty and Politics: The Rise and Decline of the Farm Security Administration* (Chapel Hill: University of North Carolina Press, 1968), p. 28; Hoover and Ratchford, *Economic Resources,* p. 284.

prices of cotton plummeted from 20.2 cents in 1928 to 6.5 cents in 1932 and tobacco per pound fell to a low of 8.4 cents by 1931. Governor Gardner's "Live at Home" plan to encourage subsistence farming through an emphasis on food crops helped rural families survive the early years of the Depression, but it did not cause a sufficient reduction in cotton and tobacco production to affect prices. After 1929 agricultural leaders made futile efforts to organize a tobacco growers' cooperative under the control of the Federal Farm Board. Not enough farmers demonstrated interest in the discipline of a cooperative, and by 1931 attempts at forming one ceased.[4]

From 1929 to 1932, farm leaders and politicians settled on acreage reduction as a solution to the agricultural dilemma. Governor Gardner joined other southern governors in promoting regional cooperation in voluntary cotton and tobacco acreage reduction. Voluntary efforts, however, floundered and Governor Gardner, opposed to compulsory crop control, refused to call a special session of the legislature to enact such a measure. Also, Gardner, who had no veto power, feared that an unruly General Assembly might change tax laws. Without the cooperation of all states in the region, moreover, a crop control scheme would not work.[5]

When state efforts at agricultural recovery failed, the focus shifted to Washington after March 4, 1933. Congress debated the president's proposed Farm Relief bill, which called for production controls and benefit payments to be worked out by the secretary of agriculture with each group of growers. The state's congressional delegation, except for Bailey, voted for it. First district congressman Lindsay Warren, in the House since 1924, a skilled parliamentarian with close ties to House leadership, enthusiastically backed the crop control measure. Many growers and the Greenville market were in his eastern district, and tobacco was important for him. He became one of the AAA's strongest supporters in Congress. Tar Heel congressmen defended it in partisan and crisis terms. Rules Committee chairman Edward W. Pou limited debate to six hours, despite Republican protests. He likened present circumstances to the Revolution and Civil War. "I pray Almighty God that we may never see such conditions again. . . . The nation is in the

4. U.S. Department of Agriculture, *Agricultural Adjustment, 1933 to 1935: A Report of the Administration of the Agricultural Adjustment Act, May 12, 1933 to Dec. 31, 1935* (Washington, D.C.: U.S. Government Printing Office, 1936), p. 119; Badger, *Prosperity Road*, pp. 26–29, 37, 65.

5. Clarence Poe to Bailey, January 31, 1932, Bailey Papers; Corbitt, ed., *Public Papers and Letters of Gardner*, pp. 225, 227; Badger, *Prosperity Road*, pp. 31–32, 34, 37; Tindall, *Emergence of the New South*, p. 357.

condition of a patient sadly requiring the operation of a blood transfusion." Roosevelt, he argued, was the "great surgeon" for this task. For his farm program J. Walter Lambeth called Hoover, "the Ethelred the Unready of modern times." Republicans "slumbered while the country went on the rock." Roosevelt was the "captain" now, "a judicious worker in the good cause." J. Bayard Clark, more cautious, declared that the farm bill "and much of the other legislation of the extra session of Congress, is not just as I would have it," but he was willing to waive his objections because the emergency was "desperate enough to justify the application of remedies that will either cure or kill." Others in the delegation, including Senator Robert Reynolds, quietly supported it.[6]

Josephus Daniels, champion of the eastern North Carolina tobacco farmers, joined the chorus of support. One of the most influential backers of the AAA was Clarence H. Poe, prominent North Carolina farm leader and editor of the *Progressive Farmer*, by 1930 the largest farm publication in the South with a circulation of over a million a month. Poe favored the vigorous New Deal farm policies because he believed that only the force of the federal government could solve the southern agricultural crisis. Poe also advocated the old Populist idea of currency inflation as a means to improve commodity prices. Yet Poe was a Jeffersonian agrarian reformer for whom the AAA, which favored the large commercial farmers over the small family farmer, posed a dilemma. Poe agonized as he witnessed the AAA improving farm prices and at the same time driving tenants off the land.[7]

Senator Josiah Bailey voted against the administration's Farm Relief bill. Torn between the textile interests who opposed the AAA's processing tax and Tar Heel farmers who favored the other features, Bailey bowed to pressure from the former. To textile magnate Charles A. Cannon, Bailey exclaimed, "I am receiving letters telling me that it is my duty not to think, not to try to be right, not to exercise my judgment, but to blindfold myself and stand by the President. . . . I was not built that way," he insisted.[8] Bailey did not like the processing tax on cotton, and he did not believe the secretary of agriculture should have such broad taxing power. He also complained about the higher tariff rates and the

6. *Congressional Record*, 73d Cong., 1st sess. (1933), pp. 766, 2562, 2693–94, 2736, 3080, 3082; Badger, *Prosperity Road*, pp. 53, 216; Hunter, "AAA between Neighbors," p. 545.

7. Poe to Bailey, December 8, 1931, Bailey Papers; Joseph A. Coté, "Clarence Hamilton Poe: The Farmer's Voice, 1899–1964," *Agricultural History* 53 (January 1979): 31, 39; Cronon, "Southern Progressive," p. 166.

8. Bailey to C.A. Cannon, April 1, 1933, Bailey Papers.

large salaries to be paid to AAA experts. Bailey's distaste for crop controls, however, remained the central reason for his opposition. He argued that such arrangements violated a farmer's basic liberty.[9]

Bailey looked to other New Deal policies as well as ideas of his own to solve the problems of North Carolina farmers. Crop controls and benefit payments alone, he realized, would not be sufficient. The senator applauded Roosevelt's inflationary moves and believed going off the gold standard was the "wisest act of the administration." Since the state exported about 60 percent of its cotton and tobacco, a cheapened dollar that would increase world trade would also aid the state's farmers with higher prices and larger markets. Roosevelt's withdrawal from the World Economic Conference during the summer of 1933 and his opposition to stabilization of the world's currencies pleased Bailey. To encourage agricultural exports, Bailey suggested that the federal government pay a bounty or subsidy for cotton and tobacco exports to expand foreign markets and reduce production abroad. Senator Bailey also believed that a balanced federal budget, tax relief, and a credit program would ease the economic burdens encountered by farmers. He endorsed the Farm Credit Administration, calling it "one of the really great creations of the New Deal."[10]

Cotton was the first commodity for which the Department of Agriculture developed and implemented an adjustment program. Only one month after the enactment of the AAA, Secretary Henry A. Wallace, with the assistance of the agricultural Extension Service, sought to enlist more than one million cotton producers in a campaign to plow under about ten million acres of cotton. The undertaking became a model for later crop control campaigns. The 1933 AAA cotton program called for voluntary crop reduction, and the government paid benefits to participating growers. A processing tax of 4.2 cents a pound levied against the cotton textile mills financed the scheme. Wallace set the week of June 26 as the time for farmers to sign up, and Governor Ehringhaus urged North Carolina's 150,000 cotton producers to join the New Deal effort.[11]

Major responsibility for the sign-up rested with the state agricultural

9. Bailey to R.C. Holland, January 11, 1933, to W. C. Cavenaugh, May 5, 1933, Bailey Papers; Moore, *Bailey*, p. 97.

10. Newspaper clipping, *Winston-Salem Journal*, December 22, 1932, Bailey to R. C. Holland, January 11, 1933, Bailey press release, [June–July 1933?], Bailey to FDR, August 31, 1933, to W. I. Myers, August 2, 1934, to Poe, April 11, 1935, Bailey Papers.

11. C. A. Cobb to Hugh C. Middleton, June 27, 1933, to Ehringhaus, June 29, 1933, D. S. Murphy to W. D. Hall, September 25, 1933, AAA Papers; Badger, *Prosperity Road*, p. 44.

Extension Service and its director Ira O. Schaub, a dean at North Carolina State College. The Extension Service, an arm of the land-grant colleges, had field staff capable of administering AAA programs. Schaub cooperated, unlike Extension Service directors in the North and East, because association with the cotton and tobacco programs strengthened his organization. County governments, encouraged by the AAA's success, granted more funds for county agents. Schaub named county control committees and paid their expenses, selected additional county agents for the drive, and held conferences to instruct these officials about the program. Extension personnel enlisted various other agricultural agencies in the cause: agriculture commissioners, cotton cooperative associations, farm organizations, farm press, home demonstration clubs, Future Farmers, and farm credit agencies. During the week of June 26, the Extension Service held community meetings to explain the AAA cotton program and enlisted farmers. Federal officials asked that extension agents emphasize the financial rewards for crop reduction and make conservative acreage and yield estimates. To encourage the sign-up, the AAA mounted a major publicity drive in the state's press. The agency's publicity official declared confidently that every cotton farmer in North Carolina who subscribed to a newspaper knew about the details of the AAA cotton program. By the time the drive ended in September, the state's Extension Service had spent over $175,000 to persuade Tar Heel cotton farmers to plow under cotton in the fields.[12]

AAA crop reduction efforts brought modest results. Nationwide, 73 percent of farmers signed an agreement to reduce production voluntarily for the 1933 crop season. In North Carolina only 51 percent acquiesced, the lowest for any cotton state, perhaps because North Carolina cotton farmers already had reduced their acreage 50 percent since 1920 in response to increased costs and a declining world market. Many had turned to other crops. The state's growers did not view further restrictions with enthusiasm because they would be hurt more than farmers in states that had not already reduced acreage.[13]

Under the 1933 AAA cotton program the price per pound averaged 10.2 cents, up substantially from the 6.5 cents for 1932. The farm value of

12. C. A. Cobb to I. O. Schaub, June 17, 1933, F. H. Jeter to Cobb, June 24, 1933, R. G. Tugwell to Schaub, June 27, 1933, Cobb to Chester C. Davis, September 9, 1933, AAA Papers; Badger, *Prosperity Road*, pp. 43–44.

13. U.S. Department of Agriculture (USDA), *Agricultural Adjustment: A Report on the Agricultural Adjustment Administration, May 1933 to Feb. 1934* (Washington, D.C.: U.S. Government Printing Office, 1934), p. 19; North Carolina Department of Agriculture, *Biennial Report, 1934–1936*, p. 9; Hunter, "AAA between Neighbors," pp. 541, 545.

the 1933 crop, including seed, lint, benefit payments, and profits on options, increased 101.5 percent over 1932. With only about half the state's cotton farmers participating, North Carolina, which ranked seventh in cotton production, placed ninth in receipts of AAA cotton benefits for 1933. The state received $2.8 million out of a total of $112 million in cash benefit payments. Nationally for 1933, one million growers took 10.4 million acres, representing about 4.4 million bales, out of production. Many cotton farmers also took advantage of advances on cotton options at 4 cents a pound and loans for 10 cents per pound on unsold cotton through the Commodity Credit Corporation.[14]

Yet increased cotton prices were only half those before the Depression, and despite the voluntary reduction, the cotton states produced more bales in 1933 than the previous year. To compound the problem, cotton exports declined almost one million bales from 1932 to 1933. In November 1933, George N. Peek, AAA administrator, announced the 1934 cotton adjustment program, designed to deal with the mounting surplus of cotton. The plan called for a 40 percent reduction in cotton acreage, which meant a twenty-five-million-acre limit. The AAA continued the benefit payments, financing them through the processing taxes, and continuing administration through the Extension Service.[15]

Against the wishes of Secretary Wallace and President Roosevelt, Congress passed the Bankhead Act in April 1934, and compulsory crop control replaced the voluntary AAA cotton program. Only Bailey in the Tar Heel delegation voted against it. He had proposed, and the Senate adopted, five amendments to weaken it, but the conference committee eliminated them. Senator Robert Reynolds voted for the measure but criticized its underlying principle of compulsory control. He could not understand why farmers would want to cut production, especially in time of need. The government could save money, he joked, by bringing back the boll weevil to destroy cotton. A proper solution, Reynolds argued, would be an increase in the money supply so Americans could buy the surplus. He thought underconsumption, not overproduction, was the problem. Reynolds estimated that 75 percent of cotton farmers wanted control, and he obliged them. Farmers overwhelmingly supported control as a means to block increased production by those not participating in the voluntary reductions. To discourage noncooperating farmers from producing more cotton, the act called for a tax on all cotton

14. Bailey to [AAA-USDA], February 23, 1934, Bailey Papers; USDA, *Agricultural Adjustment*, p. 19; USDA, *Agricultural Adjustment, 1933 to 1935*, p. 119.

15. USDA, *Agricultural Adjustment, 1933 to 1935*, p. 119; USDA, press release, November 29, 1933, Bailey Papers; Hoover and Ratchford, *Economic Resources*, p. 308.

in excess of a national quota. The tax-exempt quota was based on 1928–32 production figures, and for 1934 North Carolina's limit was about half a million bales out of the national quota of ten million. Eighty-four percent of the state's growers participated in the 1934 program, in contrast to the 51 percent in 1933. Most signed up before passage of the Bankhead Act. Cotton farmers sought aggressive means to attack the surplus problem fueled by continuing overproduction and declining exports. Voluntary control did not correct the surplus; it only brought an increase in prices.[16]

Senator Bailey continued to walk a political tightrope with the farmers of North Carolina by voting against the popular Bankhead Act, and for his opposition columnist Drew Pearson labeled him the "outstanding Democratic critic of the New Deal." To answer his critics, Bailey argued against compulsory control of cotton production because it violated a farmer's basic liberty. If the federal government could regulate crop production, it could control anything else. He reminded farmers that the Bankhead measure was not part of the administration's program. Bailey argued persuasively that the quota system based on the last five years instead of the last ten years worked against North Carolina, which had been practicing voluntary reduction over the last decade. Compulsory reduction also would harm small family farmers and tenants. If the United States limited its production, Bailey feared other nations would increase theirs and put the United States at a further disadvantage. Expanding the cotton market at home and abroad was the best solution, Bailey suggested. Farmers who wished to produce unlimited pounds and cotton textile interests applauded Bailey's stance.[17]

Bailey stubbornly fought the operation of the Bankhead program and in September 1934 called on Secretary Wallace to suspend it. Several cotton state senators joined Bailey in his fight. He pointed out that the restrictions greatly reduced farmers' incomes, and the state was about 150,000 bales below its normal yearly cotton production. Tar Heel farmers, Bailey continued, had to purchase additional tax-exempt certificates from other states to market their cotton. His biggest complaint

16. U.S. Department of Agriculture, *Agricultural Adjustment in 1934: A Report of the Administration of the Agricultural Adjustment Act, Feb. 15, 1934 to Dec. 31, 1934* (Washington, D.C.: U.S. Government Printing Office, 1935), pp. 48–49, 51–52; Paul A. Porter to Secretary [Wallace], February 8, 1934, AAA Papers; Hunter, "AAA between Neighbors," p. 541; Leuchtenburg, *Franklin D. Roosevelt and the New Deal*, p. 75; *Congressional Record*, 73d Cong., 2d sess. (1934), pp. 5482, 5485–87, 5503–4, 5494, 5712, 6775–76; Pleasants, "Robert Reynolds," pp. 198–99; Moore, *Bailey*, p. 104.

17. Bailey to John H. Bankhead, July 23, 1932, Bailey press release, April 5, 1934, Bailey to Clayton Ross, April 12, 1934, to Drew Pearson and Robert S. Allen, June 15, 1934, Bailey Papers; Moore, *Bailey*, p. 105.

against the current AAA program was that it had not brought a dramatic improvement in cotton prices in the long run. In 1934 American cotton exports dipped about three million bales from the previous year, and the 1934 exports were only about half of the 1932 total. World production and consumption of cotton had increased, but world consumption of American cotton had declined. The remedy, as Bailey saw it, was not to restrict cotton production but to promote cotton as an export by paying farmers export bounties.[18]

Wallace refused to suspend the Bankhead control program, although he acknowledged that it did adversely affect small producers and new cotton farmers. He recommended that North Carolina allocate its cotton quota in a manner beneficial to the family farm. But Wallace and other AAA officials remained adamant about continuing the compulsory feature of the crop plan. Despite any hardships caused by the acreage reduction, Wallace reaffirmed his commitment to the broad purposes of the program, and he was convinced that an overwhelming majority of cotton producers and cotton state congressmen endorsed the measure. Interests other than the farmers, Wallace believed, wanted it ended. In December 1934, after one year's experience with compulsory control, the cotton farmers voted overwhelmingly in a referendum to continue it. In a 60 percent turnout nationwide, 90 percent voted for it, and in North Carolina 92.5 percent favored it. Those results proved that Wallace had a more accurate reading of North Carolina farmers' sentiments than did Bailey. True to his pattern, Bailey favored the interests of the state's businessmen over those of the farmers.[19]

The 1934 cotton adjustment program resulted in farmers withholding 14.6 million acres from production, and the national yield amounted to 9.6 million bales, down 3.4 million bales from 1933. The price per pound averaged 12.4 cents for the year, and with this higher price, 79 percent of parity, total cash income from production and benefit payments approximated that of the previous year, despite the drop in production. With 84 percent of its growers participating, North Carolina had received over $4 million in benefit payments by December 1934, well above the $2.8 million for 1933.[20]

Compulsory crop control under the Bankhead Act continued through

18. Bailey to Wallace, September 20, 1934, Bailey Papers; Hoover and Ratchford, *Economic Resources*, p. 308.

19. Wallace to Bailey, October 2, 1934, to Robert R. Reynolds, October 2, 1934, C. A. Cobb to John H. Kerr, October 11, 1934, AAA press release, December 19, 1934, AAA Papers; USDA, *Agricultural Adjustment in 1934*, p. 54.

20. USDA, *Agricultural Adjustment in 1934*, p. 50; USDA, *Agricultural Adjustment, 1933 to 1935*, p. 119; AAA Memo, "Short Statement on Cotton," September 19, [1936], AAA Papers; Hunter, "AAA between Neighbors," p. 541.

1935 with 96 percent of North Carolina growers participating. Secretary Wallace called for a 25 percent reduction from the 1928–32 base acreage, which took fourteen million acres out of production. The 1935 allotment for North Carolina amounted to more than half a million bales out of the national quota of almost eleven million bales, up slightly from 1934. Although the price of cotton dropped a little more than one cent a pound from 1934 to 1935, growers produced one million bales more in 1935 than the previous year so that total cash income from production and adjustment payments reached its highest level since the beginning of the AAA cotton program. From 1933 to 1935 the federal government paid North Carolina cotton farmers $13.8 million in benefit payments alone.[21]

Tenants' complaints against landlords mounted under the cotton control program. By September 1934, the adjustment committee had investigated 53 complaints from North Carolina and adjusted 32 of them. Arkansas, however, registered the most complaints with 477, Texas had 368, and Georgia 151. Although some tenants benefited from price increases and benefit payments, many others suffered from the acreage reductions, which drove them off the land. Many of the tenants who maintained farming arrangements failed to receive a fair share of the AAA payments. The AAA administered the cotton program through the landlord, who in turn handed the government checks to his tenants. Agriculture officials defended the structure as necessary to secure the cooperation of the landowners in acreage production. Charles A. Sheffield, assistant state extension director, traveled throughout the cotton counties and concluded that many landlords were not observing the provisions of the AAA contracts. He recommended that the Department of Agriculture study the situation and correct the injustices or a majority of the farmers would lose their respect for the government program. In response, the AAA conducted a fact-finding survey and set up district review committees to investigate and correct the problems.[22]

Textile interests in the state continued to fight the 4.2 cents a pound processing tax on cotton throughout 1935. Before the agriculture lobby realized it, and without holding hearings, the General Assembly, pressured by textile companies, rushed through a resolution calling for repeal of the tax. Agriculture Department officials in Washington re-

21. AAA press release, November 28, 1934, AAA Papers; USDA, *Agricultural Adjustment, 1933 to 1935*, pp. 119, 124–25, 128, 296; Hunter, "AAA between Neighbors," p. 541.

22. Statements by Charles A. Sheffield, May 27, 1935, and by the AAA administrator, May 27, 1935, AAA Papers; David E. Conrad, *The Forgotten Farmers: The Story of Sharecroppers in the New Deal* (Urbana: University of Illinois Press, 1965), pp. 206, 209; Saloutos, *American Farmer and the New Deal*, p. 102.

minded textile manufacturers that their problems antedated the New Deal so they could not blame the AAA. Furthermore, AAA officials pointed out that cotton consumption had increased since the beginning of the New Deal controls; 1935 consumption was up 3.4 percent over 1934. Farmers with larger incomes, the AAA administrators noted, would buy more and surely aid business. In January 1936 the Supreme Court sided with the industry in declaring the processing tax unconstitutional. The decision in the *Butler* case invalidated the AAA financing scheme, and Congress promptly repealed the Bankhead Act.[23]

The AAA cotton program for 1933–35 achieved its goal of raising the price of cotton through restricting production, even though tenants and textile executives may have suffered. Prices per pound jumped from 6.5 cents in 1932 to 11.1 cents in 1935, and production declined from 13 million bales in 1932 to 10.6 million in 1935. Cash farm income from production and adjustment payments almost doubled from 1932 to 1935. Although the New Deal revived prices, cotton continued its overall downward trend. In 1935 cotton dropped to third place in cash value among North Carolina's crops, behind tobacco and corn. The state's 1923 cotton crop brought $157 million; 1935's dipped to $33 million. North Carolina cotton growers were plagued by increased costs, expansion of production outside the United States, and a declining world market. Cotton exports dropped from 8.4 million bales in 1932 to 5.9 million in 1935. Cotton no longer brought agricultural prosperity for North Carolina, and farmers turned to other crops.[24]

In the summer of 1933 cotton and wheat adjustment programs attracted most farmers' attention, and even in North Carolina tobacco growers, manufacturers, and politicians paid little attention to the implications of the AAA for the tobacco crop. The Agricultural Adjustment Act, passed by Congress on May 12, 1933, included tobacco as a basic commodity in the domestic allotment plan. Through the quiet efforts of southern tobacco state congressmen, the AAA based parity price goals on the 1919–29 period rather than the traditional 1909–14 because the prices for the more recent period were higher. Processing taxes on cigarettes would finance the tobacco program, yet the manufacturers complained little. Textile interests had been more vocal in their opposi-

23. Poe to FDR, April 10, 1935, statement, Paul R. Preston to opponents of the processing tax, June 3, 1935, AAA Papers; USDA, *Agricultural Adjustment, 1933 to 1935*, pp. 137–38.

24. North Carolina Department of Agriculture, *Biennial Report, 1934–1936*, p. 9; USDA, *Agricultural Adjustment, 1933 to 1935*, p. 119; Hoover and Ratchford, *Economic Resources*, pp. 308, 320; Hunter, "AAA between Neighbors," p. 545.

tion to the cotton processing tax. As with the AAA cotton plan, Secretary Wallace counted on the Extension Service to implement the tobacco program. Growers, manufacturers, and AAA officials assumed during the summer of 1933 that it was too late for any assistance for the 1933 crop and focused their attention on reducing the acreage for 1934.[25]

North Carolina tobacco farmers needed help in 1933, and the urgency neutralized concerns over federal intervention. Rather, they sought it. The previous year the South's approximately four hundred thousand tobacco growers had an average income of $250 per family, and total gross income from the crop dropped from $161 million in 1928 to $68 million in 1932. North Carolina farmers produced about 40 percent of the nation's tobacco, and the decline severely damaged the state's economy. Tobacco growers faced several basic problems. The lack of competition among tobacco companies with their secret grading system, an auction warehouse marketing arrangement, and the perennial tendency to overproduce led to low prices. Also, in recent years, farmers failed to adjust supply and demand through voluntary acreage reductions or grower cooperatives. Compounding the problems, tobacco exports fell from 525 million pounds in 1930 to 319 million in 1932. On the bright side, tobacco was in a better position for an adjustment program than any other major crop. Cigarettes were relatively inexpensive and habit-forming; domestic demand, therefore, remained stable. With heavy advertising, cigarette manufacturers increased domestic consumption even after 1929 and reduced the growers' dependence on exports. Tobacco, despite its problems, enjoyed a healthier market situation than other major commodities.[26]

Tobacco farmers demanded quick action, and intense pressure from them by late summer 1933 forced the AAA to take action to improve tobacco prices for the current marketing season. On July 28, John B. Hutson, chief of the AAA tobacco section and a key man for the federal government, met in Raleigh with twenty-nine growers from eastern North Carolina's bright-leaf tobacco belt, and these farmers pressed for near parity prices for the 1933 crop and for long-term acreage controls. Farmers believed that a processing tax levied on the tobacco companies should finance the acreage reductions and supplement prices for the current marketing period. Since foreign buyers purchased more than

25. Badger, *Prosperity Road*, pp. 38–41.

26. Ben Kilgore to P. N. DeGrace, August 7, 1934, AAA Papers; USDA, *Agricultural Adjustment, 1933 to 1935*, p. 187; Hunter, "AAA between Neighbors," p. 567; Badger, "New Deal and North Carolina," pp. 174–75; Hoover and Ratchford, *Economic Resources*, p. 343.

half of the flue-cured tobacco, the processing tax would be a problem because the AAA could levy no tax on exports.[27]

Nonetheless, the growers, landlords and tenants alike, animated by an intense hatred of the tobacco companies, pushed for a processing tax. For 1932 the manufacturers' profits more than doubled the gross income of the growers. Jonathan Daniels, now leading the liberal battles in the state while his father, Josephus, served as Roosevelt's ambassador to Mexico, pleaded with Secretary Wallace to do something for the tobacco farmers of eastern North Carolina, who were unorganized, leaderless, and at the mercy of the tobacco companies. Daniels warned Wallace not to depend on the good faith of the companies voluntarily to increase the prices paid to farmers. To do so would be "leaning upon a reed," he argued. Wallace and others in the AAA hoped pressure by growers would force the manufacturers to enter into an adjustment program with the Agriculture Department. Typically, through 1935 the AAA encouraged grass-roots pressure to achieve its objectives, and when growers disagreed with the AAA, agriculture officials ignored them.[28]

On August 29, 1933, eastern North Carolina tobacco markets opened at the low price of ten cents a pound, although the quality of the leaf merited a higher price. Grower discontent mounted after the discouraging market news, and farmers, AAA officials, and politicians moved quickly to resolve the problem. In Washington on August 30, agriculture authorities held an informal conference with the tobacco company executives about the adjustment program, but the meeting produced no agreement. John Hutson described the tobacco buyers and exporters as "arrogant as any group of industry leaders in the United States." While growers went on relief in certain areas, Hutson pointed out to Wallace, the industry enjoyed prosperity even during the Depression. Although the AAA could not secure the voluntary assistance of the companies, still tobacco growers almost unanimously insisted on acreage reductions and benefit payments, Hutson concluded. Moreover, flue-cured tobacco farmers in the Carolinas wanted the AAA tobacco program announced soon.[29]

The following day, August 31, two thousand tobacco growers held a mass meeting in Raleigh to protest the low prices and to call for the closing of the tobacco markets until prices could reach at least twenty

27. Memo, C. C. Davis, July 29, 1933, John B. Hutson to James H. Holloway, August 7, 1933, AAA Papers.

28. Jonathan Daniels to Wallace, August 10, 25, 1933, AAA Papers; USDA, *Agricultural Adjustment, 1933 to 1935*, p. 187; Badger, *North Carolina and the New Deal*, pp. 25–26.

29. John B. Hutson to Wallace, August 30, 1933, AAA Papers.

cents a pound. Lawrence V. Morrill, Jr., a North Carolina state Department of Agriculture official, who pressed Hutson for action on the 1933 crop and organized growers in eastern North Carolina, planned the rally. Promoted in the pages of the *News and Observer* by Jonathan Daniels, the meeting produced resolutions calling for parity, acreage reduction, and government tobacco graders to replace the company ones. Governor Ehringhaus, considered no friend of the growers because of his association with Gardner and the state's business interests, surprised them by calling for a marketing holiday on September 2. He suspended sales until the federal government acted to ensure parity prices for the 1933 crop.[30]

Unable to reach a voluntary agreement with the tobacco companies on higher leaf prices and not particularly concerned about farmers' protests, AAA officials announced on September 1 an adjustment program for tobacco. They assessed a processing tax on the companies starting in October and called for acreage reduction for the 1934 crop. In effect, the AAA gave up on the 1933 crop and hoped that the promise of reductions in 1934 would contribute to higher prices for the current marketing season. Undaunted, Governor Ehringhaus led a delegation of growers to Washington to meet with Agriculture Department officials about rescuing the prices for 1933. On September 4 and 5 Ehringhaus, grower representatives, and members of the state's congressional delegation persuaded AAA authorities to seek parity prices for 1933; in exchange farmers had to sign up immediately for a 30 percent reduction in the next year's crop. For the first time the government assumed responsibility for the 1933 crop, and Governor Ehringhaus confounded his critics by emerging as a forceful leader for the interests of tobacco growers.[31]

While Ehringhaus and state farm leaders encouraged growers to sign up for acreage reduction, the AAA had to convince tobacco companies to pay parity prices for 1933. Ehringhaus's job proved much easier than Secretary Wallace's. On September 6, in Raleigh Ehringhaus and Hutson inaugurated the sign-up in conjunction with a meeting of delegates from tobacco counties assembled to organize the North Carolina Tobacco Growers' Association. Those growers enthusiastically signed up and worked with county agents to promote enrollment in the plan. Edward Y. Floyd, extension tobacco specialist, led the sign-up, aided by

30. USDA, *Agricultural Adjustment*, p. 79; Corbitt, ed., *Papers of Ehringhaus*, pp. 70–72; Badger, *Prosperity Road*, pp. 47–48, 51–52.

31. Corbitt, ed., *Papers of Ehringhaus*, pp. 72–73; USDA, *Agricultural Adjustment*, p. 79; Badger, *Prosperity Road*, pp. 52–54.

businessmen and newspaper editors in the east who believed the program would bring some recovery. By September 20, 95 percent of the tobacco growers had signed up for the AAA crop controls, yet Ehringhaus delayed reopening the markets until the AAA and the companies could agree on parity prices for 1933. The governor warned that if markets reopened without assurances of parity prices, the result could be disastrous. Given the intransigence of the tobacco executives, some agriculture authorities wanted a showdown with the companies over a voluntary price agreement for this year. They could threaten the companies with licensing requirements and inspections of financial records to see if profits justified price increases if they continued to resist a compromise on the marketing plan. AAA officials believed that public opinion was on their side and that the opposition of the tobacco trust made the public more likely to support the president's agricultural program. The public would blame the industry for any failure to reach an agreement.[32]

On September 15, the AAA presented a proposal to the buyers aimed at achieving parity. This progress in negotiations and the overwhelming success of the sign-up campaign led Ehringhaus to announce that markets would reopen on September 25. By the time sales were resumed, government and industry leaders in Washington had not reached an agreement. As the days passed, the situation in North Carolina market towns became increasingly tense and critical. Ehringhaus feared that unless prices improved violence might erupt. Angry farmers had already blocked markets in Kinston. The governor hoped that better-quality tobacco and the fact that some warehousemen were limiting sales might improve leaf prices. When the AAA and the companies had not settled on an agreement by October 6, two weeks after the markets reopened, Ehringhaus urged immediate action to alleviate the marketing crisis for flue-cured tobacco. Already the state's farmers had sold half the tobacco crop at far below parity, and the governor knew that continued uncertainty would lead to more distress in eastern North Carolina.[33]

After wrangling over licensing, cigarette prices, and government access to company books, on October 12, 1933, the AAA and the tobacco industry finally concluded a 1933 marketing agreement that guaranteed an average parity price of at least seventeen cents a pound. In the

32. Victor Christgau to George N. Peek, September 14, 1933, AAA Papers; Badger, *Prosperity Road*, pp. 54–58; Badger, *North Carolina and the New Deal*, p. 18.

33. Chester C. Davis to John B. Hutson, September 27, 28, 1933, Ehringhaus to George N. Peek, October 6, 1933, AAA Papers; Badger, *Prosperity Road*, p. 57.

arrangement, effective through March 31, 1934, companies agreed to purchase an amount equal at least to the pounds used by the manufacturers during the previous year, which ended June 30, 1933. In return the tobacco companies could raise cigarette prices, although Secretary Wallace insisted on access to company records to check on compliance and to determine whether the industry could justify price increases. In the end the AAA's threat to enter the warehouses and compete with the manufacturers in purchasing tobacco had convinced industry leaders to reach an agreement with the government. John Hutson, chief of the tobacco section, and George Peek, AAA director, backed the accord, but Jerome Frank, AAA counsel, fought for tougher terms with the tobacco companies. Roosevelt, eager for results, endorsed the plan. About one month after the marketing agreement, prices advanced slowly, mainly because exporters and independent buyers purchased more than 50 percent of the flue-cured crop. The foreign companies could not increase their prices as quickly as domestic buyers, although they promised to honor the marketing agreement.[34]

North Carolina's politicians rushed to claim credit for the 1933 tobacco price deal with the companies. Lindsay Warren, working with the tobacco warehousemen, had pushed for reopening the markets before the final agreement, believing a delay would hurt farmers and business. Ehringhaus had followed his suggestion. Congressman John H. Kerr, from the tobacco-growing eastern second district, had to overcome widespread allegations that he supported the manufacturers' proposals in the negotiations. Although he had not accompanied the growers to Washington for their conference with the Agriculture Department, Kerr reminded farmers of his efforts earlier on behalf of the Farm Relief bill that set 1919–29 as the basis for tobacco parity prices. He claimed that during the September marketing crisis he pushed for the seventeen-cents-a-pound price agreement. Franklin W. Hancock, Jr., whose fifth district included growers and tobacco companies, pushed for sign-up completion first, as most growers wanted. He criticized the final agreement as a "sop to the grower and a flop by the AAA." In lieu of the marketing deal, Hancock proposed a stabilization plan under which the government would purchase tobacco and resell it to tobacco companies. Senator Bailey, who voted against the AAA legislation and went fishing in Morehead City during the September crisis,

34. John B. Hutson to J. J. Perkins, November 4, 1933, AAA Papers; "Marketing Agreement for Flue-cured Tobacco," [October, 1933], Bailey Papers; Badger, *Prosperity Road*, pp. 63, 65; Badger, *North Carolina and the New Deal*, pp. 18–19; Saloutos, *American Farmer and the New Deal*, p. 96.

later argued that he had a strong record of support for tobacco growers' interests.[35]

Governor Ehringhaus gained the most from the episode. One year earlier, he had been an unpopular gubernatorial candidate in the east because of his association with corporate interests and the Gardner machine; by the fall of 1933, as governor, he emerged as a champion of the tobacco growers. After farmers in a mass meeting in Raleigh jeered his policies, he called for the market holiday they demanded and surprised them further by leading a delegation of growers to Washington to secure an agreement for the 1933 crop prices. He personally led the sign-up campaign for 1934 acreage reduction. Prodded by pressure from growers and Ehringhaus's leadership, the AAA joined in the effort to secure government backing for higher tobacco prices. By the end of September, Ehringhaus had successfully battled the tobacco companies, unified the farmers, enlisted the aid of the AAA in raising prices, and secured a long-term plan for acreage reduction. The governor earned the admiration of easterners.[36]

In addition to Ehringhaus and the AAA, others contributed significantly to the 1933 marketing agreement. Jonathan Daniels advertised the mass meeting in Raleigh and consistently rallied the farmers. The North Carolina Tobacco Growers Association, whose executive committee the AAA recognized as the official State Tobacco Advisory Board, organized growers into a pressure group, although the association was more a creation of the AAA than representative of Tar Heel rank-and-file growers. Even the manufacturers must be credited with entering into a voluntary arrangement with the farmers, which they obviously did not have to do. With the cooperation of government, growers, and industry, the agreement became a reality and a success in the market. December 1933 figures revealed that income from the 1933 tobacco crop was twice that for 1931 and two and a half times that for 1932. Prices per pound averaged 15.3 cents for 1933, up significantly from the 11.6 cents for 1932 and 8.4 cents for 1931. Although the average by December 1933 had not reached the seventeen cents pledged by the buyers, growers still were pleased, especially since acreage for flue-cured tobacco increased 50 percent from the previous year. Depression and bad weather had wrecked the 1932 crop.[37]

35. Kerr to W. B. Douglas, February 16, 1934, Box 5, and "Statement of John H. Kerr," May 4, 1936, Box 8, Kerr Papers; Badger, *Prosperity Road*, pp. 53, 62, 64, 66–67.

36. Newspaper clipping, *Rocky Mount Telegram*, October 14, 1933, Governors' Papers (E); James C. Daniel, "North Carolina Tobacco Marketing Crisis of 1933," *North Carolina Historical Review* 40 (July 1964): 370–71; Badger, *Prosperity Road*, pp. 66, 71.

37. Wallace to Bailey, February 27, 1935, AAA Papers; Badger, *Prosperity Road*, pp. 65, 69–70, 220.

With the 1933 marketing season under control, the AAA focused its attention on the 1934 crop. In September 1933 about 95 percent of North Carolina tobacco farmers signed a tentative contract to reduce their 1934 acreage by 30 percent. The agreement was only temporary, however, and the Department of Agriculture had not specified the actual amount of the rental and benefit payments. In November 1933 the AAA announced that for the 1934 flue-cured tobacco adjustment program tobacco production would be restricted to five hundred million pounds for the year, and in return the AAA would distribute an estimated $17 million to growers in rental and benefit payments, the financial reward for signing a contract to reduce production. It would pay a farmer "rent," $17.50 for each acre withheld from production, and also compensate the grower up to 12 percent of the total value of tobacco sold, calculated on a maximum average price of twenty-one cents a pound.[38]

During the winter of 1933–34, flue-cured tobacco farmers in North Carolina once again signed up voluntarily to restrict their acreage. Although the sign-up proceeded more slowly than the previous one, eventually about 95 percent participated. Since 1933 prices had been so high, growers worried that the 5 percent who did not sign up would be tempted to produce excessive amounts and ruin the scheme. These farmers wanted some means to punish uncooperative growers. The tobacco section of the AAA sought a compulsory measure for tobacco similar to the Bankhead Act for cotton. They feared overproduction by nonparticipating farmers and wanted to tax the nonsigners to reduce their income. That way, cooperating farmers would have higher incomes than noncooperating ones. A significant difference in incomes would make crop control more attractive. Tobacco section officials persuaded Wallace that a financially attractive voluntary program would be too expensive.[39]

With this pressure from growers and the AAA tobacco section, tobacco state congressmen developed a compulsory crop control plan for 1934 similar to that for cotton. North Carolina's second district congressman, John H. Kerr, backed by the entire state congressional delegation, led the drive in the House for a measure that would heavily tax the tobacco produced by farmers not participating in the program. Kerr estimated that 90 percent of tobacco growers wanted such a tax. Kerr represented the largest tobacco-growing district in the nation and hoped

38. USDA press release, November 18, 1933, Bailey Papers; Badger, *Prosperity Road*, pp. 72–73.

39. Badger, *Prosperity Road*, pp. 74–80.

to recover from the political damage he had suffered during the previous year's marketing crisis. Growers and political opponents charged that he had supported the tobacco companies' position earlier. Facing a tough Democratic primary fight in 1934, Kerr wanted to establish himself clearly as a friend of the tobacco farmers and as their leader in Congress. Kerr introduced the compulsory control measure in Congress and guided it through the Agriculture and Rules committees. He successfully fought efforts to exempt small tobacco producers from the tax because such an exemption would have critically weakened the program. Fellow Tar Heel congressmen Lindsay Warren and William Umstead fought for such exemptions, and the bill was threatened by pressure from growers to increase the tax on nonsigners. Farmers wanted a tax as high as 50 percent, comparable to the Bankhead Act, but AAA officials and congressmen such as John H. Kerr preserved a lower tax rate of 25 to 33.3 percent.[40]

Others in the delegation pressed for control of the tobacco crop. According to Warren, the Kerr bill simply gave "justice and protection" to those who signed the agreement to restrict production. North Carolina farmers had responded admirably to the previous year's distress. Rather than resorting to violence, they had cooperated with government agencies. Warren, however, was still ambivalent: "I admit that legislation of this nature has been far away from the views many of us have heretofore held. I wish that it was not necessary." Ultimately for Warren the emergency justified the measure. If it were "regimentation," then those regimented, the farmers, wanted it. Franklin W. Hancock, Jr., representing the largest tobacco manufacturing district in the United States, endorsed the Kerr bill as necessary. To the charges of compulsion, he declared: "Liberty can mean little to a man who is bound in economic slavery." But he did not think subsidizing decreased production was a permanent solution. Eventually, agriculture would have to increase production and expand markets.[41]

The Kerr bill passed the House, and Senator Ellison D. "Cotton Ed" Smith of South Carolina sponsored it in the Senate. Senator Bailey was a pivotal figure in its passage. Earlier he had voted against both the Farm Relief bill and the Bankhead Act, and he made no secret of his opposition to compulsory crop control, which he felt not only restricted a farmer's liberty to use his land as he saw fit but unduly penalized small farmers as

40. Ibid., pp. 81–85, 113; *Congressional Record,* 73d Cong., 2d sess. (1934), pp. 10646, 10667, 12366; Henry A. Wallace to Kerr, May 1, 1936, Kerr Papers.

41. *Congressional Record,* 73d Cong., 2d sess. (1934), pp. 10651, 10653.

well as sharecroppers. The Kerr bill closely resembled the Bankhead measure, but it contained two exceptions that made it more agreeable to Bailey. Nonsigners had a grace period in which to sign up, and the tax on tobacco produced by nonsigners would be much less than for cotton. Bailey had already voted against two key New Deal farm measures and dared not oppose one supported so overwhelmingly by the state's growers and the entire congressional delegation. In addition, Bailey faced reelection in 1936, and he feared that a champion of the tobacco farmers such as Ehringhaus or Warren might oppose him. In the end, Bailey swallowed his objections and voted for the Kerr-Smith Act. On June 28, 1934, the measure became law.[42]

In 1934, North Carolina enjoyed the best tobacco crop since 1919. Under the Kerr-Smith program, which applied to the 1934 and 1935 seasons, the AAA assessed a penalty tax of 25 percent of the price on tobacco sold by noncooperating farmers, but compliance was high and few taxes were collected. The Extension Service administered the tobacco program and handled the logistics of contracts, government checks, applications for tax exemption, surveying fields, marketing cards, sign-up campaigns, and grower referenda. As a precaution, the Agriculture Department sought a marketing agreement with the tobacco companies for 1934, as in 1933. Negotiations produced no results, however, and the manufacturers assured agriculture officials that increased consumption and reduced acreage would result in satisfactory prices. The prediction proved right. The 1934 average price was 27.3 cents a pound, almost double the 15.3 cents for 1933. Total receipts for the 1934 tobacco crop were three and a half times those for 1932. One farmer's five acres of tobacco that earned him $11.30 in 1932 yielded $1,472.00 in 1934.[43]

The Kerr-Smith program gave North Carolina tobacco farmers a formula for success. Acreage for 1934 was 25 percent below the base acreage and production was eighty million pounds below world consumption. It was little wonder that in December 1934 the state's growers voted 98.9 percent in favor of continuing compulsory crop control and 87.5 percent of North Carolina's eligible farmers participated in the referendum. By the end of 1934, the tobacco farmers had realized their hopes of 1933 by following through on their pledge to reduce acreage. Grass-roots pressure from growers for a mandatory control program stirred agriculture officials and politicians. The AAA tobacco section also

42. Bailey to George H. Miller, June 20, 1934, Bailey Papers; Badger, *Prosperity Road*, pp. 86–89.

43. V. A. Christgau to Ehringhaus, July 30, 1934, AAA Papers; *Raleigh News and Observer*, December 30, 1934; Badger, *Prosperity Road*, pp. 90–95.

sought control legislation as a way to finance rental and benefit payments and used pressure from growers to persuade a reluctant Agriculture Department to implement compulsory controls. Secretary Wallace discovered a tactic that effectively curbed production, a tax on nonparticipants under the Kerr-Smith Act. By 1934 both Senator Bailey and Representative Kerr, who had been aloof to farmers' interests a year earlier, had learned the political wisdom of acceding to demands for mandatory controls.[44]

By 1935, however, growers and tobacco state politicians had divided over the issue of government grading of tobacco on the warehouse auction floor. Buyers from the tobacco companies determined the grade or quality of the leaf, hence the price paid. Grades were secret and not standard from one company to the next. Growers argued that government grading would lead to better prices, but warehousemen and buyers resisted. The unity achieved in the battles for production control dissipated. In 1933, at the beginning of the AAA, agriculture spokesman Clarence Poe expressed appreciation for the Agriculture Department's support of an official government grading program. Poe believed it was a first step in improving tobacco prices, and the department could finance it through a processing tax on the warehousemen. Expenses would be minimal, Poe argued, and growers needed the standardization of prices to free them from the abuses of the tobacco buyers.[45]

Secretary Wallace agreed that government grading would eliminate price inequalities but would not necessarily improve the price significantly. It would encounter serious obstacles. The grading standards of tobacco buyers and manufacturers varied so that it would be difficult to agree on one. Even growers, influenced by the warehousemen and buyers, were lukewarm about government grading, and Wallace believed that they would need much convincing that a change was necessary. For the 1933 marketing season, the Bureau of Agricultural Economics paid for tobacco graders in markets in Farmville, Washington, Oxford, and Henderson at a cost of about $60,000, financed by processing taxes. Also, for selected markets the bureau provided grading services for growers who were willing to pay for it. The program had little impact because few farmers participated, and buyers ignored the grades.[46]

44. USDA, *Agricultural Adjustment in 1934*, p. 146; USDA, *Agricultural Adjustment, 1933 to 1935*, pp. 206–7; Badger, *Prosperity Road*, pp. 97–98.

45. Poe to Wallace, August 13, 1933, AAA Papers; Poe to Wallace, August 18, 1933, Bailey Papers; Badger, *Prosperity Road*, p. 19.

46. Wallace to Poe, September 5, 1933, and John B. Hutson to W. I. Westervelt and Chester C. Davis, October 23, 1933, AAA Papers; Badger, *Prosperity Road*, p. 105.

Secretary Wallace did not push government grading, not wanting to alienate the warehousemen who had cooperated with the AAA during the 1933 marketing crisis and with the establishment of the 1934 NRA code for warehousemen. The threat of congressional legislation providing for government grading encouraged tobacco warehousemen to work with the federal government to eliminate certain abuses. In July 1934, warehousemen agreed to a code that restricted the selling speed, permitted growers time to reject an auction bid, licensed weighmen, and outlawed rebates. The code amounted to self-regulation, however, because the warehousemen's associations elected members of the code authority and the administrator, Con Lanier, was a good friend of the warehousemen. Because the code failed to provide for government grading, that controversy persisted.[47]

Growers won a victory in 1935 when, after much debate among growers, warehousemen, and politicians, Congress passed the Flanagan bill, which called for government grading of tobacco. Previously, warehousemen had successfully fought off such regulation, which they feared as a first step toward cooperative marketing. They argued that it was too expensive, and many growers opposed the measure. Larger growers, who were used to being treated preferentially by warehousemen to attract sales, tended to oppose the Flanagan measure, while the smaller farmers resented the favoritism and backed government grading. Jonathan Daniels, a strong proponent of the Flanagan bill, complained that warehousemen circulated petitions against the measure among farmers and intimidated them into signing. Such petitions, he argued, did not represent the true feelings of growers. Both Daniels and Clarence Poe continued to press for compulsory grading.[48]

Tobacco farmers and warehousemen vied for the politicians' allegiance, and North Carolina's congressional delegation split three ways on the issue. Harold Cooley and Frank Hancock pushed for a strong compulsory grading program and fought off amendments that would have weakened it. On the House floor Hancock attacked the "buyers, warehousemen and the market pets," large influential growers who got preferential treatment, as a "tobacco combination." Farmers, especially tenants, had little protection against expert buyers, rapid sales, and lack of competition for various grades, he argued. John H. Kerr, William B. Umstead, and J. Bayard Clark opposed the Flanagan legislation and

47. Badger, *Prosperity Road*, p. 106.

48. Jonathan Daniels to Bailey, April 3, 1935, Poe to [members of the North Carolina General Assembly], April 10, 1935, Bailey Papers; Badger, *Prosperity Road*, p. 107.

tried unsuccessfully to kill it by supporting amendments making tobacco grading optional. Kerr defended warehousemen and buyers, saying they were not "crooks, thieves, and tricksters." Tobacco growers, who were not "ignorant and incompetent," did not want some "'brain trust' expert" grading their tobacco. Furthermore, he believed that farmers in his second district, who grew one-fifth of the world's bright-leaf flue-cured tobacco and sold one-fourth of it at warehouses, opposed the measure. The bill, according to Kerr, would break up the warehouse system, not increase the price of tobacco, and cost the government $2 million. Kerr, curiously inconsistent in his approach to the AAA, stated that tobacco growers wanted to be left alone. Even if they wanted the measure, he would not vote for it. The House rejected Kerr's amendment requiring a two-thirds vote among second district growers before it could be implemented there. Umstead offered an amendment that sought to make grading optional. He did not oppose government grading and planned to vote for the bill, with or without his amendment, but he did not want to "ram it down the throats" of growers. Umstead's amendment failed; in the North Carolina delegation only Cooley, Hancock, and J. Walter Lambeth voted against it. In Oxford voluntary government grading had brought higher prices, he reminded his colleagues. Clark, decrying the dissension among North Carolina congressmen, warehousemen, and growers, favored the Umstead amendment. For him, the Flanagan bill, even with a "little synthetic referendum" or a "shirttail fiat of the Secretary of Agriculture," was compulsory and unacceptable. The AAA and the Kerr Act were, in contrast, "absolutely necessary" and overwhelmingly demanded.[49]

Lindsay Warren and Robert Doughton, torn between the pressures from growers and warehousemen, steered a middle course. Neither voted on the Umstead amendment. Warren, who had supporters on both sides of the issue, successfully offered an amendment that required a two-thirds majority in a referendum in a market area before the government could implement grading. The Flanagan measure would not accomplish anything, according to Warren, and growers in eastern North Carolina would not vote for it. Graham A. Barden backed Warren's amendment and mildly supported Flanagan. Tobacco companies had "built up a monopoly that is beyond the control of the farmer," and Barden believed that the government should control them. Answering Hancock's attacks on warehousemen, Barden noted that most "scalp-

49. *Congressional Record*, 74th Cong., 1st sess. (1935), pp. 11807–8, 11867–70, 11887–92; Hunter, "AAA between Neighbors," p. 552; Badger, *Prosperity Road*, p. 109.

ers," tobacco buyers and companies, lived in Hancock's district. In a more mediating mood, Barden defended both the farmers from charges of being "poor" and "ignorant" and the warehousemen of being "thugs and thieves." The Flanagan bill passed the House without a recorded vote. Senator Bailey, in one of his rare flexible moods, did not voice a strong opinion about it. Though personally opposed to compulsory grading, Bailey deferred to the wishes of the growers, farm leaders, and the Agriculture Department. The referendum provision satisfied him, and he voted for the Flanagan bill.[50]

Secretary Wallace had been cool toward government grading, and he angered Tar Heel growers by calling for a 20 percent increase in acreage for the 1935 AAA tobacco program. In 1934, prices had been seven cents above parity, and Wallace insisted that they be brought in line with those for other crops and other areas of the economy. The federal government had a responsibility to consumers and manufacturers, Wallace pointed out. Increased production for 1935 would bring tobacco prices down to about twenty cents a pound, which Wallace considered to be the parity price. He and the AAA officials did not want tobacco farmers to be too dependent on a government program that achieved artificially high prices through rigid production controls. Wallace reminded farmers that the AAA was a temporary, emergency adjustment program, not a permanent one. Despite strong opposition from growers and politicians, Wallace held firm on his goal of increased production for 1935.[51] The AAA, not growers, still set agricultural policy through 1935.

Predictably, farmers in North Carolina, spoiled by the high prices for tobacco in 1934, fought the AAA's efforts to bring down the price by increasing acreage. As in the two previous crop seasons, they protested through mass meetings and lobbying efforts. Jonathan Daniels attacked the AAA for its turnaround and claimed that above-parity prices would not injure consumers. Governor Ehringhaus pressured Washington once again on behalf of the growers, but this time he was criticized by Wallace. The secretary denounced those "political manipulators" who sought personal power and selfish interests over general economic recovery. It was rumored that Ehringhaus would be a candidate for the U.S. Senate in 1936 against Bailey, and he demanded an apology from Wallace for the indirect attack. The governor insisted he was loyal to the

50. Bailey to Paul Thompson, March 13, 1935, to Jonathan Daniels, April 8, 1935, to A. P. Thorpe, Sr., August 14, 1935, Bailey Papers; Hunter, "AAA between Neighbors," p. 552; *Congressional Record,* 74th Cong., 1st sess. (1935), pp. 11886–87; Badger, *Prosperity Road,* pp. 109–10.

51. Badger, *Prosperity Road,* pp. 114–15.

AAA and had no political ambitions. Wallace resisted the pressure by claiming that further reductions would send supplies below consumption levels and encourage foreign countries to produce more tobacco.[52]

When the markets opened in the fall and prices dipped to fifteen cents, Ehringhaus's fears seemed confirmed, and he wanted government action to improve prices. Wallace refused and cited the poor quality of the leaf as the reason for the low prices. At the end of the 1935 marketing season, Wallace's tactics proved successful as prices averaged twenty cents a pound for 1935. Tobacco growers had little to complain about as they viewed total receipts for the 1935 crop. Although prices dropped seven cents a pound from 1934, the increased production brought total receipts to $162.2 million, up from the $151.7 million in 1934. The AAA had resisted pressure from growers in 1935 and succeeded in raising farm income.[53]

In June 1935, 98.2 percent of tobacco farmers voting in a referendum favored continuing production controls. By December 1935, 85 percent of the farmers had signed up to reduce acreage for the years 1936 to 1939. Success of the AAA tobacco program from 1933 to 1935 ensured growers' future support. Federal government intervention had substantially improved the marketing position of tobacco producers. Prices had jumped from 8.4 cents in 1931 to 20 cents by 1935. By the end of 1935, the AAA had funneled over $15 million to North Carolina growers in rental and benefit payments. As farmers' incomes increased, the relationship between growers' returns and manufacturers' profits returned to pre-Depression levels, and for 1935 the farmers' income surpassed the tobacco companies' profits.[54]

Improved prices and restricted acreage showed that the AAA had achieved its objectives for flue-cured tobacco. Pressure from the growers, leadership from the state's politicians, and cooperation from the AAA brought substantial changes in tobacco production and marketing. In 1933 tobacco companies agreed with growers and the government to pay a certain price for the crop. In 1934 Congress punished noncooperating farmers by taxing their tobacco through the Kerr-Smith compulsory control program. Growers increasingly favored acreage reductions, as indicated by their enthusiastic sign-ups and referenda on

52. Ehringhaus to Wallace, April 3, 1935, Governors' Papers (E); editorial, *Raleigh News and Observer*, February 16, March 17, 1935; Badger, *Prosperity Road*, p. 116.

53. Ehringhaus to Wallace, September 12, 1935, and Wallace to Ehringhaus, September 18, 1935, AAA Papers; Badger, *Prosperity Road*, p. 118.

54. USDA, *Agricultural Adjustment, 1933 to 1935*, pp. 187, 296; Badger, *Prosperity Road*, pp. 65, 118, 121.

the issue. In 1935 growers scored another triumph with passage of the Flanagan government grading measure. Economic and political success came hand in hand, as the state's politicians carefully cultivated growers' support. Even conservatives such as Senator Bailey dared not stray too far from their interests. North Carolina flue-cured tobacco growers in 1935 had to be happy with the results of the New Deal's agriculture policies.[55]

North Carolina peanut and potato farmers also sought production control plans from the AAA, but they never achieved the success of the cotton and tobacco growers. The state ranked third nationally in peanut acreage and production and suffered economically when the crop's prices dropped to a half a cent per pound in 1932, down from a nickel a pound during the 1920s. Peanut growers feared that New Deal cotton and tobacco acreage controls would lead those farmers to turn to peanuts, increasing production and further lowering prices. In April 1934 peanut farmers won a victory when the AAA declared their crop a basic commodity, which meant that land taken out of cotton and tobacco production could not be planted in peanuts. The AAA had no power of enforcement, however, because it had only a voluntary peanut crop control plan and never controlled prices and acreage.

Potato farmers fared even less well. Congressman Warren, instrumental in the peanut legislation, joined with Senator Bailey in 1935 to secure passage of the Potato Control Act, modeled after the Kerr-Smith Tobacco Act. But the effort to help the eastern North Carolina potato farmers received no aid from the AAA. The Agriculture Department refused to administer it because potato growers were scattered geographically and marketed their crop differently from cotton and tobacco growers, which would make enforcement and monitoring difficult.[56]

By 1935 the AAA program for all crops had revived North Carolina agriculture. In cash farm income, the Tar Heel State had the highest percentage of increase from 1932 to 1934, moving from sixteenth among the states to fifth. Crop values increased 106.5 percent over 1932. North Carolina ranked fifth nationally in crop values, behind only Texas in the South. From 1933 to 1935 the AAA spent $33.1 million in the state, mostly in rental and benefit payments. Eastern tobacco counties, Edgecombe, Johnston, Nash, Pitt, Robeson, and Wilson, received the largest amounts, over a million dollars each. This prosperity enabled North

55. Harold B. Rowe, *Tobacco under the AAA* (Washington, D.C.: Brookings Institution, 1935), p. 247.

56. Hunter, "AAA between Neighbors," pp. 561–62, 565.

Carolina farmers to purchase new clothes and cars. New Deal officials noted a 32.7 percent increase in automobile registrations from 1933 to 1935. The AAA programs for North Carolina's two major crops, cotton and tobacco, along with good weather, brought economic recovery.[57]

"In three years we'll all be sharecroppers, and the government will be the landlord," complained a large farmer from Seaboard, North Carolina. "I see the handwriting on the wall. There's no way out for we farmers." His southern rural individualism and tradition of local control and states' rights, however, yielded to federal intervention in agriculture. His ambivalence was typical of many North Carolinians. "It's a fact that the government program has done a lot for farmers," he concluded. "I don't know what in the world we'd have done without the government help." Though the AAA did not solve all agricultural problems, fourteen-cent cotton and twenty-cent tobacco increased farmers' enthusiasm for the New Deal. By 1935 a strategy of parity and production control had helped the South more than any other region because of tobacco and cotton, although the AAA designed its program primarily for western wheat, corn, and livestock farmers. But in a few months, "nine old men" brought chaos again to American agriculture.[58]

57. *UNC Newsletter*, September 25, 1935, PC 246.9, Ehringhaus Papers (P); AAA memo on Rental and Benefit Payments, May 12, 1933, to July 1, 1936, [n.d.], Bailey Papers; "Report of Semi-Annual Coordinating Meeting of Representatives of Federal Departments and Agencies in North Carolina," December 18, 1935, NCERA Papers; North Carolina Department of Agriculture, *Biennial Report, 1934–1936*, p. 9; USDA, *Agricultural Adjustment, 1933 to 1935*, p. 395.

58. Cash, *Mind of the South*, pp. 373–75; Hunter, "AAA between Neighbors," pp. 567, 569; Tindall, *Emergence of the New South*, p. 403; Terrill and Hirsch, eds., *Such as Us*, pp. 67, 70.

CHAPTER 4

Agriculture after Butler, *1936–1940*

The Supreme Court's invalidation of the AAA's processing tax on January 6, 1936, marked a transition in New Deal agriculture policy. One month before *United States* v. *Butler,* 85 percent of flue-cured tobacco growers voted to continue production controls through 1939. Nashville farmers called the Supreme Court decision a "death blow to our hopes." Representative Lindsay Warren, announcing the decision in the House, called it a "sickening and deadly blow. . . . The farmers of the nation will never return to the economic slavery that existed prior to 1933," he added. Earlier he had defended the processing tax as a "matter of simple justice to agriculture." Farmers did not want "starvation prices," but they did not want a dole either. The processing tax, he insisted, was part of the farmers' price. Representative Harold Cooley declared that "the Supreme Court voted against the Triple A by a vote of 6 to 3; the farmers voted for the Triple A by a vote of 19 to 1, yet the Triple A is no more." In previous debate over the AAA, Cooley conceded that farmers would surrender some freedom because of the emergency. He declared to the House that though "governmental regulation is repugnant, I am also conscious of the fact that poverty, desolation, and foreclosures are likewise quite repugnant." Representative Frank Hancock called the Court's position "untenable and absurd." A *Raleigh News and Observer* editorial, "Back to Despair," captured the mood.[1]

Cotton and tobacco farmers demanded a substitute, and Congress responded with the Soil Conservation and Domestic Allotment Act of 1936, which sought voluntary control through soil conservation. Compulsory crop control was not tried again until the AAA Act of 1938. In the late 1930s, through the Resettlement Administration and the Farm Security Administration, the New Deal, moving beyond its focus on recovery with higher crop prices, targeted the tenancy problem and made efforts at reform. Although these efforts were modest, Tar Heel

1. Corbitt, ed., *Papers of Ehringhaus*, pp. 223–24, 408–9; Coté, "Clarence H. Poe," p. 37; Badger, *Prosperity Road*, pp. 121–23; *Congressional Record*, 74th Cong., 1st sess. (1935), pp. 6224–28, 9483, and 74th Cong., 2d sess. (1936), pp. 97, 2570, 5195.

farmers, led by their new and conservative pressure group, the Farm Bureau, fought the New Deal reform. Just as vehemently, power companies resisted the Rural Electrification Administration's drive to provide electricity for rural areas. North Carolina tobacco farmers, exhibiting conservatism, frustration at the New Deal, and hopes for higher income, rejected compulsory control for 1939. They believed the crisis had ended. Tar Heel farmers wanted the New Deal only on their limited terms of immediate economic self-interest.

One month after the Supreme Court decision, Congress passed the Soil Conservation and Domestic Allotment Act, which met farmers' demands for controls, critical for North Carolina after increased acreage and a surplus from the previous crop. Congressman Harold Cooley, elected in 1934 and a member of the Agriculture Committee, called it "far from an adequate substitute" for the AAA, which had brought "happiness to the hearthstones of North Carolina farms." In congressional debate, he took swipes at the Supreme Court, saying the Constitution should go "hand in hand with the progress of the human mind." Furthermore, Cooley insisted that agriculture was a national, not a local, problem. This bill was the best under the circumstances, for it did bring needed control. Representative Clark shared similar views with the House. Though not as effective as the AAA, it was "constitutional legislation" and the "maximum power of the Congress" for farm relief. Despite fear that there would be insufficient funds for it, the state's tobacco congressmen strongly supported the measure. The federal government would pay farmers to plant soil-building crops and to take certain soil-depleting crops, including tobacco, out of production. Other features distinguished the new program from the old. Congress financed the strictly voluntary program through appropriations, and emphasis shifted from production control to genuine conservation, unlike the previous AAA, which showed little interest in what farmers did with idle land. Under the conservation program, the government offered contracts for entire farms, rather than for a single commodity. The Agriculture Department administered the program through regional divisions, rather than through commodity sections. Locally, elected committees implemented the soil conservation measures, but in North Carolina, the Extension Service maintained its control of administration.[2]

2. U.S. Department of Agriculture, *Agricultural Conservation, 1936: A Report of the Agricultural Adjustment Administration under the Provisions of the Agricultural Adjustment Act and the Soil Conservation and Domestic Allotment Act and Related Legislation from Jan. 1, 1936 to Dec. 31, 1936* (Washington, D.C.: U.S. Government Printing Office, 1937), pp. 1, 4–6; Badger, *Prosperity Road*, pp. 123–26; *Congressional Record*, 74th Cong., 2d sess. (1936), pp. 2361, 2462–64.

The Agriculture Department promised to pay growers of flue-cured tobacco five cents per pound, up to a maximum of 30 percent of the base acreage, for tobacco taken out of production in the soil conservation program. Governor Ehringhaus urged tobacco farmers to plant voluntarily only 70 percent of their tobacco base acreage, and growers argued that the government must allocate $50 million for tobacco if the plan were to succeed. In North Carolina between 75 and 80 percent of the tobacco growers joined the 1936 program and reduced their acreage 23 percent. Tobacco constituted 136,100 of the 611,100 acres diverted from crops for the year. The state's farmers used soil-building practices on 1,045,200 acres in 1936, despite the late start and general lack of interest in this aspect of the conservation effort.[3]

Several farm leaders and congressmen in the state wanted compulsory crop control through a compact arrangement with other tobacco-growing states because they viewed the voluntary conservation scheme as inadequate. Congress would have to authorize those states to devise their own control schemes. In February 1936, the North Carolina Farm Bureau, pressing for such controls, organized primarily in the eastern tobacco counties with the cooperation of the old AAA tobacco committees. The American Farm Bureau Federation, organized much earlier, used the drive for control to increase its membership.

Congressman John Kerr introduced a bill calling for a compact among several southern states to limit tobacco acreage, and his colleagues in the state's congressional delegation, Bailey, Warren, Cooley, and Doughton, joined him. Warren's arguments in favor were typical for the delegation. Congress had to act quickly because of the looming threat of overproduction and surplus. Tobacco growers would be "returned to that state of serfdom that existed prior to 1932," he added. Warren estimated that 99¾ percent of the state's growers wanted it, and the federal government should act because North Carolina paid large amounts in tobacco taxes. Hancock attested that, contrary to the Supreme Court's *Butler* decision, agriculture was a national, not a local, problem. Soil conservation would help in the long term, but the compact would provide immediate control. Cooley directed the bill through the House. One senator threatened to filibuster the compact bill if Robert Reynolds did not forgo a filibuster of a bill on aliens. Reynolds relented, and the compact legislation passed. Once Congress passed the compact legislation, Kerr urged Governor Ehringhaus to call a special session of the North Car-

3. USDA, *Agricultural Conservation, 1936*, pp. 43, 193, 195; Corbitt, ed., *Papers of Ehringhaus*, pp. 223–24, 408–9; Badger, *Prosperity Road*, pp. 124–25.

olina legislature so that the state could pass compulsory crop control similar to that in other southern states. Farm leaders, particularly in the east, cited "great unrest among the farmers" and pressed for a compulsory contract "with teeth in it." Along with politicians, farmers urged Ehringhaus to call a special session for that purpose.[4]

For several weeks, Ehringhaus resisted the pleas for a special session of the General Assembly to pass compact legislation. Though an ardent supporter of the tobacco growers' cause in 1933, Ehringhaus believed that compact legislation would not be the most practical solution for the current crop season. On March 7, 1936, he declared that such a measure required congressional action and similar laws from other southern states, and without such cooperation a special legislative session would be useless. By March 1936, Virginia had passed a compact bill, but Georgia, ruled by the strong anti–New Dealer Eugene Talmadge, refused. South Carolina waited for North Carolina, the leading flue-cured tobacco state, to act first. On March 16, Ehringhaus called for voluntary crop reductions similar to those of 1933 and asked growers to sign up to reduce their tobacco production to 70 percent of the base acreage. This short-term alternative to the compact plan failed to attract support in North Carolina or in any other southern tobacco state.[5]

Governor Ehringhaus had political reasons for not calling a special session. In 1933 Ehringhaus's efforts on behalf of tobacco farmers did not conflict seriously with established political and economic interests in the state. In 1936 that was no longer true. While farmers and their political allies lobbied for compact legislation, other New Dealers in the state wanted North Carolina to comply with the social security program. Resisting both pressures, Ehringhaus feared that others in the legislature would take advantage of a special session to repeal the sales tax. Since 1933 the governor had used the sales tax and budget cuts to balance the state's budget, and he, along with the conservative economic interests in the state, did not want to risk a repudiation of those fiscal

4. Kerr to Ehringhaus, March 14, 1936, Box 8, Kerr Papers; Bailey to Ehringhaus, March 16, 1936, Bailey Papers; Ehringhaus to Pitt County Acreage Control Committee, March 23, 1936, J. H. Blount to Ehringhaus, March 26, 1936, J. S. Manning to Ehringhaus, April 10, 1936, Governors' Papers (E); Christina McFadyen Campbell, *The Farm Bureau and the New Deal: A Study of the Making of National Farm Policy* (Urbana: University of Illinois Press, 1962), p. 95; Badger, *Prosperity Road*, pp. 126, 137; *Congressional Record*, 74th Cong., 2d sess. (1936), pp. 4456, 5105, 5195, 5916; Pleasants, "Robert Reynolds," pp. 260–61.

5. Ehringhaus to Pitt County Acreage Control Committee, March 23, 1936, Governors' Papers (E); Corbitt, ed., *Papers of Ehringhaus*, pp. 217, 223–24; Badger, *Prosperity Road*, pp. 127–30.

policies he had fought for so successfully in 1933 and 1935. Ehringhaus also believed that Ralph McDonald, a leading opponent of the sales tax in the 1935 General Assembly and a candidate for governor in 1936, would use a special session to his political advantage. Some friends of Ehringhaus, such as congressmen Lindsay Warren and William Umstead, feared that his refusal would harm the chances of the organization's candidate for governor, Clyde R. Hoey. Unlike 1933, when tobacco farmers faced a much greater crisis and he championed their cause, Ehringhaus refused to act in 1936.[6]

Growers tried one final time to persuade the governor to call a special session to enact compact legislation. Led by Jasper E. Winslow of the Farm Bureau Federation, six thousand farmers gathered on April 21 in Riddick Stadium at North Carolina State College in Raleigh to protest his inaction. Previously, such mass meetings had brought prompt action from state and federal officials, most memorably in 1933. In an hour-and-a-half speech before hostile farmers and farm leaders, Ehringhaus dashed their hopes for compact legislation in 1936. Declaring that he had "a bellyfull of public office," Ehringhaus lashed out at state and federal agricultural officials for having backed increased acreage the previous year, which he considered the cause of the tobacco farmers' current problem. He also pointed to flaws in the compact proposal. It offered no protection against the interstate movement of tobacco by noncooperators into noncompact states and did not penalize noncooperators sufficiently. He encouraged the growers to reduce their acreage to 70 percent and participate fully in the soil conservation program. Obviously bitter toward the farmers and agricultural leaders for what he considered a betrayal, Ehringhaus became a willing scapegoat and taunted the crowd by pleading, "If there are some who would prepare a cross and Calvary for me, that is all right."[7]

On the same day that Ehringhaus defended himself before angry farmers in Raleigh, Congress passed the Kerr compact bill, which enabled states to control tobacco acreage. But this action changed the situation very little for farmers and only increased the acrimony between Ehringhaus and the tobacco congressmen. Doughton, Kerr, and Cooley expressed amazement at Ehringhaus's attacks in the Raleigh speech and pressed once again for a special session. But without the cooperation of Ehringhaus and the legislatures of South Carolina and Georgia, they

6. Roy T. Cox to Warren, April 11, 1936, Box 16, Warren Papers; Badger, *Prosperity Road*, pp. 127–28, 130.

7. Corbitt, ed., *Papers of Ehringhaus*, pp. 238–58; *Raleigh News and Observer*, April 22, 1936; Badger, *Prosperity Road*, pp. 130–31.

realized that this late in the planting season their scheme for compulsory crop control could not succeed for 1936. Ehringhaus and Kerr, in bitter attacks, blamed each other for the farmers' problems. Calling the Kerr Act a "plucked parrot" and a "toothless, grinning and impotent skeleton," Ehringhaus continued to point out that the compact plan could not control tobacco production by noncooperating farmers in noncompact states. He criticized Kerr for supporting increased acreage the previous year and claimed that Kerr did not endorse his request for more funds for tobacco farmers under the conservation program. Facing reelection, Kerr continued the public battle with the governor, begun in 1933, over who best represented the cause of the growers. He denied supporting increased acreage for 1935 and still believed in a compact plan as the most practical replacement for the AAA.[8]

The results of the 1936 crop season vindicated Governor Ehringhaus. South Carolina and Georgia did not legislate compulsory acreage reduction, and further reductions by North Carolina would have worked to the advantage of those other tobacco-growing states. Disease, bad weather, and the voluntary conservation program resulted in a 1936 flue-cured crop of 682.9 million pounds, down from the 811.2 million pounds for 1935. For 1936 prices averaged 22.2 cents a pound, higher than for 1935, but total income dropped $10 million from 1935. The federal government paid state farmers a total of $647,074 for all crops for participating in the 1936 conservation program and $1.1 million in rental and benefit payments to tobacco farmers.[9]

In 1937 advocates of compulsory crop control tried again to secure compact legislation among the several southern tobacco states. The North Carolina legislature passed a compact measure, but the legislatures in Georgia and South Carolina failed to reciprocate, and the movement ended. The campaign had faltered under emergency conditions in 1936, after the invalidation of the AAA, and it failed under more prosperous conditions in 1937. In congressional debate Representative Cooley pushed for "compulsory control" because soil conservation had not worked. He disliked the idea of "permanently controlling American agriculture by federal legislation." Even though control was "obnoxious," it was not as bad as "bankruptcy and starvation." He argued for an

8. Corbitt, ed., *Papers of Ehringhaus*, pp. 325–28, 331; "Statement of John H. Kerr," May 4, 1936, Box 8, Kerr Papers; *Raleigh News and Observer*, April 23, May 4, 1936; Badger, *Prosperity Road*, pp. 130–32.

9. Ehringhaus to W. E. Hooks, September 23, 1936, Governors' Papers (E); USDA, *Agricultural Conservation, 1936*, pp. 143–44; Badger, *Prosperity Road*, pp. 118, 124–25, 132, 147.

agricultural program financed from general revenues. Senator Reynolds sought less reduction for small tobacco growers. "We are all now . . . interested in the little man, because the little men have the votes," he joked to colleagues, who laughed when he reminded them of the 1938 elections.

Results for the 1937 crop season showed even further improvement. Flue-cured tobacco farmers received an average of twenty-three cents a pound for a bumper crop of 866 million pounds, and the total income from flue-cured sales reached $199.2 million, the second highest in history. The federal government paid North Carolina farmers a total of $8.3 million for all crops in the 1937 conservation program and paid tobacco farmers a little over $3 million for soil-diverting efforts from January 1937 to June 1938. In the 1937 program, the average farmer earned $81.93, but in the South the average fell to $69.68.[10]

Not until February 1938, however, did Congress pass compulsory crop control legislation to replace the first AAA. In the Agricultural Adjustment Act of 1938 lawmakers struck a balance between the earlier AAA and the soil conservation program. The new plan called for an "Ever Normal Granary" for storing crop surpluses to protect the supply against poor harvests as well as bumper crops. Secretary Wallace believed such a program would regulate the supply and stabilize farmers' incomes. The 1938 act also provided for parity payments, taxes on crops sold in excess of marketing quotas, a continuation of the soil conservation program, and loans on stored commodities. By using marketing quotas rather than production controls, agriculture officials hoped to avoid difficulty with the courts.[11]

Disagreements among farmers, agriculture leaders, and tobacco state politicians delayed passage of the measure for almost a year. Farm Bureau officials, believing Wallace's Ever Normal Granary would lower prices, sought higher commodity prices through strict production controls. The state Farm Bureau, thwarted in its drive for a compact among tobacco states, continued to lobby for a control program to replace the original AAA. Poorly organized and too heavily associated with large

10. U.S. Department of Agriculture, *Agricultural Adjustment, 1937–1938: A Report of the Activities Carried on by the Agricultural Adjustment Administration under the Provision of the Agricultural Adjustment Act of 1938, the Soil Conservation and Domestic Allotment Act, the Marketing Act of 1937, the Sugar Act of 1937, and Related Legislation, from Jan. 1, 1937 through June 30, 1938* (Washington, D.C.: U.S. Government Printing Office, 1939), pp. 49, 290, 294; Badger, *Prosperity Road*, pp. 133–36, 147; *Congressional Record*, 75th Cong., 2d sess. (1937), pp. 659–60, 1156.

11. USDA, *Agricultural Adjustment, 1937–1938*, pp. 17, 103–5; Badger, *Prosperity Road*, p. 144.

farmers, merchants, and warehousemen, the state Farm Bureau never gained much support from rank-and-file farmers, and the abrasive personality of its leader, J. E. Winslow, alienated many of the state's politicians. On the national level, however, Farm Bureau leaders persuaded Secretary Wallace to accept more rigid production controls and quotas in exchange for their support of his Ever Normal Granary.[12]

Clarence Poe also favored compulsory crop control, but he insisted on a just system with fairer allotments than under the original AAA. He believed that the new program should not reduce acreage across the board but should vary the restrictions to benefit the small family farms that produced a diversity of crops and livestock. He argued that agricultural policy penalized the small farmer who earlier had reduced tobacco acreage voluntarily and diversified into other crops. Senator Bailey also sympathized with small farmers and tenants, yet he used such sympathy as a reason to vote against the 1938 AAA measure. "If you would apply the principles and policies of the agriculture act to all other activities of our people," Bailey complained to the editor of the *Charlotte Observer*, "you would have Fascism." According to Bailey, the bill would freeze the agricultural status quo because large farmers would maintain their advantage over tenants and small farmers. Allotments, Bailey pointed out, constituted a vested interest, and land with an allotment would become too expensive for poor farmers.[13]

Largely through the work of Congressman Harold Cooley, the tobacco section of the 1938 AAA provided for compulsory crop control although Congress rejected controls for other crops. Agriculture Committee chairman Marvin Jones deferred to tobacco congressmen on such matters. Cooley, Warren, and Kerr were powerful congressional allies of the tobacco growers. Robert L. Doughton and, earlier, Edward W. Pou were more prominent politically but never played key roles in tobacco legislation. After Pou's death in 1934, J. Bayard Clark from the seventh district moved to the Rules Committee, and he expedited the handling of tobacco measures. The 1938 AAA Act required that the secretary of agriculture announce a marketing quota in November for the following crop season if the total supply of tobacco exceeded the reserve supply level. Growers had to approve the marketing quota by a two-thirds vote in a referendum to be held within thirty days after the announcement of the quota. Production totals for the past five years served as the basis for

12. Badger, *Prosperity Road*, pp. 137–40, 144-46.

13. Bailey to John Hester, November 8, 1937, to the editor, *Charlotte Observer*, May 9, 1938, clipping, *Progressive Farmer*, December 1938, Bailey Papers.

the state's marketing quota, and the government would levy a 15 percent tax on tobacco sold in excess of a farmer's quota. For any growers with a base production under thirty-two hundred pounds, the quota would not reduce their production below their average for the last three years. To assist small farmers further, the quota made allowances for acres diverted under the AAA programs.[14]

Secretary Wallace faced several logistical problems in implementing the marketing quotas for 1938. The measure had been passed in February, only a couple of months before planting season, and he quickly announced the marketing quota of 748 million pounds, 487 million for North Carolina flue-cured growers, and called for a referendum on March 12. AAA officials realized that they would not have farmers' individual marketing quotas available until the fall, and for the present they decided to use the acreage allotments under the conservation program to guide farmers in their spring planting. Without knowing their quotas for the current crop season, 86.2 percent of the flue-cured tobacco farmers favored the marketing quota for 1938. Apparently concerned about the bumper crop in 1937 and the weakness of the conservation program, 89.6 percent of North Carolina growers voted for it.[15]

After the referendum, the AAA experienced more problems with the 1938 crop. As planned, AAA officials released acreage allotments under the soil conservation program as a guide for farmers until marketing quotas could be prepared by early fall. Farmers protested strongly when the AAA issued the acreage allotments to them during or even after planting time and about inequities in the allotments. More complaints followed the issuance of the marketing quotas. As expected, some farmers did not distinguish carefully between the interim acreage allotment and the marketing quotas for the new 1938 program and consequently produced more than they could market. Unfortunately for them, Secretary Wallace believed the AAA had administered the conservation allotments too loosely, and he wanted the marketing quotas regulated more carefully. Marketing quotas created an administrative nightmare. Some farmers did not receive their quotas until after the marketing season started; others complained about the way the AAA determined the quotas; and many pointed to the wide variations in

14. Badger, *Prosperity Road*, pp. 53, 83, 146, 149, 153, 190–91, 215–16.

15. USDA, *Agricultural Adjustment, 1937–1938*, p. 113; U.S. Department of Agriculture, *Agricultural Adjustment, 1938–1939: A Report of the Activities Carried on by the Agricultural Adjustment Administration, July 1, 1938 through June 30, 1939* (Washington, D.C.: U.S. Government Printing Office, 1939), pp. 65–66; Badger, *Prosperity Road*, pp. 150–51, 158.

quotas among similar farms. Market results brought more dissatisfaction. Flue-cured growers earned 22.2 cents a pound, down from 23 cents in 1937, and because of the poundage restrictions, total income from the crop dropped $24.8 million from 1937. From July 1, 1938, to June 30, 1939, the AAA spent a total of $21.9 million in the state for all crops and paid the state tobacco farmers an estimated $3.9 million under the conservation program.[16]

In December 1938, tobacco farmers had an opportunity to vent their frustrations by voting on the referendum on 1939 marketing quotas. Edward Y. Floyd, state AAA administrator, led the campaign for continued controls in the state, and he asked fellow AAA committeemen to hold meetings and to seek the support of bankers, merchants, warehousemen, and civic organizations for controls. Floyd planned a radio campaign, newspaper articles, four district meetings, and a climactic state meeting with Secretary Wallace as speaker. Quota supporters mounted a good campaign at the state and district levels, but efforts lagged seriously at the local level. County agents and AAA county committees spent most of their time sending marketing quotas to farmers before the referendum, as promised. But opponents of control did not campaign vigorously either. Eugene Talmadge of Georgia spoke before the North Carolina Anti-Compulsory Control Association in Raleigh, but he drew an audience of only fifteen hundred, not the ten thousand expected. Senator Bailey urged farmers to reject controls because he believed that with the increasing demand for tobacco, growers would lose their foreign markets if there were further crop reductions. Foreign production would increase, he argued, if the United States persisted in controls. He also pointed out that crop controls worked to the advantage of the large farmers.[17]

In the referendum, flue-cured tobacco growers rejected marketing quotas for 1939, the only time they ever voted against controls. Overall only 56.8 percent, 57.3 percent in North Carolina, favored controls, short of the necessary two-thirds. Bailey viewed the results as a repudiation of compulsory control but not a rejection of federal assistance for agriculture as had been the case for the voluntary soil conservation program. He warned farmers not to interpret the verdict as justification for increased production. Bailey believed the AAA made a tactical error

16. USDA, *Agricultural Adjustment, 1938–1939*, pp. 91, 125; Badger, *Prosperity Road*, pp. 160–64.

17. H. I. Ogborn to W. H. Stevens, November 1, 1938, E. Y. Floyd to W. G. Finn, November 8, 1938, AAA Papers: "To the Farmers of N.C.," November 21, 1938, Bailey Papers; Badger, *Prosperity Road*, pp. 166–68.

by issuing quotas to farmers before the vote, thereby losing votes. Most observers, however, interpreted the outcome not as a rejection of controls but as a vote against the way the AAA administered the 1938 program. The vote results also revealed that small farmers opposed the controls more than did landlords and tenants. For 1936 and 1937 farmers received good prices with voluntary controls under the conservation program, and in 1938 with compulsory controls, prices dropped slightly. For 1939 growers obviously wanted to take a chance on unrestricted production.[18]

The experiment with no controls proved disastrous, and by the fall of 1939 growers once again opted for compulsory restrictions. Heartened by the Supreme Court's approval in April 1939 of the 1938 AAA Act, proponents of control secured changes in the tobacco program even before the 1939 marketing season: provisions for an early referendum, replacement of poundage with acreage quotas, and assistance to small farmers. Prices were still lower early in the marketing season, and no clamor arose for a referendum that would bring back controls. On September 8, 1939, however, Great Britain announced its withdrawal from the American tobacco market because of the war with Germany, and all associated with flue-cured tobacco quickly appreciated the seriousness of the situation. From 1934 to 1938 the British Imperial Tobacco Company purchased about one-third of the flue-cured crop and about 25 percent of North Carolina's tobacco. The loss of the state's largest customer prompted the warehousemen to close the markets the next day.[19]

With the warehouses closed, tobacco officials moved quickly to resolve the crisis. As the first priority, they scheduled a referendum on 1940 crop controls for early October. Growers had to reassure the buyers and the government by voting for controls for 1940 before the AAA could conclude an agreement to end the current marketing crisis. In a September 28 address, Governor Hoey revealed the government's plan, which called for the Commodity Credit Corporation (CCC) to purchase tobacco on behalf of the British Imperial Tobacco Company. With CCC funds, the Imperial buyers would purchase their normal amount, and

18. USDA, *Agricultural Adjustment, 1938–1939*, p. 65; Bailey to Poe, December 12, 1938, "To the Farmers of N.C.," December 15, 1938, Bailey Papers; Hunter, "AAA between Neighbors," pp. 567–68; Badger, *Prosperity Road*, pp. 169–71, 174.

19. U.S. Department of Agriculture, *Agricultural Adjustment, 1939–1940: A Report of the Activities of the Agricultural Adjustment Administration, July 1, 1939 through June 30, 1940* (Washington, D.C.: U.S. Government Printing Office, 1940), p. 46; Corbitt, ed., *Papers of Hoey*, pp. 293–99; Badger, *Prosperity Road*, pp. 176–80.

though the CCC owned the tobacco, Imperial would have options to purchase it up to July 1, 1941. But before the government could implement the program, Hoey warned the farmers, it needed a vote for controls in the upcoming referendum. Supporters of control mounted a vigorous campaign, and on October 5, 89.9 percent of the growers, 90.8 percent in North Carolina, voted for the return of controls. Undoubtedly, the crisis resulting from the British withdrawal from the markets played a crucial role in the vote for controls. On October 9, the government signed the deal with Imperial, and the next day markets reopened.[20]

Flue-cured growers faced another problem in the fall of 1939—low prices for their largest crop in history. From 1929 to 1938 flue-cured production averaged 709 million pounds, but in 1939 with no controls it reached 1.1 billion pounds. Before the markets closed, the price averaged 14.5 cents a pound and by season's end it was 14.9 cents, a significant drop from the previous year's 22.2 cents. The increased production compensated for the low price because total receipts fell only $1 million below the 1938 figure. The government paid North Carolina farmers who participated in the 1939 voluntary conservation program for flue-cured tobacco $1.3 million.[21]

In 1940 the European war brought more uncertainty to the state's tobacco farmers. Great Britain, seeking trade advantages, began to purchase Turkish leaf and announced an embargo on American tobacco imports. Because of the huge crop in 1939, AAA officials cut 1940 allotments 35 percent and again wanted growers to vote on future controls to reassure buyers and the government before the 1940 marketing season. In the July 1940 referendum, 86.1 percent of flue-cured growers, 87.1 percent in North Carolina, opted for an unprecedented three-year control program. The AAA again secured a deal with the British companies for the 1940 crop. In 1940 the price jumped to 16.4 cents a pound, but total receipts dropped a third from 1939, largely because of the allotment cuts. To assist tobacco farmers in their worst season since 1933, the AAA spent a total of $16.2 million in the state from July 1939 to June 1940 on all commodity programs. By the end of 1940 supporters of tobacco control could count their accomplishments since the defeat of controls in December 1938: they had changed the basis for

20. USDA, *Agricultural Adjustment, 1939–1940,* pp. 46, 48; Corbitt, ed., *Papers of Hoey,* pp. 293–99; Badger, *Prosperity Road,* pp. 180–83, 187–88.

21. USDA, *Agricultural Adjustment, 1939–1940,* pp. 45, 133; Corbitt, ed., *Papers of Hoey,* pp. 293–99; Badger, *Prosperity Road,* p. 188.

quotas from poundage to acreage, switched the base period for parity from 1919–29 to 1934–38, and secured crop control for three years.[22]

Cotton growers also participated in the federal government's agricultural programs in the years 1936–40. The *Butler* case ended compulsory crop control for cotton, and the 1936 Soil Conservation and Domestic Allotment Act assisted cotton as well as tobacco farmers. In the cotton belt, the conservation program for 1936 covered an estimated 76 percent of the total cropland, and North Carolina farmers took 390,600 acres of cotton out of production. In turn, the government promised to pay five cents a pound on normal yield per acre to farmers for diverting acreage from cotton up to 35 percent of the total base acreage. Drought kept the 1936 yield down to 12.3 million bales; prices averaged 12.3 cents. In the special cotton price-adjustment plan from August 1935 to August 1936, North Carolina ranked eighth among nineteen states with its receipts of $1.6 million. In cotton rental and benefit payments for 1936 North Carolina received $817,626.[23]

In 1937 cotton farmers produced a record 18.9 million bales, and the price fell to 8.4 cents. Growers demanded controls, and Congress granted their wish with the 1938 AAA, which provided for allotments, marketing quotas, commodity loans, and referenda. Using the previous five years as a guide, the AAA set a national allotment of approximately twenty-eight million acres, and North Carolina's share of one million acres ranked ninth among the cotton states. Each farmer had a marketing quota, and the AAA levied a two-cent-per-pound penalty for marketing in excess of the quota. For the next two years the national quota remained roughly the same, and cotton farmers voted overwhelmingly for marketing quotas for each year 1938 to 1940. For 1939 only 65 percent of North Carolina's cotton farmers voted for quotas, but the less than two-thirds approval did not change the overall verdict for the cotton belt because the rest of the cotton states favored controls more strongly. Under the 1938 conservation program, the AAA paid state cotton farmers $6.9 million, and for 1939, $8.9 million, which included conservation and price-adjustment payments.[24]

Unfortunately, cotton growers experienced problems the AAA could

22. USDA, *Agricultural Adjustment, 1939–1940,* p. 104; Badger, *Prosperity Road,* pp. 189–90, 192–94.

23. USDA, *Agricultural Conservation, 1936,* pp. 43, 47, 76, 144, 193; Tindall, *Emergence of the New South,* p. 406.

24. USDA, *Agricultural Adjustment, 1937–1938,* pp. 109, 111; *Agricultural Adjustment, 1938–1939,* pp. 51, 125; *Agricultural Adjustment, 1939–1940,* pp. 9, 41–43, 103, 133; Tindall, *Emergence of the New South,* pp. 406–7.

not solve. Receipts for cotton in 1939 amounted to only 39 percent of those for 1929, and income from cotton hit its lowest point since 1933. Harvested cotton acreage in the South declined from 44.7 million in 1929 to 22.8 million in 1939. In 1929 cotton provided 46 percent of cash farm receipts in the South, but in 1939 it was only 29.2 percent. Cotton lost ground because of controls, competition from synthetics, and farmers switching to other crops, as well as increased foreign production, which diminished American cotton exports from 5.9 million bales in 1935 to 1.1 million in 1940. In an effort to help, the government in 1939 subsidized foreign cotton sales and sold or bartered its cotton stocks with European nations. Consequently, exports reached an artificial high of 6.1 million bales in 1939. The war improved the domestic market. Cotton consumption in North Carolina during the first ten months of 1940 increased 7 percent from the previous year.[25]

The AAA succeeded in improving the relative position of North Carolina agriculture. For each year between 1934 and 1939 the state's flue-cured tobacco farmers earned three times as much for their crop as they had in 1932. Flue-cured tobacco prices from 1934 to 1940 averaged 97 percent of the 1920–29 level. All the states in the South, except North Carolina and Florida, experienced a decline in agriculture from 1929 to 1939, but largely because of the improvement in tobacco, North Carolina increased its share of the South's cash receipts from farming from 9 percent in 1929 to 14.1 percent in 1939. While the per capita value of farm products nationally in 1939 equaled only 70.7 percent of the 1929 figure, North Carolina's reached 90.8 percent. In addition, between 1930 and 1948 the value of North Carolina farmland increased twice as fast as the national average. Tobacco-marketing towns, Wilson, Greenville, and Kinston, grew faster than any other North Carolina towns in the 1930s except for the manufacturing centers of Hickory and Reidsville. Overall the AAA spent $84 million in the state from 1933 to 1939, and, more important, it played a dominant role in marketing cotton and tobacco. Production controls enabled the state's farmers to adjust their crops to the demand.[26]

Although the AAA restored prices and raised incomes, all North

25. "WPA: Monthly Report of Employment and Economic Conditions—N.C.," November 1940, WPA Papers; Hoover and Ratchford, *Economic Resources*, pp. 308, 320; Tindall, *Emergence of the New South*, pp. 408–9, 429.

26. U.S. Department of Commerce, Bureau of the Census, *Sixteenth Census of the United States: 1940, Agriculture*, Vol. 3: *General Report* (Washington, D.C.: U.S. Government Printing Office, 1943), p. 37; *Population*, Vol. 1: *Number of Inhabitants* (Washington, D.C.: U.S. Government Printing Office, 1942), p. 772; Hoover and Ratchford, *Economic Resources*, pp. 104–5; Badger, *Prosperity Road*, pp. 196, 199, 208.

Carolina farmers were not happy with production controls. Farmers who planted only three or four acres in tobacco or cotton, largely overlooked by historians more interested in tenants, resisted controls consistently throughout the 1930s. One small farmer in Wilson County complained to Jonathan Daniels: "Tobacco's all right if you got a big allotment and tenants to do the work. That's dandy and sugar candy. . . . The little farmers and the tenants get the sweat and he gets the cream." A small landlord from Seaboard objected: "The government farm program hasn't helped me much. . . . Some big farmers has profited by it. . . . All I drawed last year for co-opin' with the government was $25, and half of that went to the sharecropper. . . . It's enough to make folks sore to see how some gobble it up, how farmers . . . are gettin' rich on the government." A "two-horse" farmer from Pleasant Hill confessed: "The farm program mixes me up; I ain't never understood how it works. I got a check from the gov-mint last spring, but it was so little I done forgot what 'twas."[27]

North Carolina, ranked second in farm population but last in cultivated acres per farm, was a state of small farms, and the small growers fought controls designed primarily to aid large commercial farmers. In 1933 among large landowners, small farmers, and tenants, the small farmers were the slowest to sign up. Throughout the decade they complained to the politicians, especially to sympathetic Senator Bailey. In 1938, despite favorable changes in the AAA program, small farmers were largely responsible for the defeat of control. These farmers persisted in resenting production cuts, and the association of commercial farmers and their allies—the Farm Bureau, the agricultural Extension Service, and warehousemen—with control intensified the opposition. Theodore Saloutos pointed to another source of frustration: mechanization in agriculture and swift technological changes, not the AAA, led to the consolidation of farms and the increase in the size and number of large farms.[28]

That politicians were concerned about small family farmers indicates their strength as a group. In 1935 the average farm size in the state was 66.2 acres. Tenants and sharecroppers operated 47.2 percent of the 300,967 farms and nonwhites about 23 percent of them. A representative survey of 1,703 rural heads of households in 1935 revealed the following breakdown: 29.1 percent were owners, 22 percent renters, 24.1 percent

27. Saloutos, *American Farmer and the New Deal,* p. xiii; Daniels, *Tar Heels,* pp. 80–81; Terrill and Hirsch, eds., *Such as Us,* pp. 76–77, 112.

28. Badger, *Prosperity Road,* pp. 169, 171, 174, 204–5; Saloutos, *American Farmer and the New Deal,* p. 261.

"croppers," 9.5 percent farm laborers, and 15.3 percent were nonagricultural. North Carolina congressmen lobbied for special provisions for farmers who owned only a few acres, who obviously would suffer more from a 25 to 30 percent AAA acreage reduction program than would a large commercial farmer. Representative Barden conceded that there were mistakes and "inequalities" in the AAA program. Priority for crop increases should be given to farmers with less than three-acre allotments and those just starting in farming. "The average big grower is satisfied with his present allotment," Barden believed. Liberals like Clarence Poe and Josephus Daniels, champions of the "little men," faced a dilemma. They vigorously backed New Deal crop controls that aided mostly large commercial farmers at the expense of small farmers and tenants. Both men compromised by supporting acreage controls while favoring specific programs to assist family farms. Because of political pressure, the AAA gave the small farmer certain advantages, ranging from larger benefit payments to special allotment considerations, to offset the acreage reductions. The AAA refused, however, to set up minimum allotments and quotas based on the percentage of cultivated acres in a specific crop. Small farmers argued that if they planted a small percentage of their acres in tobacco, they should not have to reduce their acres as much as larger farmers who planted a greater percentage of their land in tobacco. Despite the arguments, the AAA retained the base-acreage principle for the allotments. To do otherwise, its officials believed, would injure the tenant farmer as well as the large commercial farmer.[29]

Unlike recent historians, North Carolina politicians and AAA officials demonstrated little interest in the problems of tenants and sharecroppers, the rural poor who had little political clout. Most serious was displacement of tenants as a result of acreage reduction programs. North Carolina ranked thirty-ninth nationally in the percentage of farms operated by tenants; fifteen eastern counties had a tenancy rate above 60 percent in 1933; thirty-one counties had tenancy rates of 40 to 60 percent. Tenancy prevailed in eastern tobacco counties and cotton counties in the southern piedmont. In February 1934 Lorena Hickok, a

29. Coté, "Clarence H. Poe," pp. 38–39; Cronon, "Southern Progressive," p. 166; Bailey to Poe, February 26, 1934, Bailey Papers; Badger, *Prosperity Road*, pp. 204–6; U.S. Department of Commerce, Bureau of the Census, *Sixteenth Census of the United States: 1940, Agriculture*, Vol. 1: *First and Second Series State Reports*, Part 3: *Statistics for Counties* (Washington, D.C.: U.S. Government Printing Office, 1942), p. 290; C. Horace Hamilton, "Relation of Agricultural Adjustment Program to Rural Relief Needs in North Carolina," November 22, 1935, Box 791, General Correspondence, AAA Papers; newspaper clipping, *Sampson Independent*, February 28, 1935, Graham A. Barden, letter to constituents, May 11, 1936, Barden Papers.

federal relief official, reported to her boss, Harry Hopkins, that approximately ten thousand tenants in the eastern section had no crop arrangement with a landlord. A fifty-year trend of increasing tenancy in the cotton and tobacco areas of the South was reversed with the Depression and New Deal. Displaced tenants threatened to overburden relief rolls.

Although certain eastern counties suffered, displacement of tenants never became as serious a problem for North Carolina as for other southern states. In the state during the 1930s the number of tenant farms declined only 10 percent, but from 1930 to 1935 the number of owner-operated farms increased by almost the same amount. Sociologist C. Horace Hamilton, in a study of representative counties, concluded that conditions for sharecroppers and renters improved under the New Deal. Higher prices for tobacco and the increased need for labor limited the number of displaced tenants in North Carolina. Arkansas fared worst with a 32 percent drop in tenant farms, but Georgia's experience resembled North Carolina's. A 1934 Adjustment Committee report covering 320 counties in thirteen cotton states found no wholesale displacement of tenants. Perhaps historians have placed too much blame on the AAA for removing tenants from the land. Depression and the return of urban unemployed to farms caused greater problems. Substantial displacement took place before the New Deal; 1932 was the peak year for North Carolina. The AAA caused problems when acreage controls prevented tenants from reentering agriculture after being displaced from 1929 to 1932.[30]

Although North Carolina tenants and sharecroppers may have been spared large-scale displacement, they did encounter discrimination from the AAA and the landlords. A black sharecropper from Pleasant Hill complained: "We never got no rental checks. Some has got gov-ment money on dey crops, but ain't none come to us. I don't know how it works. We never had no help from de gov-ment." The AAA administered the programs through landlords, who distributed AAA funds to tenants.

30. For a discussion of tenancy and the New Deal in North Carolina see Chapter 6. Hickok to Hopkins, February 14, 1934, Box 11, Hickok Papers; Hobbs, *North Carolina*, p. 335; Gordon W. Blackwell, "The Displaced Tenant Farm Family in North Carolina," *Social Forces* 13 (October 1934): 66, 69; Conrad, *Forgotten Farmers*, pp. 205, 209; *Sixteenth Census of the United States: 1940, Agriculture*, Vol. 1: *First and Second Series State Reports*, Part 3: *Statistics for Counties*, p. 390; Kirk, Cutler, and Morse, eds., *Emergency Relief in North Carolina*, p. 313; Badger, *Prosperity Road*, pp. 200–204; Hamilton, "Relation of Agricultural Adjustment Program to Rural Relief Needs in North Carolina," AAA Papers; *UNC Newsletter*, November 20, 1935, PC 246.9, Ehringhaus Papers (P); Saloutos, *American Farmer and the New Deal*, p. 102; Holmes, *New Deal in Georgia*, p. 263.

Landlords received all the rental payments, while the tenants, despite protests from landlords, shared in the benefit payments and, of course, the price increases. Tobacco tenants fared better than cotton tenants because the owners' rental payments were smaller and tenants' benefit payments proportionally higher. To avoid sharing benefit payments, a landlord could shift a tenant to wage-labor status or evict him. Other temptations for discrimination existed because landlords sold crops for tenants and handled the credit. Authorities for the AAA typically acquitted landlords of contract violations, publicly minimized complaints, and claimed that in many cases landlords justifiably dismissed unreliable tenants. Secretary Wallace, defending the AAA, argued that favoring the landowners was necessary to secure their cooperation in acreage reduction; moreover, the AAA sought parity, not tenancy reform. Despite widespread discrimination against tenants, there was no noticeable discontent among tenants in North Carolina.[31]

Tenants, a virtual American peasantry, would not find relief from the AAA. Those like John Easton, a tenant farmer like his parents before him, who lived in a "weather-beaten gray" one-room filling station near Wilson, sought assistance elsewhere. "If you know anything about tenant farming," he reminded an interviewer, "you know they do without everything all year hoping to have something in the fall." Though a staunch supporter of the New Deal, Easton complained, "We've got mighty little of the government money." Tenants fared badly under the AAA for several reasons. Because of the urgency, the AAA had one program for all growers. The focus on commodity prices and farming as a business benefited landlords and commercial farmers. The AAA was not designed with humanitarian or democratic aims. Large farmers feared the loss of cheap labor or competition from "rehabilitated" farmers if tenancy were reduced. Some in the agricultural establishment thought that the labor surplus in rural areas, which was increased by the mechanical cotton picker, should motivate some tenants to move off the land to the cities. Furthermore, since tenants, as part of the scattered rural poor, were not visible, they were easy to ignore. Black tenants caused even less concern.[32]

The New Deal devised strategies other than the AAA to help tenants and sharecroppers. But as Michael S. Holmes concluded, "From the

31. Tindall, *Emergence of the New South*, p. 413; Conrad, *Forgotten Farmers*, pp. 205–9; Badger, *Prosperity Road*, pp. 200–201, 203; Terrill and Hirsch, eds., *Such as Us*, p. 89.

32. Federal Writers' Project, *These Are Our Lives*, pp. 3–4, 11; Kirkendall, "The New Deal and Agriculture," p. 98; Saloutos, *American Farmer and the New Deal*, pp. 86, 98, 150, 261–62.

FERA to the FSA stretched a road littered with inadequate planning, uninformed social workers, and unrealistic utopian communities." Conservative opposition in the state to aid for the rural poor, plus Washington's lack of commitment, spelled failure for tenancy programs. The FERA's rural rehabilitation division first brought relief to rural families. Beginning in April 1934 the North Carolina Emergency Relief Administration (NCERA) eventually funneled $3.5 million into the program for forty thousand needy North Carolina families; the agency hoped to restore farm families on relief to self-sufficiency. Initially the NCERA transferred ten thousand rural relief families to the rural rehabilitation division. Officials supplied the tenants with farm implements and livestock, worked with landlords to set sharecropping agreements, and assisted in such details as arranging credit, cooperative marketing, and home economics.[33]

The NCERA also relocated families, sometimes from the city, to submarginal land areas and started small industries at various work centers where clients could work off their debt to the NCERA; public relief work provided additional income. Rural rehabilitation established three cooperative farms in Wake, Halifax, and Tyrrell counties, where a total of 135 families lived on sixty-five hundred acres. These farm colonies failed because of bad management, poor land, and inadequate funds. In May 1935 state relief officials fired rural rehabilitation manager George Ross Pou.[34]

Simultaneous with the NCERA's rural rehabilitation, the Interior Department's subsistence homesteads program offered similar assistance. Penderlea, in Pender County, was the first, and most expensive, New Deal farm colony. Hugh MacRae, a wealthy Wilmington businessman, for years sought government funds for his agricultural colonies, and in November 1933 Secretary Ickes approved $1 million for his Penderlea, a community for three hundred families with ten-acre farms, which championed "homeownership and . . . a socially satisfying rural community as contrasted with . . . farm tenancy." MacRae, a graduate of Massachusetts Institute of Technology, an engineer, and railroad and utilities entrepreneur, had organized his first rural community in 1905 and since then had established several colonies for immigrants as well as Amer-

33. "Report of N.C. Rural Rehabilitation Corporation, April, 1934 to November, 1936," December 30, 1936, Governors' Papers (H); Kirk, Cutler, and Morse, eds., *Emergency Relief in North Carolina,* pp. 281, 313–14, 372; Morgan, "Step toward Altruism," p. 169; Holmes, *New Deal in Georgia,* p. 294.

34. "Report of N.C. Rural Rehabilitation Corporation, April, 1934 to November, 1936," December 30, 1936, Governors' Papers (H); Morgan, "Step toward Altruism," pp. 169–72.

icans. A member of the Farm City Corporation, MacRae worked with Gifford Pinchot and Elwood Mead, and Ickes seriously considered offering him an administrative position in Washington. By 1934 relations between Ickes and MacRae soured. Though MacRae managed Penderlea, he resented federal controls, especially after May 1934, when Ickes federalized all subsistence homesteads. No longer ruler of his agrarian utopia, MacRae resigned in 1935, blaming Washington for Penderlea's troubles. Subsistence homestead officials, however, charged him with selecting poor land for the project, carelessly spending a third of the $1 million, and planning farms that were too small.[35]

In April 1935 Roosevelt, by executive order, established the Resettlement Administration and under this new agency consolidated the Rural Rehabilitation Division of the FERA, Subsistence Homesteads of the Interior Department, and the AAA Land-Use Planning Program. Roosevelt charged Rexford G. Tugwell with responsibility for the rural poor. By 1935 New Deal efforts had achieved mixed results. Rural Rehabilitation had been innovative but proved inadequate. Subsistence Homesteads was little more than an experiment. In 1935 in North Carolina approximately twenty thousand rural families remained on relief.[36]

During its two years of operation the RA offered three programs for rural indigents: rural rehabilitation, resettlement, and land utilization. Of these Tugwell placed immediate emphasis on rehabilitation for those families who remained on productive land yet needed financial assistance to continue farming. For those who could not obtain credit from other agencies, the RA made loans and grants for livestock, equipment, and supplies. The RA also loaned money to cooperatives and communities and provided a debt adjustment service for farmers. By June 1937 the RA had advanced $3.2 million in loans to eighty-five hundred farm families in North Carolina, and only three hundred families received a total of $70,000 in grants.[37]

35. MacRae to Ickes, February 11, 1935, R. G. Johnson to Ehringhaus, August 17, 1936, Governors' Papers (E); William S. Powell, *The North Carolina Gazeteer* (Chapel Hill: University of North Carolina Press, 1968), p. 92, 140, 312, 432, 511; Paul K. Conkin, *Tomorrow a New World: The New Deal Community Program* (Ithaca: Cornell University Press, 1959), pp. 105, 109, 277–84.

36. Marsha Thompson, "Services of the Resettlement Administration," PC 1523.2, Ferree Papers; Baldwin, *Poverty and Politics*, pp. 84, 92; Paul E. Mertz, *New Deal Policy and Southern Rural Poverty* (Baton Rouge: Louisiana State University Press, 1978), pp. 44, 256, 258; *Sixteenth Census of the United States: 1940, Agriculture*, Vol. 1: *First and Second Series State Reports*, Part 3: *Statistics for Counties*, p. 290.

37. Thompson, "Services of the RA," PC 1523.2, Ferree Papers; George S. Mitchell to Hoey, June 5, 1937, Governors' Papers (H); Baldwin, *Poverty and Politics*, pp. 93, 108.

The RA's long-term projects, resettlement and land utilization, proved formidable. The RA purchased good land and developed farmsteads on it. By July 1936 the RA had approved six rural resettlement projects to accommodate 1,132 families in North Carolina at a cost of $7.5 million. As of June 1937 only three of the projects were under way, all in the eastern section: Penderlea, with revised plans for 150 units of twenty acres each; Roanoke Farms, with eighteen thousand acres for 250 families; and the Farm Tenant Security Farms, with eight thousand acres for 100 families. For the three projects the RA had allotted $3.1 million by June 1937.[38]

Once the RA removed families from unproductive areas, the agency retired the submarginal land from farming through its land-use program. Instead of leaving poor farmers trapped in a vicious cycle of cultivating worthless land, the RA adapted the land for forests, grazing, recreation, and wildlife reserves. In North Carolina the RA had five land retirement projects totaling 152,925 acres with a budget of $1.3 million. Two projects included a thirty-thousand-acre lakes and recreational facilities project near Elizabethtown and a sixty-thousand-acre nurseries and fish hatchery project near Hoffman. By July 1936, 122 of the 173 families living on the submarginal land of the project areas still had not been resettled by the RA.[39]

In late 1936, 81 percent of North Carolinians responding to a Gallup poll favored government loans to enable tenants to purchase farms. Despite the apparent enthusiasm, the RA community-building program encountered opposition. Governor Ehringhaus fought the transfer of $3 million from the Rural Rehabilitation Division of the NCERA, legally a state agency, to the RA. Ehringhaus and the state's attorney general refused to yield even after the RA assumed control of this division of the old NCERA. In April 1936 Tugwell relented and returned control of the North Carolina Rural Rehabilitation Corporation to the state. Such fights with federal authorities hampered the RA's work in North Carolina. Because of the pressures, Tugwell confessed, "It was all done awkwardly and wastefully." Tugwell encountered severe logistical problems in conducting the resettlement programs; the RA did not have the organization, time, or funds for such a large-scale program. Solving the problem of tenancy would take decades, Tugwell argued. Besides, he

38. Mitchell to Hoey, June 5, 1937, Governors' Papers (H); "The Program of the RA," July 1936, p. 4, Bailey Papers; Thompson, "Services of the RA," PC 1523.2, Ferree Papers; Conkin, *Tomorrow a New World*, pp. 284–85.

39. Mitchell to Hoey, June 5, 1937, Governors' Papers (H); "The Program of the RA," July 1936, p. 4, Bailey Papers; Thompson, "Services of the RA," PC 1523.2, Ferree Papers.

preferred suburban "greenbelt" communities to the resettlement projects. By June 1937 the RA in North Carolina had spent only $4.4 million and had loaned $3.2 million. Nationally it had resettled only 4,441 families of the anticipated 500,000. In addition, there were the patronage headaches. Representative Graham A. Barden complained to the regional director that his district was "not getting a fair break on the job situation." Those who did have jobs were paid half the amount nondistrict residents received. Furthermore, he did not want the RA office in Goldsboro moved.[40]

Clearly the RA failed to solve the problems of sharecroppers and tenants in the South, and to meet those needs Congress in the summer of 1937 passed the Bankhead-Jones Farm Tenant Act. Under this legislation the RA became the Farm Security Administration charged with helping tenants become landowners. The law provided for homestead communities for tenants and camps for migrant workers, as well as short-term rehabilitation loans and long-term farm purchase loans.

When proponents of the Bankhead bill first introduced it in 1935, they considered Senator Bailey one of the major opponents of the legislation. He complained about the costs of the resettlement projects already in progress and argued that spending more than $3,000 per person would not solve the problem. Furthermore, he did not believe tenants could repay their $6,000 debt from farming the twenty-five to fifty acres they received. He attacked the Bankhead measure as too expensive; tenancy was a problem, but the national debt was a greater one. Bailey supported the move to cut the appropriation in half, from $1 billion to $500 million. In addition to the expense, Bailey disliked the structure of the proposed agency and wanted more controls placed on the program.[41]

Progressive Farmer editor Clarence Poe, along with Josephus Daniels, lobbied vigorously for the bill and eventually persuaded Bailey to vote for it. Poe, a longtime advocate for the small family farm, worried about the impact of rising farm costs, increased mechanization, and competition from large landowners. He also hoped the Bankhead Act could help transform sharecroppers and tenants into small farmers. Poe

40. "Report of N.C. Rural Rehabilitation Corporation, April, 1934 to November, 1936," December 30, 1936, Governors' Papers (H); Morgan, "Step toward Altruism," pp. 172–76; Rexford G. Tugwell, *The Democratic Roosevelt* (Baltimore: Penguin Books, 1957), p. 424; Leuchtenburg, *Franklin D. Roosevelt and the New Deal*, p. 140; Tindall, *Emergence of the New South*, p. 424; Conkin, *Tomorrow a New World*, p. 146; Barden to George S. Mitchell, March 24, 1937, Barden Papers.

41. Bailey to Clarence Poe, April 25, 1935, to Howard Odum, May 9, 1935, to J. Edward Kirbye, November 21, 1935, Bailey Papers; Mertz, *New Deal Policy and Southern Rural Poverty*, p. 148; Baldwin, *Poverty and Politics*, p. 3.

pointed out to Bailey that the FSA would not be an expenditure by the government but an investment. Since the Bankhead program would not be a relief agency, its "dependable" tenants would be good risks. Finally, Poe reminded Bailey that the measure meant only a change in status for farmers, not an increase in the number of farmers or in production. Harold Cooley, one of North Carolina's strongest New Deal congressmen, also from an eastern district with a high percentage of tenancy, showed reluctance for rural poverty measures. Cooley recognized tenancy as a serious problem but warned his House colleagues not to "burn down the house to get rid of the rats." He called the FSA "rural slum clearance." Cooley believed that higher prices through the AAA programs were the best weapon against tenancy and rural poverty. No member of the state's congressional delegation in the House, including Cooley, voted against the measure. The Senate passed it with a voice vote.[42]

Led by Will W. Alexander, the FSA provided loans for selected sharecroppers and tenants to purchase farms. In the period 1938–40 the FSA approved $3.3 million in loans for 691 borrowers in North Carolina; nationally $69 million went to 12,053 borrowers. Despite this commitment, the FSA failed, and the Penderlea experiment illustrated why. In April 1938, 141 families resided in the project, which had a community center, school, clinic, store, warehouse, and furniture shop. One year later one-sixth of the homesteaders had left the project; by 1943 Penderlea had experienced a 100 percent turnover, and nine units were sold to clients. Penderlea, the New Deal's most expensive farm colony, cost $2.2 million. Critics claimed that a unit in Penderlea cost $35,000, while a comparable farm in the area sold for only $3,000. Tenants complained of complicated financial arrangements and broken promises; higher rent instead of the opportunity to buy caused low morale. Historian Paul Conkin observed that they had "little understanding of government processes." Homesteaders did not take a government debt as seriously as private debts, and many resented the paternalism of project directors. Verses by a schoolboy in the project were telling:

> On the farm we have busted pumps
> And lots of trouble burning stumps,

42. Poe to Bailey, May 1, 1935, Bailey Papers; Coté, "Clarence H. Poe," p. 38; Mertz, *New Deal Policy and Southern Rural Poverty*, pp. 148, 180–81; *Congressional Record*, 75th Cong., 1st sess. (1937), pp. 6476–78, 6582–83, 6762; Badger, *North Carolina and the New Deal*, p. 88.

Barden, but unfortunately this meant "'cream-skimming', and an early end to rural electrification development in North Carolina, as soon as the cream is skimmed and we find it impossible to develop the thin territory." Rural electrification favored the more populous piedmont over the east. By 1939 four times as many counties in the piedmont had 30 percent or more coverage than in the east. On the positive side, private companies played the leading role in electrifying rural North Carolina, and rates dropped well below the national average. In the final analysis, however, the entrance of the federal government into the field created a competitive atmosphere that prodded the utilities to act. Regardless of who brought it, farmers enjoyed a better quality of life with electric power.[55]

Power companies and the American Farm Bureau Federation in North Carolina limited New Deal agricultural programs in the state. As Anthony J. Badger aptly concluded, the state's experience underscored the "limits of agrarian liberalism." In the end, Tar Heel farmers acted not as reformers embracing centralized agriculture but as an interest group demanding a solution for their economic needs. New Dealers, particularly in the late 1930s, accommodated large landowners and commercial farmers, which was necessary for agricultural recovery. These prominent farmers could hardly object to efforts for higher prices. Before the New Deal, North Carolina farmers had unsuccessfully sought production controls. The AAA brought rental and benefit payments, and acreage restriction made it difficult for farmers not already growing tobacco to break into it. The local, decentralized administration of the AAA, facilitated by the geographical concentration of tobacco farmers, favored the large farmers.

Even the AAA's success in achieving parity for tobacco, the state's most valuable crop, was wrought with ironies. As the tobacco program brought economic recovery, Tar Heel farmers became more cautious. Richard S. Kirkendall noted that "forces of resistance had become very strong." Tobacco growers voted against controls for 1939. The Farm Bureau, representing commercial farmers, held its greatest membership drives in North Carolina, Georgia, and Arkansas. Initially enthusiastic about the New Deal, the Farm Bureau fought reforms that favored cities, labor, and the rural poor and sought to keep agricultural

55. "Biennial Report of the NCREA to Governor Hoey," July 1, 1939, Governors' Papers (H); Boyd Fisher to Carmody, October 17, 1938, Box 144, REA Papers; editorial, *Raleigh News and Observer*, January 13, 1939; Brown, "Rural Electrification," pp. 193–94; Muller, *Public Rural Electrification*, p. 2; Badger, "North Carolina and the New Deal," p. 73; memo, Boyd Fisher to Barden, December 8, 1938, Barden Papers.

policies focused on the "businessman" farmer. North Carolina tobacco congressmen voted againt more relief spending and legislation to regulate wages and hours. When the New Deal expanded to assist tenants and sharecroppers, discriminated against and displaced by the AAA, the Farm Bureau and Congressman Harold Cooley led the fight against the FSA. As tobacco farmers enjoyed higher prices and special privileges, they became less hostile to warehousemen and tobacco companies, whom they previously blamed for their problems.[56]

Higher tobacco prices, the goal of the New Deal, helped create long-term agricultural problems. North Carolina, like most of the South, abounded in small farms, and the AAA froze patterns of low per capita agricultural productivity. When tobacco was profitable, growers had no reason to diversify. In 1932 56 percent of the state's cash farm income came from tobacco and cotton; by 1940 the amount had increased to 64 percent. By 1939 income in the state from livestock, fruits, and vegetables was about the same as in 1929. Acreage allotments froze the existing relationships among landlords, tenants, sharecroppers, and small farmers. In short, the AAA brought economic recovery to Tar Heel agriculture, but not reform. New Deal efforts at reform, such as the RA and FSA, struggled against inadequate funding and conservative opposition. Private power interests thwarted REA assistance to rural cooperatives; consequently, by 1940 the state lagged behind the nation in rural electrification.[57]

Despite its shortcomings, the New Deal, in the words of Theodore Saloutos, "constituted the greatest innovative epoch in the history of American agriculture." The AAA brought permanent federal intervention on behalf of North Carolina farmers. An understanding of opposition to New Deal agricultural programs helps in making a realistic assessment of its achievement. The Roosevelt administration, despite the odds, changed American and North Carolina agriculture. Growers resisted radical measures, and only a limited program proved possible.[58]

56. Campbell, *Farm Bureau and the New Deal,* pp. 94, 100; Kirkendall, "New Deal and Agriculture," pp. 103–5; Badger, *Prosperity Road,* pp. 198, 217–18, 223, 229.

57. *Sixteenth Census of the United States: 1940, Agriculture,* Vol. 1: *First and Second Series State Reports,* Part 3: *Statistics for Counties,* p. 290; Hoover and Ratchford, *Economic Resources,* pp. 284, 291; Mertz, *New Deal Policy and Southern Rural Poverty,* p. 44; Badger, *Prosperity Road,* pp. 199, 203, 207, 214, 217, 223, 230; Saloutos, *American Farmer and the New Deal,* p. 268; Heinemann, *Depression and New Deal in Virginia,* p. 128.

58. Saloutos, *American Farmer and the New Deal,* pp. xiv, 269–70; Badger, *Prosperity Road,* p. 235. For a discussion of long-term effects of the AAA such as mechanization, see Pete Daniel, "The New Deal, Southern Agriculture, and Economic Change," in *The New Deal and the South,* ed. James C. Cobb and Michael V. Namorato (Jackson: University Press of Mississippi, 1984), pp. 37–61.

CHAPTER 5

Varieties of Relief

While the NRA and AAA aided businessmen and farmers in the 1930s, New Deal relief programs brought vital material assistance to thousands of needy North Carolinians. The Federal Emergency Relief Administration and the Works Progress Administration spent millions in the state. Direct and work relief also stirred hope among the poor and permanently enlarged federal and state responsibility for welfare. Social security, a major reform that altered the relationship between government and workers, included some public assistance for certain needy groups.

But the striking feature of the relief story in North Carolina was the strength of local forces that limited the New Deal's early efforts at creating a welfare state. Farmers and businessmen, seeking help through the AAA and NRA, resisted relief because it threatened a cheap labor supply and the middle-class work ethic. State politicians, from the governor on down, opposed state matching funds for relief or delayed compliance when faced with the inevitable, as in the case of social security. Partisan politics, particularly patronage battles, and county resistance to the centralized administration, all hobbled the relief effort in the state. Not surprisingly, North Carolina ranked a lowly forty-third in per capita receipt of FERA grants; the only southern state to fare worse was Virginia at forty-seventh. In per capita WPA spending, North Carolina ranked last in the nation. New Deal relief efforts focused more on urban industrial unemployment, than on the chronic rural poverty that remained from pre-Depression days. Conservative political and economic opposition further neutralized the promise of New Deal relief for predominantly poor and rural North Carolina.[1]

1. Press release, National Emergency Council for North Carolina, [n.d.], "Relief Statistics" from Census Bureau, FERA, and Internal Revenue Service, 1935, Bailey Papers; Kirk, Cutler, and Morse, eds., *Emergency Relief in North Carolina*, pp. 46, 48–49; Tindall, *Emergence of the New South*, p. 473; James T. Patterson, *America's Struggle against Poverty, 1900–1980* (Cambridge, Mass.: Harvard University Press, 1981), pp. 42, 68, 75; Trout, *Boston*, pp. 171–72, 310; Barbara Blumberg, *The New Deal and the Unemployed: The View from New York City* (Lewisburg, Pa.: Bucknell University Press, 1979), p. 288; Badger, *North Carolina and the New Deal*, p. 47; Morgan, "Step toward Altruism," p. 394.

In the waning months of the Hoover administration, the federal government established the precedent of federal, state, and local cooperation in relief work. From October 1932 until May 1933, Reconstruction Finance Corporation loans funded relief activities in North Carolina. To administer these funds, Governor Gardner established the Governor's Office of Relief, and during its tenure, which extended through the first few months of Governor Ehringhaus's administration, it handled over $8 million. Gardner requested $7 million, and the RFC made almost $6 million available. Local public and private sources matched the loans with over $2 million. In a move that foreshadowed state resistance to matching New Deal relief funds, the General Assembly in 1933 appropriated no matching funds for the federal loans. The state spent only $55,000 of the RFC money for administrative purposes. Local political subdivisions, therefore, spent the bulk on relief activities, about three-fourths going for work relief with public works projects paying the "prevailing" wage and the other fourth for direct relief. GOR also aligned its relief activities, financed through the RFC, with local Red Cross chapters, welfare organizations, community chests, and Associated Charities. RFC funds supplemented the relief budgets of these various charities, and in the state's cities and counties these private organizations contributed to relief needs.[2]

Despite the lack of professional personnel and the loss of its director, Fred W. Morrison, midway through its operations, GOR left a creditable record of pioneering in federal relief in the state in the transitional period from Hoover to Roosevelt. The relief effort in the state under GOR peaked in the winter of 1932–33. The agency began in October 1932 with a caseload of 56,697; 1933 opened with 25 percent of North Carolina's population on some form of relief. In February, the caseload reached its zenith with 176,124 or 27.3 percent of the state's inhabitants receiving assistance. The lack of agricultural jobs during the winter months swelled the relief rolls, and according to GOR director Fred Morrison, 22.5 percent of the state's aid went to unemployment relief. As spring approached and farm work became more available, the relief figures dropped dramatically. In April farmers demanded and GOR agreed that relief activities should not compete with agricultural needs for labor during the spring through fall crop season. By June, at the close of the RFC program, the caseload declined to a little over a hundred thousand, about 16 percent of the population. During the months of

2. Ronald B. Wilson to William B. Umstead, May 1, 1933, "Summary Report of Funds Allocated by the RFC to North Carolina for Relief," May 28, 1936, Governors' Papers (E); Morgan, "Step toward Altruism," pp. 58, 60–61, 65; Kirk, Cutler, and Morse, eds., *Emergency Relief in North Carolina*, pp. 41, 45.

RFC funding, local relief agencies in the state aided some ninety thousand transients. On June 1, 1933, officials transferred all RFC funds to the FERA.[3]

Despite its best efforts, GOR, working with RFC loans, could not deal adequately with the state's relief situation. In May 1933, therefore, Congress created the FERA, a major federal program involving grants, not loans, to states for direct relief. Senator Josiah Bailey, appalled at the idea of the dole, voted against direct relief by the federal government, an action that revealed his conservative convictions and emerging opposition to the New Deal. He supported retrenchment and budget-cutting. Writing to Governor Ehringhaus, he expressed alarm that the RFC through GOR spent over $1 million a month for relief in North Carolina. Not wishing to appear anti–New Deal, Bailey argued that the relief measure discriminated against North Carolina because the money would go to areas that could raise matching funds. North Carolina, he contended, could not afford it. In the Senate, Reynolds voted for the measure, and no member of the House from North Carolina voted against it.[4]

Bailey's opposition to the FERA intensified when Roosevelt placed Harry L. Hopkins in charge of the agency. Senator Bailey disliked Hopkins personally and in private referred to him as an ex-Republican and a socialist. Also, during the first Hundred Days sectionalism strengthened Bailey's antipathy for the New Deal when Secretary of Labor Frances Perkins remarked that a social revolution would occur in the South if all southerners would start wearing shoes. Angry at Perkins's comment, Senator Bailey defended the South. He did not appreciate liberal northerners disparaging the region, nor did he relish their directing relief efforts there. Once Congress passed the FERA appropriation, however, Bailey, sensing the political benefits, had plenty of ideas about how to spend it in North Carolina. Despite his earlier comments to the governor opposing relief, he suggested to Ehringhaus that they plan together how to use the funds. His ideas included a roads program, Smoky Mountain Park development, flood control, reforestation, and coastal improvements. Throughout the 1930s, Bailey's philosophical opposition to the New Deal rarely prevented him from seeking the state's full share of benefits.[5]

3. Kirk, Cutler, and Morse, eds., *Emergency Relief in North Carolina*, pp. 24–25, 37; *Raleigh News and Observer*, February 1, December 31, 1933; Morgan, "Step toward Altruism," pp. 64, 68.

4. Bailey to Ehringhaus, March 29, 1933, to E. H. Powell, April 1, 1933, Bailey Papers; Moore, *Bailey*, p. 97: *Congressional Record*, 73d Cong., 1st sess. (1933), pp. 1042, 2130.

5. Bailey to Ehringhaus, May 28, 1933, clipping, *North Carolina Christian Advocate*, June 1, 1933, Bailey to D. C. Cooke, April 25, 1935, Bailey Papers; Moore, *Bailey*, p. 96.

Through the FERA, Congress strengthened state and local relief. Initially, Congress appropriated $500 million, then an additional $950 million, for direct aid to states. The states had to pay one-third of the relief costs and the federal government two-thirds. If the matching grants were insufficient, the FERA also provided direct grants to states. The FERA required that the states use the funds for direct and work relief. To administer those grants, the state created the North Carolina Emergency Relief Administration in June. Unlike the RFC-GOR program, which funneled federal loans to local governments and private charities and was completely state-controlled, the federal government directed policies and funding for the NCERA. The state had to request funds, and the FERA acted on those applications. Once the federal agency made the grant, the state through the NCERA had full authority to administer the funds for relief activities it developed on its own.[6]

Washington imposed other regulations relating to state relief efforts. Although the NCERA broke with tradition as a relief organization officially apart from the welfare department, the federal administration insisted that the state agency work with county welfare directors because the FERA wanted its funds administered only by public agencies. If a county did not have a superintendent of welfare, the state appointed a relief administrator. If a county or city had only private welfare agencies, the state converted their personnel into public employees to meet federal directives. Hopkins's office in Washington also had to approve the selection of state relief personnel and their salaries because they were paid with federal funds. The FERA required that the state agency meet certain standards in its accounting and record system. Washington insisted on auditing all grants.[7]

For director of the NCERA, Ehringhaus selected Annie Land O'Berry of Goldsboro, a surprise choice. Ronald Wilson, acting director of GOR since Morrison's resignation in April, had been expected to receive the appointment but instead became O'Berry's executive assistant. Roy M. Brown, a professor from Chapel Hill, accepted the post of director of the NCERA's Social Service Division, and Annie Kizer Bost, director of the state welfare department, became his top assistant. A large number of officials from the welfare department filled the ranks of the NCERA. FERA director Harry Hopkins approved the selections,

6. Kirk, Cutler, and Morse, eds., *Emergency Relief in North Carolina*, pp. 14–18, 26; Morgan, "Step toward Altruism," pp. 74–75, 88, 115.

7. Hopkins to State Relief Administrators, September 26, 1933, Governors' Papers (E); Kirk, Cutler, and Morse, eds., *Emergency Relief in North Carolina*, p. 29; Morgan, "Step toward Altruism," pp. 76, 90–91.

and these state officials had to work with Hopkins and Aubrey L. Williams, his assistant and chief liaison for state relations, and J. Alan Johnstone, the southern field representative for the FERA.[8]

The naming of O'Berry as the state relief administrator represented a patronage coup for Ehringhaus. Under the Hoover presidency and during RFC relief, the state Democratic administration demanded, and gained, control over relief agencies. Following the election of a Democratic president, that same patronage policy continued. Ehringhaus appointed O'Berry without consulting the state's congressional delegation, and Senator Bailey and Congressman Doughton protested strongly. O'Berry brought impressive professional and political credentials to the job. She was vice-chair of the Democratic State Committee and in 1927 was elected president of the North Carolina Federation of Women's Clubs. She had been trained at the New York School of Social Service, did local relief work in Goldsboro, and served as a field supervisor for GOR. Ehringhaus named her for political reasons. In the midst of a controversy over the relief wage rate, the governor wanted someone with strong political support, not a professional administrator like Wilson. Her husband and brother both served in the state legislature, and her father-in-law had been state treasurer under Gardner. Her responsibility as of August 1933 was to lead the NCERA, which eventually included 220 state office employees and some 2,000 county-level assistants.[9]

In August Ehringhaus appointed Howard W. Odum of the University of North Carolina to head the five-member Emergency Relief Commission. Like the NCERA, the commission represented the New Deal's commitment to a professional, even academic, nonpolitical approach to relief. Odum, director of the Institute for Research in Social Science, was a Democrat but not an active one. Although he voted for Roosevelt in 1932, Odum retained some sympathy for Hoover, whom he had served as assistant director of the Committee on Social Trends. Odum's experience with the Hoover committee, which produced its two-volume report in 1933, fortified his faith in voluntarism. An old Progressive and "reluctant New Dealer," according to historian Michael O'Brien, Odum increasingly feared the centralizing trends of the 1930s and instead preached a gospel of regionalism. Odum offered Hopkins a long-term

8. Ehringhaus to Hopkins, August 5, 1933, Governor's Papers (E); Morgan, "Step toward Altruism," pp. 77–78, 86, 89; Kirk, Cutler, and Morse, eds., *Emergency Relief in North Carolina*, p. 26.

9. Ronald E. Marcello, "North Carolina Works Progress Administration and the Politics of Relief" (Ph.D. dissertation, Duke University, 1968), pp. 19–21; Morgan, "Step toward Altruism," pp. 79–82, 96n.

relief program, but Hopkins, more interested in short-term success, ignored it.[10]

Annie O'Berry insisted that the NCERA have nonpolitical academic and professional personnel, a stance that pleased Harry Hopkins but infuriated certain Democratic politicians in the state. Senator Bailey, from the east and eager to mend fences in the west in preparation for the 1936 election, thought the state Democratic party should handle relief, and he placed immense pressure on O'Berry to remove Republicans from relief posts in some western counties where the GOP dominated. Democrats in Wilkes County blamed Republican Emergency Relief Administration (ERA) relief workers for GOP gains in 1934. O'Berry, asserting her autonomy over relief, refused to make the NCERA partisan.

Congressman Robert L. Doughton, from the western ninth district, a center of some Republican strength, clashed frequently with O'Berry on the handling of relief jobs and patronage. Doughton fought a frustrating and losing battle, not just with O'Berry but also Ehringhaus and Hopkins. Doughton, nicknamed "Muley," insisted that O'Berry rehire a political and personal friend in the Ashe County ERA office. Upset with O'Berry's independence and refusal, Doughton referred to her as "obstinate," "bull-headed," and "that woman at Raleigh." Aubrey Williams, assistant administrator for FERA, accused Doughton of causing more trouble over relief than any other house member. Both Doughton and Bailey called for O'Berry's dismissal. Backed by Hopkins and Ehringhaus, O'Berry survived the dissatisfaction with her patronage policy and succeeded in building a thoroughly professional relief unit. Roy M. Brown, who served in GOR and NCERA, testified that the governor never interfered with the selection of relief personnel. For example, two field representatives were Republican and another a socialist. The rest apparently were Democrats.[11]

North Carolina's ERA followed the more typical national pattern of relief free from political interference. O'Berry's achievement in overcoming pressures from Bailey and Doughton and her support from Ehringhaus stood in contrast to the experience of Gay Shepperson,

10. O'Brien, *Idea of the American South*, pp. 48–49, 60, 80–81; Marcello, "North Carolina Works Progress Administration," pp. 19–20; Morgan, "Step toward Altruism," pp. 103–5.

11. Marcello, "North Carolina Works Progress Administration," pp. 20–23, 27–34, 38–39, 43; Roy Melton Brown, "The Growth of a State Program of Public Welfare," p. 35n, unpublished manuscript, 1951, North Carolina Collection, University of North Carolina Library, Chapel Hill.

Georgia ERA director, whose battles with anti–New Deal Governor Eugene Talmadge almost destroyed federal relief in the state. After conflicts over funds and personnel, Hopkins federalized relief in January 1934 and removed Talmadge's influence. Similar problems in Oklahoma, Louisiana, Ohio, and Massachusetts forced Hopkins to assume strict federal control over relief.[12]

All was not rosy for North Carolina officials, however, and the FERA wrangled over funding for relief. Governor Ehringhaus insisted that the state could not afford the required matching funds for the federal grants. In fact, since the beginning of the Depression the state spent little on relief. Shrinking tax revenues and the state's assumption of financial responsibility for all schools and roads left little for relief. The state and counties jointly, through the public welfare departments, cared for a small number of dependents, counties provided homes for indigents, and churches along with private charities cared for other needy persons. After 1929 the state legislature appropriated sums ranging from $32,500 to $55,000 annually for a mother's aid program in which counties matched the funds. For the fiscal year 1931–32, after the state takeover of all roads, the State Highway Commission spent over $7 million on road construction and maintenance, an indirect contribution to relief.[13]

Hopkins continued to pressure O'Berry for state matching funds, without which North Carolina could only depend on the FERA's discretionary or direct grants. Federal relief officials agreed to match on a 75 percent basis rather than the usual two-thirds. Still, the governor remained silent about supplying more money for relief. Ehringhaus earlier rejected a suggestion by his previous relief director, Fred W. Morrison, that the General Assembly permit counties to levy an additional five-cent property tax to provide matching relief funds. Since the General Assembly in 1933 scrapped the state ad valorem property tax and replaced it with a sales tax, the governor knew such legislation would be impossible to pass, although counties had their property taxes alleviated through the state takeover of the schools and roads.[14]

Eventually, Hopkins stopped demanding matching funds from North

12. Tindall, *Emergence of the New South*, p. 474; Holmes, *New Deal in Georgia*, pp. 30–33, 311; Trout, *Boston*, p. 162; Patterson, *New Deal and the States*, pp. 62, 71.

13. "Statutory Provisions for Financial Relief in North Carolina, January 1, 1930 to July 1, 1934," WPA Papers; North Carolina State Board of Charities and Public Welfare, *Biennial Report, 1928–1930*, pp. 28, 30, *Biennial Report, 1930–1932*, pp. 24, 26; North Carolina State Highway Commission, *Ninth Biennial Report, 1931–1932*, pp. 125, 139; Kirk, Cutler, and Morse, eds., *Emergency Relief in North Carolina*, p. 22.

14. Fred Morrison to Ehringhaus, May 13, 1933, Ehringhaus to Morrison, May 15, 1933, Governor's Papers (E); Morgan, "Step toward Altruism," pp. 108–9, 111.

Carolina. In late August 1933 he toured the South and realized that the region had great relief needs, particularly during nonharvest times. He acknowledged, sympathetically, that since the South was in worse financial shape than the rest of the nation, the federal government had to assume a greater proportion of the burden there. After the FERA investigated North Carolina, the agency provided money without matching funds. In the winter of 1933–34, federal relief funds flowed into the state. In ability to pay, the FERA classified North Carolina in the upper section of the lowest category of states. It weighed such factors as the state's size in land and population, per capita income, percent of unemployment, number of tenant farmers and blacks, amount of state and local debt, per capita highway mileage, rank in retail sales, and automobile registration. In those categories the FERA gave the state poor marks generally, but it noted that North Carolina's crops brought above-average prices and that the state levied no property tax.[15]

But the problem did not go away. In late 1934 and early 1935, state officials clashed again with the FERA over relief funding. Hopkins requested that North Carolina supply $3 million as a condition for receiving federal funds. Roosevelt and Hopkins, alarmed over the burgeoning relief costs and disappointing results, wanted the burden shared more with all the states. Partly in response to this pressure, Governor Ehringhaus recommended, and the 1935 General Assembly passed, a $1.5 million allocation for road maintenance as a relief measure. The governor complained to Hopkins that the state could do no more, because it had the second highest debt in the country. At first Hopkins and Aubrey Williams balked at the proposal because the State Highway Commission, not the NCERA, would control and spend the $1.5 million. But after a few months, they accepted that sum as the state's required matching funds for FERA grants. Otherwise, North Carolina contributed nothing to unemployment relief under the FERA. The state's one hundred counties did little better with their 6.3 percent share of the cost of relief. Though in 1933 they spent almost $2 million on all relief, in 1934 and 1935 the amounts dropped to $189,000 and $48,000 respectively. North Carolina's record was typical of the southern states, except Texas, which paid for 80 percent of its unemployment relief.[16]

15. Lent D. Upson to Hopkins, November 15, 1934, Governors' Papers (E); Don C. Reading, "New Deal Activity and the States, 1933–1939," *Journal of Economic History* 33 (December 1973): 799; Morgan, "Relief and Welfare in North Carolina," pp. 110–11; Kirk, Cutler, and Morse, eds., *Emergency Relief in North Carolina*, p. 45.

16. "FERA Report: First Quarter, 1934," Ehringhaus to Hopkins, December 28, 1934, April 20, 1935, Governors' Papers (E); Aubrey Williams to O'Berry, April 17, 1935, WPA Papers; Kirk, Cutler, and Morse, eds., *Emergency Relief in North Carolina*, pp. 45, 47; Badger, *North Carolina and the New Deal*, p. 47.

The FERA also clashed with Tar Heel farmers over relief wages. On July 21, 1933, Hopkins announced in his Rule No. 4 that all work relief would pay a minimum wage of thirty cents an hour for an eight-hour day and a workweek of thirty-five to forty hours. Previously, state officials had the authority to adjust wages on relief projects to local standards, which, of course, were low in North Carolina. Under the RFC-GOR program, wages ranged from fifty cents to a dollar for an eight- to ten-hour day. The highest farm wage was about a dollar a day, and the hourly wage amounted to about twelve and a half cents an hour. GOR director Ronald Wilson, backed by the state administration, so opposed the FERA wage guidelines that he ended relief work in August 1933, allowing only projects in progress to be completed.[17]

That same month O'Berry assumed control of NCERA and confronted Hopkins directly with the problem. She pointed out that GOR crops had to be harvested or they would rot in the fields and that the relief workers had to do the harvesting. Farmers complained that high relief wages weakened character and lured recipients from jobs that paid less. O'Berry, afraid that farmers would be angry if the FERA paid thirty cents an hour for agricultural labor, wanted a lower wage. Although Hopkins appreciated that relief work could be unfair competition for farm labor, he had to be careful about making any concessions involving lower wages because the federal government insisted that industry through the NRA codes pay higher wages.

Hopkins, bowing to rural pressure, permitted the NCERA to pay a "prevailing wage." He also suggested to O'Berry that she terminate all work relief projects until after harvesting in areas that might compete with farm labor. As a consequence, O'Berry stopped work relief in North Carolina except for a few urban areas. O'Berry was sympathetic to the farmers and realized that they could not afford to pay the higher wages. In 1934 both Hopkins and O'Berry agreed that the NCERA had to curtail relief to employable persons in the agricultural areas during harvest time. Farmers thus won a victory over New Deal relief policies. They could expect ample labor for cotton picking and tobacco harvesting. Hopkins and O'Berry clearly expected relief clients to take available farm work, even if it meant being paid thirty-five cents a day to pick strawberries.[18]

While North Carolina farmers complained that the FERA wages were too high, state labor officials protested to O'Berry that they were too low.

17. Morgan, "Step toward Altruism," pp. 93–95.

18. Hopkins to O'Berry, September 17, 1934, O'Berry to Hopkins, September 21, 1934, NCERA Papers; Morgan, "Step toward Altruism," pp. 96–99, 160–61; Badger, *North Carolina and the New Deal*, pp. 44–45.

In May 1934 at a state labor conference, union leaders argued that the FERA's prevailing wage caused some private employers to lower their wages for skilled labor. Labor representatives claimed that since the FERA paid only seventy-five cents an hour for skilled labor in a work relief project, private employers would not pay more. State union officials blamed O'Berry for lowering the wage scale. O'Berry responded by claiming that the NCERA had been very fair to labor. Wage-rates committees in every county determined wage levels for relief projects, and in almost all counties these committees set a prevailing rate that equaled the union rate. She explained that some employers complained that the FERA wage scale was too high and that their workers were quitting to take relief jobs.[19]

Wide variations in relief wages among counties and adjoining states posed problems for federal and state officials. O'Berry recognized the difficulty of using the overall structure for determining the prevailing wage scale for relief projects. She preferred a statewide pay scale instead of the county ones because the counties set wages lower than the NCERA wanted them. Also, differences from county to county encouraged people to move to counties with high scales. People doing identical work in adjacent counties could receive different pay. Each county usually determined its wage scale, and in the more populous counties, such as Mecklenburg and Forsyth, the NCERA paid relief workers about twenty-seven dollars a month for unskilled labor. The minimum for unskilled labor in North Carolina, located in FERA Region Four, was nineteen dollars a month. Virginia, in Region Three, had a twenty-one-dollar minimum.[20]

During the textile strike of September 1934, Hopkins and O'Berry again encountered protests from farmers and businessmen when the NCERA authorized local agencies to furnish relief to the families of striking wage earners after a careful investigation revealed need. Hopkins insisted that the FERA would not judge the merits of the labor dispute but only provide aid where needed. O'Berry ordered a policy of work relief for those who could work and direct relief for those who could not. She wanted no distinction made between union and nonunion clients. In the state's urban areas of the piedmont, public sentiment favored the NCERA relief policy. During the peak period of the strike,

19. E. L. Sandefur to Hopkins, April 16, 1934, WPA Papers; "Conference with Statewide Committee of Labor Unions," May 8, 1934, O'Berry to Hopkins, September 28, 1934, NCERA Papers.

20. "Conference with Statewide Committee of Labor Unions," March 20, 1934, NCERA Papers; *Raleigh News and Observer,* May 26, 1935.

the NCERA added almost seven thousand cases to its rolls as a result of labor unrest. After the strike settlement in late September 1934, the textile mills reabsorbed about one-half of those workers, and the rest became permanent relief cases.[21]

Despite the controversies over farm labor, wages, and aid to strikers, the NCERA from 1933 to 1935 maintained a solid record of achievement in administering relief free from corruption and politics. From the receipt of the first FERA grant on May 29, 1933, until the agency officially ended in May 1936, the relief organization spent almost $40 million in federal funds and about $700,000 in local funds. The agency served more than direct relief needs. Almost $30 million went to general relief, while several millions funded public works, rural rehabilitation, various education projects, a cattle program, and distribution or surplus commodities. The Social Service Division emerged as the major NCERA agency for administering relief, and its goal was to provide clothing, rent, household necessities, and other commodities for needy families. From April 1934 to March 1935, the agency spent over $11 million; by April 1935 the staff had grown to about eleven hundred.[22]

In addition to the general relief program of the Social Service Division, the NCERA formed two other important agencies in April 1934: the Rural Rehabilitation program and the Works Division. Replacing direct relief with work relief became the most significant task of the NCERA during its last two years. The Works Division faced problems when it took over public works projects from the defunct Civil Works Administration, created by the president for the winter of 1933–34. The Works Division lacked money for materials, and local communities usually could not afford to furnish them. The FERA permitted only one member of a family to work for the division, and then only for a limited number of hours. Officials had difficulty starting projects in certain areas because there were few skilled and semiskilled workers and because the relief population was geographically scattered. State and local governments sponsored works programs, and the NCERA stressed "worthwhile" projects as opposed to "makework" ones. By May 15, 1934, the NCERA approved all the most important former CWA projects.[23]

21. O'Berry to Alan Johnstone, September 13, 1934, to Hopkins, September 22, 1934, WPA Papers; Hopkins to all State Emergency Relief Administrators, September 13, 1934, "Relief Cases due to the Strike," October 18, 1934, NCERA Papers.

22. "FERA Grants to the State of North Carolina, May 23, 1933 to February 11, 1936," WPA Papers; Kirk, Cutler, and Morse, eds., *Emergency Relief in North Carolina*, pp. 14–18, 26, 55, 123, 125, 128, 135, 139, 372.

23. Kirk, Cutler, and Morse, eds., *Emergency Relief in North Carolina*, pp. 59, 151, 158.

The NCERA Works Division had a project in every county, and construction constituted 43 percent of the work load. By December 1935 the Works Division sponsored construction of schools, hospitals, airports, ball parks, amphitheaters, sewers, and roads. It also set up malaria control projects in over half the state's counties, planted trees, and built fish hatcheries and ponds.[24]

In addition to direct and work relief, the NCERA administered numerous minor programs. For example, the relief agency granted $129,797 to North Carolina Fisheries, Inc., a self-help fishing cooperative, for the state's 3,500 coastal fishermen on relief. Another NCERA program funneled $622,777 into six urban areas to care for 122,144 vagrants, despite local criticism that the government aided "criminals" and deprived more worthy clients of needed jobs. The NCERA purchased more than one hundred thousand cows from the drought-stricken Midwest for over $3.5 million and fattened the cows, sold some to other states, slaughtered the rest, and distributed the meat to relief clients. The agency spent several million dollars on education programs providing work for unemployed teachers, financial aid to college students, and funds for adult education programs and nursery schools.[25]

In April 1935, Congress passed the Emergency Relief Appropriations Act, and that marked the demise of the NCERA. Discouraged by its expense, New Deal officials looked with disfavor on direct relief; instead, they established the Works Progress Administration for work relief and created the Resettlement Administration to take over the NCERA's rural rehabilitation program. On December 1, 1935, the federal government discontinued grants to states for direct relief and abandoned this responsibility to the states.[26]

The NCERA did not die quietly, however. While Washington gradually trimmed her agency's operation, O'Berry fought back with energy and determination. Originally, the NCERA had administrative units in all one hundred counties. By the fall of 1934, to reduce expenses and increase efficiency, it had consolidated into thirty-one district units. In September 1935 the NCERA reduced itself to eight districts to coincide with the new WPA organization. To strengthen her dying agency, O'Berry recommended to Hopkins that the NCERA take over the state

24. Ibid., pp. 154, 164–67, 173–203, 229–42.

25. "North Carolina Self-Help Corporation Report: June 18, 1935 to December 31, 1936," January 4, 1937, Governors' Papers (H); Kirk, Cutler, and Morse, eds., *Emergency Relief in North Carolina,* pp. 60–62, 327, 331; Morgan, "Step toward Altruism," pp. 176, 179–81, 184.

26. Kirk, Cutler, and Morse, eds., *Emergency Relief in North Carolina,* p. 21.

welfare department. Already, the NCERA employed welfare department personnel, mostly in an advisory capacity, in several counties, and the dual relief efforts represented needless duplication. Regional relief administrator Gertrude Gates agreed that the NCERA should take over all the welfare programs in the state. The state welfare director, Annie Kizer Bost, Gates pointed out, was a newspaperwoman, not a trained social worker, and therefore inadequate for the job. Gates did not consider O'Berry qualified for long-term relief administration either, but she was "less inadequate" than Bost. She argued that the old county welfare system was too inefficient, too costly, and too independent of state control.[27]

Bost predictably fought to preserve her authority and department, and local forces defeated this centralizing trend of the New Deal. She had on her side local traditions, county groups, and prominent welfare officials from the University of North Carolina faculty, Howard Odum and Roy Brown. The struggle between Bost and O'Berry grew so bitter that Bost eventually forced NCERA workers to resign their welfare department positions. She wanted no more dual relief and welfare officials. By February 1, 1935, Bost had won her battle when the FERA turned over "unemployables" to county welfare departments, in anticipation of the new social security program that would provide for them. In addition, the state legislature provided $32,000 a year for the welfare department to handle the extra expense. O'Berry, having lost her jurisdictional battle over welfare, complained bitterly by the end of 1935 that the situation in the state was desperate. She knew relief clients who had been cut off arbitrarily because of lack of funds and who were now suffering. O'Berry pointed out that some counties paid "unemployables" only one or two dollars a month, and some none at all.[28]

In two years of relief work, O'Berry spent millions of local and federal funds with two-thirds going into the hands of clients and the rest paying administrative expenses. She performed her task with honesty, energy, efficiency, and little partisan politics. A thorough professional, she exhibited a progressive attitude and solid administrative abilities. Her FERA superiors viewed her as competent but cautious. Her carefulness sometimes caused her to miss the spirit, the urgency, of the programs. At times her conviction that only she could do certain jobs led to

27. O'Berry to Hopkins, November 8, 1934, WPA Papers; Kirk, Cutler, and Morse, eds., *Emergency Relief in North Carolina*, pp. 29, 31; Morgan, "Step toward Altruism," pp. 192–203, 393.

28. O'Berry to Harriet Elliot, October 15, 1935, NCERA Papers; Morgan, "Step toward Altruism," pp. 192–203, 220–29; Badger, *North Carolina and the New Deal*, pp. 47–48.

pettiness, bickering, and anger. Despite opposition, she imposed minimum wages and maximum hours for work relief and gained concessions from Hopkins on wage rates. But she lost her battle for control over welfare, later failed to land the job of state WPA director, and could not convince Washington that the ERA should administer social security.

O'Berry and the NCERA suffered from Governor Ehringhaus's lack of vigor in pursuing FERA funds and his unwillingness to cooperate with federal officials concerning relief. In late 1935, when the government liquidated the NCERA, Ehringhaus feared that the overwhelming financial burden for relief would now fall on the state welfare department. Finally, O'Berry experienced difficulty because of the ambiguous nature of the NCERA. Hopkins funded the agency, but Ehringhaus appointed O'Berry as director. The governor aptly described her as "Orphan Annie" and her agency as "neither fish nor fowl." Ehringhaus remarked that she had never been accepted by the federal government or supported by the state. He added, "It is, and has for sometime like Mohammed's coffin been floating betwixt heaven and earth."[29]

Although the FERA poured millions into the state, the NCERA found that it could not satisfy all the relief needs or resolve the root causes of the state's poverty. Relief officials estimated that for the years 1933–36 some fifty thousand North Carolinians could not live for a year without help, and approximately twenty to thirty thousand were unemployable. In February 1934 Lorena Hickok, a field investigator for Hopkins, reported that ten thousand displaced tenants in eastern North Carolina crowded relief offices in towns like Wilson, while others remained in the rural areas living in shacks. She visited three such families in the countryside: one in a hovel that resembled a "corn crib," another with eight children in a shed that rented for seventy-five cents a week, and a third in a tobacco barn. The father and his two daughters lived in the barn while he searched for a job. "Seems like we just keep goin' lower and lower," the sixteen-year-old daughter told Hickok. Shortly they would have to move from the barn with no place to go, no money, and no work. In February 1934, when 22.2 percent of the population nationally was on some form of relief, a high point in welfare for any time in American history, Lorena Hickok witnessed extreme cases of need.

A survey of the state's unemployable relief cases in January 1935 revealed that about half were blacks and over one-half were past age

29. Loula Dunn to M. J. Miller, November 4, 1935, WPA Papers; "Minutes of Special Meeting of Board of Directors of N.C. Rural Rehabilitation Corporation," December 31, 1936, Governors' Papers (H); Reading, "New Deal Activity and the States," p. 804; Kirk, Cutler, and Morse, eds., *Emergency Relief in North Carolina*, p. 50; Morgan, "Step toward Altruism," pp. 115, 122–123, 194–95, 292–94.

sixty-five. In January 1933 about 25 percent of the state's population received relief, but in November 1933 the percentage dropped to 10, and it hovered around 10 and 11 percent through the first six months of 1935. For the period 1933–35, North Carolina, like Virginia and Georgia, had about 10 percent of its population on relief. In Alabama, Mississippi, Tennessee, Arkansas, Louisiana, and Texas 10 to 15 percent were on relief, while in South Carolina and Florida 15 to 20 percent received benefit payments.[30]

Relief in urban and rural areas proved inadequate; the declining numbers on relief did not indicate recovery. In early fall 1934, an examination of 204 relief families in High Point showed that the average benefit per week for a family of five amounted to $4.80. Seventy percent of those receiving aid had been unemployed for over a year. In 1934 the NCERA concluded that of 3,600 relief families in eleven representative North Carolina counties about half were capable of making a living at farming if they could be rehabilitated. For 1933 the income of those 3,600 relief families averaged $133 per household. For the entire NCERA program, average yearly benefits per relief person climbed from $19.53 in 1933 to $27.11 in 1934, up to $32.98 by 1935.[31]

Relief statistics for 1933–35 clearly pointed to a geographical bias within the state, favoring the more populous piedmont with its industrial and urban unemployment. Of the top eight counties in relief numbers, the piedmont contained five, the east two, and the west only one. For one month, November 1934, the NCERA spent 38 percent of its unemployment relief funds in only eight of the state's one hundred counties and in three of its cities. Two of the cities and six of the eight counties were in the piedmont. The areas of the state with the highest percentage of the population on relief, however, were in the extreme west and east. Of the seventeen counties in which more than 17.5 percent of the population was on relief, ten were eastern coastal tobacco-growing counties with a large black population, five were mountain counties, and only two lay in the piedmont region.[32]

30. "Survey of Unemployable Relief Cases in North Carolina," January 1, 1935, WPA Papers; Kirk, Cutler, and Morse, eds., *Emergency Relief in North Carolina*, pp. 34, 37; *Raleigh News and Observer*, December 31, 1933; Richard Lowitt and Maurine Beasley, eds., *One Third of a Nation: Lorena Hickok Reports on the Great Depression* (Urbana: University of Illinois Press, 1981), pp. 188–90; Patterson, *America's Struggle against Poverty*, p. 57.

31. "Study of the Unemployment Condition in High Point, N.C.," [August–September, 1934?], WPA Papers; Kirk, Cutler, and Morse, eds., *Emergency Relief in North Carolina*, pp. 41, 285–87.

32. "Expenditure of Funds: FERA," Senate Document No. 56, 74th Cong. 1st sess., May 1, 1935, WPA Papers; Kirk, Cutler, and Morse, eds., *Emergency Relief in North Carolina*, pp. 54, 144.

North Carolina compared unfavorably with other states, even in the South, in relief activity and receipt of FERA grants. Nationally, North Carolina ranked twenty-fourth in total FERA grants, and in the South, six states received more. In per capita FERA grants, North Carolina ranked a lowly forty-third, and the only southern state to fare worse was Virginia at forty-seventh. For the years 1933–35, North Carolina's per capita expenditure for relief was $8.78, which was less than half the amount spent by New York, Pennsylvania, and Illinois. In contrast, total per capita federal revenue for North Carolina was twice the figure for New York, mainly because of the large amount of federal cigarette taxes paid in North Carolina. State officials complained regularly that North Carolina gave more to Washington than it received in federal benefits.[33]

On November 9, 1933, President Roosevelt by executive order created the Civil Works Administration, which, in contrast to FERA, was a completely federal operation, although the state FERA officials became federal CWA employees for administrative purposes even though they retained their old NCERA duties. NCERA director Annie O'Berry also ran the CWA in the state. The budget was $400 million, and Harry Hopkins wanted quickly to employ four million people on extensive public works projects. As a relief agency, the CWA took half its workers from the relief rolls and the other half from those who needed jobs but did not have to prove need.

Workers greeted the CWA with enthusiasm. The CWA paid much higher wages than the FERA. Unskilled workers earned forty-five cents an hour minimum while skilled labor received $1.10 an hour for a thirty-hour-week maximum. The CWA wages, much higher than those paid by private industry, attracted not only the unemployed but also those currently employed in private industry. Many workers eagerly gave up their jobs and registered with the Reemployment Service. In her contact with relief clients Lorena Hickok sensed a surge in their morale. Many unemployed were "tickled to death," she reported to Hopkins. Charles H. Gilmore, CWA administrator in Charlotte, observed that a year before work relief paid fifty cents a day and now the CWA paid forty-five cents an hour. With the passing months, however, high CWA relief wages heightened the expectations of those on relief and they demanded more; many wanted sixty-five cents or $1.10 an hour. Administrators ran into trouble as clients' attitudes hardened. Modest requests

33. "Relief Statistics" from Census Bureau, FERA, Internal Revenue Bureau, 1935, Bailey Papers; Kirk, Cutler, and Morse, eds., *Emergency Relief in North Carolina*, pp. 46, 48–49.

for temporary help turned into angry demands for their share of government assistance. White-collar relief clients, bitter over having to take "that kind of job," were even angrier at the CWA when work relief was not available.[34]

As the CWA raised the hopes of those on relief, it intensified the opposition of landlords and businessmen to the New Deal. High CWA wages competed with private industry. A mill worker under the NRA code earned $13 or $14 for a forty-hour workweek whereas someone on work relief earned $12 or $13 for only twenty-four or thirty hours a week. "It gets everybody all sort of mixed up and dissatisfied," Lorena Hickok observed. She also noted that landlords, "panicky" that relief threatened their rural labor surplus, were "raising a terrific howl against CWA." "They won't play ball," Hickok complained. Paternalistic landlords, aided by improving cotton and tobacco prices thanks to the AAA, resisted New Deal relief or better terms for their tenants and sharecroppers.[35]

For eighteen weeks, the CWA was North Carolina's biggest industry. During its existence, from November 1933 to April 1934, the CWA spent $12,155,000 in the state and at its height employed more than 78,000 persons. The state never reached its maximum allotment of more than 83,000 positions under the program. This relief program, funded entirely by Washington, filled a real need in the state, where financially strapped city, county, and state governments could not provide substantial employment through public works. The agency strove to spend 70 percent of its budget on labor costs and the rest on materials and therefore tackled generally lighter construction projects than other New Deal work relief programs.[36]

The Agency supported a variety of projects, but 18 percent consisted of road and highway work. The CWA spent 10 percent of its funds on malaria control, drainage programs that provided an opportunity to employ large numbers of common laborers immediately and at the same time combat a health problem in the state. The CWA's third largest construction activities were school projects, and fourth was the construction of some fifty thousand sanitary privies. The agency attempted numerous other programs such as planting over seven hundred thou-

34. Kirk, Cutler, and Morse, eds., *Emergency Relief in North Carolina*, pp. 67, 75; Morgan, "Step toward Altruism," pp. 117–18, 120, 126–28; Lowitt, ed., *One Third of a Nation*, pp. 188, 192–93.

35. Lowitt, ed., *One Third of a Nation*, p. 187.

36. Kirk, Cutler, and Morse, eds., *Emergency Relief in North Carolina*, pp. 41, 105; Morgan, "Step toward Altruism," pp. 122, 129–30; *Raleigh News and Observer*, April 1, 1934, North Carolina Collection Clipping File through 1975.

sand bushels of oysters along the coast and pioneering in public rural electrification, constructing two rural electric lines.[37]

As soon as the CWA got under way, Roosevelt and Hopkins seemingly decided to curtail it. Originally, they intended it as a temporary works program for the winter of 1933–34, but its high wages and federal funding quickly made the CWA prohibitively expensive. Roosevelt, bowing to pressure to economize, wanted the CWA ended by March 31, 1934, and its functions turned over to other New Deal agencies. Lorena Hickok visited North Carolina and reported that farmers and businessmen favored terminating the CWA in March 1934. She also favored ending the CWA as soon as possible, especially in rural areas and small towns, where CWA funds had been "wasted." Hickok argued that in the Carolinas and Georgia unemployment was not an emergency except in the few industrial centers. Besides the cost, Hickok recommended closing down the CWA because of the attitude of relief recipients: "The more you do for people, the more they demand." Joining the assault on the CWA, Senator Bailey told Hopkins that the work relief projects in Raleigh were worthless. Others criticized the agency's hiring procedures, its high wages, and its distribution of funds. Hopkins agreed with the complaints about the agency and feared that the CWA would make relief clients too dependent on the government and be bad for morale. He and the president made the final decision to end the agency.[38]

O'Berry disagreed with Hopkins and wanted the CWA continued but with changes to make the agency more acceptable. State relief adviser Howard Odum and *Raleigh News and Observer* editor Jonathan Daniels agreed with her. O'Berry wired Hopkins that there was widespread approval for reducing CWA wages to thirty cents an hour minimum for unskilled and seventy-five cents for skilled, more in line with NRA code wages. Still, she pointed out, these amounts were slightly above prevailing wages in the state. O'Berry's action drew the ire of state labor officials, who protested vigorously to Hopkins about the lower CWA wages. The North Carolina State Federation of Labor asked for an investigation and the establishment of an appeal system and called for O'Berry's firing.[39]

37. O'Berry, "Summary of CWA Projects in North Carolina under the ERA," [January 26, 1935], Bailey Papers; Kirk, Cutler, and Morse, eds., *Emergency Relief in North Carolina*, p. 107.

38. Hopkins to O'Berry, January 17, 1934, WPA Papers; Morgan, "Step toward Altruism," pp. 139–40, 142–43, 145, 148, 152; Lowitt, ed., *One Third of a Nation*, pp. 156, 158, 187–88, 193.

39. O'Berry to Hopkins, March 8, 1934, J. A. Pinkston to Hopkins, April 10, 1934, E. L.

Despite resistance, Hopkins gradually phased out the CWA by March 31, 1934. As early as January 1934, officials reduced CWA clients to fifteen-hour workweeks in some rural areas. On March 9, the CWA employed only thirty-eight thousand after a peak of over seventy-eight thousand. Guidelines called for releasing the "least needy" first, along with those who had another family member working. Hopkins, again facing local pressure, ordered major reductions in areas where seasonal employment opportunities existed, and as of March 2 wages fell to prevailing rates in local communities but not to less than thirty cents an hour. When the agency closed at the end of the month and its operations were transferred to the NCERA Works Division, only twenty-three thousand remained on its rolls, and the CWA had completed only 25 percent of its approved projects. Former CWA relief clients resented the FERA work relief wages that usually amounted to half of the CWA wages. The CWA provided crucial aid to North Carolina for the winter of 1933–34, but it ended too quickly to have any long-term achievement. On the national level, Roosevelt worried about the expense. On the state level, O'Berry feared criticism of mismanagement, and though she avoided the taint of corruption, her agency fell short of its goals.[40]

Throughout 1935 President Roosevelt and Congress made dramatic changes in federal relief policy. In January 1935 Roosevelt presented Congress with a bold plan of public works to employ 3.5 million people at a cost of almost $5 billion. He insisted that work relief wages be higher than the relief dole yet lower than prevailing wages. The federal government, according to Roosevelt, should turn over direct relief clients or unemployables to state and local authorities. In April Congress passed his work relief bill, and one month later Roosevelt, by executive order, created the Works Progress Administration. North Carolina's congressional delegation voted for the conference report, except for Bailey, who did not vote. Representative Alfred Lee Bulwinkle criticized the speed with which the measure passed and the broad authority it gave the president. He thought the "integrity" of the House was at stake, as well as his oath of office as a member of the House. On December 1, 1935, the federal government discontinued grants to states for direct relief. Federally controlled work relief replaced direct relief financed by federal

Sandefur to Hopkins, April 16, 1934, WPA Papers; Morgan, "Step toward Altruism," p. 146.

40. Hopkins to Howard Odum, February 17, 1934, Odum Papers; Hopkins to Odum, February 28, 1934, WPA Papers; Morgan, "Step toward Altruism," pp. 122, 139–40, 151–53; Kirk, Cutler, and Morse, eds., *Emergency Relief in North Carolina*, pp. 70, 112, 135.

funds administered by state agencies. With the FERA winding down and the WPA projects gearing up, relief rolls in North Carolina declined dramatically, from 74,155 in January 1935 to 42,919 in November 1935.[41]

Senator Reynolds played an uncharacteristically active role in the Senate's wrangling over the "prevailing wage" amendment to the work relief bill. He sided with liberals in supporting the McCarran amendment, which directed that relief wages reflect those in private industry in an area. "Let us spend billions to create new wealth and save humanity," Reynolds urged his colleagues. If the amendment did not pass, Reynolds warned that the "obnoxious dole" would continue. Conservatives, like Bailey, opposed the higher wage principle as too costly and harmful to industry. Reynolds found himself in the unusual position of opposing the president, who threatened to veto the work relief bill with the McCarran amendment as too expensive. The amendment initially passed, but the Senate reversed itself later. Reynolds and Huey P. Long were the only southerners to vote for it.[42]

The WPA operated differently from the previous federal relief agency. Under the FERA the federal government made grants to the states, and state agencies like the NCERA administered the relief program. Governor Ehringhaus appointed professional and generally nonpolitical relief personnel. Blamed for relief problems and unable to do much about them within the structure of the FERA, congressmen sought several changes in New Deal relief policy, and with the creation of the WPA they realized their goals. Congress made the WPA a totally federal agency and state WPA officials federal employees. WPA chief Harry Hopkins approved each state project separately, rather than making lump-sum grants to states. Because the appointment of each state WPA official earning more than $5,000 required Senate confirmation, control of relief patronage passed from governors to congressmen. Hopkins had to cooperate with a state's congressmen on projects and patronage, and at the same time he could use WPA funds as leverage to keep the congressmen in line with Roosevelt's New Deal policies.[43]

From the beginning, political and patronage battles plagued the WPA in North Carolina. Governor Ehringhaus lobbied vigorously for NCERA director Annie O'Berry to head the new relief agency, but the new

41. Kirk, Cutler, and Morse, eds., *Emergency Relief in North Carolina*, pp. 21, 37; Leuchtenburg, *Franklin D. Roosevelt and the New Deal*, pp. 124–25; *Congressional Record*, 74th Cong., 1st sess. (1935), pp. 851, 5135, 5150.

42. *Congressional Record*, 74th Cong., 1st sess. (1935), pp. 2711, 2724–26, 2728, 3702, 3704, 3717–18, 3724; Pleasants, "Robert Reynolds," pp. 219–23; Moore, *Bailey*, p. 111.

43. Marcello, "North Carolina WPA," pp. 46–50, 248–50.

congressional power over patronage gave the governor little chance for success. Ehringhaus complained that Hopkins avoided him and would not even talk about the matter on the telephone. Even with the governor's support, O'Berry never had a serious chance of being selected. She was unacceptable to the congressional delegation. Congressman Robert L. Doughton had bitterly attacked O'Berry as relief director for spending too much in eastern North Carolina, but the largest amounts had gone to piedmont counties. Doughton and other politicians from the western part of the state, along with Senator Bailey, denounced her for appointing Republicans to various relief posts in the NCERA. O'Berry had been nonpartisan in relief appointments, and politicians openly sought patronage opportunities that Ehringhaus and O'Berry denied them in the NCERA. In a further blow to O'Berry's chances, Hopkins stated that as a general policy he favored appointing men as state WPA chiefs because the director would be cooperating with contractors in work relief projects. Also, Hopkins explained that he preferred not to name state ERA directors to head the WPA, although in fourteen states he avoided political factions and Senate confirmation problems by doing just that. O'Berry was not one of the exceptions to the policy. Although she had done a competent job, despite the state's lack of enthusiasm for relief, critics charged, perhaps for political reasons, that her performance as a relief director was only average and that her fear of corruption caused her to move too slowly.[44]

Representative Doughton and Senator Bailey, too powerful for Ehringhaus and O'Berry, exerted the most influence in securing the nomination of George Coan. In April 1935 Doughton succumbed to pressure from the White House not to leave Congress and run for governor of North Carolina. Roosevelt wanted his friend to remain at the helm of the powerful Ways and Means Committee, and as a partial payment of a political debt the president acceded to his choice for state WPA director. Bailey gained some needed favor with the administration by voting against efforts to require the WPA to pay prevailing wages, which Bailey and the administration believed would be too expensive. Robert Reynolds, the junior senator from North Carolina and usually a strong supporter of the New Deal, broke with the administration on the issue. Facing reelection in 1936, Bailey sought to strengthen his political

44. "Minutes of a Special Meeting of the Board of Directors of the N.C. Rural Rehabilitation Corporation," December 31, 1936, Governors' Papers (H); Mary W. Dewson to Hopkins, June 7, 1935, Bailey to O'Berry, October 31, 1935, WPA Papers; Morgan, "Step toward Altruism," pp. 244, 247–48, 250; Marcello, "North Carolina Works Progress Administration," pp. 54–55, 61–62, 66, 245, 248.

ties, particularly in the western section of the state, through WPA patronage. He joined western politicians in their opposition to O'Berry's appointment and deferred to Doughton in the naming of the WPA chief for the state.[45]

At Hopkins's suggestion, Doughton and Bailey presented him with a list of men acceptable to them as the new relief director. Hopkins believed, however, that the three conservative Democrats Bailey and Doughton suggested were too political and not sufficiently enthusiastic about the New Deal. Hopkins expressed relief when all three turned down the job. Congressman Frank Hancock, the most liberal member of the state congressional delegation, pushed for appointment of Ralph McDonald, the legislator who opposed the sales tax. Hancock submitted McDonald's name to Hopkins, and McDonald conferred with the WPA chief in Washington. McDonald, leader of the insurgents, an avid New Dealer, must have been a tempting prospect for Hopkins. His selection would have strengthened the liberal wing of the state Democratic party; however, as much as Hopkins liked McDonald's liberal and pro–New Deal views, he could not appoint him over Bailey's strong opposition. State political pressures overruled. With his reelection one year away, Bailey did not want to strengthen the state's insurgents with the patronage-rich WPA. Bailey rejected McDonald as too liberal and too antagonistic to the state's conservative Democratic organization.[46]

George Coan also enjoyed close ties to the tobacco and financial interests in the piedmont. NRA director S. Clay Williams, Reynolds Tobacco Company executive, recommended him to Congressman Doughton. Hopkins, Bailey, and Doughton found the forty-three-year-old mayor of Winston-Salem acceptable, and Hopkins announced his selection on June 5. Coan had strong New Deal credentials and experience in urban relief work. A graduate of Davidson and Harvard, Coan had pursued a business career in banking and real estate after serving as an executive at Reynolds Tobacco Company. Mayor since 1929 of the state's second largest city, Coan gained a reputation as a good New Dealer. He reorganized city government and established a resettlement program, which transferred seven hundred families, mostly black, from the city to farms. Coan had worked on the PWA advisory board and enthusiastically

45. Bailey to O'Berry, October 31, 1935, WPA Papers; Morgan, "Step toward Altruism," pp. 244–46; Marcello, "North Carolina Works Progress Administration," pp. 55, 58, 61, 64, 255–56.

46. Bailey to O'Berry, October 31, 1935, WPA Papers; Bailey to Robert L. Doughton, June 27, 1935, Bailey Papers; Marcello, "North Carolina Works Progress Administration," pp. 67–71.

supported New Deal programs in the city. Hopkins clearly viewed Coan as more acceptable than Doughton and Bailey's first three choices, and Doughton and Bailey applauded the rejection of O'Berry and McDonald respectively.[47]

Coan's selection as WPA chief for the state by no means ended the battles over relief patronage. Two weeks after his appointment, Coan stated that he would only "consult" with the congressional delegation over the selection of the eight district directors. He had an understanding with the congressmen that they could make patronage recommendations for the district offices, while the senators would do the same for the state office in Raleigh. The eight WPA districts cut across the state's eleven congressional districts, and since this structure weakened the influence of each congressman, Hopkins hoped to minimize the political squabbling over patronage. Expecting more patronage with the shift from the state ERA to the federal WPA, the congressional delegation expressed disappointment with Hopkins and Coan's plan for relief.[48]

Patronage squabbles persisted nevertheless. Doughton pressured Coan over relief patronage just as he had O'Berry. He protested a WPA project in Boone which he argued only furthered the political career of the Republican mayor and resented the appointment of a Republican as assistant director for District Six. Senator Reynolds complained that Hopkins and Coan left him "out in the cold" on WPA personnel matters. Fifth district congressman Frank Hancock made the selection of WPA officials a significant issue. A loser with the McDonald bid and denied patronage appointments also by Coan and Hopkins, he charged that Senator Bailey dominated WPA patronage. Sensitive to the charges, Bailey in August 1935 publicly denied that he was building a political machine through patronage. Hopkins had appointed Coan, said Bailey, and he along with Doughton and Hancock had approved it. Bailey added that he only wrote letters of recommendation, and Coan made the WPA appointments in the state, which should be nonpartisan and free of patronage considerations. Hancock's attacks were undoubtedly politically motivated, since Bailey actually interfered very little with WPA appointments; Doughton had more control over patronage than anyone else. Hancock considered challenging Bailey in 1936 for his Senate seat and realized the significance of Bailey's potential influence over the

47. Coan, "Personal History Statement," February 3, 1939, WPA Papers; *Raleigh News and Observer,* June 6, 1935; Marcello, "North Carolina Works Progress Administration," pp. 72–75, 78, 251.

48. *Raleigh News and Observer,* June 19, 1935; Marcello, "North Carolina Works Progress Administration," pp. 81, 84.

WPA. By late summer 1935, several months after its creation, WPA patronage had attracted more attention than WPA projects. North Carolina WPA activity lagged behind that of other southern states, with only $39,000 allocated by August 14.[49]

Throughout the fall of 1935, Hopkins and Coan faced another battle when NCERA director O'Berry reluctantly yielded the responsibility for relief to Coan and the WPA. O'Berry's attitude changed from cooperation to resistance when she learned that Hopkins, after calling the job too rigorous for a woman, had named Gay Shepperson, a woman ERA director in Georgia, to the WPA post in the state. For Coan more than O'Berry's resentment was at work. He believed Ehringhaus, through O'Berry's obstruction, was trying to discredit the WPA and Senator Bailey as a prelude to launching a senatorial campaign in 1936. Having been passed over for the WPA job, O'Berry struggled to keep her agency alive for as long as possible. She tried to hold on to her staff, to maintain funding for the active relief rolls, and to convince skeptics that the Roosevelt administration would place the new social security program in her agency and thereby make the NCERA permanent. O'Berry and Coan even wrangled over the transfer of furniture and equipment from the NCERA to the WPA. Confusion in Washington and delays in starting the WPA fueled her hopes further. As late as November 15, 1935, the NCERA had forty-seven thousand people on its relief rolls. Hopkins had ordered all other state ERA offices closed by that date, but he omitted North Carolina because a strike in Mooresville increased the need for relief.

In December O'Berry realized the inevitable and yielded. Reduced to only four field representatives and eight districts, coterminous with the WPA districts, the NCERA finally ceased operations on December 5, on orders from Hopkins. The WPA's relief rolls were up to forty-six thousand by December. To minimize further patronage difficulties, Hopkins transferred some NCERA personnel to the WPA. Eventually, NCERA staff filled ten of the twenty-two top administrative positions in the WPA, enabling O'Berry to salvage something of her old agency, but in the process she earned the enmity of Hopkins for trying to discredit the WPA.[50]

49. Press release, August 18, 1935, Bailey Papers; *Raleigh News and Observer*, June 23, August 14, 1935, editorial, August 15, 1935; Marcello, "North Carolina Works Progress Administration," pp. 93–96, 101–2, 106.

50. O'Berry to Aubrey L. Williams, September 10, 1935, WPA Papers; Morgan, "Step toward Altruism," pp. 254, 257–58, 265, 267–69; Marcello, "North Carolina Works Progress Administration," pp. 89, 97–101; Holmes, *New Deal in Georgia*, p. 23.

Like the NCERA before it, the WPA in North Carolina struggled for money. In the first few months of its operation, Coan pushed unsuccessfully for increased funding. Matching funds were not an issue, and North Carolina depended entirely on federal dollars. By September 17, 1935, the WPA had enrolled only seven hundred, and Coan estimated that North Carolina needed around $20 million to care for the approximately fifty thousand relief cases in the state. In October, however, Hopkins reduced the state's original quota from $14 million to $8.6 million, to finance the WPA until March 1936. Coan complained that as of October, Hopkins had made only $1 million available, and $8.6 million would meet only half the state's relief needs. Coan also pointed out to federal WPA officials that North Carolina received less than one-third its due based on population, since the state ranked twelfth in population yet twenty-seventh in the allocation of WPA funds. Furthermore, Coan complained that Georgia and Alabama, both smaller in population than North Carolina, received $15 and $11 million respectively from the WPA.[51]

WPA officials in Washington responded that they based relief allotments on the number of persons who needed employment under the WPA, not on the population of the state, and they also considered the jobs other New Deal agencies provided in a state. Rural, agricultural North Carolina had little urban industrial unemployment. One WPA official pointed out to Coan that the Civilian Conservation Corps took care of 15,400 relief cases; therefore, the WPA had to handle only 34,600 cases for the state to reach its total relief quota of 50,000. Unconvinced, Coan still argued in early 1936 that North Carolina, with 1.8 percent of the nation's relief population, should receive the same percentage of the WPA funds. Coan calculated that the WPA should allocate a minimum of $17 million to the state.[52]

The federal government stopped its direct relief payments on December 1, 1935, and state and local officials expressed concern over how to satisfy the relief needs unmet by the WPA work relief. In February 1936, the North Carolina League of Municipalities reported that 104,198 families, or 14 percent of the state's population, needed assistance, but the WPA had certified only 67,190 families for jobs. As of February 8, the

51. Coan to Hopkins, August 30, 1935, to Corrington Gill, October 4, 1935, newspaper clipping, *Raleigh News and Observer*, October 8, 1935, transcript of telephone conversation, Coan and E. R. Stewart, October 9, 1935, WPA Papers; Morgan, "Step toward Altruism," p. 266.

52. Emerson Ross to Coan, October 19, 1935, WPA Papers; Coan, memo, February 10, 1936, Bailey Papers.

WPA had placed only 51,299 cases in public works jobs. County and city authorities wondered who would care for the remaining 53,000 relief cases. Since 1933 the federal government had provided for 96.7 percent of the state's relief needs, local government 3.3 percent, the state nothing. Though local governments budgeted over $2 million for welfare and relief for 1935–36, they could not afford the burden of those 50,000 additional relief cases. Declining tax collections and increasing defaults on bonded indebtedness made such an extra financial strain unlikely. Not until the social security program operated in North Carolina after July 1, 1937, did government officials assist direct relief cases not covered by the WPA.[53]

In the 1936 Democratic primaries, WPA involvement was common, more unethical than illegal, and its influence was significant in close races. Hopkins prohibited certain political activities by relief personnel: they could not run for office or raise campaign funds, nor could relief administrators or politicians require relief personnel to make campaign contributions or base their jobs on political support. Hopkins realized the difficulties in enforcing these regulations, and in North Carolina WPA officials and politicians violated them. The gubernatorial hopefuls for 1936 wanted Coan's support and all the votes he could deliver from his relief rolls of forty to fifty thousand. When McDonald asked Coan for support, there was little chance because the two had feuded when Coan was mayor of Winston-Salem and McDonald the representative from that city in the General Assembly. Furthermore, McDonald had vied for Coan's WPA job. Coan's reply to McDonald's political overture was a tart "go to hell." According to Coan, Lieutenant Governor Alexander H. "Sandy" Graham offered him a post in the Revenue Department in exchange for his support for his gubernatorial bid. Coan wanted nothing less than the State Highway Commission chairmanship, and when Max Gardner promised it to him, Coan backed Clyde Hoey, Gardner's candidate. Coan and WPA associates, Coan later reminded Gardner, "took off their coats and tore their shirts without regard for federal regulations to influence voters in favor of Mr. Hoey." Gardner entertained Coan at his Washington home and through a third party gave Coan $25,000 for distribution by the Hoey forces in the eight WPA districts. Coan also gave Gardner, through a third party, a list of fifty key WPA personnel.[54]

53. North Carolina League of Municipalities, "The Unemployment Relief Problem in N.C.," February, 1936, WPA Papers.

54. Coan to Gardner, April 9, 1937, Gardner Papers; Marcello, "North Carolina Works Progress Administration," pp. 111–13, 115–19, 129, 257–59.

There were other scattered violations of Hopkins's rules against mixing politics and relief. Senator Bailey used lists of WPA personnel in his 1936 reelection campaign, and a WPA official in Durham worked actively in his behalf. During the November general election campaign Bailey reminded the state Democratic party chairman of the Federal Emergency Council's list of hundreds of public employees who would lose their jobs if the Democrats lost. "You know how to use such a document," Bailey cautioned—with "care and discrimination."[55] Jim Rivers, District Six WPA director, personally campaigned on the job for gubernatorial candidate Hoey and Congressman Doughton and blatantly used political pressure on employees. Herbert G. Gulley, chief fund-raiser for the North Carolina Democratic party, solicited WPA personnel for campaign funds. The primary opponent of Representative Graham Barden charged that WPA political activity unduly influenced that election, but an investigation by Hopkins revealed no misconduct on the part of Barden.[56]

The effect of the WPA on North Carolina politics was ambiguous. According to Ronald E. Marcello, it had been "significant and sometimes dominant." Thousands of WPA employees could make a decisive difference in a close Democratic primary. In a general election, however, for a heavily Democratic state in which Roosevelt was very popular it was perhaps less critical. Nationally, on the issue of relief and politics Indiana had a better record than North Carolina, but those of New Jersey, Pennsylvania, Kentucky, and West Virginia were worse. During the 1938 campaign, without a contest for governor, WPA political activity declined. When Congress in 1939 passed the Hatch Act, restricting WPA political activities, and WPA enrollments declined, the agency lost political and patronage appeal.[57]

After averaging forty to fifty thousand on its relief rolls throughout 1936, the North Carolina WPA faced severe cutbacks in 1937. Hopkins reduced some funds and relief rolls just before the 1936 elections despite complaints from state politicians that such action would harm Democratic candidates. The number of WPA districts in the state was reduced from eight to five. Believing the economy had improved and fearing inflation, Roosevelt drastically cut the WPA in June 1937. In August the state WPA had only 18,600 workers enrolled and spent only $706,000, contrasted with $1.2 million in August 1936. Coan cut the staff by 15

55. Bailey to Wallace Winborne, September 28, 1936, Bailey Papers.

56. Marcello, "North Carolina Works Progress Administration," pp. 120–22, 124, 138, 130–31, 258.

57. Ibid., pp. 190–91, 219, 245, 260.

percent and in September abolished the five district offices and directed the WPA from the Raleigh headquarters.[58]

Senator Bailey's arguments for curtailment of the WPA revealed his hypocrisy and his shrewd timing. After his overwhelming reelection in 1936 Bailey emerged as a strong critic of the New Deal and the WPA in particular. Bailey complained that the WPA destroyed the work ethic, competed with business, and built a political machine for New Dealers. He advocated retrenchment, a balanced budget, and resumption of relief responsibilities by state and local governments. Though he had voted for the WPA, by early 1937 he opposed appropriations for the agency. Bailey estimated that between 1933 and 1937, the federal government had spent about $150 million in North Carolina. As a result, "we have a bear by the tail," Bailey exclaimed to a friend. If the money stopped coming, there would be a recession, he argued, but if the spending continued it would cause inflation, damage business, and create an unbearable tax burden, along with a permanent class of relief recipients. Furthermore, Washington exaggerated unemployment figures. Bailey also pointed out that the WPA favored the more populous northern states, which had higher industrial unemployment. The WPA employed 2 percent of the population of those states, he argued, but only 1 percent of the southern states' population.

In the early months of 1937, Hopkins and Bailey waged a bitter personal battle. Bailey's angry remarks in the Senate against Hopkins and the WPA and Hopkins's attacks on Bailey after a National Press Club speech, when he alleged that Bailey was on the payroll of North Carolina corporations, led to a heated exchange between the two on April 10, 1937, at the Mayflower Hotel in Washington. Witnesses, according to Marcello, heard "the biggest and bitterest stream of four-letter epithets . . . since General Hugh Johnson." Understandably, Bailey's influence over WPA patronage dropped dramatically after that date.[59]

Cutbacks in relief and other fiscal policies by the Roosevelt administration during 1937 contributed to a recession lasting several months from late 1937 to early 1938. Construction contract figures totaled slightly more than half the amount for February 1937. Textile factories consumed 34 percent fewer cotton bales than the previous year. New car

58. Ibid., pp. 135, 170–71; Leuchtenburg, *Franklin D. Roosevelt and the New Deal*, p. 244.

59. Bailey to Roosevelt, December 29, 1936, press release, May 25, 1937, Bailey to Carl Goerch, September 25, 1937, Bailey Papers; Marcello, "North Carolina Works Progress Administration," pp. 143–48, 154–55, 159, 162; Badger, *North Carolina and the New Deal*, p. 47.

registrations dipped 40.4 percent below January–February 1937. Under pressure to deal with the recession, particularly in an election year, Congress on June 21, 1938, appropriated $1.4 billion for the WPA. In October the state WPA reached a peak of 55,000 on the relief rolls and spent $2.25 million monthly. The 1938 appropriation bill authorized the WPA to employ farmers whose net cash income was less than $300 a year. In an election year, few congressmen from North Carolina advocated cutbacks as relief and the WPA became more popular.[60]

In 1939 the WPA faced its final decline. Hopkins left the agency in 1938 to head the Commerce Department, and Coan resigned as North Carolina WPA director effective April 1, 1939, to return to private business. Coan failed to receive higher political appointments. Governor Hoey refused to appoint him as State Highway Commission chairman. Bailey and Doughton publicly supported him, and partly for that reason, Hoey named someone less closely allied to the senator and congressman. In 1938 Senator Reynolds lobbied on behalf of Coan for a position on the Federal Home Loan Bank Board, but Roosevelt named Congressman Frank Hancock to the post.

In 1939 the WPA underwent a transition. George Coan had served three and a half years as chief of the agency in North Carolina, spent $60 million, and maintained an average relief roll of forty thousand. Though he mixed politics and relief too eagerly, Coan kept the agency free of scandals and fraud and overall proved to be an able administrator. Charles C. McGinnis, deputy administrator, succeeded Coan because of his engineering and administrative abilities, not politics. The Hatch Act in 1939 banned political activity by federal employees, and Congress hoped this measure would end the ugly political battles over relief. Also that same year, Congress renamed the agency the Works Projects Administration and placed it under the Federal Works Agency. After 1939, Roosevelt focused increasingly on foreign affairs and defense spending and cut funds for the WPA.[61]

In late 1940, WPA rolls declined because defense needs stimulated employment in private industry. For the second half of 1940 army and navy contracts with the state's businesses totaled $42.6 million, and the government also spent $1.4 million on WPA defense projects. Camp

60. Malcolm B. Catlin, "Relief and Economic Statistics: N.C.," April, 1938, Coan WPA Bulletin, [1938], WPA Papers; Marcello, "North Carolina Works Progress Administration," pp. 182, 185–86, 190.

61. Coan to Aubrey L. Williams, September 14, 1938, newspaper clipping, *Raleigh News and Observer*, March 14, 1939, WPA Papers; Marcello, "North Carolina Works Progress Administration," pp. 194–205, 214, 217–19, 226, 234, 244, 255.

Davis, a new $9 million antiaircraft firing center near Wilmington, employed 10,000 workers. Increased military spending created an additional 2,760 jobs at Fort Bragg in Fayetteville by November 1940. A Charlotte construction firm received a half-million-dollar contract for two hundred housing units at a military base in another state. By late 1940 the government had placed orders with manufacturers in the Hickory area totaling approximately half a million dollars. Employment in North Carolina industry increased 3.1 percent from October 1939 to October 1940, but unemployment hovered around 9 percent, including the 4 percent of the labor force on public emergency work. Fourteen percent of the state's urban nonwhites sought work in 1940. North Carolina's 9 percent compared favorably with the nationwide unemployment rate of 15.2 percent for March 1940, and six southern states, including North Carolina, had the lowest jobless rates in the country.[62]

By January 1940, the North Carolina WPA had employed 125,000 persons, an average per year of 27,700 men and women for four and a half years, and had completed 3,984 projects. It spent 85 percent of its funds on wages, and unskilled workers made up three-fourths of the labor force. Public works projects formed two-thirds of the agency's operations, and the remainder consisted of service work in the women's and professional divisions. By 1940 the state and local governments combined had contributed more than one-fourth of the project costs.[63]

From 1935 to 1940, North Carolina WPA projects touched the lives of virtually all citizens in the state. The Public Works Division constructed schools, housing for teachers called teacherages, armories, stadiums, swimming pools, gyms, and community halls. To improve transportation, the WPA built miles of roads and bridges. The agency constructed hospitals and sewers as well as privies in rural areas. In the Professional and Service Division, women found jobs in sewing rooms, school lunch programs, libraries, nursery schools, literacy classes, and as public school restroom attendants.[64]

Relief projects for women had problems, however. Thirty-seven

62. "WPA: Monthly Report of Employment and Economic Conditions: N.C.," November 1940, December 1940, WPA Papers; Howard, *WPA*, pp. 672–73; U.S. Department of Commerce, Bureau of the Census, *Sixteenth Census of the United States: 1940, Population*, Vol. 3: *Labor Force* (Washington, D.C.: U.S. Government Printing Office, 1943), p. 529.

63. Catlin, "Relief and Economic Statistics: N.C.," April 1938, Fred J. Cohn, *North Carolina WPA* (Raleigh: NCWPA, 1940), p. 2, in WPA Papers.

64. Fred J. Cohn, "WPA and Education," *North Carolina Education*, January 1940, pp. 163–64, 166, 182, Cohn, *North Carolina WPA*, pp. 4–42, Mary E. Campbell, "Narrative Report: NCWPA Professional and Service Division," May 1, 1939, in WPA Papers.

women in a sewing room project in New Bern complained vigorously to Hopkins and Representative Barden that they suffered from discrimination. Though skilled laborers, their wages were the same as for common laborers; moreover, wages had been cut from $32 to $22 a month. They also feared that their relief project would be discontinued. About 70 percent of them were the breadwinners in their families. "Women of this project must have something to eat, some kind of roof over their head and some fuel to keep us warm," they despaired. Some of the women in the project did not even have underclothes. Barden received several letters from other women complaining about the lack of work projects or that the projects were ending. He stressed to WPA officials the need to protect the rights of women but feared that they "give more consideration to a rule book than to actual conditions."[65]

For unemployed white-collar professionals, the WPA offered the innovative Federal Writers' Project (FWP), which had as its goal the production of state guides. State director of the North Carolina Writers' Project Edwin A. Bjorkman, a journalist from Asheville, had difficulty registering writers for relief. All eligible white-collar professionals had to register with the United States Employment Service, be interviewed by social workers, and demonstrate need. Only 15 percent of the project personnel could be nonrelief persons. Just as the project got underway in early 1936, a FWP field supervisor visited North Carolina and filed a report critical of Bjorkman as an editor and administrator. The federal agency faulted him for spending only $7,100 of the $41,000 available and for having his headquarters in Asheville rather than Raleigh. A later report claimed that Bjorkman had failed to consult sufficiently with Duke and North Carolina university faculty.[66]

To improve the editorial work on the American Guide series for North Carolina, federal director Henry G. Alsberg named William Terry Couch of the University of North Carolina Press as assistant director for the North Carolina project. Couch consulted scholars and focused on editorial work and Bjorkman on administrative duties. Alsberg relied more on Couch, and eventually harmony replaced strained relations. During the 1937 WPA retrenchment, Hopkins cut the staff from 117 to 54. Clearly Congress was committed to relief, not to government support of the arts. Forced to employ those on relief, the FWP in North

65. Myrtle Hardison et al. to Harry L. Hopkins and Graham A. Barden, February 13, 1936, Barden to Cleveland Davis, October 8, 1936, Barden Papers.

66. Jerrold M. Hirsch, "Culture on Relief: The Federal Writers' Project in North Carolina, 1935–1942" (M.A. thesis, University of North Carolina, Chapel Hill, 1973), pp. 8–9, 15–20, 23.

Carolina had problems obtaining qualified persons. Nevertheless, in 1939 the project produced a solid resource work, *North Carolina: A Guide to the Old North State*. Also in 1939, the FWP completed the critically acclaimed *These Are Our Lives*, a collection of biographies of common southern folk. Couch had directed the project, and in November 1939 he resigned from the FWP after Roosevelt reorganized and deemphasized the WPA. Bjorkman remained with the project until the summer of 1941. Other publications included *God Bless the Devil, Bundle of Troubles and Other Tar Heel Tales, How North Carolina Grew,* and *Raleigh: Capital of North Carolina*.[67]

The WPA's Federal Theater Project, started in August 1935, operated in states in which twenty-five or more professional theater people were on relief. In January 1939, 7,900 people worked on forty-two projects in twenty states. Hallie Flanagan, director of the Federal Theater Project, sought a resident theater group for Raleigh, and to encourage it, WPA officials for the first time moved a theater company from New York and established it in temporary residence there. To accommodate the company, the WPA used city and WPA funds to build a little theater in Raleigh. John A. Walker, state director of the Federal Theater Project, established the North Carolina Federal Theater Project headquarters in Raleigh, and his twenty or so employees provided professional assistance in community drama work in seven towns. Besides Raleigh, the project aided children's theater work in Greensboro and Charlotte and adult community drama in Wilmington, Wilson, Kinston, and Manteo. For two years the state Federal Theater Project participated in Paul Green's pioneering outdoor drama *The Lost Colony.* Walker, who had earlier been associated with the Carolina Playmakers at the University of North Carolina, left the directorship of the state Federal Theater Project in 1939 to work with Green's historical drama in Manteo.[68]

Also in North Carolina, the WPA promoted Federal Art and Music Projects, and these efforts touched thousands of lives. From 1935 to 1937, officials reported that 353,000 people participated in some phase of four Federal Art Projects in the state, visiting galleries, taking courses, or attending lectures and demonstrations. In 1939 the Federal Art Project employed thirty-three people and boasted three centers, for extension schools, and three extension galleries, and more than 106,000

67. Ibid., pp. 23, 26–27, 32, 67, 86, 92–112.

68. Hallie Flanagan to Mr. Schofield, April 21, 1936, "North Carolina Federal Theater Project of the WPA," October 1937, Flanagan to F. C. Harrington, January 14, 1939, Florence Kerr to Harrington, February 17, 1939, WPA Papers; *Raleigh News and Observer,* June 18, 1939.

people attended its activities in Wilmington, Greensboro, and Raleigh. By 1940 state WPA officials estimated that twenty-five units from the Federal Art Project had taught 1,200 schoolchildren all over North Carolina. Erle Stapleton, state director of the Federal Music Project, reported in November 1940 that his ninety-seven employees conducted 8,080 classes with enrollments of 12,521 and that attendance at public performances was up to 88,807. Though limited in funds and restricted to essentially a relief role, WPA efforts on behalf of writers, actors, artists, and musicians provided needed and worthwhile jobs and also contributed to a better quality of life in the state.[69]

National and state relief officials targeted the "youth problem" in the 1930s with a sense of mission. Both the Civilian Conservation Corps and the National Youth Administration (NYA) brought more than relief to the young, who made up one-third of the unemployed. These agencies tackled the youth problem: need for jobs, an inadequate educational system, and too much time between completing school and finding a job. A North Carolina study described it as the "drag of poverty, malnutrition, lack of recreational facilities, and lack of employment." By 1940 North Carolina had the youngest population in the nation, 46 percent under age twenty-one. Five years earlier relief officials estimated that the state's 70,857 certified relief cases averaged 3.5 children each. One-fifth of white youths and one-half of black youths lived in households with annual incomes under $500, according to a survey of 45,000 young people in eight counties. The "typical" Tar Heel youth of the 1930s left school before age sixteen for financial reasons, the survey concluded. Though most young people in the state wished to enter a profession, they would take jobs as semiskilled or unskilled laborers. The mountain area experienced the most serious youth unemployment, mill closings caused problems in the piedmont, and seasonal unemployment increased relief needs in the agricultural east.[70]

Relief authorities feared an increase in juvenile delinquency. Charles W. Taussig, chairman of the NYA's National Advisory Committee, declared that "criminals are to be found in this social no-man's land," the

69. "A Report of the Federal Art Project, December, 1936 to December, 1937," "Report of the Federal Music Project for September, 1938," "Statewide Art Project," January 15, 1940, "Report of the WPA Music Project on N.C. for November, 1940," Cohn, "WPA and Education," p. 182, Cohn, *North Carolina WPA*, p. 40, in WPA Papers.

70. For a discussion of youth programs and North Carolina blacks see Chapter 6. "Final Report: NYA for the State of N.C.," pp. 2–3, 22, Gordon W. Lovejoy, "Paths to Maturity: Findings of the N.C. Youth Survey, 1938–1940" (UNC Cooperative Personnel Study, NYA and WPA of N.C., 1940), pp. xi–xii, 39, NYA Papers; Betty Lindley and Ernest K. Lindley, *A New Deal for Youth* (New York: Viking Press, 1938), pp. ix, 8.

time lapse between school and job. Annie Kizer Bost, state welfare director, viewed the CCC as a means to fight juvenile delinquency, to prevent "an orgy of destructive and costly crimes." Walter A. Cutter, assistant state NYA director, called for strong measures to save youths from "the jail, prison camp, and the execution chamber." Another official argued that unemployment undermined the morale and ambition of young people and adversely affected their health. Unable to provide for themselves financially, young adults could not marry and "live happy family lives in the American tradition," he continued. Such circumstances led to crime, Cutter believed, and as evidence he cited FBI statistics that 37.4 percent of those arrested in 1935 were people under age twenty-five.[71]

In the CCC the Roosevelt administration combined conservation with unemployment relief for young men. Company 436 in Durham proclaimed in its newsletter that the CCC provided "clean, honest work," enabling campers to earn money and help their families. Insisting that they were not "human parasites," these enrollees preferred manual labor to "loafing." "This is a training station we're going to leave morally and physically fit to lick 'Old Man Depression.'" Given the responsibility by the United States Department of Labor, Annie O'Berry and the NCERA selected enrollees, while the army administered the camps, and the Agriculture and Interior departments provided work projects. With the NCERA as the enrollment agency, North Carolina had over one hundred local CCC recruitment offices. Local selection agents spoke before civic groups, for example, and promoted the social value of the CCC. O'Berry emphasized the government's interest in each young man as an individual, helping him with his problems and planning his future. Nationally, and for North Carolina, seventeen-year-olds constituted the largest number of applicants.[72]

Life in the camps provided a challenge for the enrollees. First they lived in tents and eventually moved to wooden barracks. Recruits rose at 6:00 A.M., reported to work by 7:45, and after a lunch break worked until 4:00 P.M. The CCC provided two sets of clothes and plenty of food.

71. Carl Thompson, "Youth Today," [1940], pp. 11–12, address, Walter A. Cutter, February 22, [?], *Youth* (April–May 1936), pp. 19–20, 22, NYA Papers; T. L. Grier to W. F. Persons, January 14, 1937, "Public Welfare Newsletter," May, 1938, CCC Papers; Lindley and Lindley, *A New Deal for Youth*, p. ix.

72. "Sample Exam for CCC State Supervisors," [n.d.], O'Berry W. F. Persons, March 5, 1935, "CCC Operation Manual for N.C., " April 1938, CCC Papers; "The Log," May 5, [1934], CCC Company 436, Durham, N.C., North Carolina Collection, University of North Carolina Library, Chapel Hill; John A. Salmond, *The Civilian Conservation Corps, 1933–1942: A New Deal Case Study* (Durham: Duke University Press, 1967), pp. 30–31.

Camp life involved more than labor. Late afternoon and evening activities centered on sports and classes. On weekends enrollees were free to make trips to town or home, or they could attend dances or religious services in the camp.[73]

During the first few months of the CCC, North Carolina had 31 camps with 6,200 enrollees. Nationally, by July 1, 1933, the CCC had established 1,300 camps with approximately 274,000 enrollees. Fourteen of the state's CCC camps operated in connection with the National Forest Service, and 11 worked in private forests. In the summer of 1934 North Carolina added 4 camps and by October had increased the total to 38; the additional camps worked primarily with the National Park Service. September 1935 marked the height of the CCC's expansion with 500,000 enrollees in some 2,500 camps. North Carolina reached a high of 16,200 enrollees in 81 camps. The U.S. Department of Agriculture's Soil Conservation Service worked with the bulk of the newly created camps.[74]

Consistent with the national reductions, after 1935 the CCC in the state played a lesser role in relief. When the FERA ended, the state welfare department took over as the CCC selection agency, and state welfare director Annie Kizer Bost lobbied vigorously for the CCC. With the number of camps and enrollees declining, she argued that despite the cost, "the CCC was not only the wisest but the cheapest thing we could do." Nonetheless, North Carolina never again matched its peak of September 1935. Throughout 1936 the state retained sixty camps; in October 1937 the number declined to forty-six; and in April 1939 to thirty-nine camps and 5,129 enrollees.[75]

From 1933 to 1939, the CCC spent $57.2 million in North Carolina employing and training 46,940 men, 87 percent of whom attended camp education and training programs. One reporter noted that the young men "have taken a new hold upon life." In those six years $12.2 million went to dependents of enrollees in North Carolina camps. The state CCC constructed 118 lookout houses and towers and spent 148,000 man-days fighting and preventing forest fires. They built 2,535 miles of truck trails and minor roads and improved 173,800 acres of forests. Their seeding, sodding, tree planting, and gully control work covered 18.2

73. Salmond, *Civilian Conservation Corps.*, pp. 135–44.

74. "Directory: CCC Camps," First Period, 1933, "Roster: Emergency Conservation Work Camps," May 1, 1934, "Directory: Emergency Conservation Work Camps," October 25, 1934, September 30, 1935, CCC Papers; Salmond, *Civilian Conservation Corps.*, pp. 45, 56, 58–59, 63.

75. T. L. Grier to W. F. Persons, January 14, 1937, "Public Welfare Newsletter," May 1938, "Directory: CCC Camps," May 1, October 5, 1936, October 1, 1937, "Brief Summary of Certain Phases of the Program in N.C., April, 1933 to March, 1939," CCC Papers.

million square yards. They built 75,300 erosion control check dams and carried out soil conservation work on half a million acres of farmland involving 3,500 farmers. The CCC contributed to recreation through work in state parks at Mount Mitchell, Morrow Mountain, Hanging Rock, and Cape Hatteras.[76]

Through the NYA, created in 1935 under the auspices of the WPA, the New Deal expanded relief for young people—male and female, those in or out of school. NYA executive director Aubrey Williams appointed Charles E. McIntosh, formerly in charge of the state's FERA student aid program, head of the North Carolina NYA, and after August 1938 John A. Lang led the agency. In the first few months, McIntosh encountered frustration and confusion. Decentralized in administration, the NYA allowed state agencies flexibility in managing student aid, work projects, job training, counseling, and placement services for young people aged eighteen to twenty-five. McIntosh, who was also responsible for the WPA Education Division, complained about Washington's slowness in approving district supervisory staff for the division, which delayed employment of 2,500 needy teachers in the education program. McIntosh also wanted education supervisors to survey the needs of youth as a preliminary step for employing youths on projects. Williams, eager to put young people to work, set aside NYA funds for WPA youth work in the state rather than wait for NYA projects. Such confusion made McIntosh "sick at heart."[77]

A North Carolina NYA official declared that the NYA must provide more than temporary relief, serve as more than a "purgatory" between poor schooling and adulthood: "It must function in terms of the future." Accordingly, the NYA initiated the student aid program first and spent most of the NYA funds on it. For the 1935–36 school year, the NYA appropriated $572,571 to assist an average of 5,907 students per month in fifty-three North Carolina colleges and 885 public schools. Students received part-time employment, scholarships, and loans on the basis of need. In June 1940 the NYA in North Carolina reached a high with an average monthly enrollment of 11,711 in the student aid program. North Carolina's allotment for 1939–40, $719,373, the largest for any school year, surpassed any other southern state except Texas and ranked twelfth nationally. In the number of employees, the state NYA placed fifteenth

76. "Public Welfare Newsletter," May 1938, "Brief Summary of N.C. Program," memo to Alfred L. Bulwinkle, May 1, 1939, CCC Papers; *Raleigh News and Observer,* April 4, 1937.

77. "Final Report: NYA for N.C.," pp. 1, 4, 6, Aubrey Williams to McIntosh, October 2, 1935, McIntosh to Richard R. Brown, November 19, 1935; NYA Papers; Leuchtenberg, *Franklin D. Roosevelt and the New Deal,* p. 129.

nationally and second in the South behind Georgia. North Carolina ranked second nationally in the number of participating schools and colleges.[78]

North Carolina fared well in the NYA program for several reasons. It had a large number of colleges that could participate. Also, the decentralized operation, unlike the CCC, favored a state with an aggressive director like North Carolina's John A. Lang. McIntosh, the first state director, was not on a par with administrators in other states. A national NYA survey gave the state's work program under McIntosh a "D" rating, one of only two awarded. In August 1938 Washington replaced him with the younger and more energetic Lang, a twenty-seven-year-old Carthage native, a University of North Carolina Phi Beta Kappa graduate. Lang previously worked for the CCC, and three years earlier, as president of the National Student Government Federation, had lobbied for the creation of the NYA. Lang made the North Carolina NYA one of the best in the South, and Eleanor Roosevelt honored him with a visit to Carthage on April 28, 1940. She spent the day surveying NYA centers in the state. Aubrey Williams's administrative style encouraged independence by state directors. Lang recalled that at state directors' conferences, which occupied much of Williams's NYA time, the national director's role was one of "exhorter," "inspirer of confidence." For Lang, it was Williams's most important contribution. Williams, concerned with broad policy, left administrative details to subordinates and by his own admission was preoccupied with his "first love," the WPA, of which he served as deputy administrator until 1938.[79]

On January 1, 1936, the NYA initiated the second major part of its efforts to reduce "rapidly rising juvenile delinquency" with its out-of-school youth work program. To teach unemployed youths a skill, the NYA established resident training centers throughout the state. North Carolina eventually had seventeen such centers where instructors taught construction, sewing, clerical, and nursing service skills. In 1941 in the resident projects, youths earned $30 a month, minus $18 for room and board. Most young people in the work program, 90 percent in 1941,

78. "Final Report: NYA for N.C.," pp. 2, 6, 11, 32–33, 35, 40, NYA in N.C. Bulletin, "Youth at Work," April 1, 1941, p. 17, NYA Papers; editorial, NCNYA, "NYA Newsletter," November 15, 1938, North Carolina Collection Clipping File through 1975.

79. *Southern Pines Pilot*, March 20, 1974, North Carolina Collection Clipping File through 1975; John Salmond, *A Southern Rebel: The Life and Times of Aubrey Willis Williams, 1890–1965* (Chapel Hill: University of North Carolina Press, 1983), pp. 121, 124–25, 137, 140; Michael S. Holmes, "The New Deal and Georgia's Black Youth," *Journal of Southern History* 38 (August 1972): 443–60.

lived at home, and for clerical and light construction work, they earned $16 a month.[80]

For the first three years, the NYA spent much less on the work projects than on the student aid program. In January 1936 most work projects started in the piedmont, the section with the heaviest youth population, and by the end of that fiscal year in June, the state had received $146,903 for an average enrollment of only 1,543 in the work projects. During 1937–38 enrollment figures remained a low 2,500. In April 1937 the NYA opened the state's first training center to train 120 white females on relief. The NYA staff provided not only instruction but also recreation and even properly chaperoned visits to a nearby CCC camp. Thirty girls received clerical training at an NYA resident center, an old twelve-room mansion in Greensboro. By 1940 ten girls had found jobs, the NYA reported, and two found husbands. A female resident at the Ellerbe resident training center eloquently testified that the NYA replaced "dull discouragement and hopelessness" with "opportunity and encouragement." She undoubtedly spoke for hundreds of others.[81]

Despite their general popularity and the enthusiasm of young people, parents, local businessmen, school officials, and politicians, the New Deal youth programs faced serious problems. Several North Carolina communities resisted the location of black CCC camps nearby; the CCC was relatively expensive; both agencies faced desertion problems and were changed by the coming war. In the summer of 1937 state NYA officials failed to maintain a work center for boys at Brevard, a junior college in the mountains. Of the fifty-six boys involved, sixteen ran away, and eventually the national office ruled that the NYA project there could not make permanent improvements on a private institution. George Rawick pointed out that in 1941 one out of five CCC enrollees left camp because of desertion or disciplinary discharge. Those who stayed faced the eventual problem of what to do after their CCC eligibility ended. Most North Carolina enrollees knew only isolated rural life and a CCC camp. They had "outgrown" home yet had no job because the CCC served primarily as a relief program.[82]

80. "Final Report: NYA for N.C.," pp. 4, 6–7, 11, NYA in N.C. Bulletin, "Youth at Work," April 1, 1941, pp. 7–9, NYA Papers.

81. "Final Report: NYA for N.C.," pp. 6–8, 55, 58, NYA in N.C. Bulletin, "Youth at Work," April 1, 1941, p. 17, NYA Papers; *Charlotte Observer,* March 24, 1940, *Greensboro Daily News,* July 21, 1940, North Carolina Collection Clipping File through 1975; C. E. McIntosh, "The National Youth Administration in N.C. July, 1935 to August, 1938," pp. 13–15, North Carolina Collection, University of North Carolina Library, Chapel Hill.

82. For a discussion of opposition to black CCC camps see Chapter 6. George Philip Rawick, "The New Deal and Youth: The Civilian Conservation Corps, the National Youth Administration and the American Youth Congress" (Ph.D. dissertation, University of

The New Deal youth programs, particularly the CCC, proved expensive because a rural state like North Carolina with a geographically dispersed population had to have camps and centers for large work projects. But even with borrowed furnishings and donated food, the camps were costly. In March 1934 the 6,800 CCC enrollees in North Carolina cost $20,000 a day to maintain. Compared to other relief agencies, the CCC had the highest annual cost per enrollee, $1,004, compared with $770–$800 for the WPA and $400–$700 for the NYA. Of course, CCC enrollees had to be housed and fed, while only some NYA participants and none of the WPA workers needed such facilities. NYA college students also worked less. For part-time work with college student aid, the NYA spent annually one-tenth as much per youth as the CCC for full-time work.[83]

Both youth agencies suffered from ambiguous identities. The CCC, closely tied to the army, and the NYA provided temporary relief and tried to solve the youth problem through training and education. During 1939 the coming war transformed the agencies to meet defense needs, and both were placed under the new Federal Security Agency. NYA job training in the work program rivaled the funding for student aid. In February 1940 the NYA employed a record 12,914 youths on four hundred projects in North Carolina. Three new large defense resident centers opened in Asheville, Durham, and Greenville with two hundred trainees each, and to serve the new shipbuilding industry, the NYA planned a center for Wilmington. During the year before Pearl Harbor, the NYA in the state trained an average of ten thousand youths per month, and seven thousand of those gained private employment. After Pearl Harbor the NYA focused mostly on war needs but continued student aid. In 1940 students at the university in Chapel Hill, largest recipient of NYA funds in the state, fought "threatened" cuts. On February 7 the university's president Frank Porter Graham reassured a protest rally, after a thousand students expressed their opposition in a petition. Reductions did not materialize, however, for a couple of years. For 1940–41 student aid, enrollments peaked at fifteen thousand, before Roosevelt on February 1, 1942, reduced the student aid program by more than a third.[84]

Wisconsin, 1957), pp. 132, 135–36; *Raleigh News and Observer,* March 19, 1939; McIntosh, "National Youth Administration in N.C.," pp. 16–18, North Carolina Collection.

83. *Raleigh News and Observer,* March 15, 1934, McIntosh, "National Youth Administration in N.C.," pp. 13–16, 26, North Carolina Collection; Lindley and Lindley, *A New Deal for Youth,* pp. 158, 212; Salmond, *Civilian Conservation Corps,* pp. 128, 219–22.

84. "Final Report: NYA for N.C.," pp. 1, 11, 14, 16–29, 34, 40, 50–58; NYA in N.C. Bulletin, "Youth at Work," April 1, 1941, pp. 3, 11, NYA Papers; newspaper clipping, *Durham Morning Herald,* April 29, 1940, Box 271.5, Lang Papers; Rawick, "New Deal and

After 1939 the character and image of the CCC changed. With the approaching war, fear of the draft increased the desertion rate. State CCC authorities fought rumors that the administration planned military training in the CCC. When in September 1940 the CCC geared to defense needs by emphasizing noncombatant training in its educational and work programs, North Carolina CCC officials cautioned against such a move. The vast majority of the state's enrollees, they pointed out, planned to return to the farm, not go into industry; therefore, they did not need the vocational training offered by the defense program. CCC reductions came more quickly than for the NYA; before the agency closed in 1942 North Carolina had a mere 850 enrollees.[85]

New Deal youth programs never aroused strong opposition from conservatives in North Carolina. Assistance to young people proved too popular, especially because the CCC was administered by the army and the NYA was relatively inexpensive. Furthermore, the agencies kept youths out of trouble and off the labor market. Support was not unanimous, however. Whites resisted the location of black CCC camps in their vicinity. Some politicians attacked Aubrey Williams and the NYA for radical activity. In October 1941 Comptroller General Lindsay Warren, a former North Carolina congressman who had supported the NYA, issued a report that criticized the agency for financial and recruiting irregularities. In June 1943 the NYA ceased operations, a victim of conservative opposition and the priorities of the war.[86]

In 1935 Roosevelt permanently expanded government's social responsibilities with the social security program, a major reform but including some public assistance or welfare provisions. The pension plan of Dr. Francis E. Townsend attracted strong support, especially among the elderly, and public pressure for some action mounted. A committee appointed by the president finished its report on a social insurance system, and in January 1935 Roosevelt asked Congress to act. The measure passed easily; no member of the Tar Heel delegation voted against it. In August Roosevelt signed it into law.[87]

The complex program primarily provided for old-age pensions and unemployment compensation. The pensions would be financed through

Youth," pp. 379–81, 387–88; Salmond, *Southern Rebel*, pp. 141, 148.

85. T. L. Grier to Superintendents of Public Welfare, September 9, 1939, Mrs. W. T. Bost and Grier to W. F. Persons, February 24, 1941, Grier to Neal E. Guy, April 29, 1942, CCC Papers; Salmond, *Civilian Conservation Corps*, pp. 176, 181, 186, 197, 210, 217.

86. Salmond, *Southern Rebel*, pp. 153–54.

87. *Congressional Record*, 74th Cong., 1st sess. (1935), pp. 6069–70, 9650; Leuchtenburg, *Franklin D. Roosevelt and the New Deal*, pp. 130–33; David A. Shannon, *Between the Wars: America, 1919–1941*, 2d ed. (Boston: Houghton Mifflin, 1979), pp. 196–97.

a payroll tax on both employers and employees and paid upon an employee's retirement at age sixty-five. Beginning in 1937, taxes, 1 percent of the first $3,000 of income, were deducted for old-age insurance, but benefits, dependent on the size of individual contributions, did not start until 1942. For those already sixty-five and retired, social security provided the Old-Age Assistance (OAA) program, in which the federal government shared the cost of the pensions equally with the states. The federal and state governments also cooperated in unemployment compensation. In addition, the law provided national aid, on a matching basis, to states for the care of dependent mothers and children, the blind, and the crippled.[88]

When he introduced the social security bill in the House, Robert L. Doughton, a floor manager for it, declared that Congress was "pioneering in a field never before undertaken," calling it a "great reform" and "permanent legislation." Social security, however, did have some drawbacks. Critics pointed out that it relied on regressive taxation for funding. Numerous categories of needy workers were not covered. Besides, the old-age pension could not sustain a decent standard of living. It did not establish a national system of unemployment compensation but enabled the states to set up unemployment compensation plans. Furthermore, unemployment compensation did not help those already unemployed, one had to have a job first, then lose it, to receive funds. Doughton himself linked the bill to relief when he told Congress that social security attacked unemployment and old-age dependency, a "large relief problem." But social security was not a substitute for relief because it would not immediately benefit those on relief but would relieve future "destitution and dependency." Social insurance, he declared, was better than the dole. The worker would earn it and therefore would have a right to it without violating self-reliance. Though he saw social security as a reform, Doughton acknowledged that the OAA provisions were "charity" and that the Aid to Dependent Children (ADC) program for households without breadwinners was necessary because the federal government had withdrawn from direct relief. Social security also cared for unemployables—the crippled, blind, and sick—whose care the federal government had turned over to the states.[89]

Fearful of the expense, Governor Ehringhaus delayed compliance,

88. Leuchtenburg, *Franklin D. Roosevelt and the New Deal*, pp. 132–33; Shannon, *Between the Wars*, pp. 196–97.

89. *Congressional Record*, 74th Cong., 1st sess. (1935), pp. 5079, 5467–70, 5476–77, 5969, 6069; Leuchtenburg, *Franklin D. Roosevelt and the New Deal*, p. 132; Shannon, *Between the Wars*, p. 197.

and North Carolina did not begin full participation until July 1937. The state tried unsuccessfully in 1935 and 1936 to comply with the unemployment compensation provisions of the social security law. The 1935 legislature adjourned before Congress passed the social security measure, but anticipating it, the state lawmakers passed the Cherry Act, which empowered the Council of State to establish an unemployment compensation program that could conform with any eventual social security law passed by Congress. This "enabling" legislation called for voluntary contributions from employers, however, not a compulsory tax, and the Social Security Board steadfastly rejected it as invalid. For months Ehringhaus tried in vain to persuade federal officials to accept the state unemployment compensation law, at least until the General Assembly convened in January 1937. He described as "unthinkable" the federal government's position that North Carolina had to pay taxes for the program but could not participate under its own law.[90]

Governor Ehringhaus clearly faced a dilemma. If North Carolina conformed to the social security program and the courts later declared the federal law unconstitutional, Ehringhaus feared that without federal funds, the state would have to finance the system alone. That prospect horrified the fiscally conservative Ehringhaus. Yet, if social security succeeded and North Carolina had no conforming legislation, the state could lose millions in revenue. Doughton urged the governor to comply. To do otherwise could not be "excused, defended or justified," he warned. The Social Security Act financed unemployment insurance through a 1 percent payroll tax, effective January 1, 1936, on employers with eight or more workers. Ninety percent of the tax would go to the state unemployment compensation program if the state complied with the social security legislation by December 31, 1936. If the state did not cooperate, all the funds went to the federal treasury. Yet for over a year, Governor Ehringhaus refused to call a special session of the General Assembly to pass the necessary legislation. He cited the expense and the closeness of the next regular session in January 1937, but he feared most of all that a special session would give the liberals, such as gubernatorial

90. Memo, B. Lotwin to Social Security Board, March 25, 1936, Central Files, Box 46, Social Security Administration Papers; "Minutes of a Special Meeting of the Board of Directors of the N.C. Rural Rehabilitation Corporation," December 31, 1936, Governors' Papers (H); Ehringhaus to members of the North Carolina congressional delegation, May 16, 1935, Governors' Papers (E); Ehringhaus to Bailey, May 16, 1935, Bailey Papers; Thomas S. Morgan, Jr., "A 'folly . . . Manifest to everyone': The Movement to Enact Unemployment Insurance Legislation in North Carolina, 1935–1936," *North Carolina Historical Review* 52 (July 1975): 285–87, 289.

hopeful Ralph McDonald, a chance to repeal the sales tax. He did not want to take that risk.[91]

On December 5, after the November 1936 election and after the Supreme Court had upheld a New York State unemployment insurance law, Governor Ehringhaus called for a special session to meet December 10. In less than a week the legislature created a three-member Unemployment Compensation Commission to administer the program for the state. The legislation had fourteen sponsors in the House, and both chambers passed it without a single opposing vote. Despite Ehringhaus's reluctance, North Carolina delayed no longer than most states. By June 1936, only ten states had complied; by November 1936, fourteen; and not until July 1937 did all states have unemployment compensation laws. On January 1, 1938, North Carolina, along with twenty-two other jurisdictions, started benefit payments, with $8 million collected the previous year and 680,000 employees covered. During the first year, 1938, the Unemployment Compensation Commission paid over $8 million to more than 200,000 workers in the state. By November 1940, the commission had collected $39.4 million and paid claims totaling $16.3 million.[92]

During 1936, his last year in office, Governor Ehringhaus resisted compliance with the OAA and ADC provisions of the Social Security Act, programs that resembled relief. North Carolina lagged behind other states. By June 1936 thirty-six states had devised public assistance plans that satisfied federal requirements. Ehringhaus wanted a federal agency to administer the social security program because he believed Washington would be less likely to leave the states with the burden for the OAA and ADC programs. Until the FERA disbanded in December 1935, he hoped it would manage the program. The governor complained that raising $3.5 to $5.5 million for compliance with social security would strain the state financially. State welfare director Annie Kizer Bost estimated that the cost of social security to the state would be $4.6 million, while social security officials placed the figure between $1.2 and $2.8 million annually. A survey of 105,000 relief families in September

91. John J. Corson to G. R. Parker, July 10, 1936, Central Files, Box 46, Social Security Administration Papers; Morgan, "A 'folly . . .,'" pp. 282–84, 286–89; Doughton to Ehringhaus, March 14, 1936, Governors' Papers (E).

92. Corbitt, ed., *Papers of Hoey*, pp. 52, 165–66, 588–89; Morgan, "A 'folly . . .,'" pp. 298–300; Arthur J. Altmeyer, *The Formative Years of Social Security* (Madison: University of Wisconsin Press, 1966), pp. 61, 82; *Journals of the House of Representatives of the General Assembly of the State of North Carolina*, Extraordinary Session 1936, Regular Session 1937, pp. 17, 19, 20; *Journals of the Senate of the General Assembly of the State of North Carolina*, Extraordinary Session 1936, Regular Session 1937, pp. 12, 16.

1935 revealed that 55,000 North Carolinians would be eligible for the OAA and ADC programs.[93]

Calling it the most "forward and advanced step in this generation," Governor Hoey on January 7, 1937, in his inaugural address, recommended full compliance with the social security legislation. The 1937 General Assembly appropriated $1 million for OAA and half a million for ADC and created the Division of Public Assistance in the state welfare department to administer the funds and on July 1, 1937, began assistance to the old and to dependent children. By September 1938 all states had complied with one or more of the public assistance programs.[94]

From 1937 to 1940, implementation of the OAA and ADC programs began in the state, but North Carolina lagged behind the rest of the nation. OAA increased from 3,433 cases in July 1937 to 35,694 recipients by June 1940. Average monthly grants increased from $9.51 in June 1938 to $10.10 by June 1940, and through January 1940 the social security program distributed over $8 million in North Carolina in OAA benefits. Beginning with 1,755 children in July 1937, ADC assisted 23,291 children by June 1940 and from June 1938 to June 1940 increased the average grant per family from $16.17 to $16.64. By January 1940 ADC had dispensed $3.1 million in benefits in the state. Though the social security grants marked an improvement over the local expenditures for relief, an average of $4.85 per relief family, during the 1936–37 interim between FERA and social security, they compared unfavorably with the rest of the nation. North Carolina OAA payments in 1940 ranked thirty-ninth and ADC grants forty-third. Grants among the states varied depending on per capita income, and the Social Security Board lacked the power to require states to spend adequate funds. The 1939 General Assembly increased the annual appropriation for OAA from $1 million to $1.5 million and ADC funds from $500,000 to $525,000 annually. For the OAA the federal government paid 50 percent and the state and counties evenly split the rest, while the federal, state, and local governments each paid about a third of the ADC program. Thirty-five percent of OAA

93. Helen R. Jeter to Miss Hoey, July 20, 1936, Ehringhaus to R. Galt Braxton, October 2, 1936, Governors' Papers (E); Kirk, Cutler, and Morse, eds., *Emergency Relief in North Carolina*, pp. 375–77; Morgan, "Step toward Altruism," pp. 271, 348–49; Altmeyer, *Social Security*, p. 59.

94. Corbitt, ed., *Papers of Hoey*, p. 20; J. S. Kirk, "Public Assistance Statistics, July–September, 1937," p. 2, Governors' Papers (H); North Carolina State Board of Charities and Public Welfare, *Biennial Report, 1936–1938*, p. 69; Morgan, "Step toward Altruism," pp. 290, 384; Altmeyer, *Social Security*, p. 74.

grants and 22 percent of ADC payments for the year 1937–38 went to blacks in the state.[95]

By January 1940, the social security program, through the ADC, OAA, Unemployment Compensation Commission, and other services, had spent $29.1 million in North Carolina and created a permanent system of relief administered by the state welfare department. Prodded by the New Deal, state governments assumed a major new responsibility for the old and needy. All did not share in this "welfare revolution," however, because social security excluded agricultural workers and domestics, a significant omission for an agricultural state like North Carolina. By June 1938, only 21.3 percent of the population in the southeastern states had registered, in contrast to 30.6 percent for the other states. As with other New Deal relief agencies, dependence on state and local participation lessened social security's effectiveness. North Carolina's inefficiency, fiscal caution, and political interference hampered the agency as conservative local forces again frustrated the New Deal.[96]

Overall, given the state's lack of cooperation, relief proved inadequate during the 1930s. Statistics reveal the stark shortcomings. In per capita FERA grants the state ranked forty-third; in WPA spending last; and in 1940 social security OAA payments placed thirty-ninth and ADC payments forty-third, although these public assistance payments ranked high in the South. Relief payments also lagged seriously behind other states. In May 1935 relief wages were the lowest in the nation. In 1937 North Carolina and only five other states paid old-age pensions of an average of under $10 a month. By 1940 the state's average monthly payment to the old was only 40 percent of New York's.[97]

The dismal performance of North Carolina during the New Deal occurred despite economic need in the state. Though statistics are inexact, estimates indicated pervasive rural poverty. For the period

95. North Carolina State Board of Charities and Public Welfare, *Biennial Report, 1936–1938*, pp. 75, 80, *Biennial Report, 1938–1940*, pp. 64–65, 68; Kirk, "Public Assistance Statistics," pp. 2, 6–10, "Distribution of Funds under the Social Security Program by Counties in N.C.," Governors' Papers (H); Morgan, "Step toward Altruism," pp. 382–83; Altmeyer, *Social Security*, pp. 59, 82.

96. "Distribution of Funds under the Social Security Program by Counties in N.C.," Governors' Papers (H); Morgan, "Step toward Altruism," pp. 386, 389, 392; Tindall, *Emergence of the New South*, pp. 487, 490; Badger, *North Carolina and the New Deal*, p. 50.

97. *Raleigh News and Observer*, May 26, 1935; Badger, *North Carolina and the New Deal*, p. 50.

1933–35, relief officials consistently talked of 10,000 displaced tenant farm families in the east, 20,000 to 30,000 unemployables, and 50,000 North Carolinians who could not survive without some help. In February 1936 the League of Municipalities estimated that 104,000 families, 14 percent of the population, needed assistance. WPA funds, as low as they were, touched about half that number of families. To make matters worse, in 1940 only 4 percent of the state's labor force worked on public emergency projects, in contrast to the 10 percent on relief from 1933 to 1935.[98]

Several factors explain the low level of relief spending in North Carolina. The New Deal relief strategy that focused on unemployment rather than chronic rural poverty missed the state's major problem. Historian James Patterson pointed out that the "most deprived" of the pre-Depression poor largely overlooked by New Deal relief were tenants and sharecroppers, one-fourth of the South's population. Relief policies favored urban industrial states with higher unemployment. These states had higher living costs, therefore higher relief rates, and also were wealthier and more able to contribute matching funds. North Carolina had no city with a population of one hundred thousand or more although the state ranked twelfth in population. The state received less in relief because it was poorer and could not afford adequate matching funds, had lower relief rates because of a lower standard of living, and as a predominantly agricultural state had a low industrial unemployment rate, therefore, less need. New Deal largesse, as a result, maintained the imbalance between rich and poor states. On June 12, 1934, in a speech at Raleigh's State Theater with Harry Hopkins on the platform, Josephus Daniels stressed that "we must spend what is necessary in the war on starvation." His son Jonathan Daniels soon afterward editorially called for a "distribution of plenty," a reconstruction of the social and economic order. Clearly, New Deal relief strategy called for no such bold action.[99]

Conservative landowners, businessmen, and politicians kept the state legislature from adequately matching New Deal relief funds. Work relief threatened both a cheap labor supply and a low-wage philosophy; it threatened the paternalism of the local power structure, the deference of the lower classes to the landowners and mill owners. Relief represented an assault on the work ethic and free enterprise. Ironically, the decentralized administration of relief through state officials like O'Berry

98. *Sixteenth Census, Population,* Vol. 3: *Labor Force,* p. 529; Howard, *WPA,* p. 672.

99. *Raleigh News and Observer,* June 13, editorial, June 14, 1934, May 26, 1935; Patterson, *America's Struggle against Poverty,* pp. 38, 42, 75; Patterson, *New Deal and the States,* pp. 55–57, 78, 198–200; Badger, *North Carolina and the New Deal,* p. 45.

and Coan encouraged accommodation to local pressures. When the state did participate, it applied its own economic or racial conditions to relief recipients, which further limited the impact. James Patterson has noted that during the late 1930s public opinion reinforced the conservative attitude toward relief: many believed that relief clients could take care of themselves if they really wanted to. For North Carolina conservatives the question was not spending more but why the New Deal was spending and wasting so much.[100]

The ambivalence of the poor toward relief made it easier for conservatives in the state to resist the New Deal. Some scholars have argued that New Deal officials designed relief programs to lessen social unrest. That may be true for centers of high unemployment like New York City, but the argument had little relevance for rural North Carolina. Even though the state had much poverty and suffering, one must, as Patterson pointed out, put the poverty of the 1930s in perspective. The rural poverty of North Carolina was relative because about half the people grew some of their food. The poor in that decade had low expectations; demands were fewer than in the post-1945 consumer culture fueled by television. Many relief recipients blamed themselves for their plight; others adhered to old values yet reluctantly accepted relief. Later in the decade attitudes hardened as many attacked the system and bitterly demanded more from the government. Recipients were both appreciative and critical of relief. They liked the gift but resented the giver, adored Roosevelt yet cursed local relief officials. One father of eight had a WPA job that paid $18.50 every two weeks, but before that the family had gone hungry sometimes. The grateful mother acknowledged that "if it hadn't been for the WPA I don't know what we would have done." A black woman, whose husband earned $12.80 a month digging up stumps for the WPA, complained that her husband "ought not to be a-workin' wid de WPA. De gover'ment's got no business a-payin' out relief money and a-givin' WPA jobs to farmers. . . . But able-bodied landers has got no business a-havin' to look to de gover'ment for a livin'." Such attitudes reduced the chances of social unrest and encouraged Tar Heel politicians to do even less for the poor.[101]

100. Patterson, *America's Struggle against Poverty*, pp. 45–46, 59, 68–69; Tindall, *Emergence of the New South*, pp. 481–82; Holmes, *New Deal in Georgia*, pp. 7, 307, 315–16.

101. Robert S. McElvaine, ed., *Down and Out in the Great Depression: Letters from the "Forgotten Man"* (Chapel Hill: University of North Carolina Press, 1983), pp. 10–12, 15–16; Robinson, *Living Hard*, pp. 66–69; Federal Writers' Project, *These Are Our Lives*, p. 24; Blumberg, *The New Deal and the Unemployed*, pp. 283–84; Piven and Cloward, *Regulating the Poor*, pp. xiii, 76–77, 95; Patterson, *America's Struggle against Poverty*, pp. 42, 45–46.

In the end, the most striking feaure of the New Deal relief experience for North Carolina was how much local forces minimized the aims of Washington officials. Though federal relief in the 1930s transformed the welfare department into a major, permanent agency and inaugurated social security, the early welfare state of the New Deal, as James Patterson observed, offered little aid, succumbed to local pressure, and did not end the Depression. The North Carolina experience graphically illustrates his conclusion.[102]

102. Patterson, *America's Struggle against Poverty,* pp. 68, 75; Trout, *Boston,* pp. 171–72, 310.

CHAPTER 6

The Irony of Reform for Blacks

In 1944 Swedish sociologist Gunnar Myrdal declared that "the New Deal has actually changed the whole configuration of the Negro problem." That positive assessment characterized historiography on blacks and the New Deal until the late 1960s, when the New Left pointed harshly to New Deal failures. Representative of the New Left attack on the liberal consensus that praised the New Deal was Barton J. Bernstein's conclusion that Roosevelt's reforms brought much injury and little assistance to blacks and "left intact the race relations of America." "Marginal men trapped in hopelessness were seduced by rhetoric, by the style and movement, by the symbolism of efforts seldom reaching beyond words," Bernstein declared.[1]

Recently, however, historians have found the New Deal record on race ambiguous: relief and recovery programs brought material benefits to blacks, contributed to a civil rights consciousness, but also discriminated against blacks, proved inadequate for their needs, and in some instances produced long-term injury. Harvard Sitkoff's assessment typified this mixed review. He noted that "something vital" began during the decade: "Negro expectations rose, black powerlessness decreased; white hostility diminished." "As such," he suggested, "the New Deal years are a turning point in race relations." Sitkoff, however, moved beyond the liberal consensus by declaring: "For civil rights, the depression decade proved to be a time of planting, not harvesting." In the end, Sitkoff admitted, "little had changed in the concrete aspects of life for most blacks." Other historians have pointed to this dual impact of the New Deal on blacks. Raymond Wolters acknowledged the "New Deal's checkered record—an amalgam of concern and assistance, on the one hand, with indifference and neglect, on the other." John B. Kirby cited the "ambivalent legacy" of the New Deal, and Nancy J. Weiss answers her own question about whether the New Deal should be praised for

1. Gunnar Mrydal, *An American Dilemma: The Negro Problem and Modern Democracy*, 2 vols. (New York: Harper and Bros., 1944), 1:74; another positive account is Arthur M. Schlesinger, Jr., *The Age of Roosevelt*, vol. 3, *The Politics of Upheaval* (Boston: Houghton Mifflin, 1960); Bernstein, "The Conservative Achievement of Liberal Reform," pp. 278–79, 281.

assistance to blacks or criticized for shortcomings by saying that both sides have merit.[2]

Most recent studies, however, center on northern urban blacks and the New Deal. A look at North Carolina suggests that though evidence does not warrant the severe New Left indictment, the adverse effects have been underestimated. In the rural South, where blacks constituted a high percentage of the population and had little political force, economic and political conservatives were powerful and the potential for racism was great, the New Deal proved less effective than in other parts of the country. The impact of relief and recovery programs, not just participation in them, determined the New Deal's effect on blacks. In North Carolina the recovery program hurt black workers, the agricultural policies accelerated movement down the socioeconomic ladder for black farmers, and relief reinforced the low status of blacks. Ironically, the New Deal, designed to help the poor, created more hardship for the state's African-Americans.

Of all the New Deal programs, the National Recovery Administration had the most adverse effect on black workers, 17 percent of North Carolina's work force in the 1930s. From the beginning, federal officials showed little concern for black workers; the NRA refused to assign specialists to work on problems specific to blacks, as did some other New Deal agencies. Codes did not cover traditional unskilled "Negro" jobs like domestic service and agricultural work.[3]

Higher NRA code wages caused blacks to lose jobs. "White men are taking our places on the trucks. White waitresses are taking our places in the restaurants. White people threaten employers if they don't let Negroes go and hire white help. . . . The Depression and now the New Deal, with its higher wages, is just forcing us Negroes out of our jobs, that's all," a bitter cashier at a black Durham bank reported to federal relief administrator Lorena Hickok. The University of North Carolina at Chapel Hill released all its black custodial employees and hired stu-

2. Harvard Sitkoff, *A New Deal for Blacks: The Emergence of Civil Rights as a National Issue*, vol. 1, *The Depression Decade* (New York: Oxford University Press, 1978), pp. ix, 328, 330; Sitkoff, "The New Deal and Race Relations," in *Fifty Years Later*, ed. Sitkoff, pp. 93–112; Raymond Wolters, "The New Deal and the Negro," in *The New Deal*, vol. 1, *The National Level*, ed. Braeman, Bremner, and Brody, p. 202; see also Raymond Wolters, *Negroes and the Great Depression* (Westport, Conn.: Greenwood Press, 1970); John B. Kirby, *Black Americans in the Roosevelt Era: Liberalism and Race* (Knoxville: University of Tennessee Press, 1980), p. 234; Nancy J. Weiss, *Farewell to the Party of Lincoln: Black Politics in the Age of FDR* (Princeton: Princeton University Press, 1983), p. 179.

3. North Carolina Department of Labor, *Biennial Report, 1934–1936*, p. 45; Sitkoff, *New Deal for Blacks*, p. 54; Wolters, *Negroes and the Great Depression*, pp. xi, 213–14.

dents. Higher NRA code wages attracted unemployed whites to traditional black jobs. Some employers fired blacks rather than pay the new wage, and others refused to pay the higher wages. Black leaders sneered at the NRA as the "Negro Run Around" and the "Negro Removal Act." Some industry leaders sought a racial wage differential as a solution. Knowing it was only an attempt to maintain a cheap labor supply, Lawrence A. Oxley, a black North Carolina relief official and assistant to Labor Secretary Frances Perkins, fought a lower NRA wage for blacks, arguing that it would brand blacks as inefficient, submarginal workers and relegate them to a lower-wage caste with the sanction of the federal government. Southern businessmen did obtain a regional wage differential, which along with provisions for lower minimums for unskilled workers, achieved the same result as a racial differential.[4]

Since almost no blacks worked in the state's textile industry, except a few truck drivers and janitors, the NRA affected mostly the state's black tobacco workers, and it failed to improve their condition. Generally, the pay and status of employees in the state's cigarette factories were far lower than for their counterparts in textiles and furniture. Since the beginning of the industry, black women had been the chief source of labor. Slightly skilled and seasonal work yielded low pay and low living standards. In 1930 the state had 19,762 employed in cigarette factories, 76.1 percent of whom were blacks. One survey of 178 black employees in the state's tobacco companies taken before the New Deal revealed that their average weekly pay totaled $10.62. That was approximately twenty-four cents an hour for a forty-four-hour week. Workers concentrated in three cities in the state and formed a huge percentage of their cities' labor force. In Winston-Salem the R. J. Reynolds Tobacco Company employed ten thousand, and the rest of the state's tobacco workers were divided between Durham and Reidsville.[5]

Industry opposition to the NRA, as well as government weakness, contributed to the ineffectiveness of the recovery program. Tobacco industry officials had good reasons for being dilatory. Since 1929 the companies had not only survived the economic crisis but emerged "depression-proof" and enjoyed prosperity throughout the 1930s. After

4. Lawrence A. Oxley, "Negroes and Wage Differential under the Codes," [n.d.], NRA Papers; Ralph J. Bunche, *The Political Status of the Negro in the Age of FDR*, ed. Dewey W. Grantham, Jr. (Chicago: University of Chicago Press, 1973), p. 608; Wolters, *Negroes and the Great Depression*, pp. xi, 213–14; Sitkoff, *New Deal for Blacks*, p. 55; Lowitt, ed., *One Third of a Nation*, pp. 194–95; Allen Francis Kifer, "The Negro under the New Deal, 1933–1941" (Ph.D dissertation, University of Wisconsin, 1961), p. 227.

5. Charles S. Johnson, "The Tobacco Worker: A Study of Tobacco Factory Workers and Their Family," 1935, introduction, pp. 20–22, NRA Papers.

1933 per capita consumption of cigarettes grew steadily. The popular ten-cent pack increased cigarette sales further.[6]

The NRA could do little for black workers in the tobacco factories until a code was framed, and the companies were in no hurry. Because the tobacco industry recovered after the early years of the Depression and did not need the NRA, the only other lure the New Deal could offer the companies to encourage NRA participation was suspension of the antitrust laws. The already oligarchical tobacco industry did not need that either. At the start of the New Deal, the Big Four companies produced about 85 percent of all cigarettes. The number of cigarette factories shrank from sixty-one in 1923 to fourteen in 1931. Cigarette production was also geographically restricted. Three states, North Carolina, Virginia, and Kentucky, manufactured 93 percent of all cigarettes, and in 1932 North Carolina alone produced 55 percent of the total.[7]

Until the industry and the NRA devised a code, the tobacco companies accepted the President's Reemployment Agreement (PRA), which operated from August 1933 to January 1935, when the code finally began operation. During this interim, employment rose 7 percent for the industry and wages increased 15 percent. Mechanization also expanded within the industry. Those trends, however, meant further losses for blacks. The percentage of black workers in the industry decreased because mechanization and higher wages increased the number of white employees. In mid-decade the number of workers jumped to 31,881 but only 72 percent were blacks, about a 4 percent decrease. A survey of 178 black employees of tobacco companies while they operated under the PRA revealed an average hourly wage increase of four cents with an average thirty-six-hour week. Despite reduced hours, the weekly pay remained approximately the same as before the agreement.[8]

The President's Reemployment Agreement did not solve the chronic underemployment and low pay in the industry. Many tobacco workers, black and white, received government relief payments to bring their income up to subsistence level. In November 1934 median relief payments per household for tobacco workers in Durham, Winston-Salem,

6. Donald F. Yakeley, "Cigarette, Snuff, Chewing and Smoking Industry," August 16, 1934, Yakeley, "Cigarette, Snuff, Chewing and Smoking Tobacco Manufacturing Industry," September 21, 1934, W. A. Harriman to President [Roosevelt], January 25, 1935, NRA Papers.

7. Yakeley, "Cigarette Industry," September 21, 1934, W. A. Harriman to President [Roosevelt], January 25, 1935, NRA Papers; Badger, "North Carolina and the New Deal," pp. 59, 63.

8. W. A. Harriman to President [Roosevelt], January 25, 1935, Johnson, "Tobacco Worker," introduction, p. 75, NRA Papers; North Carolina Department of Labor, *Biennial Report, 1934–1936*, pp. 45–46.

and Reidsville equaled $11.79 per month. One-eighth of all households on relief in those cities had one or more members who worked in the tobacco factories. Over one-fourth of tobacco workers during the years 1933–35 received relief.[9] Clearly the relative prosperity of the industry had not filtered down to the workers.

Formulation of the NRA code for the tobacco industry was further complicated by the predominantly black labor force. Blacks and whites worked in separate buildings or parts of buildings. Blacks did the more menial premanufacturing work and whites the more skilled tasks. Industry officials assumed there would be a racial wage differential. The huge numbers of blacks raised awkward questions about unionization under Section 7(a). Including blacks in the union risked violating the southern Jim Crow system, but excluding them made them potential strikebreakers. Thus the issue of race relations added one more obstacle for unionization in the industry.[10]

Code negotiations stalled on the question of the minimum wage for hand stemmers, the bulk of the labor force and made up of predominantly unskilled black women. The code committee, led by chief negotiator and president of the R. J. Reynolds Tobacco Company, S. Clay Williams, included officials from the Big Four and minor tobacco companies. At the hearings for the proposed manufacturers' code, which began in August 1934, industry leaders argued for a minimum wage of twenty-five cents for hand stemmers. Williams pointed out that the companies could not afford to pay them more because their production was substandard. Williams added that employment of these sometimes old and infirm workers was a charitable act of the companies because no one else would hire them. A higher minimum for them, he believed, would mean their unemployment and increase the relief rolls. Company officials also cautioned the NRA to consider the broader social implications of a higher minimum for these black female workers because blacks in other industries earned less and white textile workers in the same communities earned only thirty cents an hour. Williams's arguments had some merit, but his intention was to keep wages down and profits up. He even admitted to a union official that wages could be doubled without affecting the price of cigarettes.[11]

9. Johnson, "Tobacco Worker," pp. 182–84, 191, NRA Papers.

10. Ibid., pp. 125–34, C. W. Dunning, "History of the Cigarette, Snuff, Chewing and Smoking Tobacco Manufacturing Industry Code," October 1, 1935, NRA Papers.

11. William Green to Armin Riley, November 30, 1934, Walter White to C. W. Dunning, January 3, 1935, Dunning to NRA Board, January 8, 1935, W. A. Harriman to President [Roosevelt], January 25, 1935, NRA Papers; Badger, *North Carolina and the New Deal*, pp. 33–35.

Sidney Hillman, union leader and member of the National Industrial Recovery Board, and other NRA officials pushed for a minimum hourly wage of thirty-five cents. Hillman pointed out that 90 percent of the industry's workers received insufficient wages although the companies enjoyed enormous profits. At issue was how much profit the code would permit the companies. The NRA and the industry eventually compromised on a minimum of thirty cents for stemmers. President Roosevelt signed the code in February 1935, and in May the Supreme Court declared the NRA unconstitutional. The end of the code made little difference for blacks in the tobacco industry because it had operated for only a few months. In May 1935, despite the employment gains since 1930, unemployment among tobacco workers remained at a high 24 percent.[12]

Workers' attitudes toward the NRA tobacco industry code revealed the limitations and even irrelevance of the recovery program. Black sociologist Charles S. Johnson studied tobacco workers in Durham, Winston-Salem, and Reidsville and discovered that only about half knew the purpose of the NRA. One worker commented: "It's supposed to be the government, and if it is, it looks like they could make things better, because we can't hardly keep from starving sometimes." Johnson concluded that the largely illiterate black workers did not understand posted code notices. Approximately one-half of the workers who experienced pay increases and shortened hours credited the changes to the goodwill of the company or in some cases their unions. Workers complained as much about the codes as they did about the company. They resented the employers requiring the same amount of work, or even more, with the shorter hours and higher pay. Some workers did not like the shorter workweek because it reduced their actual pay, even with wage increases. Others resented the codes for other industries because they pushed up the cost of living. Black workers blamed the NRA for men replacing women and whites replacing blacks; few appreciated that high unemployment was also a culprit.[13]

Unions failed to organize in North Carolina's tobacco and textile industries. Employers generally ignored the Wagner Act, and in 1939 only 4.2 percent of the state's nonagricultural labor force was unionized, which placed North Carolina forty-seventh nationally. Reynolds Tobacco Company in Winston-Salem resisted unions; consequently, union ac-

12. "Cigarette, Snuff, Chewing, and Smoking Manufacturing Industry Code," [January 25, 1935], Dunning, "History of Cigarette Industry Code," Johnson, "Tobacco Worker," p. 78, NRA Papers; Badger, *North Carolina and the New Deal*, pp. 34–36, 38.

13. Johnson, "Tobacco Worker," pp. 82–93, NRA Papers.

tivity at the plant was negligible. The Brown and Williamson plant in the same city had a closed shop and a conservative union with 560 members. A union existed in Durham but was inactive. The black female tobacco employees represented, perhaps, the toughest challenge for organized labor in the South. Among this group, unions faced all the traditional obstacles—agrarian values, religious conservatism, employers' paternalism, deference to authority—along with racial and sexual intimidation, their lack of education, and the seasonal nature of their work. Not surprisingly, in one study of thirteen hundred tobacco workers, less than one-fifth of the black women responded positively to unions, despite low wages. Organized labor's hopes, buoyed nationally by the NRA, were not realized in North Carolina's tobacco factories.[14]

Critics attacked the NRA tobacco code as an indication of the NRA's weakness. Union official Sidney Hillman cited "miserable" wages and "gigantic profits" as the results. Companies responded to the high NRA wages and shorter workweeks by becoming increasingly mechanized. In 1939 a hundred black stemmers in Kinston lost their jobs to whites, and in Wilson machines replaced two thousand black stemmers. By 1940 half of black tobacco workers in North Carolina, Virginia, and Kentucky had lost their jobs; in North Carolina blacks constituted 54.9 percent of employees in the tobacco industry, down from 76.1 percent in 1930. By 1940 the number of white workers had increased by more than 40 percent. One of the nation's most prosperous industries had fixed its code's minimum wage at a level lower than existing cotton textile wages. One official reminded the NRA Board that as of early 1935 net profits for the industry were more than triple its total wage bill. Because many workers were on relief, this statistic angered opponents of the code. Throughout the two-year period before the code went into effect, the companies increased their prices many times over their increased production costs. The tobacco companies paid huge sums in federal taxes yet passed them on to consumers. In addition, the code appeared a year and a half after the codes for the other major industries. Then, to the consternation of industry opponents, Roosevelt named the president of Reynolds Tobacco Company, S. Clay Williams, to head the NRA.[15] That

14. Ibid., pp. 94–95, 283–84, NRA Papers; Badger, *North Carolina and the New Deal*, pp. 38–39.

15. Badger, *North Carolina and the New Deal*, p. 35; Armin W. Riley to NRA Board, January 18, 1935, NRA Papers; editorial, *Raleigh News and Observer*, February 12, 1935; *Durham Carolina Times*, September 2, 1939; Wolters, "The New Deal and the Negro," p. 183; John R. Larkins, *The Negro Population of North Carolina: Social and Economic* (Raleigh: North Carolina State Board of Charities and Public Welfare, 1944), p. 21.

move, in the closing days of the NRA, signaled Roosevelt's abandonment of the recovery program.

The NRA's adverse effect on North Carolina blacks frustrated Charles Clinton Spaulding, the state's most prominent black and the New Deal's emissary to the African-American community. Spaulding left his family's Columbus County farm for Durham, where he held menial jobs until he worked his way to the top of North Carolina Mutual Life Insurance Company, one of the world's largest black-run businesses. As patriarch of Durham's black middle class and in the tradition of Booker T. Washington, he looked to opportunity in business and education rather than politics as avenues of racial advancement. Initially enthusiastic about the NRA, he served as national chairman of the Urban League's Emergency Advisory Council to garner black support for the program. Spaulding promoted the NRA among blacks, acquainted them with codes, but was disappointed when the NRA did little to correct violations. For example, the NRA code for hotels in Durham recommended pay of $6.75 a week for Negro bellhops. Realizing the codes had no sanctions, owners reduced wages to $3.50. Spaulding protested, but NRA officials could do no more than remove the Blue Eagle, the NRA emblem, from the doors of guilty hotels. The North Carolina Commission on Interracial Cooperation, of which Spaulding was the most prominent black member, publicized and made recommendations about NRA violations. But its quiet manner accomplished little. Spaulding, though a front man for the New Deal, had little power to influence its policies.[16]

Because North Carolina was primarily an agricultural state, the NRA was destined for a minimal role at best there. The Agricultural Adjust-

16. News release, North Carolina Commission on Interracial Cooperation, October 12, 1933, "CIC," [1934], Howard W. Odum Papers; Walter B. Weare, *Black Business in the New South: A Social History of the North Carolina Mutual Life Insurance Company* (Urbana: University of Illinois Press, 1973), pp. 22, 58–59, 217–22, 253, 263; Weare, "Charles Clinton Spaulding: Middle-Class Leadership in the Age of Segregation," in *Black Leaders of the Twentieth Century*, ed. John Hope Franklin and August Meier (Urbana: University of Illinois Press, 1982), p. 189. Michael S. Holmes, in his study of the NRA and Georgia blacks, accurately pointed out that the NRA was not actively racist even though blacks suffered because of their exclusion from codes, wage losses, and displacement. He concluded, however, that in Georgia, black workers may have suffered less than whites because of fair-minded state administrators and an alliance with unions that softened the adverse effects. See "The Blue Eagle as 'Jim Crow Bird': The NRA and Georgia's Black Workers," *Journal of Negro History* 57 (July 1972): 276–83. Such was not the case in North Carolina. The unique circumstances of the tobacco workers demonstrated the inadequacy of the NRA for the state's black workers. In Virginia, which also had a large number of tobacco workers, the NRA adversely affected blacks. "Crucifying Negro workers on an economic cross," claimed one black editor. See Heinemann, *Depression and New Deal in Virginia*, p. 54.

ment Administration, by contrast, had significant consequences for African-Americans. In the 1930s blacks made up one-third of the state's population; three-fourths of them lived in the agricultural east. Roosevelt's farm policies of production and acreage controls displaced thousands of black sharecroppers and tenant farmers in that eastern tobacco region.

In February 1934, Harry Hopkins's assistant Lorena Hickok visited Wilson, North Carolina, a town of thirteen thousand in eastern North Carolina, and reported an alarming increase in the number of displaced tenants: "The intake office in Wilson today was so crowded you could hardly get into the place. Every house, every abandoned shack, is filled with them. They even break the locks off empty houses and move in." She estimated that acreage reduction had displaced ten thousand tenants in eastern North Carolina, and 60 percent of them were blacks. According to Hickok, three hundred displaced tenants and their families had moved to Wilson during the last three years, but two hundred of them came during the past winter. One welfare official declared that in at least fifty cases the landlord moved them to town and paid the first week's rent just to get rid of them. Hickok observed a desperate situation: 75 percent of these families were blacks, and they suffered from illiteracy, tuberculosis, and social diseases. Displaced tenants who remained in the country became squatters and tried to survive living in sheds, tobacco barns, hovels, and shacks.[17]

Unlike some New Deal agencies, the AAA did not address particular needs of blacks. "We never got no rental checks," a black sharecropper in Pleasant Hill complained in 1939. "Some has got gov-ment money on dey crops, but ain't none come to us. I don't know how it works. We never had no help from de gov-ment." Local authorities administered the AAA cotton program and black farmers inevitably suffered some discrimination. Some landlords kept benefit payments from black tenants. Southern black tenant farmers and wage laborers were the poorest agricultural group in the nation, yet the AAA refused to hire specialists to aid them. AAA officials listened more carefully to southern congressmen and landowners.[18]

The catastrophe for black tenant farmers in the state occurred despite the resounding success of the AAA overall. By 1935 the entire AAA program for all crops had put North Carolina agriculture back on the

17. Lowitt, ed., *One Third of a Nation*, pp. 188–90.

18. Wolters, *Negroes and the Great Depression*, pp. xi, 22–34, 79; Bunche, *Political Status of the Negro*, pp. xxv, 515; Terrill, ed., *Such as Us*, p. 89.

road to recovery. Prices for flue-cured tobacco had returned to the level of the 1920s by the end of the 1930s. In North Carolina 13,198 blacks owned their farms, and those black farmers who maintained their status undoubtedly benefited from these positive effects of the AAA.[19]

Despite the increase in tobacco and cotton prices, the AAA acreage reduction program displaced thousands of the state's tenant farmers. Jonathan Daniels, sympathetic to the tenant farmers, recognized the "ironic tragedy" and noted that the AAA "seemed to dispossess rather than serve" the rural poor. With fewer opportunities in agriculture for tenants, relief officials worried about their becoming agricultural day laborers or moving to the towns and going on relief. Nearly two million southern tenant farmers were vulnerable to the acreage reduction programs. North Carolina, in which on the eve of the New Deal forty-six out of one hundred counties had about 50 percent tenancy rates, was particularly susceptible to this adverse effect of the AAA. Eastern counties with high tenancy rates also had a heavy black population.[20]

As the AAA improved farm prices and made agriculture more attractive, blacks unfortunately suffered in the competition with whites for farming opportunities. Theodore Saloutos explained the problems blacks faced. Unemployed whites moved from cities to small, abandoned farms and engaged in subsistence agriculture. White youths, unable to find traditional opportunities in the city, turned to tenant farming. Increased mechanization further reduced agricultural jobs for blacks. With fewer acres to farm, the landlord could shift the tenant to a wage-labor status or evict him. From 1930 to 1935 the number of black-operated farms declined by 9.8 percent, a stark contrast to the period 1910 to 1925, when North Carolina led the nation in the increase in the number of black farmers. Depression and acreage controls displaced about 15 percent of black tenants but only 6 percent of whites through 1934. The ranks of black farm owners in North Carolina did not increase sufficiently to offset black farmers' overall decline in status.[21]

In 1937 C. Horace Hamilton, a rural sociologist for the Extension

19. North Carolina Department of Agriculture, *Biennial Report, 1934–1936,* p. 9; Badger, *Prosperity Road,* pp. 196, 199; John W. Mitchell to J. C. B. Ehringhaus, January 29, 1934, Governors' Papers (E).

20. Charles W. Eagles, *Jonathan Daniels and Race Relations* (Knoxville: University of Tennessee Press, 1982), p. 65; Hobbs, *North Carolina,* p. 335; Blackwell, "Displaced Tenant," p. 66; Conrad, *Forgotten Farmers,* pp. 205, 209.

21. *UNC Newsletter,* December 4, 1935, PC 246.9, Ehringhaus Papers (P); Hobbs, *North Carolina,* p. 335; Blackwell, "Displaced Tenant," p. 66; Kirk, Cutler, and Morse, eds., *Emergency Relief in North Carolina,* p. 281; Saloutos, *American Farmer and the New Deal,* pp. 189–90.

Service, studied five representative rural areas in the state and noted that for the years 1925–35 the trend for black farmers was "down the agricultural ladder and out of farming." He observed that the relative number of black owners and tenants declined, while the number of black farm laborers increased. The Depression and New Deal accelerated the move of blacks off the farm.[22]

Blacks could have been justifiably bitter, for though the AAA had a generally adverse effect on them, it helped improve the status of white farmers. From 1930 to 1935 the number of white farmers in the state increased. Although the eastern counties showed a decline because of displaced tenants, overall the number of farms increased by 8 percent from 1930 to 1935. For those same years, the number of farms operated by whites increased 14.2 percent, the largest jump in recent history. This increase took place largely in the western part of the state and in the southern piedmont cotton counties, but also in eastern tobacco counties. When whites returned to farming they usually replaced black tenants. Landlords found it easier to shift blacks from being tenants to day laborers while keeping whites as tenants.[23]

Hamilton discovered that in his sample for 1934 and 1935 there was twice as much upward mobility as downward mobility, in contrast to the downward mobility in agriculture in 1931 and 1932. Counter to the trend among blacks, whites shifted into farming and up the tenure ladder. For example, the percentage of farm laborers as heads of households dropped from 13 percent in 1932 to 9.5 by 1935. From 1934 to 1935, forty-three laborers moved up the ladder, contrasted with twenty-four owners, renters, and croppers who moved down the socioeconomic scale. Another study showed that the net increase of 12,629 owner-operated farms for 1930 to 1935 nearly equaled the number of displaced tenants. Restored prosperity for tobacco farming and the increased need for labor attracted whites to farming and reduced the number of displaced tenants in North Carolina.[24]

During 1930–35, North Carolina black farmers fared worse than

22. C. Horace Hamilton, *Recent Changes in the Social and Economic Status of Farm Families in North Carolina* (Raleigh: North Carolina Agricultural Experiment Station, 1937), pp. 60, 175.

23. *UNC Newsletter,* November 20, 1935, December 4, 1935, PC 246.9, Ehringhaus Papers (P); U.S. Department of Commerce, Bureau of the Census, "North Carolina Farms Increase 8%," May 31, 1935, Bailey Papers.

24. C. Horace Hamilton, "Relation of Agricultural Adjustment Program to Rural Relief Needs in North Carolina," November 22, 1935, Box 791, General Correspondence, AAA Papers; *UNC Newsletter,* November 20, 1935, PC 246.9, Ehringhaus Papers (P); Hamilton, *Recent Changes,* pp. 60, 174.

blacks nationally. African-American farm operators declined 8 percent nationally, 9.8 percent in North Carolina; North Carolina black sharecroppers suffered especially. While the number of sharecroppers in the United States dropped 8 percent, blacks and whites suffered equally; in North Carolina the percentage of black displacements was more than double the figure for whites.[25]

The local administration of the tobacco program also caused problems for blacks. A survey of Wilson County, North Carolina, conducted after World War II, revealed that after 1936 AAA committees reflected the interests of landowners and members of the Farm Bureau. No blacks or sharecroppers participated in the community committees. Of those interviewed, 91 percent of white owners voted in committee elections, while only 11 percent of blacks voted. Hertford County had one black community committeeman. The AAA relied on influential large farmers and the county agents of the Extension Service, who were not representative of sharecroppers or tenant farmers, black or white. In 1937 the Extension Service employed 235 black county agents in twelve southern states. There was one agent for 1,455 white farmers and one for 3,606 black farmers. Since funds for extension work for blacks were not in proportion to the number of black families, Secretary Wallace insisted that black farmers consult white agents. Black agents rarely had any supervisory authority except over other black agents, and undoubtedly intimidation in some southern states kept them from reporting problems in the distribution of AAA benefits.[26]

Even though they were generally excluded from AAA committees, blacks voted in AAA referenda, which gave them political experience, strengthened their contact with government, and at least to a small degree weakened their dependence on the landlord. Some landlords treated blacks better because their sharecroppers and tenants could turn to the AAA for assistance. Also landlords wanted tenants to vote the right way in the crop referenda in order to pile up huge majorities for control.

Dewey Grantham, however, cautioned against exaggerating the significance of blacks' participation in the AAA referenda. In Wilson County 43.4 percent of the black and 19 percent of the white tenants in-

25. A study of twenty-three cotton counties in Georgia from 1930 to 1935 revealed similarities with North Carolina. The proportion of tenants increased 12 percent, that of sharecroppers decreased 26 percent. The number of white tenants rose, but white sharecroppers, black tenants, and sharecroppers declined. See Holmes, *New Deal in Georgia*, p. 260; Saloutos, *American Farmer and the New Deal*, pp. 189–90; Badger, *Prosperity Road*, pp. 203–4.

26. Kifer, "The Negro under the New Deal," p. 148; Saloutos, *American Farmer and the New Deal*, pp. 180–87; Badger, *Prosperity Road*, pp. 222–23.

terviewed admitted that landlords pressured them to vote for the AAA program. Landlords expected them to support the acreage reduction schemes, even if it meant losing their jobs as tenants. Sharecroppers and tenants were given time off to vote and transportation to the polling places. Despite the use of the secret ballot, the informal procedures at the polling places provided opportunities for intimidation.[27]

Secretary Wallace and other AAA officials defended their treatment of tenants, both black and white. Wallace argued that the purpose of the New Deal adjustment program was not to benefit one class over another but to improve commodity prices. The AAA also pointed out that tenants gained from the benefit payments and price increases. In fact, AAA policies reflected the prevailing notion among politicians and scholars in the 1930s that too many people lived on the land, and the best interests of society would be served if some tenants and sharecroppers moved to the cities.[28]

There were other reasons for the adverse effects of the AAA on tenants black and white. With eyes on the Jeffersonian ideal and on votes, politicians were more concerned with the small family farmer than the displaced tenant. Conservatives in the AAA overcame the influence of liberals in the bureau who wanted more attention given to tenants and sharecroppers. Displaced black tenants suffered because agrarian reformers such as Clarence Poe and Josephus Daniels, along with New Dealers, supported acreage controls, most helpful to commercial farmers, but backed inadequate relief measures to assist tenants and small family farmers.[29]

After 1935 New Deal officials tried, with mixed results, to improve the AAA for tenants and sharecroppers, black and white. Blacks participated in the crop referenda. The 1937 Soil Conservation Program promised tenant farmers an equal share of benefit payments instead of the 75 percent to 25 percent landlord-tenant ratio. From 1935 to 1940, however, the displacement rate accelerated. The number of farms operated by nonwhites dropped an additional 13 percent, compared with 9 percent from 1930 to 1935. The way production and acreage controls were administered continued to deny farming opportunities for blacks.

27. Badger, *Prosperity Road*, pp. 224–27; Bunche, *Political Status of the Negro*, ed. Grantham, pp. xxv, 509, 511.

28. Tindall, *Emergence of the New South*, p. 413; Conrad, *Forgotten Farmers*, pp. 205–9; Badger, *Prosperity Road*, pp. 200–201; Saloutos, *American Farmer and the New Deal*, p. xv.

29. Coté, "Clarence Poe," pp. 38–39; Cronon, "Southern Progressive," p. 166; reprint, G. W. Forster, "In Defense of the Bankhead Act," *Law and Contemporary Problems* (June 1934), AAA Papers; Badger, *Prosperity Road*, p. 203.

Charles C. Spaulding, an agrarian at heart, lamented the social consequences of sharecroppers moving to the city but as an urban, middle-class black leader could do little to stem the migration. Ignoring the realities of the 1930s, he advised black sharecroppers to stay in the country, "raise gardens, diversify crops, apply for federal assistance, and of course to pay their debts and go to church."[30] Black tenants and sharecroppers in North Carolina had no effective spokesman.

New Deal relief programs in North Carolina brought both assistance and adversity to African-Americans. For example, the Federal Emergency Relief Administration brought tangible material benefits to needy blacks in the state. Although relief payments were meager, the federal agency was a crucial source of aid, especially since the state and local governments had little money or interest in relief, particularly for blacks. In ten eastern coastal tobacco-growing counties with a large black population a higher percentage received federal aid than in other counties. In April 1935, blacks constituted 29.1 percent of the relief population in the rural areas; they formed 65.5 percent of relief rolls in cities over twenty-five thousand.[31]

FERA relief in North Carolina was generally in line with the percentage of blacks in the population, 29 percent, but relief measures did not match their need. Relief officials estimated that in 1933 blacks made up 77 percent of the needy and over 50 percent of the state's unemployed. Even those employed earned only subsistence wages. After agriculture and domestic service, public relief became the third major black occupation. Fearful of fostering a dependence on the state, some black leaders expressed concern about the huge numbers of blacks on relief rolls. In 1940 African-Americans still suffered disproportionately in terms of low income, unemployment, and relief.[32]

Participation in relief programs, however, should not be the only

30. *Durham Carolina Times*, September 25, 1937; U.S. Department of Commerce, Bureau of the Census, *Sixteenth Census of the United States: 1940, Agriculture*, Vol. 1: *First and Second Series State Reports*, Part 3: *Statistics for Counties* (Washington, D.C.: U.S. Government Printing Office, 1942), p. 290; Weare, *Black Business in the New South*, p. 172; Wolters, *Negroes and the Great Depression*, p. 60.

31. Guy B. Johnson, "The Negro and the Depression in North Carolina," *Social Forces* 12 (October 1933): 103–4, 106; Kirk, Cutler, and Morse, eds., *Emergency Relief in North Carolina*, p. 33; Tindall, *Emergence of the New South*, p. 570; editorial, *Raleigh News and Observer*, May 4, 1933; memo, National Urban League to FDR, January 4, 1937, Spaulding Papers.

32. Larkins, *Negro Population of North Carolina*, p. 20; Johnson, "The Negro and the Depression in North Carolina," p. 104; Tindall, *Emergence of the New South*, pp. 546–49; Wolters, "The New Deal and the Negro," p. 210; Kirby, *Black Americans in the Roosevelt Era*, pp. 140, 222; editorial, *Raleigh News and Observer*, May 4, 1933.

standard for evaluating the New Deal relief experience for blacks. Discrimination accompanied the material benefits of relief. For example, a 1935 FERA study revealed that in some areas of the South, black families on relief received $8.31 monthly, whites $12.65. In 1933 University of North Carolina sociologist Guy Johnson accurately predicted that blacks would experience "new opportunities for friction—friction over work, friction over wages, friction over distribution of relief funds and jobs." Will Alexander, a leading southern liberal and executive director of the Commission on Interracial Cooperation (CIC) in 1934 complained to Howard Odum, leader in the North Carolina CIC, that southern blacks were victims of "wholesale discrimination" in the expenditure of relief funds. FERA director Harry Hopkins insisted officially on equal treatment but was "pretty hard-boiled and thinks that it isn't his business," Alexander confided. "Such a situation certainly discredits the New Deal," he lamented.[33]

Hopkins's acceptance of the principle of the prevailing wage hurt black relief workers and illustrated their expendability. Farmers did not want cheap black and white labor for harvesting crops threatened by higher relief wages. Annie Land O'Berry, director of the state relief agency, the NCERA, sided with the farmers, and Hopkins capitulated, despite his rule that all work relief would pay a minimum wage of thirty cents an hour.[34]

In 1935 the Works Progress Administration replaced the FERA and work relief continued as a major New Deal strategy against the Depression. North Carolina blacks benefited materially from the WPA programs but faced tough problems. In 1938 North Carolina blacks totaled 24.5 percent of WPA enrollees, just shy of their percentage of the population. Unemployment from 1935 to 1940 continued to hit hardest among domestic workers, farm laborers, and unskilled workers in general. The WPA had particular difficulty finding jobs for unskilled black women. A black WPA worker in Fayetteville complained of "rampant discrimination" when the WPA transferred sixteen black women from a sewing project to cleaning and yard work. Thurgood Marshall, attorney for the National Association for the Advancement of Colored People (NAACP), relayed the complaint to Hopkins, and an investigation revealed that the women had been shifted to unskilled labor because they

33. Johnson, "The Negro and the Depression in North Carolina," p. 115; Will Alexander to Howard Odum, October 13, 1934, Odum Papers; memo, National Urban League to FDR, January 4, 1937, Spaulding Papers.

34. Morgan, "Step toward Altruism," pp. 93–99, 160–61; Harry Hopkins to Annie O'Berry, September 17, 1934, O'Berry to Hopkins, September 21, 1934, NCERA Papers.

had not met standards for the sewing projects. White residents in Concord demanded that Hopkins remove a black sewing project from their neighborhood. Relief officials shifted some black women in Fayetteville from WPA rolls to picking cotton. The NAACP complained because the change meant a drop in wages from twenty-four dollars to fifteen dollars a month. In Mecklenburg County the WPA received complaints that whites, refusing to pick cotton, took the relief jobs, leaving cotton picking for blacks. The county welfare superintendent reported that of the 180 workers in cotton fields in September 1939, only twenty-five were white. Some blacks, however, eagerly sought WPA work because it usually meant better pay, shorter hours, lighter work, and year-round employment.[35]

Though it could have done more, the North Carolina WPA treated blacks fairly; its various projects helped them in countless tangible and intangible ways. "Were it not for the federal government," editor Louis Austin of the black *Durham Carolina Times* declared, "the plight of the Negro in the U.S. would be even worse than it is." Durham education officials decided to transfer funds from a black school building project to a white one. Austin, militant in his defense of black interests locally and nationally and an outspoken critic of segregation, reminded readers that the WPA had a policy against such a transfer of funds. Austin praised and attacked New Deal measures, depending on their impact on African-Americans. The WPA's Federal Music Project organized eighteen black choral groups in the state, and President and Mrs. Roosevelt selected the North Carolina Negro Chorus to perform at the White House on June 8, 1939, in a concert honoring the king and queen of England. By June 1939 in a WPA education project, volunteers had taught 2,788 adult blacks to read and write. The North Carolina Federal Theater Project assisted black theater units in Raleigh, Greensboro, and Manteo. Raleigh's Little Theater, in a WPA project, cast a black in a part and possibly became the first southern town to produce a play with a mixed, local cast. Local audiences accepted this new departure.[36]

35. Alfred E. Smith, "1935 Report, Summary of Negro Clients of Federal Unemployment Relief," December 31, 1935, Thurgood Marshall to Hopkins, January 11, 1938, E. G. Dorsey to Alfred E. Smith, March 7, 1938, M. B. Catlin, "Relief and Economic Statistics: N.C.," April, 1938, WPA Papers; Cash, *Mind of the South*, p. 418; *Durham Carolina Times*, October 9, 1937, September 23, 1939; McElvaine, ed., *Down and Out in the Great Depression*, pp. 93–94.

36. Howard Bailey to John McGee, January 30, 1937, "North Carolina Federal Theater Project of the WPA," October 1937, Florence Kerr to F. C. Harrington, February 17, 1939, Erle Stapleton to William C. Mayforth, May 26, 1939, "Resumé of Literary Work in N.C.," June 1, 1939, Fred J. Cohn, *North Carolina WPA: Its Story* (Raleigh: Federal Works Agency NCWPA, 1940), p. 41, in WPA Papers; Wolters, *Negroes and the Great Depression*, pp. xi, 214–15; editorial, *Durham Carolina Times*, April 22, 1939.

Even the New Deal's most popular relief agency, the Civilian Conservation Corps, created problems for relief administrators, politicians, and blacks. The law creating the CCC pledged no discrimination, but by the summer of 1933 southern states had enrolled only a token number of blacks. North Carolina's 9 percent contrasted sharply with South Carolina's record of 36 percent black enrollment. By the end of 1935, blacks made up less than 6 percent of the CCC enrollments nationwide. Director Robert Fechner, a southerner, insisted on segregation in the establishment of camps and placed white supervisors in charge of black camps. The CCC confined black enrollees to their home state but sometimes assigned whites to camps in neighboring states.[37]

After 1935 the CCC improved its assistance to blacks but failed to give them their fair share. In 1936 Roosevelt changed policy and permitted some black supervisory personnel in black camps, although blacks experienced no breakthrough in securing administrative positions in the CCC. *Carolina Times* editor Louis Austin in June 1939 chided Roosevelt and Fechner for not following the policy banning discrimination. He pointed out that in the black camps staff positions did not generally go to blacks. North Carolina, with eight black camps out of fifty in November 1936, had three camps with black advisers, mostly in the education program. By August 1940 blacks constituted 21 percent of the state's seven thousand enrollees, still short of their 29 percent of the population. With the improvement in the economy in 1941 the number of white enrollees declined as they found employment in private industry. Blacks faced resistance in entering private industry and pressed to join the CCC in greater numbers. State welfare director Annie Kizer Bost reported that North Carolina would have no trouble filling its quota of blacks. Bost also observed that generally blacks took better advantage of CCC opportunities, served longer terms than whites, and had proportionately fewer disciplinary discharges.[38]

In North Carolina, politicians and businessmen protested the location of black CCC camps in their communities. Whites objected to two hundred young black men, all strangers, in their midst. They expressed concern about the safety of their women and children and feared the

37. Sitkoff, *New Deal for Blacks*, p. 74; John A. Salmond, "The Civilian Conservation Corps and the Negro," *Journal of American History* 52 (June 1965): 76, 79, 82, 84; Kifer, "The Negro under the New Deal," p. 68.

38. Charles H. Taylor to Bailey, August 2, 1940, Mrs. W. T. Bost and T. L. Grier to W. F. Persons, February 24, 1941, CCC Papers; C. C. Spaulding to Bailey, November 18, 1936, Bailey Papers; Salmond, "Civilian Conservation Corps and the Negro," p. 82; Sitkoff, *New Deal for Blacks*, p. 74; Calvin W. Gower, "The Struggle of Blacks for Leadership Positions in the Civilian Conservation Corps: 1933–1942," *Journal of Negro History* 61 (August 1976): 135; *Durham Carolina Times*, June 10, 1939.

drunkenness and vices of the black campers. Fechner promised to consult each governor in advance about the location of black camps, but North Carolina Governor Ehringhaus protested frequently that the CCC acted without consulting him. Senator Josiah Bailey and Representative Lindsay Warren both faced intense pressure from constituents in Laurinburg, Butters, and Washington concerning the presence of black camps, and they sought the aid of the governor in having them removed. The location of these camps became such a problem that in 1935, when the agency expanded, Fechner established a quota system for blacks and enrolled them only as vacancies occurred. Fechner and Roosevelt decided not to risk the main purpose of the CCC for any controversial racial policies.[39]

During the late 1930s the placement of black camps continued to be a problem. Citizens in Onslow County feared one camp would be changed from white to "colored." Representative Barden implored Governor Clyde R. Hoey to prevent the change because it was the only white one in his district. One official later explained to Barden that CCC personnel visited eleven places and no one wanted a black company. Durham city and county officials were agreeable, he explained, "but the matter got into the papers and the protests became so strong that this proposal had to be given up." Townspeople in Albemarle complained that white homes bordered the proposed black camps on three sides, and they feared trouble with the enrollees. Citizens in Ramseur and Monroe expressed strong opposition to plans for black camps in their area, and Congressmen Robert L. Doughton and Alfred Lee Bulwinkle protested to director Fechner about the placement of blacks in CCC camps in Gaston, Iredell, and Stanley counties. The congressmen, like most townspeople, preferred that these white camps be closed rather than have black companies use the facilities. State officials eased the problem somewhat by placing two black companies at Fort Bragg, but in July 1938 these two companies finished their work there and again faced the difficulty of relocation. Furthermore, the camps at Fort Bragg reduced the quotas and the financial benefits for the state. Fechner, consulting with Hoey, continued to seek acceptable areas for the camps; if unsuccessful, the state faced the loss of a CCC company.[40]

39. Lindsay Warren to Ehringhaus, July 9, 1935, Ehringhaus to Warren, July 11, 1935, Ehringhaus to Josiah W. Bailey, July 22, 1935, Governors' Papers (E); Bailey to Thomas J. Dunn, August 17, 1935, Bailey Papers; Salmond, "Civilian Conservation Corps and the Negro," pp. 79–81, 84, 87.

40. Fechner to George Tyner, June 11, 1938, to Clyde Hoey, June 24, 1938, Hoey to Fechner, June 30, 1938, Charles Taylor to Hoey, July 5, 1938, CCC Papers; Josiah W. Bailey to Fechner, January 13, 1936, Fechner to Bailey, September 29, 1937, Bailey to A. Hand

Though the director was cautious and official policy prevented full participation, thousands of black young men learned skills and received employment opportunities. "Camp life has made my boy all over," one black mother from Greensboro declared, "he is a new boy." The experience not only strengthened her son's morale, she added, but the CCC checks enabled her to keep their home. Some North Carolina towns, like New Bern and Shelby, accepted black camps without complaint. During the CCC's first five years, the state's nine black camps reported no violence or significant misbehavior. Speaking for North Carolina blacks, Louis Austin recognized the CCC camps as a last resort for many boys and proudly declared them the "last word in cleanliness and order." Critical of those who opposed a black camp in a white section of Durham, Austin questioned the genuineness of white fears. "Let us all be thankful," he confessed, "that the federal government is sometimes not moved by local customs and sentiment."[41]

Similar to the CCC, the National Youth Administration provided opportunities as well as adverse results for blacks. Overall, the NYA had the best record of any New Deal agency for assisting blacks. National NYA director Aubrey Williams insisted on fair treatment of blacks, and nationally and in North Carolina, toward the end of the program, the percentage of black young people in the NYA equaled their percentage of the population. John A. Lang, appointed in 1938 as the second state director, broadened black participation in North Carolina's NYA. The NYA paid the same wages to both races. Mary McLeod Bethune, national director of the NYA's Division of Negro Affairs, participated in policy making and managed agency supervisors in twenty-seven states, although North Carolina, probably because of politics, racism, and inertia, had no Negro Advisory Committee until 1939. In 1940 the NYA in North Carolina employed nine blacks in administrative positions. Until then, the state's black youths depended completely on white bureaucratic paternalism.[42]

James, September 30, 1937, Bailey Papers; A. K. Winget to Hoey, June 15, 1938, J. S. Holmes to Hoey, June 21, 1938, Governors' Papers (H); Salmond, "Civilian Conservation Corps and the Negro," p. 84; telegram, Barden to Hoey, July 13, 1937, J. S. Holmes to Barden, October 5, 1937, Barden Papers.

41. Editorial, *Durham Carolina Times*, August 20, 1938; T. L. Grier to Mrs. W. T. Bost, October, 1937, CCC Papers; Bailey to Fechner, January 10, 1936, Bailey Papers; J. S. Holmes to Hoey, June 21, 1938, Governors' Papers (H); Sitkoff, *New Deal for Blacks*, p. 74; Jenny Snipes to [CCC], November 15, 1934, NCERA Papers; Salmond, *Civilian Conservation Corps*, pp. 220–21; Salmond, "Civilian Conservation Corps and the Negro," pp. 75–88.

42. "Final Report: NYA Division of Negro Affairs," pp. 30, 37–39, NYA Papers; Bunche, *Political Status of the Negro*, pp. 623–24; Sitkoff, *New Deal for Blacks*, p. 73; Kifer, "The Negro under the New Deal," pp. 111, 119; *Southern Pines Pilot*, March 20, 1974, North

The NYA Student Aid program assisted black students in North Carolina. By December 31, 1936, 1,456 black college students had earned an average of thirteen dollars a month from the NYA, and 2,493 black high school students received an average of $4.70 a month. For the 1938–39 school year, the NYA spent $52,650 on 710 black college students, almost 16 percent of the 4,439 enrolled in the thirteen black colleges.[43]

In its out-of-school work program, the North Carolina NYA had an innovative job training and placement service. One of the first three state units to have black vocational counselors, the state NYA worked with Spaulding's North Carolina Mutual Life Insurance Company that sought black clerical workers and salesmen. At a conference on the problems of out-of-school Negro youth, state NYA officials detailed the difficulties they faced with black young people: how to get them to develop a positive attitude toward manual labor; how to fit them into a biracial world; how to get employers to see the employee as a person who needed a decent wage; how to get the trainee to accept a job when offered one rather than making a career out of the NYA; and how to solve superiority-inferiority complexes in the work centers.

Despite the commitment to job training at the various work centers, state NYA administrators persisted in the "Negro jobs" concept, which was as degrading as a racial wage differential. Rather than training black young people for different jobs, state NYA officials wanted to change the attitudes of black youths. For example, to solve the servant problem, they had the Colored Maid Training Project. At a 1940 conference they concluded: "Recognizing the tradition that Negro thought and feeling is opposed to all kinds of manual labor as a degrading relic of slavery, the NYA, through its educational program, should emphasize the fact that work in all forms is a necessity . . . is natural and honorable and that efforts be made to dignify the particular type of work done." In a speech at the conference, state NYA administrator John A. Lang recommended that the NYA give black young people training and a needed skill, and their wages would "come along naturally." He also noted a great demand for domestic workers—good ones who could do high-quality work. If blacks did not take these jobs members of another race would, he warned, and it would be better if the blacks took them. Lang concluded: "At the same time, I want to fight for all of the things that rightfully

Carolina Collection Clipping File through 1975.

43. "Final Report: NYA for the State of N.C.," p. 4, "Final Report: NYA Division of Negro Affairs," pp. 100–103, NYA Papers; J. Percy Bond, Jr., "Negro in the NYA for N.C.," November 1939, PC 1523.3, Ferree Papers.

belong to you."[44] Once again racism limited the material gains of New Deal relief.

Initially the NYA did not give blacks their fair share of funds, but in 1941, when whites no longer needed the programs because of the World War II boom, the NYA improved its assistance to blacks in the out-of-school work program. They operated six of the state's seventeen resident work centers for blacks in places like the state normal schools in Fayetteville and Elizabeth City. In North Carolina black participation reached as high as 30 percent in the spring of 1941. With the emphasis on defense training, blacks broke into skilled jobs through the NYA's insistence, despite resistance from industry and labor. North Carolina never matched the record of the Georgia NYA, which served more blacks than any other state NYA program.[45]

In 1937 Congress established the Farm Security Administration to deal with the relief needs of displaced tenants and sharecroppers. Previous New Deal efforts to alleviate rural poverty failed, and the FSA, led by Will Alexander, renewed the goal to transform tenants into landowners. The FSA's basic program provided loans for selected tenants to purchase farms. After almost one year, the agency had spent $10 million in North Carolina. Because its national director was sensitive to racial justice, the FSA did benefit some blacks. Nat Williamson of Guilford County became the first black tenant farmer in the nation to receive an FSA purchase loan. In 1943 Ollie Burnett of Chatham County, perhaps the first black farmer in the United States to repay an FSA farm purchase loan, owned a 132-acre farm after years as a tenant. But Burnett and Williamson were exceptions, for fewer than 2,000 black tenants received purchase loans out of the 192,000 displaced black tenants. In North Carolina, though they constituted 44 percent of the tenant farmers, in 1938 blacks totaled only 25 percent of the state's participants in the FSA purchase program, 5 percentage points above the southern average. When conservative opposition to the agency strengthened by 1945, the percentage dropped to 17, 6 points below the average for the region.[46]

44. "Final Report: NYA Division of Negro Affairs," pp. 7–8, 12, 20–21, 31, 91, NYA in N.C., "Proceedings of the N.C. Conference on Problems of Out-of-School Negro Youth," Fayetteville, N.C., January 31 to February 4, 1940, pp. 12, 18, speech, February 1, 1940, NYA Papers; Kifer, "The Negro under the New Deal," pp. 116–17.

45. "Final Report: NYA Division of Negro Affairs," pp. 43, 58, 130, 212, "Final Report: NYA for N.C.," p. 70, NYA in N.C. Bulletin, "Youth at Work," April 1, 1941, pp. 7–8, NYA Papers; Kifer, "The Negro under the New Deal," p. 103.

46. M. B. Catlin, "Relief and Economic Statistics: N.C.," April 1938, WPA Papers; Baldwin, *Poverty and Politics*, p. 197; Wolters, *Negroes and the Great Depression*, pp. xi, 79; Bunche, *Political Status of the Negro*, p. 616; Lefler and Newsome, *North Carolina*,

Two black FSA projects in North Carolina provide graphic examples of southern racism and the New Deal's limitations. Frustration and failure marked the Roanoke Farms project in Halifax County, the Halifax community for whites and Tillery for blacks. Initiated by the FERA and continued by the Resettlement Administration, the black FSA project at Tillery faced numerous obstacles. Relief officials abandoned plans for the original site when landowners, for financial and racial reasons, dramatically increased their price demands. Fearing bad publicity, relief officials refused to invoke eminent domain. Plans called for two hundred farms for blacks on ten thousand acres of poor land at another location. The FSA budgeted a maximum of $1,200 per house. Agriculture Secretary Henry Wallace, more thrifty than earlier FERA and RA administrators, ordered renovation of old cottages on the site and planned cheaper model homes. Black units had one-third less land than the white project at Halifax. Tillery residents complained to FSA officials in Richmond and Washington about their incompetent white manager, their white doctor, and the fact that the Negro farm supervisor did not have an office. Black tenants, confused about the financial arrangements, resisted the FSA's cooperative system. Tenants were required to purchase through co-ops that they did not understand. The FSA held a mortgage on all their possessions and planned their economic lives to the penny. In Tillery the average price for a farm was $3,000; in the first two years only four families had a cash surplus. After five years, the Tillery experiment ended. Before 1941 no more than 125 families even resided in the settlement. After a 1943 congressional investigation the government sold homes to tenants or at a public auction.[47]

At the Pollocks Ferry Farm, another FSA project for African-Americans, participants protested when the manager replaced a black foreman with a white one. According to the FSA report, the manager of the community did not want the blacks becoming landowners; instead, he hoped the project would fail so that he could rent the place and hire blacks as field hands. Earlier, when he could have hired competent black foremen, he deliberately selected incompetent ones so they would fail,

pp. 645, 648; *Raleigh News and Observer*, September 27, 1943; *Durham Carolina Times*, July 16, 1938.

47. Howard H. Gordon to W. W. Alexander, June 12, 1940, Project Records: North Carolina, Box 435, FSA Papers; U.S. House of Representatives, Select Committee of the House Committee on Agriculture to Investigate the Activities of the Farm Security Administration, 78th Cong., 1st sess., *Hearing, Part II, June 7 to July 2, 1943* (Washington, D.C.: U.S. Government Printing Office, 1943), pp. 416–17; Kifer, "The Negro under the New Deal," pp. 179–90; Conkin, *Tomorrow a New World*, pp. 141, 335.

the report concluded. Other grievances included inadequate explanation of the contracts and confusion over dividend payments after the harvesting of crops; inaccessible loans for livestock until the first of the year; and inability to keep a portion of the corn or wheat crop for bread or use as livestock feed.[48]

There were several reasons why the FSA did not have a larger impact on North Carolina blacks. Race and economic factors undoubtedly played a pivotal role. Landlords, wanting to keep a cheap labor supply, opposed assistance to black tenants. The agricultural establishment, the Extension Service, the land-grant colleges, and the Farm Bureau, all jealously guarded their roles as supervisors of relief to tenants and sharecroppers. Others refused to be alarmed at the long-standing poverty of black sharecroppers. The lack of commitment from Roosevelt and Congress prevented the agency from meeting the need. Since the FSA provided loans, not outright grants, it amounted to only a modest banking institution. But despite its limitations, the FSA battled rural poverty more effectively than any New Deal program.[49]

The impact of the New Deal on blacks, not mere participation in relief programs, should be the standard for evaluating their relationship to the New Deal. According to that yardstick, the New Deal affected North Carolina blacks more adversely than positively. The NRA, unable to overcome the opposition of the cigarette companies, did little for the tobacco workers, the most needy in the state. The AAA accelerated the descent of black tenants and sharecroppers on the socioeconomic ladder. Relief programs brought needed material assistance but also discriminated and failed to meet the need. A report on urban black housing in North Carolina during 1939 and 1940 found 80 percent of black families ill-housed and two-thirds of black households living on less than $800 a year.[50]

In explaining why policies worked against the interests of blacks in the 1930s, historians typically point to conservative opposition, racial politics, states'-rights traditions, and the decentralized New Deal bureaucracy. All these factors operated in varying degrees in North Carolina,

48. Constance Daniel to George S. Mitchell, November 7, 1941, Project Records: North Carolina, Box 435, FSA Papers.

49. Select Committee of the House to Investigate the FSA, *Hearing, Part IV, July 3, 1943 to May 3, 1944*, pp. 1449–53; Baldwin, *Poverty and Politics*, pp. 115, 190, 193, 279; Mertz, *New Deal Policy and Southern Rural Poverty*, pp. 256, 260–61; Tugwell, *Democratic Roosevelt*, pp. 472–73; Leuchtenburg, *Franklin D. Roosevelt and the New Deal*, p. 141.

50. Augustus M. Burns III, "North Carolina and the 'Negro Dilemma,' 1930–1950" (Ph. D. dissertation, University of North Carolina, 1968), pp. 185–86.

for example opposition to higher wages and discrimination against blacks, but the dynamics of race relations also obstructed black progress. Blacks and their white liberal allies bear part of the blame, for the North Carolina experience challenged their assumption that New Deal economic reform would produce progress for blacks. Furthermore, as John B. Kirby concluded, most white liberals, more interested in the success of liberal reform than in black progress, never considered the "Negro problem" a central issue. The North Carolina Commission on Interracial Cooperation, founded in 1921, and with twelve hundred members by 1934, the largest for any state, illustrated the dilemma. Though this southern interracial organization represented progress in race relations from the Progressive Era, its cautious manner produced few practical results for blacks in the 1930s. CIC members lobbied for advisers in black CCC camps, fought some adverse effects of the NRA, and secured the right for African-Americans to ride buses.

The CIC's goal was not progress for blacks but racial harmony for social and economic progress. To that end, white extremists and black militants were resented for creating racial conflict. Though blacks outnumbered whites three to one at meetings, whites outnumbered blacks two to one in membership and dominated the organization. Howard Odum, chairman of the North Carolina CIC, and by 1937 CIC president, described the commission's role as "educator rather than . . . excited reformer." Odum, though a scholar of black culture, subjugated race problems to his concept of regionalism. A reluctant New Dealer, Odum resisted the centralizing trend of Roosevelt's reforms, and his earlier association with Hoover limited his usefulness to the New Deal. After his battles with fundamentalists in the 1920s, Odum shied away from politics. In sum, Odum was not the white liberal to challenge segregation, and faced with New Deal discrimination he sacrificed race for other goals, as did other New Dealers. Aside from teaching at the North Carolina College for Negroes in 1939, Odum had little to show for his interracial work in the 1930s.[51]

51. Memo, "Suggestions for speech to N.C. Commission on Interracial Cooperation," February 15, 1934, Governors' Papers (E); Lorena Hickok to Harry Hopkins, February 18, 1934, Box 11, Hickok Papers; Sitkoff, *New Deal for Blacks*, p. 269; "Commission on Interracial Cooperation," [1934], Odum Papers; Kirby, *Black Americans in the Roosevelt Era*, pp. 54, 221, 230–34; Morton Sosna, *In Search of the Silent South: Southern Liberals and the Race Issue* (New York: Columbia University Press, 1977), pp. 22, 38, 58–59, 63, 90; Daniel J. Singal, *The War Within: From Victorian to Modernist Thought in the South, 1919–1945* (Chapel Hill: University of North Carolina Press, 1982), pp. 150–51; O'Brien, *Idea of the American South*, pp. 48–49, 60, 80–81. Raymond Gavins has pointed out that racial progress is difficult to determine because of an "elaborate mythology of the state, a

atmosphere that he perpetuated. He did not want civil rights concerns to threaten the priority of economic recovery. Material benefits for blacks resulted not so much from their being black as from their being poor. Historians, seeking a nascent civil rights movement in the 1930s, have given perhaps too much credit to the New Deal. As Carl N. Degler observed in 1969 at the close of the civil rights movement, Gunnar Myrdal was too optimistic in his prediction of prospects for blacks in the New Deal era. For many North Carolina blacks the New Deal years brought more adversity than economic and social progress.[59]

59. Sitkoff, *New Deal for Blacks*, pp. 47–49, 190, 329; Tindall, *Emergence of the New South*, p. 541; Carl N. Degler, "The Negro in America—Where Myrdal Went Wrong," *New York Times Magazine*, December 7, 1969, pp. 64–65, 152–60.

CHAPTER 7

Conservative Rule in the State

A close examination of state government and politics during the height of the New Deal reveals a stubborn probusiness ideology that not only resisted Roosevelt's measures but set forth a conservative agenda for North Carolina. State leaders did more than react to Washington, "shadow-boxing with issues that were determined elsewhere," George B. Tindall called it. The actions of state government in the 1930s further underscored the conservative grip on policies and shattered any pretense of a progressive image. Not "especially fertile soil for New Deal ideas," James T. Patterson concluded about North Carolina. For Governor John C. B. Ehringhaus and the majority of the legislature, the overwhelming preoccupation was fiscal restraint. A balanced budget achieved through extreme retrenchment and regressive taxation was more important than relief, welfare, jobs, health, or education. For example, in 1933 the state's educational institutions experienced a 42 percent cutback. North Carolina, at times inhospitable to New Deal efforts to fight the Depression, was even less interested in the state taking measures to improve the plight of suffering Tar Heels.[1]

Governor Ehringhaus, despite any private ambivalence about the New Deal, led North Carolina down a thoroughly conservative road. Public rhetoric supportive of Roosevelt, owing to party loyalty, deference to the president's popularity, or partial sympathy for some New Deal measures, rarely translated into enthusiasm for the relief and reform programs. Josephus Daniels warned his son Jonathan that conservatives like Ehringhaus and Gardner "preach Jeffersonian democracy but they compromise with it when it runs counter to the interest of big business." Securing and preserving the sales tax overshadowed all other concerns in the Ehringhaus administration. Fearing that the legislature would repeal the sales tax, he either refused to call or delayed special sessions to deal with Depression and New Deal issues. The last governor to call a bank holiday, Ehringhaus also dismissed Roosevelt's plea in

1. Patterson, *New Deal and the States*, pp. 47, 158, 206–7; Tindall, *Emergence of the New South*, p. 649.

April 1933 for state minimum wage legislation. He abdicated the role of relief to the federal government, although he supported the NRA and secured maximum benefits for the tobacco farmers under the AAA.[2]

Ehringhaus perhaps appeared more conservative than he was because of his cautious manner. Newspaper reporter William T. Bost described the governor as one who "served his state without theatricalism in an era which was highly dramatic." Ehringhaus was one of those governors in the 1930s whom James Patterson labeled "nobodies—moderate, undramatic, yawn-inspiring men with legislative programs as pedestrian as they were unsuccessful." North Carolinians expected orators as governors, like Charles B. Aycock and Max Gardner. Ehringhaus could not match their dynamism. He faced tough decisions as a Depression governor, and according to Raleigh attorney James H. Pou, served more as the receiver for a bankrupt corporation than the chief magistrate of the Tar Heel State. Sometimes the strain showed. Jonathan Daniels remembered Ehringhaus as "thin-skinned" when he criticized the governor for not supporting the tobacco program strongly enough. In one angry speech to the state's farmers in 1936, when he flatly refused to call a special legislative session to enact tobacco controls to replace the AAA, he thundered: "No matter how hard you try you are always wrong. I have spent my health, practically, in trying to carry out the duties of that office, and . . . the happiest man in North Carolina, next January, will be the governor that goes out of office!"[3]

In January 1933, when Ehringhaus became governor, economic concerns were paramount as the state faced its worst crisis since Reconstruction. Cotton and tobacco prices dropped to five and eight cents a pound respectively. Unemployment reached an all-time high, farmers lost mortgage battles, and between October 1929 and March 1933, 215 banks with assets of over $110 million failed. State government faced a serious debt problem. In 1932 North Carolina, Louisiana, Florida, and Arkansas represented 9.5 percent of all state and local debts in the United States, and those states' debts were more than twice their resources for servicing those debts. Despite economy moves during the

2. Josephus Daniels to Jonathan Daniels, April 8, 1935, Box 2, Jonathan Daniels Papers; editorial, *Raleigh News and Observer,* April 15, 1933; James Patterson and Anthony Badger described Ehringhaus as a moderate New Dealer, while George Tindall characterized North Carolina government in the 1930s as a "peculiar blend of progressive conservatism." See Patterson, *w Deal and the States,* pp. 147–48, 158; Tindall, *Emergence of the New South,* pp. 643–45; Badger, *North Carolina and the New Deal,* pp. 62–63.

3. Corbitt, ed., *Papers of Ehringhaus,* pp. ix–x, xxi, 251–52; Patterson, *New Deal and the States,* pp. 153, 158; interview of Jonathan Daniels by Eagles, March 9–11, 1977.

Gardner administration, the 1931–32 fiscal year ended with a $7 million deficit. Financial woes threatened the state's credit. In addition, by January 1933 40 counties and 125 cities and towns in North Carolina had defaulted on bond payments.[4]

One cause of the fiscal difficulty stemmed from the state's ambitious overborrowing during the 1920s to finance public services. After 1929 the state had to pay off the debts while revenues, particularly from property taxes, declined significantly. During the Gardner administration, a state property tax, to alleviate county property taxes, created an additional financial burden for the state. The wild real estate speculation in western North Carolina and its subsequent collapse in the late 1920s added another economic burden.[5]

"There is war—economic war—ahead," Ehringhaus declared on January 5, 1933, in his inaugural address before a few thousand in Raleigh's Memorial Auditorium. Calling it an "ugly picture" and "a burden that galls and grinds and terrifies us," he announced that the state's debts totaled $9.4 million. Ehringhaus confessed to his listeners that North Carolina was paying for the "delirious drama of development marking the past decade." He cited the staggering national deficit under the Hoover administration as a further cause for alarm.[6]

In his inaugural address, Ehringhaus presented his remedy. The budget must be balanced, he argued, "beyond cavil, doubt or disputation," and there must be a substantial cutback in spending. If the state did not economize and balance the budget, it would suffer "scrip payments, financial chaos and repudiation." Following through on a Democratic party campaign promise, Ehringhaus committed himself to immediate revaluation of property and the repeal of the fifteen-cent ad valorem property tax. He defended this reform as an "equity due the landowner," although he avoided the controversial issue of what tax should replace it. There would have to be a replacement tax, Ehringhaus told his audience, because removal of the property tax would mean a loss of $4 million a year in revenues. The governor also proposed other economy measures: the voluntary consolidation of counties with counties and counties with towns and cities; abandonment of all highway

4. Lent D. Upson to Hopkins, November 12, 1934, Governors' Papers (E); Hoover and Ratchford, *Economic Resources*, p. 219; Ratchford, "Financial Crisis," p. 43; Elmer L. Puryear, *Graham A. Barden: Conservative Carolina Congressman* (Buies Creek, N.C.: Campbell University Press, 1979), p. 8; Lefler and Newsome, *North Carolina*, p. 611.

5. Ratchford, "Financial Crisis," pp. 43–44; Hoover and Ratchford, *Economic Resources*, pp. 196, 219.

6. Corbitt, ed., *Papers of Ehringhaus*, pp. 3–6, 17.

construction for the current biennium; consolidation of the prison and highway departments; and abolishment of the executive counsel position and the governor's entertainment fund.[7]

Ehringhaus faced a difficult task in translating rhetoric into reality. Besides fiscal problems of declining revenues and balancing the budget, he had to deal with political opposition from the insurgent, liberal wing of the Democratic party. His very narrow primary victory over Richard T. Fountain forced Ehringhaus to incorporate some of the liberal points in his inaugural address. Small farmers in the east had backed revaluation of property for years, but the Gardner administration balked at it. In the 1931 General Assembly, Gardner forces passed the ad valorem property tax as the basis for state support of the six-month school term. With his calls for revaluation of property, repeal of the property tax, and retrenchment measures, Ehringhaus hoped to satisfy some of the insurgents' demands.[8]

The newly inaugurated governor also suffered from his close association with the conservative Gardner machine. His critics labeled him a puppet of the former governor. Max Gardner had endorsed and actively supported Ehringhaus in the previous year's campaign, and the association remained strong, especially in the east, where neither was very popular. Easterners perceived both as favoring the state's business interests, particularly the tobacco companies, over the farmers. Although he certainly wanted his policies continued under his successor and maintained a position of political leadership as the state's national committeeman, Gardner clearly intended to give Ehringhaus his independence in running state government. He pledged not to interfere directly or indirectly with appointments made by Ehringhaus. To create some distance from the new governor, and also at Ehringhaus's insistence, Gardner did not attend an inaugural reception for governors and former governors given by President Roosevelt. Through his general prestige, political allies, and contacts with business interests, Gardner continued to dominate the state Democratic party, but he did not attempt to run the day-to-day affairs of his successor's government.[9]

Before he left office, Gardner followed the advice of a special tax commission and submitted the state's next budget. He urged an across-the-board 15 percent decrease in expenditures. He favored repeal of the

7. Ibid., pp. 3–4, 6, 8–12, 14.

8. Puryear, *Democratic Party Dissension*, pp. 156, 158.

9. Gardner to W. G. Womble, August 13, 1934, Gardner Papers; Morrison, *Gardner*, pp. 134–35, 163; Puryear, *Democratic Party Dissension*, p. 156; Key, *Southern Politics*, p. 213.

ad valorem property tax and recommended that the legislature replace the revenue by increasing income, franchise, and license taxes by 20 percent and by diverting highway funds to the general fund. Gardner even suggested refinancing the state's general fund bond maturities. The governor, of course, based his last budget on the assumption that the state would continue to support a six-month public school term.[10]

In his January 16 budget report to the General Assembly, Ehringhaus clearly separated himself from his political mentor by rejecting several of Gardner's budget recommendations for the 1933–35 biennium. He rejected Gardner's proposals for replacing the property tax with a transfer of approximately $2 million from the highway fund to the general fund. Declining car and truck sales, along with an accompanying drop in revenues from gasoline taxes and license tag sales, endangered the highway fund without an additional drain on it, Ehringhaus believed. Also, the governor did not want to refinance the state's general fund bond maturities. Although the move would compensate for some of the revenue loss, he argued that it would accentuate the state's financial instability and further damage its credit reputation. Both men wanted the property tax replaced but disagreed over the substitutes for the unpopular tax. In January Ehringhaus did not wish to commit himself to any specific alternative tax. In his budget message he stressed that any new taxes must be only an "absolute necessity," and then only emergency and temporary measures. The legislature should earmark any new taxes, he suggested, for the specific service to be funded. The budget for the 1933–35 biennium contained a $12.7 million deficit, and since he offered no immediate replacement tax plan, most political observers believed a sales tax was inevitable.[11]

Ehringhaus agreed with his predecessor about the spending cuts. Only one day after his inauguration, the General Assembly had reduced the salaries of state officials by 15 percent in line with Gardner's tax commission's recommendations and consistent with Ehringhaus's inaugural address. In his budget message to the legislature, the new governor established economy in government, a reduction in general fund expenses, as the first fiscal priority. The proposed budget for 1933 of $82 million represented a substantial drop from the $106 million for 1931. State salaries, including those of public school teachers, were about two-thirds of what they had been before 1933. Public schools suffered a $2.5

10. Corbitt, ed., *Papers of Ehringhaus*, pp. 17–21; *Raleigh News and Observer*, April 23, 1933; Puryear, *Democratic Party Dissension*, p. 157.

11. Corbitt, ed., *Papers of Ehringhaus*, pp. 17–21; *Raleigh News and Observer*, January 17, 1933.

million cut and higher education a $350,000 reduction. Highway and agriculture departments did not escape budget cuts either. Ehringhaus also hoped to economize by reorganizing and consolidating several state government agencies. This aspect of retrenchment, however, faced political opposition because liberals had criticized the Gardner administration for such moves. Opponents of the Gardner organization complained that a more centralized government in Raleigh with more appointed rather than elected officials only strengthened the conservatives.[12]

Between his January 16 budget message to the General Assembly and the inauguration of Franklin D. Roosevelt on March 4, Governor Ehringhaus emphasized his economy and retrenchment proposals. With legislative appropriations expected to be down 25 percent from 1931, North Carolina had advanced "more than any governmental unit on the continent" in reducing expenditures, Ehringhaus boasted to Senator Bailey.[13] Otherwise, Ehringhaus remained fairly quiet about fiscal matters and measures for dealing with the severe depression until March 4. There were several reasons for his tentativeness. First, he wanted to wait and see what Roosevelt would do after taking office. Federal programs designed to ease the economic crisis certainly would affect the state's efforts along the same line. In addition, Ehringhaus had not made up his mind about how to replace the state property tax and balance the budget. If he had already decided on a tax proposal, he did not wish to announce it yet. Finally, the legislative committees needed a few weeks to work on his budget proposals. Ehringhaus did not plan his next move until Roosevelt became president.

The governor's first dramatic act in dealing with the economic crisis came two days after Roosevelt's inauguration. On March 6 he announced that in conjunction with the president's national bank holiday, he was closing all the banks in the state for three days. That same day both houses of the state legislature suspended the rules and passed bills granting special powers to the bank commissioner. The governor had pushed for the measures to expand his authority to declare bank holidays. They were sponsored by Senators R. Grady Rankin, Hayden Clement, James Sprunt Hill, and Robert M. Hanes (of Wachovia Bank). Senator John W. Hinsdale fought giving the bank commissioner "as much power as a Roman dictator." Later, when Roosevelt extended the

12. Corbitt, ed., *Papers of Ehringhaus*, pp. 17–21; *Raleigh News and Observer*, January 6, 17, 1933; Puryear, *Democratic Party Dissension*, pp. 158–59.

13. Ehringhaus to Bailey, April 3, 1933, Bailey Papers.

bank holiday one more day, Ehringhaus followed suit. Even though between October 1929 and March 1933, 215 banks failed in the state and the assets of the state's commercial banks in 1933 dropped to their lowest point since 1929, Ehringhaus announced that North Carolina's banking system remained basically sound. Ehringhaus was the last of the state governors to declare a holiday, and he acted only after the financial centers of New York and Chicago followed the president.[14]

One newspaper in the state called the bank holiday the "big event of a big year." Indeed, the suspension of the operation of more than three hundred banks and branches in the state inspired public confidence that political leadership in Washington and Raleigh would resolve the lingering economic problems. On March 14, banks in North Carolina began reopening; seven clearing banks in four cities were operating on an unrestricted basis. Gradually more banks reopened as government officials expressed confidence in their financial soundness. On March 29, Senator Bailey complained to the governor that more than one hundred banks remained closed in the state. By the end of the year, however, the state had two hundred sound banks. Roosevelt, with the cooperation of Ehringhaus, substantially improved North Carolina's banking situation. Over a period of ten months, the state went from no banks to over two hundred stable ones.[15]

After the General Assembly had been in session for more than two months, Governor Ehringhaus finally ended the suspense over his proposals to balance the state's budget. On the evening of March 13, before a joint session of the legislature, in a statewide radio address, he announced his support for a general sales tax as the most practical replacement of the ad valorem property tax and to eliminate the budget deficit. With this speech the governor shifted the emphasis from retrenchment to maintaining several state agencies. Ehringhaus believed that budget cutting had gone far enough. "But there is a point, even in economy, beyond which self-respecting government cannot go," he charged. He did not want to "crucify" the state's credit, schools, and highways. Coupled with the sales tax proposal, he requested that the legislature fund an eight-month school term out of part of the sales tax revenue. This two-month extension of the school year signaled a dramatic break from Gardner's budget proposal.[16]

14. Corbitt, ed., *Papers of Ehringhaus*, pp. 65, 67, 91; Gurney P. Hood, "Chartering of Banks," [n.d.], Governors' Papers (H); *Raleigh News and Observer*, March 7, December 31, 1933; Lefler and Newsome, *North Carolina*, p. 611.

15. Bailey to Ehringhaus, March 29, 1933, Bailey Papers; *Raleigh News and Observer*, March 14, December 31, 1933.

16. Corbitt, ed., *Papers of Ehringhaus*, pp. 25–27; *Raleigh News and Observer*, March 14, May 16, 1933.

The battle over the sales tax in the 1933 General Assembly climaxed a struggle that had been building since the 1920s. In adopting a sales tax, the state succumbed to pressures for property tax relief. The movement for sales taxes in several states began in the early 1920s when state governments expanded and enlarged their public services. Citizens complained that property carried a disproportionately high share of the tax burden. Homeowners, farmers, and corporations disliked property taxes, and after 1929 farmers and homeowners especially fought for relief. Frequent foreclosures and land sales to satisfy mortgages and delinquent taxes made the property tax more than just irritating. State government soon realized that property taxes failed to yield the necessary revenues as collections declined in the early 1930s because of tax delinquencies and difficulty selling property for tax defaults. In 1931 the legislature granted the largest property tax relief in the state's history by assuming responsibility for the schools and roads throughout the state. A huge property tax burden was lifted from counties and cities and financed through a small ad valorem state property tax after the legislature failed to agree on a sales or luxury tax. In his March 13 address, Ehringhaus sought more property tax relief through repeal of the ad valorem tax and more state support for education by instituting an eight-month school term.[17]

In 1925 politicians in North Carolina first proposed a sales tax on luxuries to support public schools. During the 1926 and 1928 campaigns the state Democratic platform included planks against the sales tax. In 1930 the party omitted the anti–sales tax provision from its platform. Advocates of sales and luxury taxes fought for them bitterly and unsuccessfully in the 1931 legislature. Merchants, particularly from the commercial and industrial piedmont, opposed any general sales tax, and tobacco companies and theater owners resisted efforts to levy a luxury tax. The General Assembly could not break the deadlock, and it enacted no sales tax.[18]

Mississippi's successful experiment with the sales tax since 1930 caught the attention of several states, including North Carolina. Governor Mike Connor saved his state from fiscal ruin through an austerity program coupled with a sales tax. He brought about a minor fiscal

17. Ehringhaus to Herbert Peele, May 5, 1933, Governors' Papers (E); Corbitt, ed., *Papers of Ehringhaus*, pp. 26–27; editorial, *Raleigh News and Observer*, May 13, 1933; Josephine L. Doughton, "Passage of the Sales Tax Law in North Carolina, 1931–1933" (M.A. thesis, University of North Carolina, Chapel Hill, 1949), pp. 18, 94–95; Hoover and Ratchford, *Economic Resources*, p. 199.

18. Doughton, "Sales Tax," pp. 18, 21, 94–95; *Raleigh News and Observer*, January 1, 17, 1933.

revolution by replacing the property tax with the sales tax and federal aid as the major sources of state revenue. Southern states generally favored a luxury sales tax on soft drinks, liquor, and tobacco, but North Carolina and Virginia naturally avoided taxing cigarettes. By 1933 eleven states had either adopted or were seriously considering the sales tax. Despite the regressive nature of the tax and the organized opposition of merchants, state governments quickly realized that it was a practical and steady source of revenue.[19]

From the beginning of its session in January, the General Assembly stressed economy. In the first three days it cut salaries for government officials 15 percent and passed a resolution calling for a balanced budget and the abolition of all unnecessary departments, commissions, and functions connected with state government. A desire for tax relief drove many to push for reductions. Speaker of the House Reginald Lee Harris, operator of several Roxboro cotton mills, pledged economy in government. "Taxation has become a form of capital punishment," he told his House Democratic caucus. The leader for retrenchment in the senate was Larry I. Moore of Craven County, chairman of the joint Committee on Reorganization. He and Robert M. Hanes introduced a bill to merge the highway and prison departments, arguing it would save $400,000 annually. After committee delays and extended debate, it passed by a wide margin. Moore and Hanes also proposed that a single Public Utilities Commissioner replace the Corporation Commission. Opponents such as John Sprunt Hill attacked it as too centralized and pointed out that one official, appointed by the governor, replacing three elected ones, gave too much power to the governor. The measure sailed through the House but overcame stiff Senate opposition only after amendments. Legislators also had their minds on fiscal prudence in Washington, passing resolutions commending Roosevelt and Congress for the economy program and one in the House requesting a balanced budget without a tax increase. The only other New Deal measure it endorsed that session was the Tennessee Valley Authority (TVA).[20]

The major fiscal issue before the General Assembly was a sales tax to support public schools and to give property tax relief, or no sales tax,

19. Tate, "Easing the Burden," pp. iii–iv; Hoover and Ratchford, *Economic Resources*, p. 201; Tindall, *Emergence of the New South*, pp. 368–69; Billington, *Political South*, p. 64.

20. *Raleigh News and Observer*, January 1, 4, 5, 6, 7, 22, 1933; Puryear, *Democratic Party Dissension*, pp. 158, 160–63; *Journal of the House of Representatives of the General Assembly of the State of North Carolina*, Session 1933, pp. 106, 413, 501–2; *Journal of the Senate of the General Assembly of the State of North Carolina*, Session 1933, pp. 318–19, 446.

which would require greater economy in government. The sales tax had no champion in the legislature for the first two and a half months and was opposed by representatives Tam C. Bowie of rural Ashe County, a former Speaker, looking "plump and prosperous," according to one reporter, and R. Gregg Cherry from industrial Gaston County. For Bowie and Cherry the priority was an appropriations bill, with cuts that would make the sales tax unnecessary. Their substitute appropriations bill, at odds with the wishes of committee chairman Harriss Newman, called for $6 million less in expenditures, which meant a six-month school term. On March 16, the "economy bloc" triumphed when the House adopted the Bowie-Cherry bill by a vote of fifty-three to forty-three. According to Speaker Harris, debate over spending produced the "rawest business he had ever observed in the legislature." W. Kerr Scott, master of the state Grange, and speakers from the state Merchants' Association and the North Carolina Economy League called for more economy in government if necessary at a mass meeting in Raleigh's Memorial Auditorium with about fifteen hundred people present, including several state legislators. Scott also argued against any new taxes, especially a sales tax.[21]

That vote proved to be the high point for retrenchment. Earlier, college presidents had lobbied hard against cuts for higher education, and Graham A. Barden and Thomas O'Berry pressed their cause in the House. In addition, proponents of the eight-month school term pushed for more funds. "When a man can't legislate his mind without being written to, telegraphed to, and sworn at by people who don't know the condition of the state, things are coming to a damn poor pass in North Carolina," exclaimed Cherry, harried by education lobbyists. Edwin B. Jeffress, highway commission chairman, pleaded against the diversion of highway funds, which was likely if there were a budget deficit. With Barden and Thomas Turner leading the fight for Harriss Newman, who had been injured in an auto accident, administration forces on March 21 routed the Cherry-Bowie bloc by restoring funds for public schools with a fifty-eight-to-forty-three vote. Eventually, the senate increased school appropriations to $16 million annually, enough to fund an eight-month school term, and the conference committee approved it. The House endorsed the final appropriations bill fifty-one to forty and the Senate by thirty-four to nine.[22]

21. *Raleigh News and Observer,* March 3, 16, 17, 18, 19, 20, 1933; *North Carolina House Journal,* 1933, pp. 55, 341, 421, 431; Puryear, *Democratic Party Dissension,* pp. 168, 171.

22. *North Carolina House Journal,* 1933, pp. 592–99; *North Carolina Senate Journal,* 1933, p. 509; *Raleigh News and Observer,* March 21, 22, 1933, cited in Puryear, *Democratic Party Dissension,* p. 172, see also pp. 166–67, 172–73.

Attention then shifted to the revenue bill. Senator Hayden Clement proposed a manufacturing or production tax, and Senator John W. Hinsdale, Jr., along with Representative Harriss Newman, suggested a luxury tax to fund schools. Both bills failed because powerful forces in the state did not want such taxes. Senator Robert M. Hanes, president of Wachovia Bank, largest bank in the state, and a good friend of tobacco interests, fought the luxury tax. Momentum for the sales tax increased as the most acceptable way to balance the budget. Key lawmakers switched to its support. For example, Senators Capus M. Waynick and R. Grady Rankin had opposed it in the 1931 session. In 1933 Rankin, a textile manufacturer, chaired the Senate Finance Committee and managed the bill in that chamber. Rufus A. Doughton, brother of the congressman and House Finance Committee chairman, steered it through greater opposition. Tam C. Bowie left his sickbed to lead the House fight against the sales tax. The joint Finance Committee settled on a 3 percent general sales tax, and Bowie scored a temporary victory when his amendment to delete it from the revenue bill carried fifty-nine to forty-six. In a critical development, a special finance subcommittee chaired by Cherry reconsidered the bill and recommended a 2 percent sales tax. Cherry, now the chief advocate for the sales tax, argued that it was the only solution. The 2 percent sales tax passed the House fifty-one to forty-nine. The Senate by a one-vote margin increased the rate to 3 percent and exempted basic foods, and its version survived in conference. On May 8, the House approved it fifty-three to forty-one, and the Senate three days later agreed by a twenty-six-to-eleven margin.[23]

After a 132-day session, the third longest in the state's history of biennial sessions, the 1933 General Assembly passed a 3 percent general sales tax, which exempted meat, flour, meal, sugar, salt, molasses, coffee, and milk. This levy replaced the 15 percent ad valorem property tax and was to take effect July 1, 1933. Few legislators really wanted a sales tax, but this General Assembly, with only 49 members of the 170 returning from the 1931 session, viewed it as the most practical solution. Representative James S. Massenburg of Polk County expressed mixed feelings after voting for the revenue bill. "It is my firm belief that education and democracy are dependent one upon the other," and he believed the sales tax was the only alternative. "I subrogated my personal opinion" and voted for the "unfair and unjust" bill, he added. Senator William K. Boggan of Anson County concluded that the "unnec-

23. *North Carolina House Journal*, 1933, pp. 610, 649, 661, 675, 700, 867–68; *North Carolina Senate Journal*, 1933, pp. 580–81, 743; *Raleigh News and Observer*, February 4, 13, April 28, 1933; Puryear, *Democratic Party Dissension*, pp. 165–70, 173–76.

essary and unjust burden" on the people and the merchants violated the principles of the Democratic party and Thomas Jefferson, and he did not vote for it. The sales tax finally passed for several reasons. Proponents of the measure linked it with support for the eight-month school term and made opponents appear to favor further retrenchment, even in education. This strategy for passing the tax developed after the first month of the session, and in his March 13 speech Ehringhaus reinforced it. The public wanted lower local property taxes, and the state's assuming more financial responsibility for schools through the sales tax would achieve that goal.[24]

In the end, the merchants lost the battle of the interest groups when the legislature rejected other alternatives. Industrial leaders, insurance men, and businessmen fought any increases in corporation taxes. Some of those same groups vigorously resisted the luxury tax. Supporters of public and higher education did not want further retrenchment, the only other option if the legislature did not find a new source of revenue. Despite the lobbying pressures of thousands of merchants, the lawmakers passed North Carolina's first sales tax.[25]

Governor Ehringhaus and the other sales tax proponents had to persuade the legislature and a skeptical general public of the need for the highest sales tax in the country. Ehringhaus had an additional burden because in the 1932 campaign he had opposed such a tax. To counter the charge of opportunism, Ehringhaus reminded his critics that in 1932 he had never completely opposed the tax but supported it only as a last resort to preserve the credit of the state during the emergency. He cited the universal application of the tax and claimed that it had some relationship to ability to pay because spending was tied to income. Ehringhaus's best argument for his fiscal policies was the reduction in property taxes and the support for public education that accompanied the sales tax. At the close of the General Assembly in May 1933, with his popularity at its lowest, only one major state newspaper defended Ehringhaus. The *Greensboro Daily News*, owned by the chairman of the State Highway Commission, declared that corporations and property could no longer bear the tax burden, and the legislature had been forced to find a new way. Common people, the editor believed, might find the sales tax as tolerable as any other.[26]

24. *Raleigh News and Observer*, January 1, February 6, April 10, May 16, 1933; Puryear, *Democratic Party Dissension*, pp. 166–67, 169; *North Carolina House Journal*, 1933, pp. 701–2; *North Carolina Senate Journal*, 1933, pp. 631–32.

25. *Raleigh News and Observer*, February 13, 1933; Lefler and Newsome, *North Carolina*, pp. 612–13.

26. Ehringhaus to Herbert Peele, April 20, May 5, 1933, Governors' Papers (E); Corbitt,

Liberals in the state attacked the sales tax for shifting the tax burden from the corporations to the masses. Santford Martin, editor of the *Winston-Salem Journal*, complained that Raleigh and Washington were going in opposite directions. Roosevelt enhanced democracy under the New Deal, but Ehringhaus moved backward with the "New Oppression." Martin labeled the legislature the most reactionary of this generation; instead of granting relief for the poor, the lawmakers placed a new tax burden on them. The *Burlington Daily Times-News* described the sales tax as "blood money" being squeezed out of the forgotten men, the working class in the state.[27]

Josephus and Jonathan Daniels opposed the sales tax as too regressive. In *News and Observer* editorials they urged the legislature "to get the money where the money is." They advocated new sources of revenue such as a production tax on power companies similar to South Carolina's, but both realized that the utilities had too much influence in the state for that to happen. The Danielses promoted the luxury tax on such nonessentials as soft drinks, tobacco, and theater tickets as the most viable alternative to the general sales tax in support of the eight-month school term. Their editorials reminded readers that although the removal of the property tax reduced the burden for individuals, it also eased the tax bite for corporations. Nor did they view the sales tax as an emergency, temporary measure but knew it represented a long-term shift from property taxes. Opposition to this tax united liberals in North Carolina as no other issue could, and these New Dealers gained strength for future battles against the state's conservatives.[28]

The sales tax was also resisted by those who argued for further retrenchment as a solution to the state's fiscal problems. The *Charlotte Observer* blamed the legislature for not economizing sufficiently. Voters sent the legislators to Raleigh to spend much less, the editor insisted, and if they had kept faith with the voters the sales tax would not have been necessary. The *Observer* questioned the common assumption that small farmers would fare better under the sales tax than with the previous property taxes. Farm owners, key proponents of the property tax relief that was tied closely to the sales tax, paid only about 11 percent

ed., *Papers of Ehringhaus*, pp. 25–27, 30; *Raleigh News and Observer*, December 31, 1933; editorial *Greensboro Daily News*, May 13, 1933.

27. Editorial, *Winston-Salem Journal and Sentinel*, May 14, 1933; editorial, newspaper clipping, *Burlington Daily Times-News*, March 22, 1933, Governors' Papers (E); Puryear, *Democratic Party Dissension*, p. 176.

28. Josephus Daniels to FDR, June 1, 1933, Box 95, Josephus Daniels Papers; Josephus Daniels to Ehringhaus, March 11, 1933, Governors' Papers (E); editorials, *Raleigh News and Observer*, February 19, May 13, 1933.

of the state's tax bill under previous laws; individual property holders in cities paid about 24 percent; and corporate property, 33.8 percent. The editor suggested that, ironically, the sales tax would mean that farmers would pay a larger share of taxes. Spokesmen in the piedmont also pointed out that their section, with its greater population and heavier concentration of business and industry, would pay a larger portion of the sales tax to support the poorer, more agricultural east. Some resented the fact that through the sales tax the piedmont would help finance an eight-month school term for the eastern counties.[29]

The sales tax proved to be a more than adequate source of revenue and thus vindicated Governor Ehringhaus's approach to the state's financial crisis. It became the largest source of revenue for the general fund and helped the state balance its budget. By the end of the 1933–34 fiscal year, the state had collected $6 million in sales taxes, 26.4 percent of its revenue. In 1935 it yielded 29.9 percent. Local governments' share of the total tax burden dropped almost 25 percent, from 65.3 percent in 1933 to 43.8 percent by 1934. Revaluation of property alone reduced local property tax yields by a third. Ehringhaus also reported in 1934 that total state spending declined by a third over the previous fiscal year. As the key element in the state's financial recovery, the sales tax became easier to defend. The governor pointed out that even the federal government, with the AAA processing taxes, sought revenues in a way similar to the sales tax. North Carolina only did on the state level, he argued, what Washington did on the national level. By 1935, with its reputation as a practical source of revenue, sales taxes had been adopted by twenty-one states.[30]

The General Assembly of 1933 balanced the budget for the 1933–35 biennium by approving Ehringhaus's major financial recommendations: retrenchment, repeal of the property tax, revaluation of property, enactment of the sales tax, and an increase in income taxes. The state achieved fiscal stability in part by reducing expenditures for the various state agencies, except for public schools, and by leaving the responsibility of relief to the federal government. While the budget fell from $107 million in 1931 to $83 million in 1933, Ehringhaus boasted that North Carolina's government operating expense was one of the three lowest in the nation. As recently as 1931, the state had ranked forty-first in per capita cost of

29. Editorials, *Charlotte Observer,* May 7, 11, 13, 1933; Doughton, "Sales Tax," p. 71.

30. Corbitt, ed., *Papers of Ehringhaus*, pp. 94, 147–48; Doughton, "Sales Tax," p. 93; Patterson, *New Deal and the States*, p. 97; Lefler and Newsome, *North Carolina*, pp. 612–13.

government, and the 1933 budget moved the state even closer to forty-eighth.[31]

Governor Ehringhaus defended the austerity of state government by reminding critics of the $150 million North Carolina contributed annually to the federal government in taxes. Of the state's tax dollars, 76 percent went to the federal treasury; the rest was divided equally between state and local governments. North Carolina ranked first in per capita payment of federal taxes. Though the payment of high federal cigarette taxes by the state's tobacco companies was the reason behind the statistics, Ehringhaus frequently cited the fact as a defense for the state's declining expenditures and a reason why the national government should spend more in the state. In 1934 he pointed out that North Carolina ranked last in per capita receipts from Washington for public works and relief.[32]

Relief and labor received scant attention from the legislature. The 1933–35 budget for the State Board of Public Welfare clearly revealed the fiscally conservative mood of the legislators. For the previous biennium, the state appropriated about $40,000 annually for the department's Mothers' Aid program, but reduced the amount to $29,000 annually for 1933–35. Since the state provided no matching funds for federal relief activity and little money for its own welfare department, North Carolina left the problem of the poor and unemployed to the Federal Emergency Relief Administration. Counties also decreased their relief expenditures from $1.9 million in 1933 to $48,000 in 1935, although they continued to match state appropriations for the Mothers' Aid program. A joint resolution, requesting the state's congressional delegation to oppose Hugo Black's bill for a five-day week, six-hour day, passed the House, but it died in the Senate. A bill requiring children under sixteen to complete the sixth grade before working failed to pass in either chamber. Ehringhaus rejected as "altogether unworkable" a minimum wage law for women and minors that President Roosevelt recommended to the states. He did not even study the measure, and the legislature never considered it. Jonathan Daniels complained that the General Assembly, by approving the sale of beer, enacted the New Deal for the beer drinker but not for the forgotten man.[33]

31. Corbitt, ed., *Papers of Ehringhaus*, p. 138; Lent D. Upson to Hopkins, November 12, 1934, Governors' Papers (E); *Raleigh News and Observer*, May 16, 1933.

32. Corbitt, ed., *Papers of Ehringhaus*, pp. 95, 173–74.

33. North Carolina State Board of Charities and Public Welfare, *Biennial Report, 1932–1934*, p. 15, *Biennial Report, 1934–1936*, p. 14; Kirk, Cutler, and Morse, eds., *Emergency Relief in North Carolina*, p. 47; Corbitt, ed., *Papers of Ehringhaus*, p. 342; editorial, *Raleigh News and Observer*, April 15, 1933; *North Carolina House Journal*, 1933, pp. 171, 227, 303, 572–73.

North Carolina did little road building during the 1933–35 biennium. Shifting the emphasis to maintenance of the state's fifty-eight thousand miles of roads, the 1933 General Assembly limited the State Highway Commission's spending for construction to $190,000 annually and appropriated $6.9 million for maintenance. Before the state assumed control of all county roads in 1931, counties alone had spent about $9 million yearly on maintenance. Overall expenditures for road construction in the state increased, however, from $4.6 million in 1932–33 to $7.5 million for 1934–35 because of federal funds. In 1934 the Public Works Administration committed $14.3 million to road construction in North Carolina. With the state limiting construction and reducing maintenance funds, the State Highway Commission ended the 1933–35 biennium, ironically, with an $11.9 million surplus. Revenues from license tags and gasoline taxes exceeded the General Assembly's expectations. Fortunately, the 1933 legislature had authorized the diversion of $1 million from the highway department to the general fund to balance the state's budget. During the biennium the transfer became necessary.[34]

By establishing a statewide eight-month school term, the 1933 legislature enlarged the state's financial responsibility for public education, and Ehringhaus boasted of a "new deal in education."[35] Though designed to reduce local property taxes and to "sell" the new sales tax, the move still meant increased spending. The measure had been something of a crusade for Senator Angus D. MacLean, chairman of the Education Committee. It passed easily in the Senate thirty-three to eleven and in the House sixty-three to twenty-three. Some legislators complained that it gave the state too much power and that communities should control school and tax matters. Former governor Gardner, addressing the Raleigh Chamber of Commerce in January 1934, declared that schools and colleges, victimized by cuts during the Depression, needed more funds. He predicted "an educational and cultural New Deal in North Carolina."[36] To finance the public schools, the state spent sixty-four cents out of every tax dollar, not counting the taxes that funded the highway program. For 1933–35 the legislature allocated $16 million annually to operate the schools for eight months. Though the state cut teachers' salaries, along with those of all state employees, it significantly enlarged its role in public education.[37]

34. North Carolina State Highway and Public Works Commission, *Biennial Report, 1933–1934*, pp. 5, 8–9, 68, 111, *Biennial Report, 1935–1936*, foreword, p. 97.

35. Corbitt, ed., *Papers of Ehringhaus*, pp. 99–100.

36. Newspaper clipping, *Raleigh News and Observer*, January 27, 1934, Gardner Papers; *North Carolina House Journal*, 1933, pp. 914–16; *North Carolina Senate Journal*, 1933, pp. 109, 672.

37. Corbitt, ed., *Papers of Ehringhaus*, p. 139; Lefler, ed., *North Carolina History*, p. 469.

The legislature of 1933 wrestled with more than taxes and budget cuts. Issues such as prohibition and a new constitution, though controversial, did not split the state along pro– or anti–New Deal lines. On the question of repeal, the legislature provided for a November 7, 1933, referendum to decide whether to call a state constitutional convention. Gardner argued that Roosevelt's election made repeal inevitable, and he urged Democrats not to make it a partisan issue. Ehringhaus, though personally "dry," did not take an official position, nor did the state party chairman J. Wallace Winborne. Liberals Josephus Daniels and Santford Martin joined conservatives Cameron Morrison and Clyde Hoey in the campaign against repeal, while conservatives Josiah Bailey and New Dealer Robert Reynolds urged repeal. In November 1933 prohibition forces surprisingly won by more than two to one when voters rejected the call for a state constitutional convention. One month later, however, enough states had ratified the Twenty-first Amendment. Though not a rejection of Roosevelt or the New Deal, the strong opposition to repeal proved that state prohibition would remain for the time being, though national prohibition had ended.[38]

Another issue that cut across ideological lines was the proposed referendum in November 1934 on a new state constitution. The new constitution, a product of the Gardner administration, gave the governor veto as well as additional appointive powers and called for more legislative control over local governments. Conservatives and liberals alike attacked it as further centralization in Raleigh. Richard Fountain and Dennis Brummitt joined erstwhile enemies Josiah Bailey and Cameron Morrison in opposition. Gardner accused opponents, especially New Deal liberals, of hypocrisy. "Roosevelt had done more to abolish state lines, state rights and invade the functions of state government, than I ever thought of proposing for county government in North Carolina," Gardner complained to a friend. Support from Ehringhaus and liberals Clarence Poe and Frank Porter Graham could not overcome the opposition. The state supreme court's invalidation of the referendum on the grounds that the vote should have occurred a year earlier spared the Gardner organization defeat at the polls, but Gard-

38. Daniel Jay Whitener, *Prohibition in North Carolina, 1715–1945* (Chapel Hill: University of North Carolina Press, 1946), pp. 198–206; Puryear, *Democratic Party Dissension*, pp. 164–65, 181; *Raleigh News and Observer*, December 31, 1933; Gardner to J. Wallace Winborne, June 19, 1933, to P. Cleveland Gardner, October 11, 1933, Gardner Papers; Corbitt, ed., *Papers of Ehringhaus*, pp. 282–83; Bailey to James Farley, November 9, 1933, Bailey Papers; Pleasants, "Robert Reynolds," pp. 194–95.

ner failed to increase the power of state government through a new constitution.[39]

Although the new constitution never reached the voters, the General Assembly of 1933 passed Ehringhaus's proposals for a limited reorganization of state government despite considerable opposition. The governor cited the need for economy, but political opponents feared additional appointive powers and a more centralized state government would strengthen Ehringhaus and the conservative wing of the party. Nonetheless, the lawmakers merged the state's highway and prison departments and changed the Corporation Commission, with three elected members, to a single, appointed public utilities commissioner. After the legislature adjourned, critics charged Ehringhaus with politicizing the highway and revenue departments with his appointments.[40]

In the 1934 off-year elections the state's Democrats rallied behind the New Deal in the first election of General Assembly members since the inauguration of Roosevelt. North Carolina's Democratic party platform endorsed the New Deal recovery program and recommended studies of unemployment insurance and old-age pensions but did not mention the sales tax, an issue in practically all local legislative races. Opponents emphasized that the sales tax was contrary to the New Deal philosophy. Results in the elections encouraged those who wished to repeal the sales tax; the 107 rookie lawmakers out of the 170 members of the General Assembly might be more willing than veterans to change the course of state government.[41]

In the 1934 congressional elections Harold Cooley's victory strengthened the New Deal forces in the state. Most interest focused on that eastern fourth district seat left vacant by Edward Pou's death. Five Democrats sought to replace the late chairman of the House Rules Committee, but Cooley, a young lawyer from Nashville, won the nomination in the first primary. Facing George Ross Pou, the late congressman's son and ally of the Gardner organization, Cooley exploited

39. Bailey to I. T. Valentine, September 14, 1934, Bailey Papers; Gardner to R. R. Clark, August 16, 1934, Edwin Gill to Gardner, August 21, 1934, Gardner Papers; Puryear, *Democratic Party Dissension*, pp. 163, 182–84.

40. Newspaper clipping, *Raleigh News and Observer*, December 31, 1933, Governors' Papers (E); Puryear, *Democratic Party Dissension*, pp. 161–63; Lefler and Newsome, *North Carolina*, p. 612.

41. Editorial, newspaper clipping, *Winston-Salem Journal*, June 23, 1934, Governors' Papers (E); H. M. London, ed., *North Carolina Manual, 1935* (Raleigh: State of North Carolina, 1935), pp. 74–75; editorial, *Raleigh News and Observer*, June 1, 2, 1934, January 6, 1935.

New Deal issues and antimachine sentiments. Fountain forces helped Cooley, and after the victory Jonathan Daniels described him as a "new man" whose liberal policies followed Roosevelt's New Deal. Voters returned all incumbents, except Charles Abernethy in the eastern third district. In that race, in which Graham Barden beat Abernethy, the congressman's ill health, not the New Deal, was the issue.[42]

By 1935 Ehringhaus and the General Assembly, facing a more stable fiscal situation, were more generous; rising tobacco and cotton prices brought improvement to the state's economy, and general revenue collections for the biennium ran half a million dollars ahead of the previous legislature's expectations. Consequently, in his January 10 biennial message to the General Assembly, Ehringhaus did not mention the sales tax but instead outlined a social program that Jonathan Daniels called a "New Deal for North Carolina." New Dealers in the state, like Daniels, believed that the governor in this speech followed the pattern of Roosevelt in going from a preoccupation with recovery and relief to a focus on reform and long-term change. He urged increased appropriations for schools, especially to improve teachers' salaries and to initiate a program of textbook rentals. After stalling road building for two years, he recommended funds for highway construction to match the federal grants and requested an end to the diversion of highway funds for other state expenditures. Ehringhaus also asked the legislature to ratify the national Child Labor Amendment, pass an unemployment insurance plan consistent with federal laws, and extend the workmen's compensation law to cover occupational diseases as well as accidents.[43]

Four days after his progressive proposals to the legislature, however, Governor Ehringhaus dashed the hopes of sales tax opponents with his budget requests for the 1935–37 biennium. He wanted not only to continue the sales tax but also to eliminate the exemptions on necessities. If this were done, he argued, and business conditions continued to improve, the state would have additional revenue without any new taxes. Extra revenue would pay for the salary increases for teachers and other state employees, Ehringhaus reminded the lawmakers. Since its enactment in 1933 the sales tax produced about 30 percent of general fund revenues, therefore, the governor insisted that the tax be con-

42. T. L. Bland to Gardner, May 24, 1934, Gardner Papers; *Raleigh News and Observer*, May 27, 28, June 3, 1934, editorial, June 5, 1934; Puryear, *Barden*, p. 14; Badger, "North Carolina and the New Deal," pp. 99, 102.

43. Corbitt, ed., *Papers of Ehringhaus*, pp. 40–48; Lefler, ed., *North Carolina History*, p. 458; editorial, *Raleigh News and Observer*, January 11, July 27, 1935.

tinued. Otherwise, the legislature must find another revenue source, he contended.[44]

Most political observers believed that the General Assembly would pass the governor's sales tax package. In the past two years, respect for Ehringhaus had increased significantly since the low point in his popularity just after the adjournment of the 1933 legislature. During the 1933–35 biennium, his economic policies of retrenchment, reorganization, revaluation of real estate, and repeal of the state property tax produced a budget surplus. The state's total tax burden reached a new low in the 1933–34 fiscal year. Legislators, however, realized that budget cutting could not go on forever and that the state needed more money for schools, teachers, and its various agencies. Constituents wrote fewer letters to the lawmakers protesting the sales tax. Merchants, especially from some chain stores, did not resist as strongly as in 1933 because the sales tax eased their property taxes. Corporations did not want the sales tax repealed, for they would likely pay more under any alternate plan.[45]

Nonetheless, liberals in North Carolina fought a vigorous, though losing, battle against the sales tax. A few New Deal newspaper editors, along with a couple of legislators, led the campaign during the 1935 General Assembly. The liberals experienced a serious setback in early 1935 with the death of Attorney General Dennis Brummitt, influential opponent of the sales tax and generally believed to be the 1936 insurgents' choice for governor. Josephus Daniels continued his fight against the tax he called as "iniquitous as the old Republican tariff." Writing from Mexico City to his son Jonathan in Raleigh, Daniels complained, "Ehringhaus seems to think that it is more important to balance the budget, saying his prayers to the Great God Boodgit, than to pay teachers living salaries and give children proper educational facilities." Once Ehringhaus announced his sales tax proposal, the *News and Observer*, which earlier praised his program as a "forward-looking New Deal," termed it a "program for standing still." Both Danielses argued that the state's economic crisis had subsided and it should get revenue "where the money is." They believed, however, that Ehringhaus was too closely associated with the business interests to seek higher corporation taxes. The *News and Observer* pointed out that corporations benefited most from the shift to sales taxes. Since the enactment of the tax, corporations had paid 6.8 percent less taxes, the newspaper claimed.[46]

44. Corbitt, ed., *Papers of Ehringhaus*, pp. 52–54.
45. Ibid., pp. 35–39; *Raleigh News and Observer*, January 6, February 4, 1935.
46. Josephus Daniels to Jonathan Daniels, January 14, April 8, 1935, Box 2, Jonathan

Jonathan Daniels conferred with Ralph W. McDonald, the leader in the North Carolina House of the anti–sales tax forces, on legislative strategy and a substitute for the sales tax. After the first month of the General Assembly, McDonald, a college professor and according to one critic "a rank amateur in the political game," presented an alternate plan to the Finance Committee. The plan called for four new taxes to raise $12 million: a 6 percent tax on stock dividends; increased franchise taxes on corporations, including utilities; a boost in the tax on insurance premiums; and new occupational taxes on individuals earning over $1,000 on businesses, on chain theaters, and on chain service stations. In the committee hearings, McDonald angered chairman Gregg Cherry by charging that a few men controlled the legislature and that corporations dominated state government. McDonald warned that there would be a "political revolution" if the legislature did not eliminate the sales tax. Privately, he expressed doubts to Santford Martin, liberal editor of the *Winston-Salem Journal.* It appeared that three-fourths of the people favored the sales tax, McDonald wrote to Martin, but opposition lay under the surface. McDonald believed that leading newspapers performed a valuable service in keeping the issue before the people.[47]

In the House, Willie Lee Lumpkin, a small-town lawyer, whom one observer labeled a "left-winger from Louisburg," and in the Senate, Lee L. Gravely of Nash, Appropriations Committee chairman, joined with McDonald in opposing the sales tax. Both sides waged what Lumpkin termed a "knock down and drag out fight." Corporate interests rallied against McDonald's plan. In hearings before the joint Finance Committee, Norman Cocke, vice-president of Duke Power, testified that it would mean $311,000 more in taxes for his utility. Grady Rankin, former Senate Finance Committee chairman, a textile manufacturer, now with Duke Power, explained that the taxes would hamper the state's industrial growth. Officials from Wachovia Bank and Carolina Power and Light Company, along with those from insurance, theater, and telephone interests, attacked the measure. Earlier before the Finance Committee, tobacco company representatives fought increased corporate taxes. Viewing it as an alternative to the sales tax, the state Merchants' Association supported it.[48]

In late February, McDonald and Lumpkin lost in the committee and

Daniels Papers; editorial, *Raleigh News and Observer,* January 16, February 5, 1935.

47. Josephus Daniels to Santford Martin, January 14, 1935, Ralph McDonald to Martin, January 21, 1935, Box 2, Martin Papers; *Raleigh News and Observer,* February 13, 23, March 4, 1935.

48. *Raleigh News and Observer,* January 15, 30, February 13, 20, 22, March 18, 1935.

pledged to carry the fight to the floor. Key players in the defeat were House Finance Committee chairman Gregg Cherry of Gaston County and Senate Finance Committee chairman Harriss Newman of New Hanover County. Both championed the sales tax. House Speaker R. Grady Johnson of Pender County, a thirty-nine-year-old lawyer who favored the sales tax, had won easily for Speaker in a race in which the sales tax was not an issue. He deferred to Cherry. The joint Finance Committee in early March voted against reducing the sales tax rate from 3 percent to 2 percent, further dashing the hopes of opponents of the sales tax. Ehringhaus met a few days later with finance and appropriations chairmen from both chambers to balance revenue and spending bills. Two weeks later, in a surprise, the House voted to increase business taxes so as to lower the sales tax, now the aim of sales tax opponents in lieu of replacing it. The following day, March 21, however, with Cherry's leadership and the lobbying of oil, telephone, and power companies, the House reversed itself and routed this reprise of the McDonald plan. McDonald and Lumpkin had held the momentum for only a couple of days before their fortunes changed. For example, their amendment to increase the franchise tax on insurance companies failed sixty-six to forty-four.[49]

The issue remained volatile, nonetheless, for several weeks as both houses reversed positions frequently on the sales tax rate. On March 22, Ransom L. Carr offered an amendment to reduce the sales tax to 2 percent, and Cherry's forces triumphed, defeating it fifty-one to forty-three. That same day an amendment to exempt food lost by fifty-six to forty-one. A 3 percent rate with no food exemptions passed the second reading on a Saturday, fifty-five to twelve. Samuel E. Douglass, voting no, warned that "this House is setting a legislative incubator that will hatch the strongest Republican party seen in this state since the Civil War."[50]

The following Monday, after legislators returned from a weekend of listening to constituents, they voted fifty-two to forty-four for an amendment by William W. "Cap" Eagles and Ransom L. Carr to lower the tax to 2 percent. The next day, March 26, Ernest A. Gardner moved to reconsider the previous day's action, and the motion carried sixty-two to forty-three. Then the House defeated the Eagles-Carr amendment fifty-seven to forty-three. The revenue bill passed easily on its third reading.

49. Ibid., January 9, 15, February 27, March 2, 4, 7, 21, 22, 1935; *Journal of the House of Representatives of the General Assembly of the State of North Carolina*, Session 1935, pp. 355–56, 360; Puryear, *Democratic Party Dissension*, p. 190.

50. *North Carolina House Journal*, 1935, pp. 374–75, 379–80; Puryear, *Democratic Party Dissension*, p. 191.

McDonald voted "present," declaring that the "respect which I have for the clean, hard fight which they have made, prevents my voting 'no'." Nonetheless, he termed the sales tax the "most unfair tax" and insisted that reducing it was the least the legislature could have done. Some who voted for it cited the need for revenue, especially for schools, but still they protested the 3 percent rate and the tax on food.[51]

In the Senate, Harriss Newman threatened to fight Lee Gravely's appropriations bill if Gravely did not cease battling his sales tax bill. Newman won when the Senate easily defeated a sales tax reduction to 2 percent, but Gravely succeeded when the Senate retained the exemptions for food by a twenty-two-to-eighteen vote. The conference report eliminated all the exemptions for the 3 percent sales tax, and that version passed the Senate on the third reading twenty-seven to fifteen. Some insurgents acceded to the pressure for additional revenues for education. After conditions were placed on the diversion of funds from the highway department, the House approved the revenue bill on the third reading fifty-seven to twelve. Not only did opponents of the sales tax fail, but an effort by Senator John Sprunt Hill and Representative Victor S. Bryant, both "wets," to legalize liquor and tax it instead of food came to naught.[52]

Debate among the legislators had been vigorous. Cherry referred to the opposition plan as "hocus pocus." Senator John Sprunt Hill of Durham, debating against reducing the sales tax, declared that "the New Deal has got us in a blind alley in North Carolina. . . . There are no more rich people left in the state [to tax]. . . . They are coming down to fat back pretty soon." On the other side Lumpkin exclaimed that "there's a group in this House which won't accept a thing under God's shining sun but the 3 percent sales tax." Senator Brock Hurley of Montgomery County pointed out that passing the 3 percent sales tax "would be saying to the New Deal 'you have failed. Things are not better, they're worse.'" In the end corporate interests triumphed over merchants, farmers, and labor, the groups most opposed to the sales tax.[53]

In the major fight of the 1935 General Assembly, administration forces kept the sales tax and expanded it to include necessities. In retrospect,

51. *North Carolina House Journal*, 1935, pp. 385, 392–95; Puryear, *Democratic Party Dissension*, pp. 191–92.

52. *North Carolina House Journal*, 1935, pp. 656, 687, 698; *Journal of the Senate of the General Assembly of the State of North Carolina*, Session 1935, pp. 348, 383, 413–14, 424–25, 434–35, 502, 527; Puryear, *Democratic Party Dissension*, pp. 192–97.

53. *Raleigh News and Observer*, January 25, 30, 31, March 26, 27, April 11, 12, May 3, 1935.

the McDonald plan hit industry and business too hard, and their lobbyists responded. Legislators had questions about the fairness of the McDonald proposals, too, because income and franchise taxes on corporations in North Carolina were as high as levied by any state except Oregon. Linking it to public school funding, according to Gregg Cherry, made the sales tax "smell sweeter." The legislature had made the sales tax a permanent source of revenue for the general fund. In 1935 it yielded 31 percent, while income, franchise, and license taxes provided 56 percent.[54]

Although the 1935 legislature expanded the sales tax to necessities, it spent $6 million over Ehringhaus's recommendations. Unlike 1933, the appropriations bill passed with little difficulty. Increasing revenues, primarily from the sales tax, permitted more generous funding for state agencies. General fund appropriations for the 1935–37 biennium amounted to $64.6 million, the largest general fund allocation in the history of the state. The General Assembly authorized $2.9 million annually, matched by federal grants, for highway construction. State employees received a 20 percent pay increase. Lawmakers provided a textbook rental system for North Carolina schoolchildren. Legislators designated highway maintenance appropriations as matching relief funds and passed a voluntary unemployment insurance measure, which they hoped would comply with eventual social security legislation.[55]

Beyond increased spending for schools and roads, Ehringhaus was most progressive in his support of the federal Child Labor Amendment. Only sixteen states were needed for ratification when the 1935 lower house in North Carolina, by a margin of three votes, refused to put the measure on its calendar. Ralph McDonald and Ernest A. Gardner led the unsuccessful drive in the House. Despite backing by Roosevelt and Ehringhaus, the measure could not overcome opposition from textile interests and the state Grange, and with that mounting resistance Ehringhaus became "silent as a mouse" on the issue, according to the *News and Observer.* A bill to regulate the hours of work for boys ages

54. Ibid., January 24, March 22, May 12, 1935; A. J. Maxwell, "Comparing Tax Loads: North Carolina and Other States," November 24, 1935, Gardner Papers; Corbitt, ed., *Papers of Ehringhaus,* p. 200; Puryear, *Democratic Party Dissension,* pp. 187, 192, 197.

55. Lefler, ed., *North Carolina History,* pp. 458, 469–70; *Raleigh News and Observer,* May 12, July 27, 1935; Corbitt, ed., *Papers of Ehringhaus,* p. 199; Kirk, Cutler, and Morse, eds., *Emergency Relief in North Carolina,* pp. 45, 47; North Carolina State Board of Charities and Public Welfare, *Biennial Report, 1934–1936,* pp. 11, 14, 16–17; Puryear, *Democratic Party Dissension,* p. 186; North Carolina State Highway and Public Works Commission, *Biennial Report, 1935–1936,* foreword, p. 163; *North Carolina House Journal,* 1935, pp. 426, 741; *North Carolina Senate Journal,* 1935, p. 487.

fourteen to sixteen failed to pass a second reading in the Senate, and a forty-hour-workweek bill for men and women never made it out of Representative Benjamin Cone's Manufacturers and Labor Committee in the House. But the state did make progress in the battle against child labor. A combination of the Depression and code prohibitions reduced the number of employees under sixteen from 6,410 in 1929 to 276 by 1935.[56]

Legislators in 1935 dramatically reversed the strong prohibition verdict of the November 1933 referendum. Members from the "wet" eastern counties failed by a close vote to pass a statewide liquor law but did weaken prohibition by permitting eighteen counties to hold local option referenda on the question of liquor. On July 2, 1935, the first county-operated liquor store opened in Wilson, after twenty-seven years of prohibition.[57]

Another example of modest reform by Ehringhaus and the 1935 General Assembly was the establishment of the North Carolina Rural Electrification Authority. For years the state Grange, the rural press, and politicians had lobbied for North Carolina to establish the nation's first public-sponsored rural electrification program. In 1934 Ehringhaus had appointed a commission, headed by Clarence Poe and aided by a $25,000 FERA grant, to plan for electric cooperatives. In Hoke and Orange counties the CWA had constructed two test projects that operated successfully. Calling it a "good New Deal project," the governor requested more funds from Roosevelt. State senator Dudley W. Bagley, later director of the NCREA, introduced the bill in the House, and it passed by a voice vote in both chambers.[58]

The legislators also expressed opinions on a range of issues generally supportive of Congress and the White House. Representative Claude C. Abernathy and Senator Lee L. Gravely introduced joint resolutions requesting Congress to pass the Frazier-Lemke bill providing mortgage relief for farmers. It passed quickly, as did a similar joint resolution on

56. Corbitt, ed., *Papers of Ehringhaus*, pp. 189, 404–5; *Raleigh News and Observer*, January 6, March 10, 12, 13, 20, May 12, 1935; *North Carolina House Journal*, 1935, pp. 55, 298, 343, 351–52, 861; *North Carolina Senate Journal*, 1935, pp. 297, 347; Puryear, *Democratic Party Dissension*, p. 187.

57. *Raleigh News and Observer*, May 12, 1935, January 1, 1936; Whitener, *Prohibition*, pp. 211–13; Lefler and Newsome, *North Carolina*, p. 613.

58. Ehringhaus to FDR, November 28, 1934, WPA Papers; Kirk, Cutler, and Morse, eds., *Emergency Relief in North Carolina*, p. 365; Brown, "Rural Electrification in the South," pp. 45, 48, 58–60; Badger, "North Carolina and the New Deal," p. 73; "Report D, Federal REA: NCREA," [n.d.], Governors' Papers (E); *North Carolina House Journal*, 1935, p. 731; *North Carolina Senate Journal*, 1935, pp. 321, 454.

the work relief bill. Representative Cherry easily pushed through an unemployment compensation bill in an effort to comply with social security legislation in Congress. Business interests persuaded the General Assembly to ask Congress to eliminate the AAA processing tax, but later the House and Senate repealed the joint resolution after pressure from agricultural groups. Legislation enabling cities and towns in the state to participate in the PWA only made it through the House. Also the House alone passed a resolution requesting Congress to defeat the Flanagan bill, which provided for government grading of tobacco.[59]

Despite increased funding for state agencies in 1935 and the creation of the NCREA, North Carolina experienced no "little New Deal." Ehringhaus and the General Assembly never advocated the welfare state, regulation of business, or assistance to labor. State government instead balked at relief and compliance with New Deal measures. Ehringhaus sought a balanced budget through retrenchment and a regressive sales tax, rather than expanding public services to deal with the economic crisis. Indicative of his caution, Ehringhaus began his term with a $15 million deficit and ended it with a $5 million surplus. North Carolina's response, typical for most states, especially in the South, demonstrated what James Patterson has called the "continuing strength of traditional American beliefs in self-help, the inherent virtues of hard work, and the benevolent character of business enterprise." Despite Roosevelt's popularity and the lure of the New Deal, probusiness forces still ruled the state. Given the meager financial resources of the state, opponents could do little more than accept the conservative agenda. Liberals in North Carolina had only modest aims: opposition to both the sales tax and the Gardner machine. Their limitations mirrored those of Roosevelt and the New Deal as well.[60]

Unable to capture the state legislature and implement a little New Deal, insurgents encountered more frustrations in the 1936 elections. Despite close margins, they failed to wrest state government from the conservatives or defeat New Deal critic Josiah Bailey. In North Carolina in 1936 conservatives beat liberals in gubernatorial and senatorial primaries, remarkable for a peak New Deal year. Although unsuccessful in removing the sales tax, insurgents captured enormous popular support in the state for their opposition to it and faced 1936 with optimism.

59. *North Carolina House Journal,* 1935, pp. 74, 229–30, 261, 498, 554, 582, 898; *North Carolina Senate Journal,* 1935, pp. 60, 190, 211, 358, 428, 507, 658; *Raleigh News and Observer,* May 3, 1935; Puryear, *Democratic Party Dissension,* p. 186.

60. Corbitt, ed., *Papers of Ehringhaus,* p. xii; Patterson, *New Deal and the States,* pp. 192, 202–7; Badger, *North Carolina and the New Deal,* pp. 73–75.

Ehringhaus and his allies had to defend not only the sales tax but also the failure to call a special session of the legislature to comply with social security and establish regional compulsory crop controls. Furthermore, the organization's choice for governor was Max Gardner's brother-in-law, Clyde Hoey. Though Roosevelt's popularity was at its zenith and insurgent candidate Ralph McDonald identified openly with New Deal liberalism, the state's progressives fell short once again.

Representative Robert L. Doughton's possible candidacy for governor in 1936 posed the first threat to the Gardner organization. Insurgents in the state viewed Doughton, a representative from the western ninth district since 1910, as their strongest candidate since the death of attorney general Dennis Brummitt in January 1935. As Ways and Means chairman, Doughton solidly endorsed New Deal programs, particularly social security, and on the state level he opposed the sales tax. Although Doughton had many conservative friends in the state, his antiadministration stand on the sales tax and his New Deal record in Congress made him acceptable to the insurgents. A Doughton candidacy had the additional advantage for the liberals of removing Clyde R. Hoey, the conservatives' strongest candidate, from the race. Doughton and Hoey remained close friends, and Hoey indicated that he would not oppose Doughton. New Dealers pressured Doughton to run, and with him they fully expected to gain control of state government.[61]

Doughton had been a faithful New Deal workhorse, steering the NRA, social security, and revenue bills through the House. As chairman of the Ways and Means Committee, his major responsibility was tax legislation. In 1934 the revenue bill sought to close loopholes for the wealthy, and Doughton appealed to party loyalty for its passage. Although Democrats were not responsible for economic conditions, Doughton argued, the majority party had to raise the taxes needed by the administration. "This day to your tents, you Democratic hosts of Israel," he exhorted them. He defended the 1935 Revenue Act, popularly called the "soak-the-rich" tax. "Instead of further soaking the poor by a sales tax," Doughton challenged lawmakers to get the revenue from those "best able to pay." It would not hurt business, he insisted, and after the emergency had passed, he promised "rigid economy" in spending.[62]

61. Santford Martin to R. L. Doughton, November 1, 1934, Box 1, Doughton to Martin, August 30, 1935, Box 3, Martin Papers; Puryear, *Democratic Party Dissension*, pp. 199, 202.

62. Tindall, *Emergence of the New South*, p. 608; *Congressional Record*, 73d Cong., 2d sess. (1934), pp. 2507, 2510, 2999; 74th Cong., 1st sess. (1935), pp. 10301, 12308–10, 12312.

Doughton also appealed to New Dealers as a gubernatorial candidate by leading the 1934 legislative battle for the reciprocal trade agreement, which he called an "emergency measure to meet a great emergency." The bill gave the president the same authority in foreign trade that he already had in domestic areas, and Doughton deemed it critical to recovery. He expected critics to stress the lowering of the tariff. Doughton further strengthened his New Deal credentials by moving the Guffey-Snyder coal bill through the House in 1935. He had engineered the passage of the NRA and sought to preserve it with this "little NRA." Typically, the North Carolina congressional delegation overwhelmingly voted for New Deal measures, but on this bill five of thirteen members—Clark, Kerr, Lambeth, Umstead, and Bailey—opposed Doughton.[63]

To everyone's surprise, however, Doughton announced in April 1935 that he would not be a candidate for governor. At one point he decided to make the race but, after what he called a "terrific struggle," reversed himself. The congressman bowed to pressure from Roosevelt to remain in the House as chairman of the Ways and Means Committee. Roosevelt repeatedly requested him to stay and on one occasion personally called him to the White House. Secretary of State Cordell Hull urged him to forgo the governor's race. Just as the president did not want to risk a new anti–New Deal Ways and Means chairman, Hull feared someone whose tariff views would not conform to his. Doughton's decision to remain in Washington benefited the organization Democrats most. With support from liberals and conservatives, his candidacy would have been formidable, and though Doughton as governor would not have been an enemy, neither would he have been "one of them."[64]

By the summer of 1935, the state's insurgents and New Deal liberals had settled on Ralph McDonald as their choice for governor in 1936. The thirty-two-year-old former Salem College professor, Duke Ph.D., and leader of the anti–sales tax forces in the 1935 General Assembly made his decision public on August 19, 1935. His rise to prominence in a few months constituted one of the major stories for 1935. A North Carolina resident for the last twelve years, after moving from Illinois, McDonald resigned from Salem College in 1934 rather than succumb to pressure from the trustees to withdraw as a candidate for the legislature from

63. *Congressional Record,* 73d Cong., 2d sess. (1934), pp. 5255–56, 5259–60; 74th Cong., 1st sess. (1935), pp. 13666–67, 14084.

64. Doughton to Martin, May 3, 1935, Box 2, Martin Papers; Bailey to Doughton, July 15, 1935, Doughton to Bailey, July 18, 1935, Bailey Papers; *Raleigh News and Observer,* April 30, 1935; Puryear, *Democratic Party Dissension,* p. 202.

Forsyth County. In the General Assembly the following year he led the unsuccessful minority fight against the sales tax, and after the death of Brummitt and the withdrawal of Doughton, he became the natural choice for liberals. His gubernatorial boom began after the 1935 legislature closed and grew over the next several months as he attracted volunteers and grass-roots support. Though short on funds, McDonald nevertheless emerged as a major candidate for governor with help from Jonathan Daniels and politicians who viewed his victory as an opportunity to return to state government.[65]

In calling for a "New Deal for North Carolina," McDonald placed priority on repealing the sales tax, the most potent issue an antiadministration candidate for governor could raise. Critical of Ehringhaus's tax policies as unbalanced and damaging to the poor, McDonald favored shifting taxes more toward the wealthy and corporations. To replace the sales tax he recommended additional income, dividend, interest, and corporate taxes. Adopting the slogan "It can be done and it will be done," McDonald urged additional funds for schools. He denounced as a fraud the claim that the sales tax would pay for the eight-month school term. According to McDonald, the state's public schools suffered more after the enactment of the sales tax than before. State funding and North Carolina's national ranking in support for schools both declined, as did the teachers' salaries. McDonald charged that conservatives linked the schools and sales tax to cover up their real intention of easing the tax burden on the corporations. He also criticized the Ehringhaus administration for the previous year's budget surplus of $5 million, which he said resulted from exorbitant taxes and inadequate appropriations.[66]

McDonald simultaneously praised the New Deal and blasted the Gardner machine for thwarting it in North Carolina. He attacked conservatives who "boast loudly of their loyalty to FDR and are seeking to destroy the policies of the New Deal." "The forces of entrenched wealth are desperately trying to keep their grip on our state government," he warned one campaign audience, and he labeled Hoey the "crown prince" of the banks, tobacco companies, power interests, and textile groups. "A political sand fiddler—bought and paid for by Duke Power," McDonald called Hoey. He pledged to rid Raleigh of "swivel-chair" politicians, appointed officials qualified only by political allegiance to

65. *Raleigh News and Observer*, August 20, 1935, January 1, July 5, 1936; Puryear, *Democratic Party Dissension*, pp. 203, 213.

66. Speeches by McDonald, April 2, May 4, 1936, Governors' Papers (E); *Raleigh News and Observer*, August 2, 1935, April 3, 4, May 9, 1936; Puryear, *Democratic Party Dissension*, pp. 214, 216–17.

the machine, and to replace them with an administration wholeheartedly in support of the New Deal. Congress had already made funds available for North Carolina's old people, he reminded audiences, but Ehringhaus would not call a special session for the state to qualify for the money, nor would the governor permit a session to act on tobacco compact legislation. McDonald charged that the machine politicians, tied to the state's power interests, kept the TVA from benefiting the western section of North Carolina. To assist workers in the state, McDonald advocated a state law guaranteeing their right to collective bargaining. Not surprisingly, the North Carolina Labor Voters' League, with twenty thousand members in forty counties, endorsed McDonald and called him labor's "true friend." In the 1936 gubernatorial primary, McDonald presented himself as a clear choice between conservative, machine government and a genuine, liberal New Deal administration.[67]

McDonald's promotion of the New Deal and his attacks on the sales tax and the Gardner machine captured strong popular support by the spring of 1936. By March he had a state organization, and newspaper polls showed him gaining strength and eventually leading. At a May 26 rally that attracted thirty-five hundred people in Raleigh's Memorial Auditorium McDonald demonstrated his drawing power as an orator by filling the largest auditorium ever rented for a political speech by a North Carolina candidate for office. As McDonald emerged as the front runner, the conservatives expressed concern and lashed out against him. The *Charlotte Observer* called him politically "unsound, unsafe, and untrustworthy" and labeled his program one of "fantasies and fancies" and "fiscal flim-flams." Editorially, the *Greensboro Daily News* tried to undercut McDonald's liberal support by questioning his credentials as a radical. Merchant support contradicted his radical image, and the editor called the radical charge against McDonald a "figment in the imagination of the opposition." From the beginning, Gardner respected McDonald as "undoubtedly a man of ability" and hoped that he would damage himself by becoming more "intemperate and radical."[68]

McDonald's chief rival differed sharply in background and style. Clyde R. Hoey, a fifty-eight-year-old lawyer from Shelby, represented

67. Speech by McDonald, April 2, 1936, Governors' Papers (E); *Raleigh News and Observer*, August 2, 20, 1935, April 3, 4, 18, May 9, 12, 17, 19, 1936; Puryear, *Democratic Party Dissension*, pp. 214, 216–17; R. Mayne Albright, "O. Max Gardner and the Shelby Dynasty," Part II, *State* 51 (July 1983): 12.

68. Gardner to Josphus Daniels, October 14, 1935, to Hoey, November 2, 1935, Gardner Papers; *Raleigh News and Observer*, May 27, July 5, 1936; editorials, *Charlotte Observer*, June 4, 5, 1936; editorial *Greensboro Daily News*, June 5, 1936; Puryear, *Democratic Party Dissension*, pp. 215–16.

the older generation of "Democracy" in the state. A political veteran, Hoey had served as a state legislator, an assistant United States attorney, one-term congressman, and leader of the "dry" forces and had been one of the party's renowned orators for the past twenty years. Sam Ervin remembered Hoey primarily as "quite a speaker," one who was personally popular, not one to build a strong political organization like Gardner. Part of his political charm derived from his dress and mannerisms, "eccentric in its old-fashionedness," according to one newspaper editor. Hoey had long, flowing hair, wore a frock coat with a wing-tipped collar, high-topped shoes, a fresh red boutonniere every day, and donned a nightshirt for bed. He neither drank, smoked, nor chewed tobacco, and he taught Sunday School at Shelby's Methodist church.[69]

Though not a statewide officeholder with a record to defend, Hoey did have to guard against being linked to Gardner's political organization. Not only was Gardner his brother-in-law, but both were citizens of Shelby. No longer was there the east-west rotation of the governorship, the popular expression ran, but now one governor from the east and one governor from Shelby. Charges about the "Shelby dynasty" put the organization in a more defensive position than it had been with Ehringhaus in 1932. By 1936 the stakes were higher; through increased centralization of state government, Gardner and Ehringhaus had created a governor's office that ranked as one of the most powerful in the South, even without the veto power. The organization's strength rested with elected and appointed officials in state government, particularly the highway and revenue departments.

Basking in his influence in state and national politics, Gardner expressed no reservations about pushing his brother-in-law for the governorship. He planned, as in 1932, to play a major role in the election of the next governor. Hoey benefited from his network of political allies and his ability to raise campaign funds through his contacts in the state's business community. Gardner publicly defended himself against charges of being a "dictator" running the state by long distance telephone from Washington. He reminded everyone that he had been out of office for four years and had not interfered with the details of the Ehringhaus administration. Gardner revealed that in 1932 Hoey turned down an appointment to the United States Senate that eventually went to Cameron Morrison. Hoey, Gardner argued, could run on his own "character,

69. H. M. London, ed., *North Carolina Manual 1937* (Raleigh: State of North Carolina, 1937), p. 159; *Raleigh News and Observer*, May 15, 1935, January 7, editorial, January 8, 1937; interview with Sam Ervin by Dick Dabney, January 8, August 2, 1974.

record, and integrity." Furthermore, Gardner pointed to the good government in North Carolina under the so-called "dynasty." "Never been a breath of scandal or corruption," he boasted.[70]

Along with Gardner, the political establishment closed ranks behind Hoey. Congressman Lindsay Warren, the organization's strongest ally in the east, favored him, and Congressman Robert L. Doughton from the west supported Hoey after his own withdrawal from the race. Senator Bailey, in a reelection battle of his own, officially remained neutral in the race as a matter of political prudence, but privately he endorsed Hoey. During the runoff, with his own renomination secure, Bailey made his feelings public. Senator Reynolds, facing reelection two years hence and unwilling to antagonize the conservatives, openly backed Hoey's nomination.[71]

Strategists for Hoey feared that his identification with the conservatives and McDonald's enthusiasm for Roosevelt's very popular New Deal threatened his chances. Gardner sensed that Hoey could not win by defending Ehringhaus. "I knew he had to liberalize his platform and extend his reach," he argued. McDonald could not, according to Gardner, make Hoey look weak in his support of FDR. Edwin Gill, an aide to both Gardner and Ehringhaus, advised Hoey to address himself more to the needs of the "average man" because since the invalidation of the AAA in January 1936 farmers and workers had become increasingly "radical." Gill warned Hoey to identify more with Roosevelt, and Gardner's working relationship with the president and many New Dealers in Washington should help achieve that goal. Tyre Taylor, an RFC official and friend of Gardner's, urged Hoey to take a more liberal stand. A strong New Dealer himself, Taylor wanted Hoey to advocate the end of the sales tax, and he believed that replacement taxes on liquor, utilities, and income would enable the state to increase its spending on public services for the "oppressed and the underprivileged."[72]

70. Gardner to Wideman Kendall, June 15, 1935, press release, May 12, 1936, Gardner Papers; Michie and Ryhlick, *Dixie Demogogues*, p. 162; Daniels, *Tar Heels*, pp. 324–25; Key, *Southern Politics*, p. 213; Albright, "Shelby Dynasty," Part I, p. 27; R. Mayne Albright, "O. Max Gardner and the Shelby Dynasty," Part III, *State* 51 (August 1983): 26; interview of Thad Eure by Abrams, June 21, 1983; interview of Sam Ervin by Dick Dabney, January 8, August 2, 1974.

71. Warren to W. J. Boyd, April 6, 1936, Box 16, Warren Papers; Doughton to Martin, August 30, 1935, Box 2, Martin Papers; Doughton to Gardner, February 28, 1936, Edwin Gill to Gardner, February 29, 1936, Gardner Papers; Hoey to Bailey, April 30, 1935, Bailey to C. H. Robertson, May 21, 1935, Bailey Papers.

72. Tyre Taylor, "A Word to the Progressives of N.C.," April 1935, Edwin Gill to Gardner, May 2, 1935, Taylor to Gardner, July 15, 1935, Gill to Hoey, January 15, 1936, Gardner to Clayton Moore, November 10, 1936, Gardner Papers.

To a limited degree, Hoey followed their advice for co-opting his opponent's New Deal liberalism. He defended the sales tax as essential but promised to remove it from necessities. Hoey argued that landowners would resist a state property tax, and additional taxes on business would hamper further economic growth in the state. Also, the loss in revenue from a repeal of the sales tax would jeopardize funding for public schools as well as joint state-federal New Deal programs. Governor Ehringhaus had infuriated liberals in the state by delaying or refusing to convene a special session of the legislature for compliance with social security and tobacco compact legislation, and Hoey pledged full cooperation with the federal program to help farmers and to provide thirty dollars a month as a pension for those over sixty-five. In addition, Hoey advocated more money for schools, teachers, textbooks, and highways, and he unveiled a four-year plan to develop and advertise the state's agricultural, industrial, port, and recreational facilities. Hoey could appeal to New Dealers in the state, too, because he enjoyed the support of the state WPA director, George Coan, North Carolina's most important New Deal official in 1936. As a candidate, Hoey could reach out to New Dealers in the state and at the same time benefit from Ehringhaus's refusal to call a special session. Some Hoey supporters argued that Ehringhaus should call the session to boost his campaign among farmers and New Dealers, but the governor's stubbornness prevented a special session. Neither Ehringhaus nor Hoey wanted to provide McDonald with such a forum.[73]

Although Hoey defended the sales tax and softened his approach to the New Deal, he spent much of his time and energy in harsh attacks on McDonald. In a strategy machine candidates had used against insurgents in the past, Hoey questioned McDonald's loyalty to the Democratic party and thereby blunted McDonald's profession of loyalty to Roosevelt and the New Deal. McDonald's "vicious" assaults on state party leaders Gardner and Ehringhaus, according to Hoey, rivaled those of the Republican party. Hoey questioned his party loyalty further by claiming McDonald had never voted before 1932. Like Hoover in 1920, Hoey reminded voters, McDonald could not decide whether to join the Republican or Democratic party. Citing his liberal opponent's promises to spend more and tax less, Hoey likened him to Hoover in 1928 with his talk of a "chicken in every pot and a car in every garage." Hoey labeled McDonald

73. See chapter 5 for more on relief and politics in 1936; Warren to W. J. Boyd, April 6, 1936, Roy T. Cox to Warren, April 11, 1936, Box 16, Warren Papers; *Raleigh News and Observer*, April 23, May 13, 31, 1936; Puryear, *Democratic Party Dissension*, pp. 218–19.

"our friend, the Professor," and predicted his return to academia after the primary. McDonald's youth and inexperience and his being a native of another state disqualified him from running North Carolina, according to Hoey. Throughout the campaign, Hoey focused on the character and ability of McDonald and sidestepped the New Deal issues.[74]

Alexander H. "Sandy" Graham's presence in the primary posed a threat to the Gardner machine from the right. Pushed by conservative, antiorganization Democrats and those most antagonistic to Roosevelt, like Robert Hanes of Winston-Salem, Graham could split the conservative vote and allow McDonald to win the first primary. The forty-five-year-old Graham was a significant force in state politics. Lieutenant governor since 1933 and a Harvard Law School graduate, Graham had been active in the North Carolina House in the 1920s, serving as Speaker in 1929. Graham, like Hoey, favored the sales tax, but during the campaign he attacked the Gardner-Ehringhaus-Hoey machine. "Shall all the policies and personnel of the Ehringhaus administration be perpetuated for another four years," he shouted to one campaign audience, "under the direction of Max Gardner, the highly paid, super-lobbyist who represents special interests in Washington and runs North Carolina by long distance telephone." Believing the antimachine rhetoric attracted votes and angered by Gardner's personal efforts for Hoey, Graham intensified his attacks, which divided conservatives and encouraged the liberals.[75]

On June 6, Clyde Hoey surprised most political observers by leading in the first primary. In a record primary vote of 516,873, Hoey beat McDonald by 4,468 votes. Capturing over half of the state's counties, Hoey showed strength in the populous west, while McDonald and Graham won twenty-seven and twenty-one counties respectively, primarily in the east. McDonald expected to lead the first primary or even win the nomination outright; therefore, the narrow loss on June 6 was a psychological letdown. Since the establishment of the statewide primary in 1915, no loser in a first primary had gone on to win the gubernatorial nomination in a runoff. Nonetheless, five days after the setback, McDonald called for a runoff and, courting the Graham vote, cited the Gardner machine as the central issue. Avoiding issues such as the sales tax, both candidates engaged in vicious personal attacks. McDonald charged that underneath those long coattails Hoey hid money he re-

74. *Raleigh News and Observer,* May 9, 22, 23, 26, 31, 1936.

75. Gardner to H. W. Kendall, August 22, 1935, to Josephus Daniels, October 14, 1935, Gardner Papers; *Raleigh News and Observer,* May 11, 1935, May 9, 14, 27, 31, 1936; Puryear, *Democratic Party Dissension,* pp. 202–3, 212, 221.

ceived while serving as a lobbyist for Duke Power interests. Hoey labeled McDonald a "carpetbagger," "mail order governor," and "public enemy." With such name-calling between the two as "vicious lie," "gutter snipe," "lobbyist number one," "scoundrel," and "henchman," one newspaper described it as the "meanest, wildest campaign."[76]

Conservatives in the state lined up behind Hoey in his close, bitter runoff battle with McDonald. Max Gardner returned to Shelby and organized what he termed "the most powerful force that ever went into a political battle in this century." Working behind the scenes, using the telephone, and "putting on the pressure everywhere," Gardner pledged to "administer such a licking to [McDonald] that we will settle for sometime to come rebellion and revolution." Too busy to attend the June state Democratic convention, Gardner commanded his "army" from the "precinct up" and promised a "crushing victory." To achieve that goal, he poured $50,000 into the Hoey campaign. Sandy Graham, the loser in the first primary, remained neutral, but the bulk of his campaign leadership labored publicly for Hoey. A key financial booster for Graham, the Hanes family, donated $25,000 to the Hoey runoff campaign. Fresh from his own primary victory and free from political retaliation, Senator Bailey threw his support to Hoey.[77]

On July 4, McDonald's "crusade" to bring a New Deal to the state ended in another virtual east-west split, in which he lost by fifty-two thousand votes. He had held the spotlight and had made more "news and noise" than Hoey, but he could never match the smooth organization and financial backing of his opponent. Even the *News and Observer,* a friend of McDonald's, described his drive as the "goofiest campaign ever waged in North Carolina" and argued that his plan to repeal the sales tax and increase public services did not make sense. His shift from the sales tax issue to personal assaults on the well-liked Hoey further injured his campaign. Also, his image as an "outsider," as too young, and as too liberal cost him votes. While the *Charlotte Observer, Greensboro Daily News,* and *Asheville Citizen* promoted Hoey, McDonald could rely only

76. Thad Eure, ed., *North Carolina Manual, 1941* (Raleigh: Edwards and Broughton, 1941), p. 194; editorial, *Greensboro Daily News,* June 8, 1936; *Raleigh News and Observer,* June 10, 12, 22, 26, July 3–5, 1936; Key, *Southern Politics,* p. 212; Puryear, *Democratic Party Dissension,* pp. 226–27; Morrison, *Gardner,* p. 166.

77. Gardner to Fred Morrison, June 11, 1936, Gardner Papers; Bailey to Hoey, June 15, 1936, newspaper clipping, *Winston-Salem Journal and Sentinel,* June 21, 1936, Gardner to A. Hand James, July 7, 1936, Bailey Papers; Gardner to Warren, June 13, 1936, Box 16, Warren Papers; *Raleigh News and Observer,* June 26, 30, July 3, 4, 1936; Morrison, *Gardner,* pp. 166–67; Puryear, *Democratic Party Dissension,* pp. 224–25; interview of Capus Waynick Series D, pp. 24–26, Southern Oral History Program Collection.

on Jonathan Daniels's *News and Observer* and the *Winston-Salem Journal.* Despite these handicaps, however, only an extraordinary effort by Gardner and his organization defeated a gubernatorial candidate thoroughly identified with Roosevelt's New Deal. Hoey confided later that Gardner's assistance made the difference in his victory.[78]

Insurgents focused so much attention on the governor's race in 1936 that Josiah Bailey won renomination to the Senate with relative ease. Former lieutenant governor Richard Fountain mounted the only serious opposition. A spokesman for southern conservatism since entering the Senate in 1930, Bailey increased his political strength through control of federal patronage and funds. Though never a part of the conservative state organization, Bailey coexisted with it, shared a probusiness outlook with Gardner, and they remained close personal friends in Washington. He opposed the New Deal with remarkable political skill and managed to survive politically. Before the 1936 campaign Bailey prudently restricted his opposition to the New Deal to lengthy letters and in public utterances offered quiet support or disagreement. His votes against the AAA and compulsory crop control early in the New Deal angered the state's farmers, and by 1935 he had switched to a position of support. He infuriated others fond of the Roosevelt program by his opposition to several recovery and relief measures. In 1935 he voted against the Wagner and Guffey coal acts. To his critics, Bailey quickly pointed out his support for over 80 percent of the president's measures, having voted for the CCC, NRA, Soil Conservation, FERA, FDIC, and social security, although he voted against major legislation 58 percent of the time. In the 1934 congressional session Bailey strongly supported Roosevelt's efforts to stabilize the dollar. At the majority leader's suggestion, he presented the president's monetary policy to the Senate. The Gold Reserve Act resulted, and Bailey appeared as a defender of Roosevelt. He noted with satisfaction that the Supreme Court declared unconstitutional several programs he had opposed. Furthermore, he reminded critics that he had never voted to override a presidential veto.[79]

Despite Bailey's opposition to major New Deal legislation, moderated by his careful public speeches and concern for party loyalty, no major

78. Eure, ed., *North Carolina Manual, 1941,* p. 194; Warren to E. G. Flanagan, July 9, 1936, Box 16, Warren Papers; Hoey to Gardner, September 10, 1936, Gardner Papers; *Raleigh News and Observer,* July 5, 1936; editorial, *Greensboro Daily News,* July 3, 1936; editorial, *Charlotte Observer,* July 2, 1936; Badger, "North Carolina and the New Deal," pp. 112–16; Puryear, *Democratic Party Dissension,* p. 228; Morrison, *Gardner,* pp. 167–68.

79. Bailey to P. V. Parks, January 22, 1936, Bailey Papers; Patterson, *Congressional Conservatism,* pp. 27–29, 349; Cash, *Mind of the South,* pp. 433–34; Moore, *Bailey,* pp. v, 102, 115, 117, 123–24.

liberal figure in the state dared challenge him in 1936. In January 1935 Richard Fountain, whom Ehringhaus defeated in 1932, announced for Bailey's Senate seat, but most considered him a stalking-horse for someone else. After the 1932 race, Fountain spent months in a sanatorium after a breakdown, and some of his friends believed he had not recovered mentally. Neither Bailey nor Gardner took Fountain's candidacy seriously, and most political observers believed he had little chance. For a while, Governor Ehringhaus considered challenging Bailey, but the prospect of Bailey and Ehringhaus splitting the conservative vote and benefiting Fountain discouraged that possibility. Besides, Ehringhaus's popularity sank after the 1935 legislative session, and his poor health, along with the prospect of losing, kept him out of the race. Congressman Frank Hancock flirted with the idea of running, but his effort never got past the "trial balloon" stage.[80]

Josephus Daniels, the most prominent liberal in the state, considered a campaign against Bailey in 1936, but as in 1932, he declined. In July 1934 Daniels infuriated Mexican and American Catholics by praising the public education program of anticlerical President Plutarco E. Calles of Mexico. Father Charles Coughlin, popular Catholic radio priest of the 1930s, attacked Ambassador Daniels, and angry American Catholics demanded his resignation. A race against Bailey would be an opportunity for a graceful exit, would relieve Catholic attacks on Roosevelt, and also, if successful, would promote the New Deal in North Carolina and in the Senate. In January 1935, after surveying the political situation, Jonathan Daniels advised his father not to enter the race. Max Gardner stirred political gossip in November 1935 by conferring with Daniels in Mexico City. Some accused Gardner of trying to persuade Daniels to run so as to divert liberals' attention from the McDonald drive against Hoey, but Gardner discouraged Daniels from running. Most likely, a Daniels-McDonald team against the conservatives in the primaries would strengthen the New Dealers in the state, especially the McDonald campaign, which Gardner wanted to diminish. Max Gardner, Jonathan Daniels, Robert L. Doughton, and even the president argued that Daniels faced an uphill battle with the conservative organization and finances arrayed against him.[81]

80. Gardner to Josephus Daniels, October 14, 1935, Gardner Papers; Bailey to Gardner, December 3, 1935, Bailey Papers; Jonathan Daniels to Josephus Daniels, January 17, 1935, Box 676, Josephus Daniels Papers; Puryear, *Democratic Party Dissension*, pp. 205–6.

81. Jonathan Daniels to Josephus Daniels, January 17, 1935, Heriot Clarkson to Josephus Daniels, January 17, 1936, John D. Langson to Josephus Daniels, January 24, 1936, Box 676, Josephus Daniels Papers; Gardner to Hoey, November 2, 1935, Gardner Papers; Cronon, "Josephus Daniels," pp. 467–68, 470, 473–76, 480–81.

As late as January 1936, however, Daniels wrote his son, "I want to see him [Bailey] defeated so much that I can hardly stay here." Daniels believed that North Carolinians overwhelmingly backed the president and deserved a progressive senator. Although Bailey had softened his opposition to the New Deal since 1934, his attacks on the AAA particularly angered Daniels. If he won reelection, Daniels predicted Bailey would view it as a mandate and would join forces with the "reactionaries." Representative Lindsay Warren, though an ally of Gardner's and cordial to Bailey, urged Daniels to challenge the incumbent. Upset with Bailey's opposition to the New Deal farm programs, Warren believed Daniels would "sweep the state," particularly the east. Santford Martin, editor of the *Winston-Salem Journal,* implored him to "come home soon and assume the leadership of the liberal forces" in the state. Believing the odds against him were too great, Daniels resisted such pressures and in April 1936 decided not to run for the Senate. He also cited his pleasant situation in Mexico City, the opposition of his family, and his lifelong pledge never to run for office.[82]

Senator Bailey never expressed concern about a challenge from Daniels because he had confidence in his own support and believed that Roosevelt would not jeopardize his electoral votes in the fall by backing Daniels. With Daniels safely out of the race, Bailey remained in Washington for most of the campaign and never established a headquarters or state campaign organization. The Bailey-Fountain primary contest never generated much interest or attention, and the press concentrated on the more colorful gubernatorial battle. Believing McDonald had a better chance of winning, insurgent forces focused on his crusade against the machine. Fountain, with little organization and money, spoke out against Bailey's anti–New Deal record and called him "the fly in Roosevelt's ointment ever since his inauguration." He pointed to Bailey's alleged ties to vested interests and the Liberty League and questioned how any voters could support both the president and Senator Bailey. Fountain pledged continued efforts on behalf of the farmers, labor, and the elderly. Fountain's association with the popular New Deal and even his support from eastern farmers could not overcome Bailey's strength as an incumbent and his ties with the conservative organization. On June 6 Bailey defeated Fountain by 63,168 votes.[83]

82. Warren to Josephus Daniels, February 7, 1936, Josephus Daniels to Edward M. Land, April 8, 1936, Box 676, Josephus Daniels Papers; copy of letter, Josephus Daniels to Jonathan Daniels, January 31, 1936, Bailey Papers; Josephus Daniels to Warren, January 30, 1936, Box 15, Warren Papers; Martin to Josephus Daniels, January 28, 1936, Josephus Daniels to Martin, February 3, 1936, Box 2, Martin Papers.

83. Bailey to J. O. Carr, January 6, 1936, to C. L. Shuping, February 10, 1936, to M. G.

Bailey succeeded for several reasons. Hiding his opposition to FDR, he had campaigned as a loyal New Dealer, stressing those programs he had supported. He inaccurately claimed credit for helping tobacco farmers in the 1933 marketing crisis. To his critics he could point to a note of endorsement from James A. Farley, Roosevelt's campaign manager. Bailey's major advantage was the lack of a strong, pro–New Deal opponent. In the end Bailey's strong support throughout the state, his connection with financial interests, and the power of personality over ideology brought victory.[84]

In the 1936 primaries in North Carolina, liberal New Dealers, despite a valiant effort in the gubernatorial race, came away empty-handed once again. As in the 1932 election and in the legislative sessions of 1933 and 1935, liberalism failed to develop in the state even though Roosevelt's New Deal enjoyed enormous popular support. Foremost among the reasons for this failure was that conservative strength, in response to the insurgent-liberal challenge, peaked in 1936. Max Gardner expressed pride that North Carolina was the only state where conservatives, who had opposition, elected a governor or a senator. "Our forces are in complete control," Gardner boasted to his friend Bob Woodruff. Sensing the danger, Gardner had returned to North Carolina in the last few weeks of the gubernatorial primaries and worked hard for a Hoey victory. In this campaign, liberals were no match for the aroused conservatives.[85]

The conservatives appreciated the political popularity of Roosevelt and refused to let the insurgents and liberals paint them as enemies of the New Deal. Hoey and Bailey both "liberalized" their rhetoric and embraced Roosevelt and the New Deal. Bailey even seconded the nomination of FDR at the Democratic National Convention. In the fall campaign Hoey and Bailey continued their enthusiasm for the New Deal. The two conservative Democrats were wise to co-opt the New Deal's popularity, for in November North Carolinians cast more votes for Roosevelt than for Hoey or Bailey.

Just as conservatives in the state valued FDR's ballot-box appeal, Roosevelt also realistically accepted the clout of the conservatives and

Mann, June 24, 1936, Bailey Papers; *Raleigh News and Observer*, April 12, May 20, 23, June 12, 1936; Moore, *Bailey*, pp. 121–22; Puryear, *Democratic Party Dissension*, pp. 210–11; H. M. London, ed., *North Carolina Manual, 1939* (Raleigh: State of North Carolina, 1939), p. 103.

84. Badger, *North Carolina and the New Deal*, pp. 79–80

85. Gardner to Clayton Moore, November 10, 1936, Gardner Papers; Albright, "Shelby Dynasty," Part III, p. 8.

worked with them, thereby giving the very enemies of the New Deal some "New Deal respectability." The result was frustration on the part of the state's liberals. Congressman Frank Hancock, a New Dealer, explained to James Farley that in 1936 "the old [conservative] party machinery had to be oiled, greased, and geared to the limit to make the grade" but complained that without "a world of money and undeserved prestige on the part of many from Washington," liberals would have won. Loyal New Dealers in the state, Hancock continued, were becoming disaffected by the national administration working with anti–New Dealers in the state in appointments and using conservatives as administration spokesmen. Despite the frustrations of Roosevelt's accommodation to the conservatives, approximately one hundred liberal Democrats, including Keith Harrison of High Point and E. Johnston Neal of Raleigh, essentially McDonald's old campaign organization, met in Raleigh on September 7 to chart their course for the future. The group stressed its loyalty to the Democratic party and its intention to "clean up the party, not desert it." McDonald addressed the meeting, and all pledged to work for Roosevelt's election and for the advancement of the New Deal in the state, specifically tax and election law reform, in the 1937 General Assembly.[86]

North Carolina illustrated what James Patterson described as "not the failure of the New Dealers, but the limits in which they had to operate." Roosevelt could not liberalize the state parties, Patterson argued, because he had a "weak hand in the first place." Continuing the card-game imagery, Patterson concluded that "state politicians held too many aces." For example, Bailey confided to his campaign manager that Roosevelt, not wanting to risk losing North Carolina's electoral votes in the fall, would not support Daniels against him and divide the state party. Bailey was right; Roosevelt was not ready for that strategy in 1936. Other factors worked for conservatives and against New Dealers. State politics remained independent of national politics, and especially in the one-party South partisan loyalty and personalities were more important than ideology. So Tar Heel voters in 1936 could nominate Hoey and Bailey as well as overwhelmingly endorse Roosevelt.[87]

Furthermore, liberalism did not succeed in North Carolina in the 1930s because of its own limitations. Except for some excessive campaign

86. Frank Hancock to James A. Farley, August 18, 1936, office file 300 (Democratic National Committee), Roosevelt Papers; McDonald to Martin, August 17, 1936, Box 3, Martin Papers; *Raleigh News and Observer*, September 7, 8, 1936.

87. Bailey to C. L. Shuping, February 10, 1936, Bailey Papers; Patterson, *New Deal and the States*, pp. 156, 162–63, 191, 206–7.

rhetoric, the liberals' program for the state during the Depression rarely extended beyond opposition to the sales tax and the Gardner machine. There was not a sufficient urban-labor base to create a strong New Deal constituency. Agrarian liberalism in the east only went as far as the AAA tobacco program. North Carolina was too poor to fund an extensive welfare state, even if liberals had captured state government and tried to create a little New Deal.[88]

North Carolina liberals in 1936 also had weak candidates. The most formidable insurgent for governor would have been Dennis Brummitt, attorney general and former Speaker of the House and Democratic party chairman. His death in January 1935 was a great blow to the liberal cause. As a result, New Dealers turned to a flawed candidate, Ralph McDonald, who was easily discredited as a novice and "carpetbagger." Even his most ardent supporter, Jonathan Daniels, later viewed him as less than serious. "A flash in the pan," he recalled, "a mighty big flash at one time, but once he was defeated for governor he just disappeared off the face of the earth as far as North Carolina was concerned." Likewise, for the race against Bailey liberals had to settle for Fountain when the best candidate, Josephus Daniels, remained in Mexico. If weaker challengers came so close to ending conservative rule in Raleigh, certainly stronger liberal candidates, if they had not won, would have at least gained more concessions for the New Deal in the state.[89]

88. Patterson, *New Deal and the States*, pp. 162–63, 202–5. For North Carolina New Dealers in the 1930s, political insurgency may have been more important than liberalism. See Alan Brinkley, "The New Deal and Southern Politics," in *The New Deal and the South*, ed. Cobb and Namorato.

89. Interview with Jonathan Daniels by Eagles, March 9–11, 1977; Albright, "Shelby Dynasty," Part II, p. 10.

CHAPTER 8

Decline of Reform

In the late 1930s, conservatives in North Carolina gained strength and battled President Roosevelt and his New Deal on several fronts, while the Roosevelt administration scaled down its relief and reform programs. By 1937 the New Deal presence in the state had diminished; the WPA had only 18,600 enrollees, in contrast to 50,000 in 1936. By October 1937 the CCC had forty-six camps, down from the previous year's sixty. The 1937 General Assembly, after pressure from Duke Power lobbyists, voted against legislation enabling cities to match funds for PWA-built public power plants. Although the 1937 General Assembly complied with social security, modest benefits started July 1, 1937, for only 3,400 OAA and 1,800 ADC clients. Unemployment compensation would not start until January 1, 1938. In 1937 a drive for an interstate compact to restrict tobacco acreage failed, but tobacco farmers received twenty-three cents a pound for a bumper crop of 866 million pounds and the state's tobacco growers collected $8.3 million from the federal conservation program.

While the New Deal stalled, conservatives mounted a more open and aggressive assault on Roosevelt and his allies in the state. Buoyed by their 1936 primary triumphs, organization Democrats preserved the sales tax, the basis for the all-important balanced budget. Dispirited liberals did not challenge it in the 1937 and 1939 legislatures. In the late 1930s, Max Gardner shed much of his erstwhile ambivalence toward the New Deal and joined fellow conservatives in attacking Roosevelt. Senator Bailey emerged as the most vocal critic of the New Deal in the state. Resentful of Roosevelt's 1938 attempt to "purge" fellow conservatives in other states, few state Democratic leaders supported him for a third term. By the late 1930s, the New Deal was no longer a major political force in North Carolina.

The staunch opposition of Governor Clyde Hoey was responsible for much of the New Deal's frustrations in North Carolina after 1936. Personally popular, Hoey had an amiable, old-fashioned, casual style that belied a tough political conservatism. Brother-in-law of Max Gardner, also a resident of Shelby, a lawyer who years before helped prosecute communist strike leaders in nearby Gastonia, Hoey resisted most of the New Deal changes, especially concessions to labor. Decrying the New Deal's leftward drift, Hoey despaired: "Many disastrous things have happened which will damage tremendously the morale of the people of the United States." "It looks like the federal bureaus are undertaking to usurp all the authorities of the state," he complained. Like Ehringhaus before him, he fought an extensive welfare state and federal interference. Instead, he sought policies to ensure a balanced budget and the state's credit, all-important issues to piedmont business interests.[1]

But as in the 1936 primaries, Hoey kept the liberals off balance with progressive rhetoric. The hyprocisy was deliberate, not confusion on his part. George Tindall observed that "cohesive majority factions" like the Democratic organizations in North Carolina, Virginia, and Tennessee stayed strong in the 1930s by "bending with the winds of change." For the Hoey administration the change was mostly oratorical illusion. A few weeks before Hoey's inauguration, Gardner suggested that he "touch on liberalism in your inaugural" to fool his enemies, who expected him to continue Ehringhaus's policies. Gardner advised him to shift from preoccupation with a balanced budget and the sales tax to a more positive program of improvements for the state. In his January 1937 inaugural address, following Gardner's suggestions, Hoey called poverty the state's greatest enemy and noted that individual income was about half the national average. He announced no dramatic measures to alleviate the problem but only proposed removing the sales tax from food, asked for free textbooks for schoolchildren, called for labor legislation, and urged an advertising campaign to promote industrial development. His progressive tone misled some newspaper editors. The *News and Observer* characterized him as "liberal, realistic and intelligent" and sympathetically added: "The Governor's hair is not so long as comment has made it; his dress is not so strange." His proposals "indicate a measure of liberalism which may surprise a great many," the *Durham Sun* declared. Hoey "may turn out to be a more liberal executive than some of those who opposed him."[2]

The bitterness of the 1936 primaries led most observers to expect a long and stormy 1937 legislative session; however, thanks to Hoey's leadership and thorough organization in the House and Senate, along with an improvement in the economy that removed a sense of urgency,

1. Badger, *North Carolina and the New Deal*, pp. 68–69.
2. Gardner to Hoey, November 25, 1936, Gardner Papers; Corbitt, ed., *Papers of Hoey*, pp. 4–5, 8, 10, 15, 18, 753, 757; Tindall, *Emergence of the New South*, p. 645.

lawmakers held the shortest session since 1929. House Speaker Gregg Cherry, a veteran of fiscal wars and beginning with the 1933 legislature a proponent of the sales tax, placed administration allies in key committee posts. The near success of the insurgents in the previous summer's primaries had frightened organization Democrats. One observer declared that in contrast to previous sessions, the mood had shifted from "cringing to strutting." With conservatives in control and liberals in disarray, the bitter factionalism so typical of the decade vanished. Without a significant leader, no serious opposition to the sales tax materialized, and the legislators accepted it as permanent. They also acted quickly; the House approved both revenue and appropriations bills in one evening and approved the sales tax seventy-three to seven. In the third legislative session Willie Lee Lumpkin fought an administration revenue bill, this time with unsuccessful amendments to raise income taxes on individuals and corporations. Lesser-known members such as Virgil A. Wilson and D. Lacy McBryde focused their attacks on the sales tax. The Senate approved the revenue bill forty-one to three. North Carolina, along with twenty-seven other states by 1937, had realized its value as a practical source of revenue during the Depression. General fund revenues for the fiscal year 1936–37 increased $8 million over the previous year. The sales tax had revolutionized the role of state and local governments. With the state assuming control of schools and roads and funding them with the sales tax, state revenues by 1936 had almost doubled since 1931, and during the same period county and city revenues declined almost by half. Legislators in 1937 expressed little interest in reversing that trend by abolishing the sales tax.[3]

The 1937 General Assembly approved the largest budget in the state's history, not out of sympathy for New Deal goals, but partly to justify the continuance of the sales tax, according to Anthony J. Badger. Voice votes quickly passed the appropriations bill. Additional revenues because of improved business conditions and an increase in the income, liquor, and gift taxes financed the $79 million appropriation despite the loss of $2 million a year from the removal of the sales tax from food. Public schools received the largest appropriation for the biennium, $50 million. Although it represented a $10 million increase over the previous biennium, the state's support of public schools and colleges had not returned

3. Corbitt, ed., *Papers of Hoey*, p. 7; Lefler, ed., *North Carolina History*, p. 458; Patterson, *New Deal and the States*, p. 97; *Raleigh News and Observer*, January 9, February 12, 13, March 24, 28, and editorial, 1937; editorial, *Greensboro Daily News*, March 24, 1937; *North Carolina House Journal*, 1937, pp. 165, 179–80, 195; *North Carolina Senate Journal*, 1937, pp. 171, 213.

to pre-1930 levels. The legislature granted a 10 percent pay raise for state employees, including teachers, and provided free textbooks for elementary school children, a move Senator John Sprunt Hill of Durham denounced as "state socialism." Highway fund revenues declined $5.7 million from 1936 to 1937, and expenditures, both state and federal, for highway construction projects also dropped $1.3 million from 1936–37 to 1937–38. The legislature also allotted $250,000 to promote tourism and industry in the state.[4]

The legislature addressed social programs. After it met in a special session and passed the workmen's compensation act in December 1936, the General Assembly of 1937 complied by overwhelming majorities with the remaining social security programs. Initiated in the Senate by Gertrude Dills McKee, head of the Committee on Public Welfare, the bill passed forty-five to one. Effie Lee Griffith Hutchins sponsored it in the House, where members approved it ninety-seven to one. The *News and Observer* called the social security legislation the most important action of the 1937 legislature. Addressing the legislature, Frank Bane, executive director of the Social Security Board, likened the program to "hitching up three wild horses—state, county, and federal governments." Representative Willie Lee Lumpkin, always an administration foe, wanted coverage expanded, but representative David L. Ward, chairman of the House Appropriations Committee, wanted no financial obligation for counties. An economy bloc failed to reduce payments. Senator James A. Bell of Mecklenburg County, the only senator to vote against it, complained that it would mean "paying contributions to the damnyankees." Old-age insurance covered only half the state's workers; counties and the state shared the cost of the public assistance programs with the federal government. With funds from the 1937 legislature, the state welfare department operated the commodity distribution program. During the 1938–39 fiscal year, the welfare department distributed food and clothes with an estimated retail value of $2.7 million to relief clients. Although social security and other services marked a strong commitment by the federal, state, and local governments, North Carolina trailed thirty-nine other states in meeting its general relief needs not covered by social security. In April 1938 general relief cases in

4. Corbitt, ed., *Papers of Hoey*, pp. 95–97; North Carolina State Highway and Public Works Commission, *Biennial Report, 1937–1938*, pp. 64, 128; *Raleigh News and Observer*, January 7, 13, March 3, 24, 28, 1937; Lefler, ed., *North Carolina History*, pp. 459, 469–70; Lefler and Newsome, *North Carolina*, p. 655; Badger, *North Carolina and the New Deal*, p. 69; *North Carolina House Journal*, 1937, p. 192; *North Carolina Senate Journal*, 1937, p. 237.

the state received an average per capita expenditure of only $5.16 a month.[5]

In labor legislation the General Assembly of 1937 made little progress. Pressured by farmers and manufacturers, the House rejected the federal Child Labor Amendment fifty-eight to forty-seven, the third time it was defeated in the state since 1924. The measure did not even make it out of John Sprunt Hill's Senate Committee on Manufacturing, Labor, and Commerce. Hoey opposed it, and Representative Walter "Pete" Murphy led the fight against it in the House with the cry "protect the sovereign rights of North Carolina." In committee hearings, former representative Ulysses S. Page predicted it would mean "more than one little Yankee woman snooping around" checking on people's children. Willie Lee Lumpkin, its sponsor in the House, called it "nothing radical and nothing dangerous" to states' rights, and the state Federation of Labor also pushed for it. Under the leadership of Senator Gertrude Dills McKee, a textile manufacturer, the lawmakers passed a state law prohibiting children under sixteen from working. In the House, D. Lacy McBryde and George A. Uzzell introduced a forty-hour-workweek bill for textile and tobacco manufacturing, forty-eight hours for everyone else, except for agricultural workers and domestics. When that failed in committee, they accepted a maximum hour law, forty-eight for women and fifty-five for men, with exemptions for agricultural workers and domestics, which passed both chambers with voice votes. McBryde called it "an advance in the right direction." Not until 1959 would there be a minimum wage law.[6]

On other New Deal–related issues, the legislature had a mixed record. To replace the AAA, legislators passed a tobacco compact bill, which called for state production controls. The state rather than the federal government would control the tobacco crop, but the quotas would be set in cooperation with other states. William G. Clark pushed the measure in the Senate, while W. W. Eagles led the drive in the House. The bill passed easily, but the action was meaningless when neighboring states failed to reciprocate. The General Assembly did

5. North Carolina State Board of Charities and Public Welfare, *Biennial Report, 1936–1938*, pp. 10, 69; J. S. Kirk, "Public Assistance Statistics, July–September, 1937," p. 2, memo, A. E. Langston, March 28, 1938, Langston to R. G. Deyton, June 6, 1939, Governors' Papers (H); *Raleigh News and Observer*, January 7, 31, February 11, 28, March 6, 9, 28, 1937; *North Carolina House Journal*, 1937, pp. 191, 446; *North Carolina Senate Journal*, 1937, pp. 75, 137, 348; Badger, *North Carolina and the New Deal*, p. 50.

6. *North Carolina House Journal*, 1937, pp. 98, 108, 114, 167, 377, 711–12; *North Carolina Senate Journal*, 1937, pp. 201, 207, 263, 592, 597; *Raleigh News and Observer*, January 22, February 2, 19, March 3, 24, 1937.

loosen liquor laws by extending local option to all counties. Dry forces did not get the liquor referendum they wanted. Lawmakers, however, refused to pass legislation enabling cities to use PWA funds through a bond program after a 1935 law that allowed them to do so expired in 1937. Power companies, fearful of PWA-built public power plants, fought the legislation. The issue was revived in August 1938 when Governor Hoey called a special session of the legislature to pass a law enabling counties and cities to participate in PWA building projects. A $4.6 million bond program passed with no dissent in the Senate and by a vote of seventy-two to fifteen in the House; however, an amendment required state Utilities Commission clearance for projects, a victory for the power companies. On balance, the General Assembly of 1937 and Governor Hoey, in the early months of his term, proved that a state government dominated by business and agrarian interests and preoccupied with a balanced budget and low wages could never experience a little New Deal or generate enthusiasm for the one in Washington.[7]

Events for the remainder of 1937 marked a watershed in relations between the state's conservatives and the Roosevelt administration. The court-packing episode and recession severely ruptured consensus favoring the New Deal in the state. Up to this point conservative Democrats, despite strong private reservations, had cooperated with the New Deal. Gardner and Hoey's strategy for the 1936 primaries and the tone of Hoey's inaugural address reflected at least a conciliatory public posture toward the New Deal and liberalism. The president's popularity, the economic emergency, party loyalty, and the political and economic benefits from recovery programs required concessions from conservatives. Roosevelt's court reform bill, however, ended the pretense of harmony and quickened opposition toward the New Deal to public denunciation. Even though supporters in North Carolina linked court reform to a restoration of AAA crop controls, popular in the state, conservatives fought it without adverse political consequences.

Max Gardner's response to court packing symbolized the conservatives' exasperation with the New Deal by 1937. The former governor, important to FDR for ties to the business community and as the unques-

7. *North Carolina Senate Journal*, 1937, pp. 101–2; *Journal of the Senate of the General Assembly of the State of North Carolina*, Extraordinary Session, 1938, Regular Session, 1939, p. 39; *North Carolina House Journal*, 1937, pp. 47, 118; *Journal of the House of Representatives of the General Assembly of the State of North Carolina*, Extraordinary Session, 1938, Regular Session, 1939, pp. 13, 38; *Raleigh News and Observer*, January 12, 20, March 24, 1937; *Charlotte Observer*, August 2, 9, 11, 13, 1938; Whitener, *Prohibition*, p. 217; Badger, *North Carolina and the New Deal*, pp. 69–70.

tioned leader of North Carolina Democrats, shifted from private cooperation to private opposition to the New Deal. Publicly, Gardner maintained conciliatory relations with the president. Throughout the decade Gardner had always been a conservative, not a reactionary, and not a New Dealer at heart. If one conviction characterized his overall career from state Senate to New Deal Washington it had been the need to protect business. Gardner, as a mill owner, welcomed the early New Deal. The NRA provided the industrial self-regulation and economic rationalization that upper South textile executives sought since the late 1920s in their competition with newer mills in the Deep South. Furthermore, the state's landowners benefited handsomely from the AAA tobacco and cotton programs. Initially Roosevelt's reforms must have seemed similar to Wilson's Progressive New Freedom, which twenty years earlier had not threatened the South but had helped it. Southerners like Gardner had perhaps confused the New Deal with Progressivism and were lulled into viewing Washington as an ally. Wilson had provided federal assistance without challenging the status quo in race, class, and property relations. By 1935 the New Deal, with prolabor and increasingly antibusiness measures, had shifted to a northern-urban bias in the eyes of southern conservatives like Gardner. After Roosevelt's reelection, Gardner wrote to a friend that he regretted his prior accommodation to Roosevelt. "This movement [New Deal] will spend itself in time, but my thought is that we should go along with it, try to direct it as far as possible, yielding where yielding is wise and then finally at the proper time take a stand. But when we take a stand we will have advanced forward considerably beyond the front lines of our old intrenchment." Court reform for Gardner marked the proper time to take that stand.[8]

Gardner's affinity for the New Deal before 1937 had been for practical, not ideological, reasons. No longer ambitious for elective office since leaving the governorship, Gardner concentrated on building a clientele as a major corporate lawyer-lobbyist in Washington for North Carolina business interests. "Interested in accumulating wealth," as well as a man of "tremendous ability," was the way Sam Ervin remembered him. With clients like the Cotton Textile Institute, Duke Power, and the National Aeronautic Organization, Gardner earned a six-figure income. It was important, therefore, to his clients and for new business that he have

8. Newspaper clipping, *Winston-Salem Journal*, January 27, 1934, Gardner to Clayton Moore, November 10, 1936, Gardner Papers; I. A. Newby, *The South: A History* (New York: Holt, Rinehart and Winston, 1978), pp. 377–79.

influence in New Deal Washington. Gardner had known Roosevelt while both served as governors, had been an early, eager supporter of his presidential bid, and after 1932 enjoyed "ready entree" at the White House as a presidential adviser. The president perhaps respected Gardner's advice more because Gardner repeatedly turned down presidential appointments. He served as a useful interpreter of the New Deal to conservative businessmen such as Robert Woodruff of Coca-Cola. In addition to Roosevelt he advised Harold Ickes on legal matters, wrote some speeches for James Farley, and played golf with Marvin McIntyre. For business and personal reasons, Gardner kept secret his opposition to the New Deal in the late 1930s.[9]

His misgivings about the New Deal were strong after Roosevelt announced proposed changes for the Supreme Court. "I am thoroughly alarmed over the trend," he wrote to Josiah Bailey. He reminded his textile friend Ben Gossett that the Supreme Court had been a good friend of the South, and he expressed relief that southern Democrats opposed the president. "I have followed him [FDR] with reluctance at times and occasionally at a distance, but I had to stop cold in my tracks when he laid his hands on the Supreme Court," he wrote to Julian S. Miller, editor of the *Charlotte Observer.* To his son he complained about the "trend and motive that lies behind this" and cited the president's lack of candor about the reason for the bill, his "tricky" method, and the threat of "constitutional dictatorship" as reasons for his opposition. "The President is hell bent to have his own way," he added. In an address to the South Carolina Bar Association Gardner warned that the "twilight zone" of confusion between federal and state authority needed clarification. He noted that throughout the 1930s funding and control for public services moved steadily from local and state levels to the federal government, and states needed to assert themselves. A more liberal Supreme Court would make a reversal of that trend more difficult. Congressman Alfred Lee Bulwinkle immediately resisted it, and Governor Hoey, like Gardner, privately opposed the court plan, as did Representatives Doughton and Warren.[10]

9. Morrison, *Gardner,* pp. vii–viii, 139, 147, 156; interview of Sam Ervin by Dick Dabney, January 8, August 2, 1974; interview of Edwin Gill by Archie K. Davis, September 10, 12, October 2, 1974; Badger, *North Carolina and the New Deal,* pp. 61–62, 71–72.

10. Gardner to Bailey, February 6, 1937, to Ralph Gardner, February 10, 1937, to B. B. Gossett, July 16, 1937, to Julian S. Miller, July 17, 1937, address to the South Carolina Bar Association, March 26, 1937, Gardner Papers; Hoey to Bibb Graves, April 14, 1937, Governors' Papers (H); Badger, "North Carolina and the New Deal," pp. 80, 121–22; Badger, *North Carolina and the New Deal,* p. 86.

Senator Bailey, fearing that after capturing the presidency and Congress liberals would move against the Supreme Court, opposed Roosevelt's plan vigorously. "My regret is inexpressible," he declared in a press release. He called the scheme, which threatened the last conservative check on the New Deal, "abhorrent to the minds of thoughtful men and women." Encouraged by Justice George Sutherland, Bailey attacked the plan as a "devious ploy" in a nationwide radio address on February 13. Bailey's Senate speech on the court bill concerned Senator Joe Robinson, a proponent of the measure: "Bailey's in there and he's making a great speech. . . . He's impressing a lot of people, and I tell you I'm worried." "I had rather have made a speech like that than be a senator for fifty years," Superior Court Judge Sam Ervin wrote, congratulating Bailey on his stand. At the height of the court fight, Bailey angered New Dealers in the state by inviting Senator Millard Tydings of Maryland to address a March 3 state Democratic party victory celebration. Tydings, a Roosevelt critic, spoke of "regimentation" and "subversive trends." Later in 1937 Bailey opposed the nomination of Hugo L. Black to replace Justice Willis Van Devanter and privately urged Justices Pierce Butler, James McReynolds, George Sutherland, and Charles Evans Hughes not to retire but instead to "sacrifice," "to resist the temptation," so as to prevent a "disaster." Representative Barden also resisted court reform. "I realize that my natural tendency is more conservative," he wrote a constituent. He feared "monkeying" with the Supreme Court, changing the number of justices for ideological reasons.[11]

The president did have strong support in the state. Though in Mexico as ambassador, Josephus Daniels "led the charge" for court reform in the state through personal appeals and editorials in his *News and Observer.* Since their cabinet relationship in the Wilson administration Daniels and Roosevelt had been close, especially after 1930. Roosevelt visited the Daniels home in Raleigh on his way to Warm Springs, Georgia. Daniels had had a remarkable career, and as Otis L. Graham, Jr., has noted, one that did not fit a pattern. Similar in many respects to his hero Bryan, Daniels was evangelical, dry, and provincial, and his newspaper had a rural constituency. Yet Daniels grew more radical over the years,

11. Press release, [February 1937]; Bailey to Henry Wilson, February 8, 1937, to Justice Sutherland, February 26, 1937, to Justice Pierce Butler (and same letter to Justices McReynolds, Hughes, and Sutherland), September 25, 1937, to FDR, October 4, 1937, Bailey Papers; *Raleigh News and Observer,* March 4, 1937; editorial, *Charlotte Observer,* March 8, 1937; Moore, *Bailey,* pp. 130–31, 137; Patterson, *Congressional Conservatism,* p. 96; interview of Sam Ervin by Dabney, January 8, August 2, 1974; Barden to A. H. Edgerton, January 18, 1937, Barden Papers.

and as Graham observed, "his ardent New Dealism is astonishing." His enthusiasm for the New Deal sprang from more than mere party loyalty, for his battles with plutocracy that originated in the Progressive Era intensified through the 1930s. If the New Deal had a fault, for him it was too conservative. According to Daniels, the judiciary was thwarting the democratic wishes of the people, and it had to be changed. Angry with liberals who defected, Daniels argued that New Deal policies were "hanging in the balance."[12]

His son Jonathan Daniels, also eager for a fight, rallied support for Roosevelt and publicized a speech by Interior Secretary Harold Ickes that pro–New Deal Democrats in the state promoted to counter Tydings's address the week before. On March 12, approximately two thousand persons in Raleigh's Memorial Auditorium heard Ickes, in a speech carried by NBC, attack the previous week's dinner as "sad tidings" and declare that the president would purge the Court of "usurped powers." Tobacco interests in the state linked court reform to a return of AAA crop controls, which had restored relative prosperity to North Carolina tobacco farmers before the Supreme Court invalidated it. In 1936 substitutes for the AAA had not worked. Jonathan Daniels argued that a constitutional amendment would take ten to twenty years to pass; in the meantime farmers might starve to death. With constituent support as high as 95 percent in tobacco-growing areas, and with Farm Bureau pressure, many Tar Heel congressmen backed Roosevelt. Frank Hancock, first in the delegation to give unqualified support, was on the steering committee for the bill and delivered an NBC radio address on its behalf. Representative Cooley vigorously defended the president in the House. The New Deal and the Democratic party regarded human life as more important than property rights, he argued. He characterized some recent Supreme Court decisions as "carbuncles upon the constitution" and hoped that new justices would "carve the offending growth from the body of . . . organic law." Senator Reynolds viewed the court plan as utilitarian, a way to change a court too protective of bankers and big corporations. In addition to Hancock, Cooley, and Reynolds, Zebulon Weaver and John Kerr, along with former governor Ehringhaus, endorsed the measure; only five of the thirteen members of Congress from the state took such a stand. The General Assembly, with quick voice votes, easily passed a resolution in favor of the court plan and

12. Cronon, "Southern Progressive," pp. 169–71; interview of Jonathan Daniels by Eagles, March 9–11, 1977; Morrison, *Josephus Daniels*, pp. 153, 174–75; Otis L. Graham, Jr., *An Encore for Reform: The Old Progressives and the New Deal* (New York: Oxford University Press, 1967), pp. 7, 114–15, 119.

requested the state's congressional delegation to vote for it. A Gallup poll revealed that only 51 percent in the state favored it, about the national average. Most in the delegation remained silent, however, during the controversy. The Tar Heel response to court packing, however, illustrated Roosevelt's national problem: presidential popularity and constituent pressure were not enough to change congressional votes, even in North Carolina when tied to an important tobacco program. Conservative business interests had prevailed again.[13]

By the end of 1937 a recession had stiffened the conservatives' opposition to the New Deal. In February 1938, construction contracts awarded in the state equaled only slightly more than half the figure for February 1937, while new car registrations dropped 40.4 percent and the number of cotton bales consumed in textile production fell 34 percent from the previous year. For the long term, Gardner argued that Roosevelt must change his attitude toward business, perhaps through a revision of tax laws. The private sector could not promote economic recovery, he complained, because of the "straight jacket" the New Deal had put on business. Gardner, however, blamed Roosevelt's cuts in public spending for the recession, revealing again his desire for federal largesse but not federal control. For the short term, he believed that if there were no more bold, public spending to end the slump, North Carolinians would "chill on the New Deal."[14]

Recession on the heels of the court-packing episode led Senator Bailey to his most dramatic rejection of the New Deal, and by late 1937 he had become nationally prominent in his opposition to Roosevelt. Since 1933 Bailey had been at odds with the New Deal, his resistance tempered only by pressure from tobacco growers and political realities of the solid South. His biographer said he was "devoted to ideals of individualism, hard-work, self-help, sound money, a balanced budget, strong local government, and administrative efficiency." By 1934 he had voted against three of the ten major New Deal measures, recognized the

13. Address by Frank Hancock, March 2, 1937, Bailey to North Carolina General Assembly, April 17, 1937, Gardner Papers; Josephus Daniels to FDR, April 5, 1937, PPF 86, Roosevelt Papers; *Raleigh News and Observer*, March 4, 13, 28, 1937; Cronon, "Southern Progressive," pp. 168–71; Morrison, *Josephus Daniels*, p. 193; Pleasants, "Robert Reynolds," pp. 308, 310; Badger, *Prosperity Road*, pp. 141–43; Badger, *North Carolina and the New Deal*, p. 86; *Congressional Record*, 75th Cong., 1st sess. (1937), pp. 1978–81; *North Carolina House Journal*, 1937, p. 691; *North Carolina Senate Journal*, 1937, p. 565; Tindall, *Emergence of the New South*, p. 622.

14. Malcolm B. Catlin, "Relief and Economic Statistics: N.C.," April 1938, WPA Papers; Gardner to William C. Appleton, October 28, 1937, to Doughton, November 5, 1937, to Julian S. Miller, November 15, 1937, to W. D. Anderson, November 22, 1937, speech to Gastonia Chamber of Commerce, January 27, 1938, Gardner Papers.

shallowness of many of the recovery programs, and decided that the Depression would end only if the federal government concentrated on restoring business. Fearing political retribution, Bailey concealed his objections through 1936, limiting his opposition to a few votes, and won reelection in 1936 as a Roosevelt "supporter." A few days after that victory, however, Bailey warned James Farley: "I am going to follow conservative lines." Since his Senate actions had not hurt him politically, the 1936 results stiffened his resistance to Roosevelt's programs. By 1939 Bailey was the seventh most conservative Democrat in the Senate.[15]

Bailey survived politically amid overwhelming Tar Heel enthusiasm for Roosevelt and the New Deal because of his shrewd political skills. "Astute, intelligent, and persistent," according to James Patterson, he kept his opponents off guard with a strong organization and on-again, off-again support for the president. Bailey's hypocrisy frustrated his political foes. Josephus Daniels warned Roosevelt that if Bailey were reelected, he would "fly the coop." He had never really favored any liberal policies, Daniels added, and he only praised the president to get votes, then joined the reactionaries. "Bailey could sit still and be a greater demagogue, pretending to be a Democrat when he was a complete reactionary Republican," Jonathan Daniels argued. To him, Bailey was "off the reservation" about two-thirds of the time. Once, to call attention to his duplicity, Jonathan Daniels for a few months ran Bailey's speech, seconding Roosevelt's nomination in 1936, on the *News and Observer* editorial page, while Bailey opposed the New Deal publicly. Daniels characterized it as "Chinese water torture," and finally Bailey urged him to stop it.[16]

Contemporaries, even foes, acknowledged his political acumen. "He was an able man, but oh, so damn conceited. He thought he was the most brilliant man that ever went to the Senate," recalled Jonathan Daniels. "He strutted even when he sat down," he added. W. J. Cash conceded that in ability, even integrity, Bailey was on a "higher level" with a "better background than usual for a southern senator." Thad Eure, a political friend, characterized him as a smart debater, a "deep thinker," a person of "sound judgment." He could and sometimes did, Eure recalled, take both sides of an issue, and one could not tell which side he

15. Bailey to James Farley, November 10, 1936, Bailey Papers; Moore, *Bailey*, pp. 78, 107–8; Patterson, *Congressional Conservatism*, pp. 27n, 82–83.

16. Patterson, *Congressional Conservatism*, pp. 29, 50; Josephus Daniels to Roosevelt, January 5, 1937, Box 96, Josephus Daniels Papers; interview of Jonathan Daniels by Eagles, March 9–11, 1977; interview of Jonathan Daniels by Singal and Tindall, March 22, 30, 1972.

favored. Sam Ervin, also an ally, described him as "very able," a "constitutional scholar," someone "politically very much on his own." Unlike other officeholders, according to Ervin, Bailey did not have the "political itch."[17]

By 1937 Bailey's opposition to the New Deal was public, overt, and total as he shed any pretense of cooperation with Roosevelt. As James Patterson noted, Bailey saw issues in simple terms and like other conservatives sought a pre-1933 America, devoid of federal power, encroaching bureaucracy, deficit spending, aggressive labor unions, and welfare programs. Bailey recognized that the South had problems, but as W. J. Cash pointed out, he was more concerned with "legalisms than realities." His remedies were those that favored the landowners and commercial and industrial interests. Bailey's career, however, did contain some persistent threads of Wilsonian liberalism. In the 1930s, as he had as a prewar Progressive, Bailey believed in competition for business, deference to states' rights, and politics with a moral tinge. Bailey's demeanor was even Wilsonian. His biographer described him as a "man of studied dignity," "proud and haughty," and an appearance that "hinted at the Baptist minister." But Bailey, as a former southern Progressive, discovered that the hard-nosed economic features of the New Deal, unlike Wilsonian liberalism, threatened the status quo in the region.[18]

By the end of 1937, Bailey had fought court packing as a threat to the Court's ability to check the New Deal. He was also convinced by the recession that the federal government could not end economic distress. With the Supreme Court's increasing approval of the New Deal he believed that now only Congress could thwart Roosevelt's designs. In December 1937 Bailey and a coalition of conservative Republican and Democratic senators issued a "Conservative Manifesto," which was both probusiness and anti–New Deal. "We propose to preserve and rely upon the American system of private enterprise and initiative, and our American form of government," they declared. Bailey, draftsman of the document, called for investment of savings, not emergency public spending; probusiness tax policies; a balanced budget; end of government competition with private enterprise; just relations between capital and labor; maintenance of states' rights; and a return to private and local relief. The conservative solution in brief was that "private enterprise, properly

17. Interview of Jonathan Daniels by Eagles, March 9–11, 1977; Cash, *Mind of the South*, p. 434; interview of Thad Eure by Abrams, June 21, 1983; interview of Sam Ervin by Dabney, January 8, August 2, 1974.

18. Cash, *Mind of the South*, p. 434; Patterson, *Congressional Conservatism*, pp. vii–viii, 28; Moore, *Bailey*, pp. v, 3.

fostered, carries the indispensable element of vigor." As Bailey wrote later to the vice-president of the Southern Railway, the issue was politics versus business.[19]

Over 1.5 million copies of Bailey's "recovery program" circulated throughout the country, but the obstacles for conservatives uniting against the New Deal were formidable. For Bailey and fellow southerners there were twin burdens of association with the Republicans in the bipartisan effort and the perception of party disloyalty, a stinging charge for Bailey since he defeated Simmons in 1930 over the latter's refusal to back Al Smith. Bailey's persistence, nonetheless, revealed the primacy of his probusiness views over party. To defend himself against the charges of party disloyalty, he placed full-page ads in newspapers proclaiming, "Senator Bailey chooses the hard way." Shifting the burden, Bailey questioned Roosevelt's party loyalty because he had aided non-Democrats, had admitted to voting Republican, and had appointed Republicans to his cabinet. Bailey also pointed out that Josephus Daniels, to whom party loyalty approached fanaticism, had advocated fusion with Populists in North Carolina in the 1890s. Instead of party loyalty, Bailey challenged critics to deal with the issues of the manifesto.[20]

Despite the mounting conservative criticism of Roosevelt, the ambitious conservative coalition floundered and anti–New Deal Democrats in North Carolina did not challenge proponents of the president's reform program in the state's 1938 primaries. In the only statewide race, Senator Reynolds sought reelection, and unlike some other states, North Carolina experienced no liberal-conservative primary duels. Anti–New Dealers avoided a fight because Roosevelt, despite all his problems and enemies, remained personally popular in the state. Gardner and Bailey instead aided Senator Walter F. George of Georgia in his struggle against a Roosevelt-backed primary opponent. Both Gardner and Bailey wrote speeches for Senator George, and Gardner, who valued George as a great friend of the textile industry, worked with his contacts in Washington on behalf of George's campaign. At one point Gardner suggested that in response to any attacks from Roosevelt, George should remind audiences that the president had voted for a

19. "An Address to the People of the United States by Certain Members of the Senate," December 1937; Bailey to E. R. Oliver, May 18, 1938, Bailey Papers; Patterson, *Congressional Conservatism*, pp. 99, 190–91, 202, 204; Moore, *Bailey*, pp. 155, 159.

20. Bailey to the editor, *Raleigh News and Observer*, December 28, 1937, to John D. Gold, February 19, 1938, Bailey Papers; Patterson, *Congressional Conservatism*, pp. 198–200, 207, 255; Moore, *Bailey*, pp. 144–45, 151, 159; Michie and Ryhlick, *Dixie Demagogues*, p. 161.

Republican president, Theodore Roosevelt, in 1904. Gardner's efforts on behalf of George remained secret because publicly he continued to support the president. "What we need is a very broad tolerance in the Democratic Party," Bailey reminded Roosevelt. Just as conservatives accepted some Republicans and socialists in the national administration, now New Deal Democrats had to tolerate conservatives, he added, or the party would suffer. Roosevelt's "purge" in 1938 threatened conservative Democrats in the South, like Gardner and Bailey, who tolerated a New Deal victory on the national level, Josephus Daniels pointed out angrily, as long as their own positions of power in the state remained secure.[21]

In 1938 Senator Robert Reynolds, a loyal New Dealer for five years, faced a primary challenger, Congressman Frank Hancock, who had equally liberal credentials. Their race, therefore, revolved around personalities and issues other than ideological ones. Since entering the Senate, Reynolds voted for virtually all Roosevelt's measures, strongly supporting tax and relief ones. In Congress Reynolds had pressed for inflation. In 1933 he endorsed economist Irving Fisher's "stamp money," and he voted for the veterans' bonus, a prevailing wage for work relief, and wage and hour legislation for its inflationary results. In addition to the veterans' bonus and prevailing wage issues, Reynolds opposed President Roosevelt in 1938 by seeking repeal of the undistributed profits tax. Earlier, he had tried unsuccessfully to exempt small businesses from wage and hour legislation. After 1935 Reynolds paid most attention to immigration restriction and deportation of alien criminals, an issue for him because of competition for relief and jobs. He traveled abroad frequently, took his senatorial duties lightly, and the political establishment in the state did not take him seriously. "Erratic and irrelevant," V. O. Key labeled him. The state's most prominent "wet," Reynolds remained a powerful orator, a charismatic personality, and a folk hero to many North Carolinians. Jonathan Daniels described him as a "demagogue who is clown, not master," a "persuasive jackass." "He was just nothing," Daniels exclaimed. He had supported Reynolds through 1938 because the senator was a strong New Dealer, and he did not want the "conservative Bailey crowd" to capture the seat. During the 1936 campaign, Reynolds had logged six thousand miles and had given seventy-five speeches in support of Roosevelt. But to Daniels's dismay

21. Gardner to John A. Sibley, July 12, August 8, 1938, to Russell Leonard, July 18, 1938, to Bob Woodruff, January 13, 1939, to Ben Gossett, January 16, 1939, Gardner Papers; Bailey to Walter F. George, July 14, 1938, "Remarks of Senator Bailey," [1938], Bailey Papers; Cronon, "Southern Progressive," pp. 174–75.

Reynolds "weirdly disintegrated as an opponent of the war and the administation." In 1938 conservatives in the state considered him still too popular and chose not to challenge him. Predicting an overwhelming victory, Reynolds cited his seniority and support of the New Deal as reasons for his reelection. Claiming that millions of aliens took jobs that Americans should have, Reynolds pledged to deport those illegally living in this country.[22]

Frank Hancock, fifth district representative, ideologically the most ardent New Deal advocate in the state congressional delegation, had contributed significantly to housing and banking legislation. With the large urban center of Winston-Salem in his district, he pushed for federal action in housing. "The housing situation in this country amounts to an indictment of our whole civilization," he complained to House members. Lower mortgage interest rates were vital to housing recovery, he believed. In 1934 Congress created the Federal Housing Administration (FHA), which helped middle-class families modernize their homes or build new ones. Not only would Americans have better housing, but building trades and private lending institutions could recover. "The building and loan associations . . . have toted their part of the burden throughout this depression," he reminded colleagues. In 1936 Hancock protested that the FHA had not accomplished its original purpose. Only a few manufacturers of durable goods and a few big banks had benefited, not the building trades. The president, by design, favored stimulating the private sector with the FHA, but the emphasis shifted in 1937 to public, low-cost housing with the Wagner-Steagall Act, which created the United States Housing Authority. For Hancock that was going too far; he dismissed such programs as "permanent socialistic housing schemes." The federal housing program was too expensive, and his solution was to clear the slums and let the poor secure private housing in "decent, second-hand houses." If the government would stimulate home building through private financing, the resulting upward mobility would make more low-rent housing available to low-income families, according to Hancock. In the state congressional delegation, Cooley and Bailey joined him in voting against the housing bill.[23]

22. Pleasants, "Robert Reynolds," pp. 180, 196, 218–20, 222, 224, 271, 274, 279, 283–84, 298–99, 326, 340–41, 722; interview of Jonathan Daniels by Eagles, March 9–11, 1977; *Raleigh News and Observer,* May 18, 1938; Jonathan Daniels, *Tar Heels,* p. 323; Michie and Rhylick, *Dixie Demagogues,* p. 222; Cash, *Mind of the South,* p. 433; Key, *Southern Politics,* p. 206; *Congressional Record,* 73d Cong., 1st sess. (1933), pp. 1028, 1033, 1035; 75th Cong., 1st sess. (1937), pp. 7662–63, 7878, 7887–88, 7948.

23. *Congressional Record,* 73d Cong., 2d sess. (1934), pp. 11206, 11208, 11380–82; 74th Cong., 1st sess. (1935), pp. 3244, 3309–10; 74th Cong., 2d sess. (1936), pp. 4425, 4430,

Hancock's vigorous support of the Banking Act of 1935 had revealed his strong New Deal sympathies. "The Financial Emancipation Proclamation of the Twentieth Century," he labeled the measure, which gave the federal government greater centralized control over banking, currency, and credit. Hancock, who described his monetary views as "pretty liberal," saw it as a necessary shift of economic power from Wall Street to Washington. The bill would thwart "the callous and ruthless manipulation of a few greed-blind bankers." All members of the state delegation voted for it. In a hard-hitting campaign speech in 1936, Hancock attacked the "corporate aristocracy" in Winston-Salem and the state whose "stool pigeons" in Washington posed as friends of the average man and the New Deal but back home fought Roosevelt's advances except when it benefited them. Winston-Salem financial interests deserted Hancock. His district also included one of the largest concentrations of tobacco companies, but he sought a reduction in tobacco taxes for those interests. With high cigarette taxes the "government had its mouth on a wet teat," he declared. Cheaper cigarettes would increase tobacco consumption and help the prices for growers.[24]

Hancock, a liberal in state and national politics and a McDonald supporter in 1936, had few substantive issues to use against Reynolds, a fellow New Dealer. Instead, he attacked his absenteeism and frequent junkets, credited him with a bill to legalize barrooms in the District of Columbia, revealed that Reynolds employed a Virginian in his Senate office, called him a playboy lacking in senatorial dignity, and denounced his crusade against aliens as a fake. Hancock claimed that Reynolds had only seniority as a defense for reelection. He accused Reynolds of sympathies with William Randolph Hearst when he voted against the president on foreign policy matters such as the World Court, the St. Lawrence Waterway, and immigration legislation. Hancock lived in Oxford, only fifty miles from Raleigh, and the tradition since antebellum days of having one senator from the east and one from the west hurt Hancock's chances. He tried to overcome the geographical issue by attacking Senator Bailey, whom he believed supported Reynolds out of self-interest. According to Hancock, having two eastern senators would endanger Bailey's reelection in 1942, and Bailey wanted to avoid the problem. Furthermore, Hancock reasoned, Bailey preferred Reynolds

4679; 75th Cong., 1st sess. (1937), pp. 9249–50, 9294; Pleasants, "Robert Reynolds," p. 305; Moore, *Bailey*, pp. 139–40.

24. *Congressional Record*, 73d Cong., 2d sess. (1934), pp. 6492–95; 74th Cong., 1st sess. (1935), pp. 6733–35, 6738, 6740, 6925–26, 7270–71, 11935; 74th Cong., 2d sess. (1936), pp. 10043–46; Badger, *North Carolina and the New Deal*, p. 80.

as a colleague because he posed little threat to his "domination" of the state's congressional delegation. Hancock pledged to stand up to Bailey and defend President Roosevelt. Although former governor Ehringhaus, former senator Morrison, and Congressman Doughton endorsed Hancock, one of the quietest statewide races in a generation ended in a smashing victory for Reynolds. He outdistanced Hancock by 118,000 votes.[25]

The congressional primaries in 1938 attracted little interest, and no issue divided candidates along liberal-conservative lines. All candidates ran on a platform supporting the New Deal. In the November general election, all Democratic congressional candidates, including Senator Reynolds, won in the lowest voter turnout since 1926. Four of the eleven House members ran unopposed, and apathy, along with rain, kept the number of voters down. In 1939, the GOP increased its number in the legislature to ten members, up from six in 1937.[26]

During the 1939 General Assembly, with liberal and conservative factionalism virtually nonexistent, a short, quiet, harmonious session contrasted with the long, bitter, stormy legislatures of the mid-1930s. Governor Hoey set the tone with his address to the assembly. With no mention of the national administration, he proclaimed: "We believe that economy is still a virtue in government." In the first three months of 1939, the legislators accomplished little, and the state's fiscal policies remained generally the same. Led by House Speaker David L. Ward, a thirty-five-year-old lawyer, the legislators made the sales tax permanent; it would no longer require renewal every two years. With a state surplus of $14.1 million at the beginning of the 1938–39 fiscal year, Governor Hoey and the legislators wanted no changes in the state's taxes. This General Assembly finalized the fiscal revolution begun by the 1933 legislature, when depression economics and politics demanded a practical source of revenue and property tax relief. In 1940 sales taxes, for all states that levied them, represented 53 percent of state revenues, contrasted with 43 percent in 1931. In the South property tax revenues fell from 56.5 percent of total revenues in 1932 to 33.9 percent in 1942.[27]

25. Newspaper clippings, *Greensboro Patriot,* May 30, 1938, *Henderson Daily Dispatch,* June 1, 1938, *Charlotte Observer,* June 11, 1938, Box 374.1, newspaper clippings, *Charlotte Observer,* October 14, 1937, *Raleigh News and Observer,* October 14, 1937, *Oxford Public Ledger,* October 15, 1937, scrapbook 374.4, Hancock Papers; *Raleigh News and Observer,* May 21, 27, June 1, 4, 1938; Pleasants, "Robert Reynolds," pp. 338, 340–41, 354–55.

26. *Raleigh News and Observer,* June 3, 4, 6, July 4, November 1, 2, 8, 9, 1938.

27. Corbitt, ed., *Papers of Hoey,* pp. 34, 55; Patterson, *New Deal and the States,* p. 97; Hoover and Ratchford, *Economic Resources,* p. 198; *Raleigh News and Observer,* January 6, 10, April 4, 1939.

in 1936 and 1937, blamed Roosevelt for capitulating to labor. John L. Lewis and the CIO, according to Bailey, were communist-inspired. "The WPA has collapsed of its own rottenness," Bailey declared in early 1939, and he predicted that other New Deal measures, like wage and hour legislation, would "fall of their own weight." The Fair Labor Standards Act, Bailey argued, cost thirty-five thousand persons in the state their jobs.[31]

In addition to all the other threats from Washington, the 1938 report by the National Emergency Council (NEC) that the "South represents right now the nation's number one economic problem" further angered southern conservatives. Liberals in the state such as Santford Martin, Frank Graham, and Jonathan Daniels agreed with the statement and hoped that the publicity would help in the battle against the region's poverty. Conservatives, however, were resentful and defensive. "Frankness compels me to say that I would never recognize North Carolina from the description given in the report," Governor Hoey insisted. This report pointed to the fundamental contradiction in the anti–New Dealers' position. As Anthony Badger has observed, men like Hoey and Bailey denied the state's poverty when New Dealers argued for progress and reform, but at the same time pled poverty as an excuse for not increasing taxes and financing New Deal relief and recovery efforts. Conservatives in Congress like Bailey also hypocritically demanded fiscal responsibility from Roosevelt but voted for huge expenditures, especially for agriculture, which required deficit spending. Bailey and other southern conservatives wanted the New Deal largesse for southern agriculture but not for the urban North. In response to the NEC report Bailey argued that if the president really believed it, why did the New Deal spend less per capita for relief in the South than elsewhere. For example, Pennsylvania with nine million people, Bailey pointed out, received more WPA aid than the South, with twenty-nine million inhabitants. If the federal government would end its interference in business and provide equal treatment in agricultural policies, Bailey would gladly have accepted an end to federal spending in the region.[32]

31. Bailey to H. B. Jennings, August 4, 1937, to Herbert Hoover, October 18, 1938, to Farley, November 11, 1938, to Carl Goerch, January 23, 1939, Bailey Papers; Max Gardner to Ralph Gardner, March 8, 1937, Gardner Papers; *Raleigh News and Observer*, January 3, 1939; Moore, *Bailey*, p. 168. According to Alan Brinkley, conservatives were very perceptive about New Deal threats to their interests. See Brinkley, "The New Deal and Southern Politics."

32. Martin to Gilbert T. Stephenson, December 1, 1938, Box 4, Martin Papers; address, September 10, 1938, Bailey Papers; Moore, *Bailey*, p. 168; Mertz, *New Deal Policy and Southern Rural Poverty*, pp. 233–34, 261; Jonathan Daniels, "Democracy Is Bread," *Virginia Quarterly Review* 14 (Autumn 1938): 485, 489–90; Patterson, *Congressional Conservatism*, pp. 248, 328; Badger, *North Carolina and the New Deal*, p. 71.

Southern conservatives also recognized a threat to race relations as the economic benefits of the New Deal attracted blacks to the Democratic party. Bailey viewed the prospects of blacks in the party as "extremely distasteful," "the lowest depths of degradation." Bailey blamed men like Ickes and Hopkins for the national party reaching out for black votes in northern cities, and he estimated that about twenty thousand blacks in North Carolina voted in the 1936 primaries. Bailey feared that black power in local elections would lead to black officeholders and patronage demands.[33]

Amid their frustrations in the late 1930s, the state's conservatives hoped for a respite from battles over the New Deal, for none expected Roosevelt to accept renomination for a third term. "Another Roosevelt would destroy us," declared Bailey. Cordell Hull and Paul V. McNutt impressed him as solid compromise choices, but by mid-1939 Bailey wanted a campaign against a third term, not aimed directly against FDR but pushing John Nance Garner's nomination. Max Gardner, who persisted in his guise of private opposition but public support for the New Deal, predicted Roosevelt would not seek a third term. Despite resistance to court packing and secret assistance to Senator George in the 1938 "purge," Gardner, for professional and political reasons, maintained close ties to the White House. After the president named Hopkins secretary of commerce, Gardner served as his adviser for his Senate confirmation hearings. Curiously, Gardner enjoyed a close, almost "father-son" relationship with columnist Drew Pearson, and the conservative Gardner's compatibility with the liberal Pearson illustrated Gardner's considerable skill in moving in both worlds in the late 1930s. By the summer of 1939 Roosevelt's strategy of silence had opponents off balance. As Gardner admitted to Pearson, there was no "well-defined movement" in North Carolina for 1940. To Robert Woodruff of Coca-Cola, Gardner wrote in February 1940 that Roosevelt would not seek a third term for fear of a Republican Congress after 1940. As late as July 1, 1940, Gardner argued to business friend John Hanes that Roosevelt would decline in favor of Hull because he did not want to battle Republican Wendell Willkie.[34]

33. Bailey to Emil Hurja, February 13, 1936, to Pomeroy Nichols, February 2, 1938, to R. G. Cherry, March 1, 1938, to Ralph W. Gardner, September 24, 1938, Bailey Papers; Warren to J. D. Grimes, May 23, 1936, Box 16, Warren Papers; *Raleigh News and Observer*, October 13, 1936; Billington, *Political South*, pp. 77–78, 80; Patterson, *Congressional Conservatism*, p. 257.

34. Bailey to Gardner, October 4, 1938, August 17, 1939, to C. L. Shuping, July 8, 1939, Bailey Papers; Gardner to Robert Woodruff, January 13, 1939, February 20, 1940, to Drew Pearson, June 28, 1939, to John Hanes, July 1, 1940, Gardner Papers; Morrison, *Gardner*, p. viii; Patterson, *Congressional Conservatism*, p. 289.

Believing that Roosevelt would not run, Governor Hoey supported Cordell Hull. Yet, since a Democratic gubernatorial primary was in progress, joining forces with other conservatives in a strong campaign against a third term would have been awkward. In a May 1939 private lunch with Roosevelt, Gardner received the president's blessing for a Hoey favorite-son candidacy. But by the spring of 1940, with Roosevelt's renomination assured, that tactic seemed empty. Still opposed to a third term, Hoey confided to Bailey that he did not want the convention to draft Roosevelt or go on record for a third term. Hoey insisted, however, that if Roosevelt announced as a candidate, he would support his renomination. Bailey could not forgive so easily. To avoid a vote on the third term, he did not want to be a delegate to the national convention in Chicago. Bailey described himself as in "constant opposition" to FDR in North Carolina, but by the fall campaign Bailey was supporting the president.[35]

By 1940 the increasing importance of the war effort more than opposition to the New Deal had brought a decline in the activities of New Deal agencies in North Carolina. In the state WPA enrollees dropped as Roosevelt cut WPA funds but increased defense spending, and employment rose in private industry. The CCC and the PWA suffered severe reductions. Only the NYA was thriving. In June 1940, 11,711 young people participated in the student aid program; however, NYA officials geared the job training in the work programs to defense needs. Even the popular New Deal agricultural programs encountered hardships in the late 1930s. In 1938 compulsory crop controls, after a three-year lapse, returned with the second AAA, but when tobacco income dropped, frustrated growers rejected market quotas for 1939. That strategy failed, too, and the next year they voted to reinstate controls.

The New Deal played out for several reasons. The economic crisis had subsided, and the war turned attention from domestic reform. North Carolina reflected this new mood. From July to December 1940 army and navy contracts for North Carolina firms totaled $42.6 million. During the first ten months of 1940, cotton consumption jumped 7 percent from the previous year, retail furniture sales 8 percent, and department store sales 10 percent. As of March 1940 just under 10 percent of the state's population was unemployed or on work relief. Four years of Governor Hoey's probusiness policies and the war effort brought results. Over four hundred new industries moved to the state and spent

35. Gardner to Hoey, May 31, 1939, Gardner Papers; Hoey to Bailey, April 24, 1940, Bailey to C. L. Shuping, May 11, 1940, Bailey Papers; Corbitt, ed., *Papers of Hoey*, pp. 542–43.

$125 million on industrial expansion. Tourist business increased from $36 million annually to $102 million following the state's first advertising campaign. Fittingly for Hoey, the state in June 1940 enjoyed an $8 million surplus.[36]

In judging the impact of the New Deal in North Carolina, one must distinguish between the federal and state programs. An enormous largesse came from Washington. By 1938 grants and loans for the state had totaled almost $440 million, which New Deal opponents did not turn down for all their philosophical objections.[37] Economically in the short term, the AAA was the most important agency for the state. Tobacco controls succeeded in bringing higher prices and raising farm income. Overall, tobacco under the AAA performed better than other crops in the South and the nation. Cotton, with increased competition from abroad and from synthetics, did not fare as well with reductions. With tobacco's success and the resulting need for labor, displacement of tenants proved less of a problem than elsewhere in the South. Not surprisingly, farmers had embraced production controls enthusiastically but did not support New Deal agricultural programs beyond increased prices for their commodities. Through the Farm Bureau, "middle-class" farmers fought relief efforts for the urban North as well as efforts like the FSA to alleviate tenancy in the state. In the agricultural crisis, tobacco growers acted in their own economic self-interest. Washington had intervened in agriculture, not to reform it but to improve prices.

For the long term, federal agricultural policy produced significant changes. The AAA further entrenched the large landowners and commercial farmers, and production controls made entry into farming more difficult. As historian Pete Daniel observed, "The AAA created a revolution in the rural South." Government intervention brought reduced acreage, which diminished the need for labor. Consequently, sharecropping waned, especially in the cotton South. Higher commodity prices and the income from the government farm programs, making machines affordable, in the postwar period contributed to the shift from sharecropping to more commercial agriculture. For tobacco, Daniel pointed out that change came generally in the 1970s.[38]

36. "WPA: Monthly Report of Employment and Economic Conditions—NC," November 1940, Federal Works Agency, WPA, "Monthly Report of Employment and Economic Conditions:," December, 1940, WPA Papers; Corbitt, ed., *Papers of Hoey*, pp. xiv–xvii, 558–59; *Raleigh News and Observer*, December 29, 1940; North Carolina Department of Labor, *Biennial Report, 1938–1940*, p. 59; Howard, *WPA*, pp. 672–73.

37. Press release, National Emergency Council for North Carolina, [n.d.], Bailey Papers; Howard, *WPA*, p. 672.

38. Daniel, *Standing at the Crossroads*, pp. 121, 123; Pete Daniel, "Going among

The other New Deal agency with a significant economic impact was the NRA. The NRA symbolized North Carolina's response to the New Deal: initial enthusiasm for reasons of economic advantage turned to frustration and resistance once problems mounted. North Carolina, the most industrialized southern state, had problems at the onset of the Depression. Textiles suffered from low prices, overproduction, and cutthroat competition, and so businessmen welcomed the codes, which formalized the trade association strategies promoted since the 1920s. In the short term, the NRA brought a measure of recovery: per capita income, profits, and wages rose, unemployment declined, the work-week shortened, and child labor ended. The enthusiasm was short-lived. In 1934 economic statistics dipped, and businessmen realized that the NRA meant bureaucracy, higher wages, strikes, and unions, and for textiles, the AAA caused higher cotton prices along with the additional burden of processing taxes. Tobacco companies, enjoying high prices and not needing the NRA, fought it and reached a code agreement only a few months before the Supreme Court declared the NRA unconstitutional. Few business leaders in the state mourned the demise of the NRA in 1935. During the years 1936–37, the state's economy returned to 1929 levels, and for the long term, spurred by World War II demand, North Carolina maintained industrial supremacy in the South. In 1945 Texas temporarily replaced it as the leading southern state in value added by manufacturing. The NRA and the Wagner Act promise to labor was never realized.[39]

The New Deal transformed the state welfare department into a major, permanent relief agency, handling some of the social security programs. The NCERA had worked with county welfare personnel. Through public works projects the New Deal left a substantial record of physical achievement. Yet North Carolina ranked very low per capita in receipt of relief funds. Local forces had restricted the welfare state. Farmers and businessmen fought relief, especially high wages for work relief, as a threat to cheap labor and the work ethic. Politicians in Raleigh, led by governors Ehringhaus and Hoey, balked at providing state matching funds for relief. Ehringhaus delayed for about two years before calling for a special session of the legislature to comply with social security. Often patronage battles over relief agencies concerned governors and congressmen more than the purpose of the programs.

Strangers: Southern Reactions to World War II," *Journal of American History* 77 (December 1990): 888, 896–97.

39. Tindall, *Emergence of the New South*, pp. 694, 696–97, 700.

In addition to the economy, the New Deal affected North Carolina in various other ways. Scholars have concluded that the urban South changed little in the 1930s. "In the urban South the forces of conservatism successfully resisted—at least temporarily—the challenges to traditional political, social, and economic conditions," Roger Biles asserts. Urbanization declined almost to the level of the 1890s, and southern cities were ill-equipped to handle the relief burden, David R. Goldfield has observed.[40]

North Carolina's urban population inched upward from 25.8 percent in 1930 to 27.3 percent in 1940. There were, however, some signs of urban vitality. The manufacturing cities of Hickory and Reidsville grew the fastest, followed by the tobacco market towns of Wilson, Greenville, and Kinston, stimulated by the success of the AAA. Public works projects brought physical improvements. The state's two relief administrators had experience in urban relief before assuming their positions: Annie Land O'Berry of the NCERA in Goldsboro and George Coan of the WPA as mayor of Winston-Salem, the state's second largest city. Through the Federal Housing Administration, 25,519 families in North Carolina had received $31.4 million in financing by the end of 1939. The state, however, ranked at or near the bottom in FHA activities for the Southeast, and critics blamed state regulations that limited the participation of building and loan associations in FHA programs. For public housing under the United States Housing Authority (USHA), by 1940 North Carolina had commitments for eleven projects, totaling $9.7 million. Charlotte, the state's largest city, had three projects approved. For New Bern, where two-thirds of all dwellings were substandard, the USHA planned a project with 434 units. In the end, the New Deal offered little to urban North Carolina, a rural state with no city with a population over one hundred thousand. The 1940s, with the economic demands of World War II, proved to be a decade of growth.[41]

The New Deal in North Carolina also had implications for race, class, and gender. Relief in the 1930s aided blacks, a higher percentage of the poor, but the assistance proved inadequate. African-Americans suffered discrimination, lost jobs to whites when wages rose under the NRA, and

40. Roger Biles, "The Urban South in the Great Depression," *Journal of Southern History* 56 (February 1990): 72–74, 99–100; David R. Goldfield, *Cotton Fields and Skyscrapers: Southern City and Region, 1607–1980* (Baton Rouge: Louisiana State University Press, 1982), pp. 142, 149–50, 181–82.

41. Hugh T. Lefler and Albert Ray Newsome, *North Carolina: The History of a Southern State* (Chapel Hill: University of North Carolina Press, 1954), p. 540; Tindall, *Emergence of the New South,* p. 696; L. G. Pfefferkorn to Graham A. Barden, February 16, 1939, Stewart McDonald to Barden, February 21, 1939, April 29, 1940, press release, Federal Works Agency, USHA, May 1, 1940, Barden Papers.

resisted change, which limited the New Deal. Max Gardner, with his conservative state government in place on the eve of the New Deal, set the tone for the decade. The state's response to the Depression—retrenchment, minimal relief effort, and property tax relief—never fundamentally changed after 1933, despite the New Deal. With a strong political organization Gardner perpetuated those policies for the rest of the decade with a handpicked successor, Ehringhaus, followed by Hoey, Gardner's brother-in-law. After 1933 the sales tax assured a balanced budget and tax relief for property owners and corporations. Remarkably for governors without the veto power or right of succession, both Ehringhaus and Hoey prevailed on controversial fiscal matters such as the sales tax. Perhaps in North Carolina a tough, probusiness ideology and loyalty to Gardner's political organization transcended New Deal issues at the state level. The legislature did not expand relief and public works programs but resisted coordination with Washington in those areas. Though North Carolina experienced no little New Deal, the popularity of Roosevelt and his programs forced the conservatives in Raleigh to accommodate some so as to receive funds from Washington. Roosevelt's cooperation with the conservatives weakened the hand of the state's New Dealers, also hurt by poor candidates and an ideology that rarely stretched beyond opposition to the sales tax and Gardner's organization.

In a southern context, North Carolina's political response was a moderate conservatism, not extreme like that of Governor Eugene Talmadge of Georgia, nor as alienated from the New Deal as Senators Carter Glass and Harry F. Byrd of Virginia. But Governors Olin D. Johnston of South Carolina and E. D. "Ed" Rivers of Georgia succeeded in bringing more New Deal reforms in state government. Among southern states, North Carolina, along with Florida, improved agriculturally in the 1930s, while the rest of the South declined. Unlike the Deep South states with large plantation farms, North Carolina remained a state of small farms that recovered thanks to the AAA tobacco program. Upper South mill owners, as in the Tar Heel state, more readily embraced the NRA because they wanted to end the ruinous competition with lower South mills. Even though the New Deal accepted the southern wage differential, southern mills lost ground to New England ones under the NRA. Restrictions imposed by the NRA codes violated the New South creed of industrial growth. In relief statistics, North Carolina remained near the bottom in the region.

Despite the strong impact of the New Deal on North Carolina, the most salient characteristic of federal-state relations in the 1930s was conservative constraints on liberal reform. "The New Deal produced neither federal dictation, a completely cooperative federalism, nor a new state progressivism. Instead . . . a rather flat mixture of achievement, mediocrity, and confusion," concluded James Patterson. The conservative surge that erupted by the late 1930s had been building since 1933. Dependence on state and local governments for cooperation, funds, and administration limited the New Deal's impact. In per capita allocation of New Deal expenditures for 1933–39, the state ranked last in the nation. In 1940 in per capita income North Carolina ranked forty-third nationally, little change from forty-fifth in 1929. The Old North State traveled the road it did in the 1930s because states'-rights, probusiness, conservative traditions, and Roosevelt's deference to them, limited the change brought by the New Deal.[48]

Despite its limitations, the New Deal set in motion forces that would alter the configuration of the state's politics in the immediate postwar period. Reformers, frustrated so long in the 1930s, interrupted the probusiness, conservative rule in the state with the election of W. Kerr Scott as governor in 1948. Scott's appointment of Frank Porter Graham, University of North Carolina president, to the United States Senate, created a high tide for liberalism in the state's leadership. North Carolina's underclass, mostly farmers, lifted by continuing New Deal programs and a war-era economic boom, served as an important constituency for Scott and Graham. But New Deal concessions to labor, higher taxes for welfare, and implicit support for blacks generated opposition and galvanized an alliance between businessmen and conservative Democrats for the postwar era, exemplified by the Dixiecrat movement in 1948. That development foreshadowed the eventual fracturing of the Democratic party and the emergence of a two-party system in North Carolina.[49]

48. Reading, "New Deal Activity and the States," p. 794; Hoover and Ratchford, *Economic Resources*, p. 50; Badger, *North Carolina and the New Deal*, p. 91; Patterson, *New Deal and the States*, pp. 162–63, 202–7.

49. James C. Cobb, *Industrialization and Southern Society, 1877–1984* (1984; rpt. Chicago: Dorsey Press, 1988), pp. 150–53; Lamis, *Two-Party South*, p. 144.

Bibliographical Essay

Records of the New Deal bureaucracies in National Archives, Washington, D.C., are critical sources of information on federal activities in the states. Since the materials are enormous in quantity and uneven in quality, the researcher must rely on the assistance and judgment of archivists for best use of the sources. Some collections are organized better than others: the AAA by subject and general correspondence, the NRA by industry, and much of the WPA by state. Records of the cotton textile, furniture, and tobacco industries are easily accessible in the NRA Papers. Records for North Carolina are most substantial in the AAA, NRA, and WPA Papers. The CCC, NYA, FSA, REA, and Social Security Administration Papers are smaller collections and have less material on North Carolina, mostly scattered throughout the files. Those agency records generally have useful annual summaries. PWA records are thin because Harold L. Ickes, the director, had the agency's records destroyed. The Harry A. Slattery Papers in the Special Collections Department, Duke University Library, Durham, North Carolina, cover his years as REA administrator, 1939–44, and were not useful.

In the New Deal archives, reports compiled by agency bureaucrats usually contain far more information than correspondence. Hours, sometimes days, of routine research were rewarded by the discovery of such gems as a study by black sociologist Charles S. Johnson in the NRA Papers. His "The Tobacco Worker: A Study of Tobacco Factory Workers and Their Family," written in 1935, provides a wealth of detail about black workers and the NRA in North Carolina. "Relation of Agricultural Adjustment Program to Rural Relief Needs in North Carolina," in the AAA Papers, written in 1935 by rural sociologist C. Horace Hamilton, analyzed the impact of the AAA on tenants and sharecroppers in the state. In the NYA Papers, Gordon W. Lovejoy's "Paths to Maturity: Findings of the N.C. Youth Survey, 1938–1940" is a detailed examination of Tar Heel young people. The records of several agencies are excellent concerning efforts on behalf of blacks.

In the North Carolina State Archives in Raleigh, the Governors'

Papers have the most substantial materials on state activities and relations with New Deal agencies. The Gardner and Ehringhaus papers are especially useful, but Hoey's Papers are not, perhaps because of his more casual approach to government and his opposition to the New Deal. The Hoey Papers in the Special Collections Department, Duke University Library, deal with his postwar senatorial career. At the State Records Center in Raleigh, the North Carolina Emergency Relief Administration Papers provide extensive information on welfare and relief efforts.

The personal papers of Senator Josiah W. Bailey in the Special Collections Department, Duke University Library, are both bulky and informative, a mine of lengthy letters carefully explaining his conservative views on the New Deal. Equally activist, but in support of Roosevelt, Josephus and Jonathan Daniels exhibit sympathy for tenant farmers and mill workers and anger at tobacco companies and mill owners. Their papers are at the Library of Congress and the Southern Historical Collection, University of North Carolina, Chapel Hill, respectively. Together, the Bailey and Daniels collections illustrate the clashing views of the 1930s in the state. O. Max Gardner's extensive private papers, in the Southern Historical Collection, reveal a man torn between his conservative instincts and pragmatic cooperation with Roosevelt. The Lindsay C. Warren and John H. Kerr papers, also in the Southern Historical Collection, help unravel the details of New Deal legislation, bureaucracies, and politics from a congressman's point of view. The papers of the following North Carolina congressmen were of minimal value: Robert L. Doughton, Harold D. Cooley, and Carl T. Durham, all in the Southern Historical Collection; Franklin W. Hancock, Jr., in the East Carolina Manuscript Collection, East Carolina University, Greenville, North Carolina; Graham A. Barden in the Special Collections Department, Duke University Library; and Edward W. Pou in the North Carolina State Department of Archives and History, Raleigh. The best source for the views of Doughton, Hancock, Warren, and Cooley on various legislative issues of the New Deal era is the *Congressional Record*, since they engaged in debates occasionally, especially on agricultural matters. More helpful were the papers of state NYA director John A. Lang in the East Carolina Manuscript Collection and state Democratic stalwart James O. Carr in the Southern Historical Collection.

Papers of politicians Richard T. Fountain and Allen J. Maxwell, both in the East Carolina Manuscript Collection, and newspaperman Santford Martin in the Special Collections Department, Duke University Library, give a greater understanding of antimachine-insurgent politics. Charles C. Spaulding's Papers, housed at the North Carolina Mutual Life Insurance Company, Durham, disclose a great deal about his New Deal activities as a black businessman and his work in the black community. He tried to accommodate whites and placate more militant blacks. The papers of the NAACP in the Library of Congress also record struggles by North Carolina African-Americans in the 1930s. In his papers at the Southern Historical Collection Howard W. Odum, a leader of the Commission on Interracial Cooperation, deals with the racial problems of the Depression–New Deal era from the white liberal perspective. At the Roosevelt Library in Hyde Park, New York, the president's papers, the Democratic National Committee's materials, and especially Lorena Hickok's observations about politics and relief contributed to the North Carolina New Deal story.

The transcripts of interviews in the Southern Oral History Program Collection at the University of North Carolina at Chapel Hill provide a lively, personal glimpse into the New Deal era that supplement the manuscript sources. Charles W. Eagles's interview with Jonathan Daniels, crusading New Deal editor of the *Raleigh News and Observer,* and an interview with Daniels by Daniel J. Singal and George B. Tindall cover a wide range of political issues. Richard Dabney's interview with Samuel J. Ervin, Jr., an ally of the Gardner organization during the 1930s, sheds light on the workings of state politics, as does the interview with Edwin M. Gill, longtime state treasurer, by Archie K. Davis. Jacquelyn Dowd Hall interviewed University of North Carolina sociologist Guy B. Johnson, active in the interracial movement during the New Deal and also an expert on race. In addition, Thad Eure, whose long tenure as secretary of state began in the 1930s, shared with the author insights about his mentor Max Gardner and politics in general for the period. Published oral histories such as Federal Writers' Project, *These Are Our Lives* (Chapel Hill: University of North Carolina Press, 1939); Tom E. Terrill and Jerrold Hirsch, eds., *Such as Us: Southern Voices of the Thirties* (New York: Norton, 1978); John L. Robinson, *Living Hard: Southern Americans in the Great Depression* (Washington, D.C.: University Press of America, 1981); Ann Banks, ed., *First Person America* (New York: Knopf, 1980); and Robert S. McElvaine, ed., *Down and Out in the Great Depression: Letters from the "Forgotten Man"* (Chapel Hill: University of North Carolina Press, 1983), present the views of the lower classes during the New Deal era.

For this study, the *Raleigh News and Observer,* the *Charlotte Observer,* and the *Greensboro Daily News* were read extensively for the years 1932 to 1940. The *News and Observer* is the major daily for the east, while the Charlotte and Greensboro papers cover the piedmont. Various other newspapers in all areas of the state were researched for selected events and topics by consulting scrapbooks in several manuscript collections and the North Carolina Collection Clipping File at the University of North Carolina Library in Chapel Hill. The *Raleigh News and Observer* covered the New Deal in the state with detail and enthusiasm. Unabashedly pro–New Deal, both father and son Daniels, through their newspaper, enlivened the debates with conservatives over the direction North Carolina should take. Other newspapers such as the cautiously conservative *Charlotte Observer* and the *Greensboro Daily News,* had solid but bland coverage of the 1930s. Louis E. Austin's black newspaper, the *Durham Carolina Times,* attacked both conservatives and New Dealers when they adversely affected black interests.

Publications by both national and state government agencies record vast statistical information essential to evaluating their achievements during the Depression and the New Deal. Particularly useful are annual United States Department of Agriculture reports on the AAA. For data on public works, the Federal Works Agency, *The First Annual Report: Federal Works Agency 1940* (Washington, D.C.: U.S. Government Printing Office, 1940), and the Public Works Administration, *America Builds: The Record of the PWA* (Washington, D.C.: U.S. Government Printing Office, 1939), are valuable. Biennial reports produced by the state departments of Agriculture, Conservation and Development, Labor, Charities and Public Welfare, and the Highway Commission are both comprehensive and convenient sources for government statistics. *Recent Changes in the Social and Economic Status of Farm Families in North Carolina,* written by C. Horace Hamilton and published in Raleigh by the North Carolina Agricultural Experiment Station in 1937, detailed the impact of New Deal agricultural policy on the state's farmers—landowners, tenants, sharecroppers, and farm laborers. Especially useful for studying the NCERA is J. S. Kirk, Walter A. Cutter, and Thomas W. Morse, eds., *Emergency Relief in North Carolina: A Record of the Development and the Activities of the North Carolina Emergency Relief Administration, 1932–1935* (Raleigh: Edwards and Broughton, 1936). The published papers of Governors Gardner, Ehringhaus, and Hoey make key documents accessible, even though most items are routine. The *Journal* of the General Assembly of North Carolina records the fiscal and political conservatism of state politicians.

Secondary literature on the New Deal era has shifted both its focus and interpretations in the past few decades. For works that celebrate the change brought by the New Deal, see Richard Hofstadter, *The Age of Reform: Bryan to F.D.R.* (New York: Vintage Books, 1955); Carl N. Degler, *Out of Our Past: The Forces That Shaped Modern America* (New York: Harper and Row, 1959); and William E. Leuchtenburg, *Franklin D. Roosevelt and the New Deal, 1932–1940* (New York: Harper & Row, 1963). At a symposium in 1983 Leuchtenburg persisted in his positive assessment of the New Deal; see Leuchtenburg, "The Achievement of the New Deal," in *Fifty Years Later: The New Deal Evaluated,* ed. Harvard Sitkoff (Philadelphia: Temple University Press, 1985), pp. 211–31. Other essays in the volume also praise the New Deal's achievements. For scholars who see less change in the 1930s see Arthur S. Link, *American Epoch: A History of the United States since 1900,* 3d ed. (New York: Knopf, 1967), and Richard S. Kirkendall, "The New Deal as Watershed: The Recent Literature," *Journal of American History* 54 (March 1968): 839–52. For a leftist indictment of the New Deal, see Barton J. Bernstein, "The New Deal: The Conservative Achievements of Liberal Reform," in *Towards a New Past: Dissenting Essays in American History,* ed. Bernstein (New York: Pantheon Books, 1968), pp. 263–88.

In the late 1960s, James T. Patterson shifted New Deal studies away from the president and Congress with his innovative *The New Deal and the States* and concluded that the New Deal encountered enormous obstacles that limited its effectiveness. Recent state and local studies of the New Deal have further denigrated the Roosevelt era as a time of basic change. See Patterson, *The New Deal and the States: Federalism in Transition* (Princeton: Princeton University Press, 1969); and John Braeman, Robert H. Bremner, and David Brody, eds., *The New Deal,* vol. 2, *The State and Local Levels* (Columbus: Ohio State University Press, 1975). According to the chapters on Massachusetts, Virginia, Oklahoma, and Colorado, the New Deal had minimal results in those states, but Louisiana and Pennsylvania were exceptions. For an excellent collection of essays on the New Deal overall, see vol. 1, *The National Level.* In the urban North, where the New Deal had the best chances for success, scholars have found that local forces thwarted change. See Charles H. Trout, *Boston, the Great Depression, and the New Deal* (New York: Oxford University Press, 1977); Bruce M. Stave, *The New Deal and the Last Hurrah: Pittsburgh Machine Politics* (Pittsburgh: University of Pittsburgh Press, 1970); and Jo Ann E. Argersinger, *Toward a New Deal in Baltimore: People and Government in the Great Depression* (Chapel Hill: University of North Carolina Press, 1988).

In the South, less hospitable to reform, the New Deal struggled even more for less results. Scholars have emphasized the limits of Roosevelt's programs, especially for the short-term. See James C. Cobb and Michael V. Namorato, eds., *The New Deal and the South* (Jackson: University Press of Mississippi, 1984); Michael S. Holmes, *The New Deal in Georgia: An Administrative History* (Westport, Conn.: Greenwood Press, 1975); Roger Biles, *Memphis in the Great Depression* (Knoxville: University of Tennessee Press, 1986); Biles, "The Urban South in the Great Depression," *Journal of Southern History* 56 (February 1990): 71–100; Douglas L. Smith, *The New Deal in the Urban South* (Baton Rouge: Louisiana State University Press, 1988); Ronald L. Heinemann, *Depression and the New Deal in Virginia: The Enduring Dominion* (Charlottesville: University Press of Virginia, 1983); Jack Irby Hayes, Jr., "South Carolina and the New Deal, 1932–1938" (Ph.D. dissertation, University of South Carolina, 1972); and Roger D. Tate, Jr., "Easing the Burden: The Era of Depression and the New Deal in Mississippi" (Ph.D. dissertation, University of Tennessee, 1978). In the western states, despite drought and agricultural crises, the Roosevelt "revolution" never took hold. See Francis W. Schruben, *Kansas in Turmoil, 1930–1936* (Columbia: University of Missouri Press, 1969); and Michael P. Malone, *C. Ben Ross and the New Deal in Idaho* (Seattle: University of Washington Press, 1970). To the New Deal's credit, it did stimulate some reform on the state level. See Robert R. Ingalls, *Herbert H. Lehman and New York's Little New Deal* (New York: New York University Press, 1975). Governor Culbert L. Olson in California, however, did not fare as well. See Robert E. Burke, *Olson's New Deal for California* (Berkeley: University of California Press, 1953).

George Brown Tindall's *The Emergence of the New South, 1913–1945* (Baton Rouge: Louisiana State University Press and the Littlefield Fund for Southern History of the University of Texas, 1967) is the most comprehensive treatment of the South in the Depression and New Deal era. His *The Persistent Tradition in New South Politics* (Baton Rouge: Louisiana State University Press, 1975) clarifies further the South's unique political configuration. Also helpful is his article "The 'Colonial Economy' and the Growth Psychology: The South in the 1930's," *South Atlantic Quarterly* 64 (Autumn 1965): 465–77. W. J. Cash's classic *The Mind of the South* (New York: Vintage Books, 1941) includes insights about the Depression and New Deal. For a thoughtful analysis, see Pete Daniel's *Standing at the Crossroads: Southern Life since 1900* (New York: Hill and Wang, 1986). Another standard study, V. O. Key, Jr., *Southern Politics in State and Nation* (New York: Vintage Books, 1949), gauged the influence of business in North Carolina politics, and more recent studies have updated the analysis of regional and state politics.

See Jack Bass and Walter DeVries, *The Transformation of Southern Politics: Social Change and Political Consequence since 1945* (New York: Basic Books, 1976); Alexander P. Lamis, *The Two-Party South* (New York: Oxford University Press, 1984); and Earl Black and Merle Black, *Politics and Society in the South* (Cambridge, Mass.: Harvard University Press, 1987). For general appraisals of recent southern politics Dewey W. Grantham, Jr., *The Democratic South* (Athens: University of Georgia Press, 1963), and Grantham, *The Regional Imagination: The South and Recent American History* (Nashville: Vanderbilt University Press, 1979); Frank Freidel, *FDR and the South* (Baton Rouge: Louisiana State University Press, 1965); and Monroe Lee Billington, *The Political South in the Twentieth Century* (New York: Charles Scribner's Sons, 1975), all are first-rate. In *The New Deal and the South* (Jackson: University Press of Mississippi, 1984), ed. James C. Cobb and Michael V. Namorato, the essays minimize change brought by the New Deal to the South. David R. Goldfield's *Cotton Fields and Skyscrapers: Southern City and Region, 1607–1980* (Baton Rouge: Louisiana State University Press, 1982) places in context the New Deal's impact on the urban South. For a gold mine of useful statistics about the South for this era, consult Calvin B. Hoover and Benjamin U. Ratchford's *Economic Resources and Policies of the South* (New York: Macmillan, 1951). For a focus on ideas in southern history relevant to the 1930s, see Daniel J. Singal's *The War Within: From Victorian to Modernist Thought in the South, 1919–1945* (Chapel Hill: University of North Carolina Press, 1982) and Michael O'Brien *The Idea of the American South, 1920–1941* (Baltimore: Johns Hopkins University Press, 1979).

Both the quality and quantity of sources on North Carolina during the Depression–New Deal era are impressive. The best brief account is Anthony J. Badger's pamphlet *North Carolina and the New Deal* (Raleigh: North Carolina Division of Archives and History, 1981). Elmer L. Puryear's *Democratic Party Dissension in North Carolina, 1928–1936* (Chapel Hill: University of North Carolina Press, 1962) is a good guide to state politics for that period. Another important contribution is Richard L. Watson, Jr.'s "A Southern Democratic Primary: Simmons vs. Bailey in 1930," *North Carolina Historical Review* 42 (Winter 1965): 21–46. See also his "Furnifold M. Simmons: 'Jehovah of the Tar Heels'?," *North Carolina Historical Review* 44 (April 1967): 166–87, for important political background.

Many North Carolinians active in the 1930s are subjects of biographies. John Robert Moore in *Senator Josiah W. Bailey of North Carolina: A Political Biography* (Durham: Duke University Press, 1968) and

Joseph L. Morrison in *Governor O. Max Gardner: A Power in North Carolina and New Deal Washington* (Chapel Hill: University of North Carolina Press, 1971) and *Josephus Daniels: The Small-d Democrat* (Chapel Hill: University of North Carolina Press, 1966) cover the most important figures for the New Deal in the state. James T. Patterson in his *Congressional Conservatism and the New Deal* (Lexington: University of Kentucky Press, 1967) highlights further Bailey's conservative role in the United States Senate. For more on Josephus Daniels, see Otis L. Graham, Jr., *An Encore for Reform: The Old Progressives and the New Deal* (New York: Oxford University Press, 1967), and articles by E. David Cronon, "A Southern Progressive Looks at the New Deal," *Journal of Southern History* 24 (May 1958): 151–76, and "Josephus Daniels as a Reluctant Candidate," *North Carolina Historical Review* 33 (October 1956): 457–82. His son Jonathan Daniels wrote candidly about the state in *Tar Heels: A Portrait of North Carolina* (New York: Dodd, Mead, 1947). R. Mayne Albright wrote about his political contemporary Max Gardner in articles for the *State*, "O. Max Gardner and the Shelby Dynasty," Part 1, 50 (April 1983): 8–11, 27; Part II, 51 (July 1983): 10–13; Part III, 51 (August 1983): 8–11, 26. Grace Rutledge Hamrick, *"Miss Fay:" A Biography of Fay Webb Gardner* (Boiling Springs, N.C.: Gardner–Webb College, 1978), tells the story of Max Gardner's wife and the state's first lady. For a detailed account of North Carolina's other senator in the 1930s, see Julian M. Pleasants, "The Senatorial Career of Robert Rice Reynolds" (Ph.D. dissertation, University of North Carolina, 1971). Elmer L. Puryear also has written *Graham A. Barden: Conservative Carolina Congressman* (Buies Creek, N.C.: Campbell University Press, 1979), a biography of one Tar Heel congressman of the New Deal era. Warren Ashby's *Frank Porter Graham: A Southern Liberal* (Winston-Salem: John F. Blair, 1980) tells the story of the University of North Carolina president who fought for liberal causes but not those directly involving the New Deal. Aubrey L. Brooks in *A Southern Lawyer: Fifty Years at the Bar* (Chapel Hill: University of North Carolina Press, 1950) reminisces about his life and state politics.

For general scholarly works on North Carolina history, see William S. Powell, *North Carolina through Four Centuries* (Chapel Hill: University of North Carolina Press, 1989); Hugh T. Lefler and Albert Ray Newsome, *North Carolina: The History of a Southern State* (Chapel Hill: University of North Carolina Press, 1973); Samuel H. Hobbs, Jr., *North Carolina: Economic and Social* (Chapel Hill: University of North Carolina Press, 1930); Lindley S. Butler and Alan D. Watson, eds., *The North Carolina Experience: An Interpretive and Documentary History*

(Chapel Hill: University of North Carolina Press, 1984); and Thad L. Beyle and Merle Black, *Politics and Policy in North Carolina* (New York: MSS Information Corporation, 1975).

Other works include Don C. Reading's article "New Deal Activity and the States, 1933–1939," *Journal of Economic History* 33 (December 1973): 792–810, which documents the impact of federal programs in North Carolina; John L. Bell, Jr., *Hard Times: Beginnings of the Great Depression in North Carolina, 1929–1933* (Raleigh: North Carolina Division of Archives and History, 1982), a pamphlet that covers the onset of the Depression; and Daniel J. Whitener in *Prohibition in North Carolina, 1715–1945* (Chapel Hill: University of North Carolina Press, 1946) deals with an issue important to the New Deal era. For incisive analysis on the question of North Carolina's image, progressive or conservative, see Richard N. Current, "Tarheels and Badgers: A Comparative History of Their Reputations," *Journal of Southern History* 42 (February 1976): 3–30, and William H. Chafe, *Civilities and Civil Rights: Greensboro, North Carolina, and the Black Struggle for Freedom* (New York: Oxford University Press, 1980). For a thorough account of North Carolina historiography, what has and has not been written, see Jeffrey J. Crowe and Larry E. Tise, eds., *Writing North Carolina History* (Chapel Hill: University of North Carolina Press, 1979).

A critical overall assessment of the NRA is Bernard Bellush, *The Failure of the NRA* (New York: Norton, 1975). Three monographs that deal thoroughly with subjects important to the NRA are Irving Bernstein, *Turbulent Years: A History of the American Workers, 1933–1941* (Boston: Houghton Mifflin, 1970), on workers in the 1934 strikes; Louis Galambos, *Competition and Cooperation: The Emergence of a National Trade Association* (Baltimore: Johns Hopkins Press, 1966) on the Cotton Textile Institute before and during the NRA; and Ellis W. Hawley, *The New Deal and the Problem of Monopoly* (Princeton: Princeton University Press, 1966). *New Deal Labor Policy and the Southern Cotton Textile Industry, 1933–1941* (Knoxville: University of Tennessee Press, 1986), by James A. Hodges, is a critical assessment of New Deal labor policy with examples of North Carolina problems. For a vivid portrait of the cotton mill workers' world, see Jacquelyn Dowd Hall, James Leloudis, Robert Korstad, Mary Murphy, LuAnn Jones, and Christopher B. Daly, *Like a Family: The Making of a Southern Cotton Mill World* (Chapel Hill: University of North Carolina Press, 1987), and Jennings J. Rhyne, *Some Southern Cotton Mill Workers and Their Villages* (Chapel Hill: University of North Carolina Press, 1930). On the cigarette industry, see Nannie M. Tilley, *The R. J. Reynolds Tobacco Company* (Chapel Hill: University of North Carolina Press, 1985); Richard B. Tennant, *The American Cigarette Industry: A Study in Economic Analysis and Public Policy* (New Haven: Yale University Press, 1950); and Ben F. Lemert, "Tobacco Manufacturing Industry in North Carolina," mimeo, NYA of North Carolina, 1939. William Stevens, *Anvil of Adversity: Biography of a Furniture Pioneer* (New York: Popular Library, 1968), is a treatment of James E. Broyhill.

For the AAA in North Carolina, see Anthony J. Badger's *Prosperity Road: The New Deal, Tobacco, and North Carolina* (Chapel Hill: University of North Carolina Press, 1980), a superb study of a New Deal program on a local level. His Ph.D. dissertation, "The New Deal and North Carolina: The Tobacco Program, 1933–1940" (University of Hull, 1974), includes additional useful information. Three fine articles supplement Badger's work: Robert F. Hunter, "The 'AAA between Neighbors': Virginia, North Carolina, and the New Deal Farm Program," *Journal of Southern History* 44 (November 1978): 537–70; James C. Daniel, "North Carolina Tobacco Marketing Crisis of 1933," *North Carolina Historical Review* 41 (July 1964): 370–82; and Joseph A. Coté, "Clarence Hamilton Poe: The Farmer's Voice, 1899–1964," *Agricultural History* 53 (January 1979): 30–41. Clarence Poe's *My First 80 Years* (Chapel Hill: University of North Carolina Press, 1963) has a disappointing chapter on the Depression era. He shared few insights about agriculture for that critical decade. An interim account of the New Deal tobacco program is Harold B. Rowe's *Tobacco under the AAA* (Washington, D.C.: Brookings Institution, 1935). For an overview of the AAA, see Theodore Saloutos, *American Farmer and the New Deal* (Ames: Iowa State University Press, 1982). For solid information and technical analysis, see Samuel Thomas Emory, *Bright Tobacco in the Agriculture, Industry and Foreign Trade of North Carolina* (Chicago: University of Chicago Libraries, 1939).

Several studies focus on various other agricultural topics for the 1930s. Paul L. Conkin's *Tomorrow a New World: The New Deal Community Program* (Ithaca: Cornell University Press, 1959) includes Penderlea Homesteads in North Carolina in this account of New Deal community programs. For detailed information on tenants in the state, see Gordon W. Blackwell, "The Displaced Tenant Farm Family in North Carolina," *Social Forces* 13 (October 1934): 65–73. Overview treatments of tenants and sharecroppers for the 1930s are David E. Conrad's *The Forgotten Farmers: The Story of Sharecroppers in the New Deal* (Urbana: University of Illinois Press, 1965) and Donald H. Grubb's study of the Southern Tenant Farmers' Union, *Cry from the Cotton: The Southern Tenant*

Farmers' Union and the New Deal (Chapel Hill: University of North Carolina Press, 1971). Sidney Baldwin describes the efforts of the Farm Security Administration on behalf of tenants and sharecroppers in *Poverty and Politics: The Rise and Decline of the Farm Security Administration* (Chapel Hill: University of North Carolina Press, 1968). For a study of commercial farmers, see Christina McFadyen Campbell's *The Farm Bureau and the New Deal: A Study of the Making of National Farm Policy* (Urbana: University of Illinois Press, 1962). Stuart Noblin, *The Grange in North Carolina, 1929–1954: A Story of Agricultural Progress* (Greensboro: North Carolina State Grange, 1954), has little on the New Deal. The REA aided rural America, and for that story, see D. Clayton Brown, *Electricity for Rural America: The Fight for REA* (Westport, Conn.: Greenwood Press, 1980); for the South, see his Ph.D. dissertation, "Rural Electrification in the South, 1920–1955" (University of California at Los Angeles, 1970); and for North Carolina, see his article "North Carolina Rural Electrification: Precedent of the REA," *North Carolina Historical Review* 59 (April 1982): 109–24. Frederick W. Muller's *Public Rural Electrification* (Washington, D.C.: American Council on Public Affairs, 1944) is a good general source for the REA.

The study of relief in North Carolina during the 1930s must begin with two excellent dissertations: Thomas S. Morgan, Jr., "A Step toward Altruism: Relief and Welfare in North Carolina, 1930–1938 (Ph.D. dissertation, University of North Carolina, 1969), and Ronald E. Marcello, "North Carolina Works Progress Administration and the Politics of Relief" (Ph.D. dissertation, Duke University, 1968). Some of their findings are more accessible in articles: Morgan, "A 'folly . . . manifest to everyone': The Movement to Enact Unemployment Insurance Legislation in North Carolina, 1935–1936," *North Carolina Historical Review* 52 (July 1975): 283–302; Marcello, "The Selection of North Carolina's Works Progress Administration Chief: A Division over Political Patronage," *North Carolina Historical Review* 52 (Winter 1975): 59–76, and Marcello, "The Politics of Relief: The North Carolina WPA and the Tar Heel Elections of 1936," *North Carolina Historical Review* 68 (January 1991): 17–37. Women played key roles in relief. See Sarah Wilkerson-Freeman, "From Clerks to Parties: North Carolina Women in the Advancement of the New Deal," *North Carolina Historical Review* 68 (July 1991): 320–39. William Foy Lisenby, "An Administrative History of Public Programs for Dependent Children in North Carolina, Virginia, Tennessee, and Kentucky, 1900–1942" (Ph.D. dissertation, Vanderbilt University, 1962), has one chapter on child welfare in North Carolina before the New Deal. Paul E. Mertz in his *New Deal Policy and*

Southern Rural Poverty (Baton Rouge: Louisiana State University Press, 1978) treats several issues related to relief. Other general sources that deal with relief in the 1930s are James T. Patterson's *America's Struggle against Poverty, 1900–1980* (Cambridge, Mass.: Harvard University Press, 1981); Frances Fox Piven and Richard A. Cloward, *Regulating the Poor: The Functions of Public Welfare* (New York: Pantheon Books, 1971), which focuses on public welfare's functions; and Barbara Blumberg, *The New Deal and the Unemployed: The View from New York City* (Lewisburg, Pa.: Bucknell University Press, 1979), a study of relief in New York City.

Relief agencies have been carefully examined. See John A. Salmond, *The Civilian Conservation Corps, 1933–1942: A New Deal Case Study* (Durham: Duke University Press, 1967), and George Philip Rawick, "The New Deal and Youth: The Civilian Conservation Corps, the National Youth Administration and the American Youth Congress" (Ph.D. dissertation, University of Wisconsin, 1957). For a contemporary and interim account of the NYA refer to Betty Lindley and Ernest L. Lindley, *A New Deal for Youth: The Story of the National Youth Administration* (New York: Viking Press, 1938). Aubrey W. Williams's leadership of the NYA is examined in John A. Salmond's *A Southern Rebel: The Life and Times of Aubrey Willis Williams, 1890–1965* (Chapel Hill: University of North Carolina Press, 1983). A compendium of the WPA is Donald S. Howard, *The WPA and Federal Relief Policy* (New York: Russell Sage Foundation, 1943). Solid treatment of social security can be found in Arthur J. Altmeyer, *The Formative Years of Social Security* (Madison: University of Wisconsin Press, 1966). For additional relief activities in North Carolina, see Jerrold M. Hirsch, "Culture on Relief: The Federal Writers' Project in North Carolina, 1935–1942" (M.A. thesis, University of North Carolina, 1973), and the unpublished manuscript by Roy Melton Brown, "The Growth of a State Program of Public Welfare," in the North Carolina Collection at the University of North Carolina Library in Chapel Hill. Lorena Hickok's observations about relief needs in the state, written for her boss Harry L. Hopkins, can be found in Richard Lowitt and Maurine Beasley, eds., *One Third of a Nation: Lorena Hickok Reports on the Great Depression* (Urbana: University of Illinois Press, 1981).

Several sources explore the subject of North Carolina blacks in the 1930s. For a general overview, see Augustus M. Burns III, "North Carolina and the Negro Dilemma, 1930–1950" (Ph.D. dissertation, University of North Carolina, 1968), and William A. Mabry, *The Negro in North Carolina Politics since Reconstruction* (New York: AMS Press,

1940). Charles W. Eagles has carefully traced the attitude of one white liberal newspaper editor on race in *Jonathan Daniels and Race Relations* (Knoxville: University of Tennessee Press, 1982). Charles C. Spaulding, prominent black leader and New Dealer, and his Durham business, are the subject of Walter B. Weare's *Black Business in the New South: A Social History of the North Carolina Mutual Life Insurance Company* (Urbana: University of Illinois Press, 1973), and Weare, "Charles Clinton Spaulding: Middle-Class Leadership in the Age of Segregation," in John Hope Franklin and August Meier, eds. *Black Leaders of the Twentieth Century* (Urbana: University of Illinois Press, 1982), 167–89. Two articles by sociologist Guy B. Johnson provide information and contribute to the policy debate about blacks in the 1930s: "The Negro and the Depression in North Carolina," *Social Forces* 12 (October 1933): 103–15, and "Does the South Owe the Negro a New Deal?" *Social Forces* 13 (October 1934): 100–103. Robert Cannon's "The Organization and Growth of Black Political Participation in Durham, North Carolina, 1933–1958" (Ph.D. dissertation, University of North Carolina, 1975) has a brief treatment of non–New Deal issues. An excellent source of data on blacks in the state for the 1930s is John R. Larkins, *The Negro Population of North Carolina: Social and Economic* (Raleigh: North Carolina State Board of Charities and Public Welfare, 1944). A useful anthology is Jeffrey J. Crowe and Flora J. Hatley, eds., *Black Americans in North Carolina and the South* (Chapel Hill: University of North Carolina Press, 1984).

General sources on blacks in the New Deal era help place the North Carolina experience in a proper context. The starting point is the classic two-volume study by Gunnar Myrdal, *An American Dilemma: The Negro Problem and Modern Democracy*, 2 vols. (New York: Harper and Bros., 1944). For the best recent scholarship, see Harvard Sitkoff, *A New Deal for Blacks: The Emergence of Civil Rights as a National Issue*, vol. 1, *The Depression Decade* (New York: Oxford University Press, 1978), and Raymond Wolters, *Negroes and the Great Depression* (Westport, Conn.: Greenwood Press, 1970). Also an excellent general source of information is Allen Francis Kifer, "The Negro under the New Deal, 1933–1941" (Ph.D. dissertation, University of Wisconsin, 1961). For blacks and New Deal politics, consult Nancy J. Weiss, *Farewell to the Party of Lincoln: Black Politics in the Age of FDR* (Princeton: Princeton University Press, 1983), and Ralph J. Bunche, *The Political Status of the Negro in the Age of FDR* (Chicago: University of Chicago Press, 1973), edited by Dewey W. Grantham, Jr. On the theme of race and liberalism, two important works are Morton Sosna, *In Search of the Silent South: Southern Liberals and the Race Issue* (New York: Columbia University

Press, 1977), and John B. Kirby, *Black Americans in the Roosevelt Era: Liberalism and Race* (Knoxville: University of Tennessee Press, 1980). Two articles with a helpful overview are Richard M. Dalfiume, "The 'Forgotten Years' of the Negro Revolution," *Journal of American History* 55 (June 1968): 90–106, and Leslie H. Fishel, Jr., "The Negro in the New Deal Era," *Wisconsin Magazine of History* 48 (Winter 1964–65): 111–26. On blacks and the CCC two useful accounts are Calvin W. Gower, "The Struggle of Blacks for Leadership Positions in the Civilian Conservation Corps: 1933–1942," *Journal of Negro History* 61 (April 1976): 123–35, and John A. Salmond, "The Civilian Conservation Corps and the Negro," *Journal of American History* 52 (June 1965): 75–88.